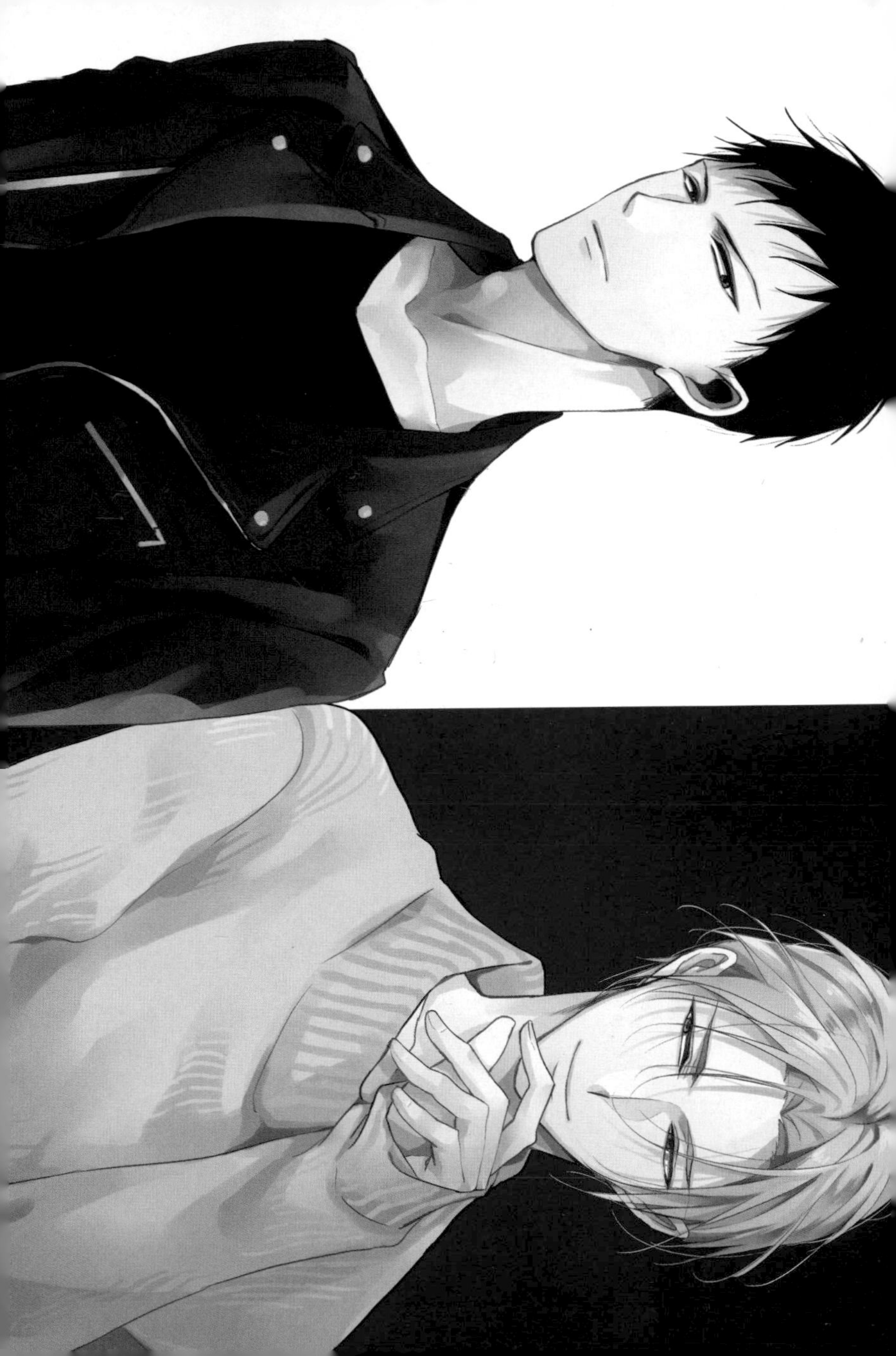

Contents

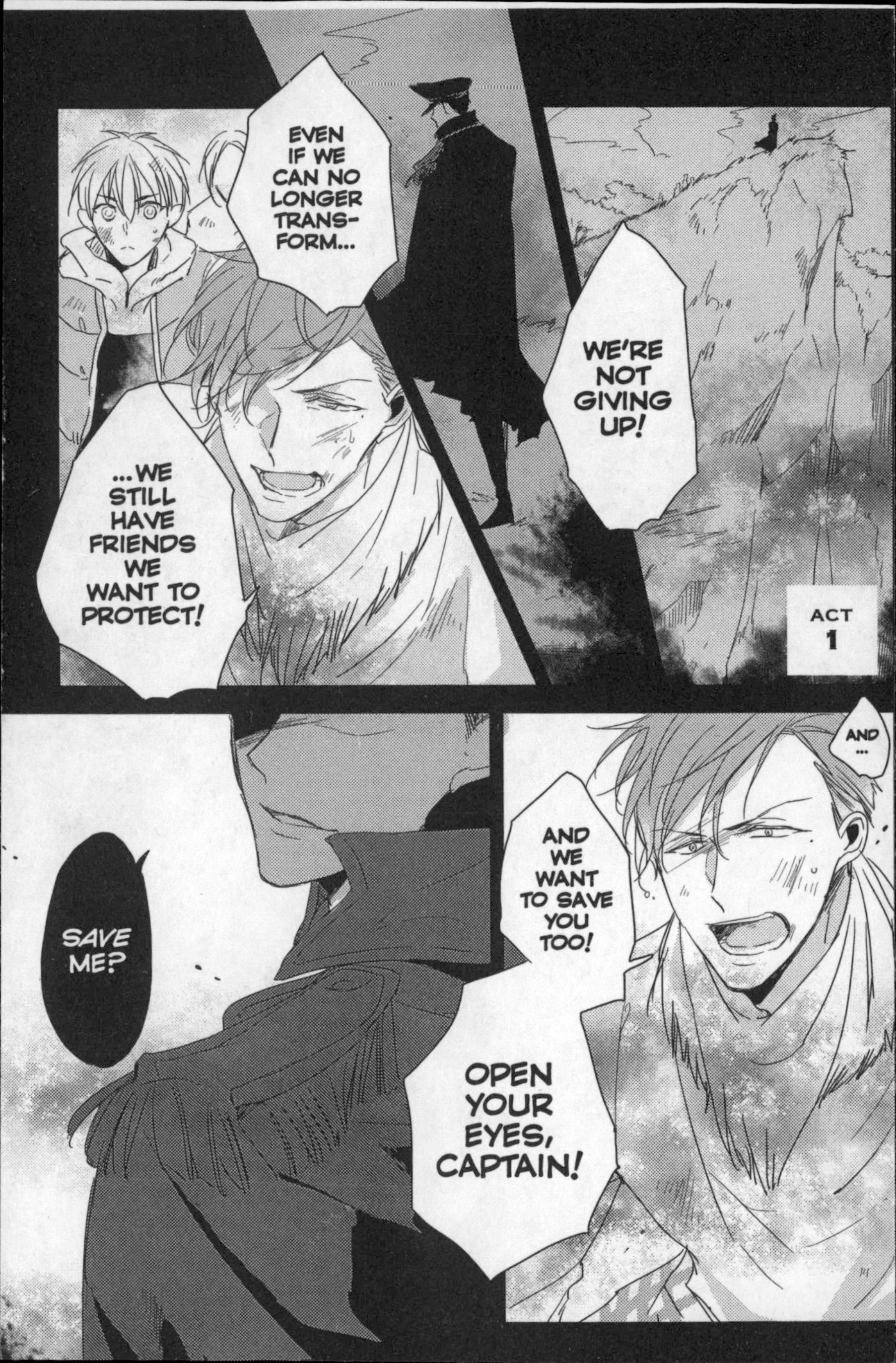
WE'RE NOT GIVING UP!
ACT 1
EVEN IF WE CAN NO LONGER TRANS-FORM...
...WE STILL HAVE FRIENDS WE WANT TO PROTECT!
AND...
AND WE WANT TO SAVE YOU TOO!
OPEN YOUR EYES, CAPTAIN!
SAVE ME?

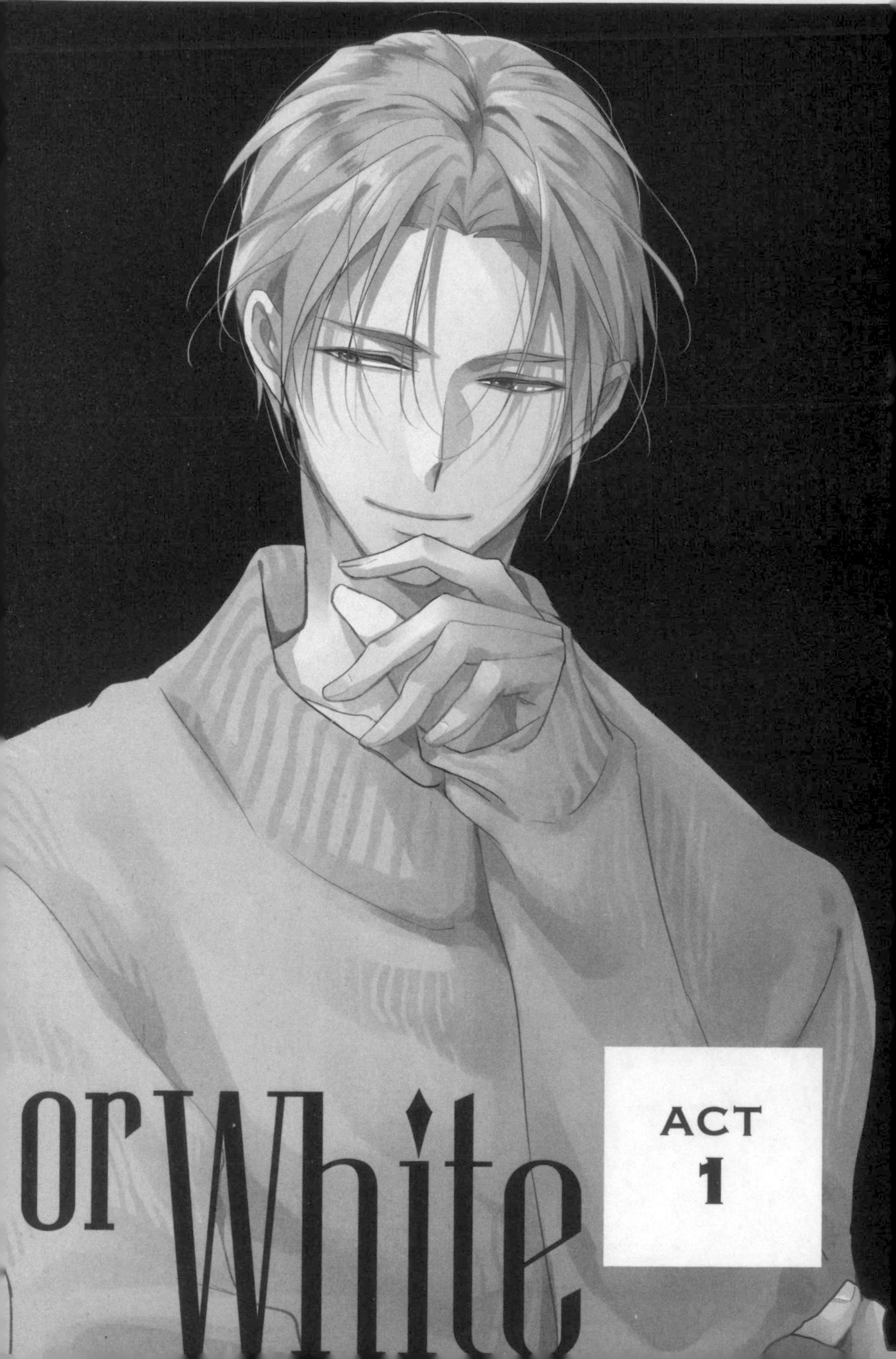
or White
ACT
1

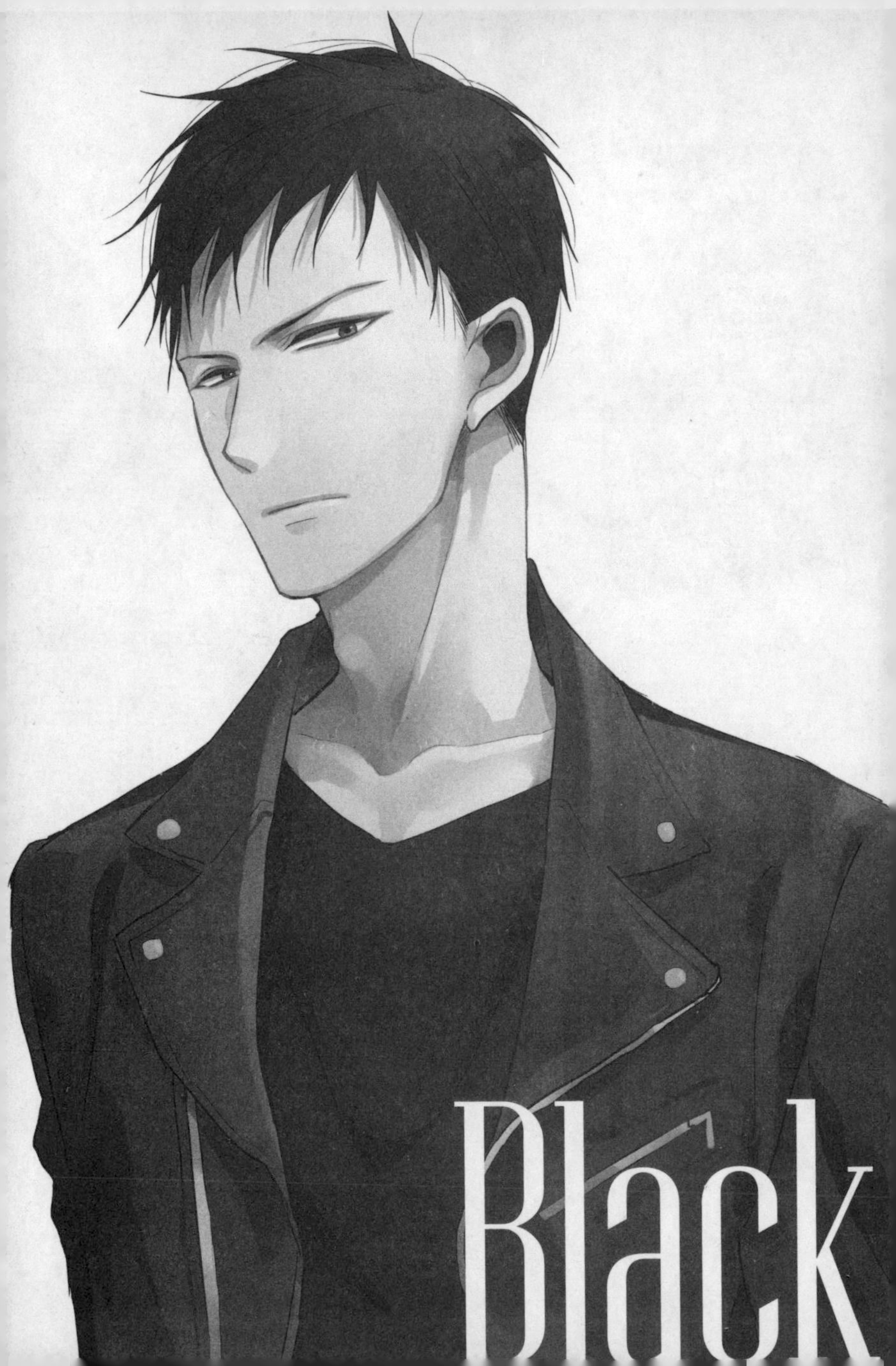
Black

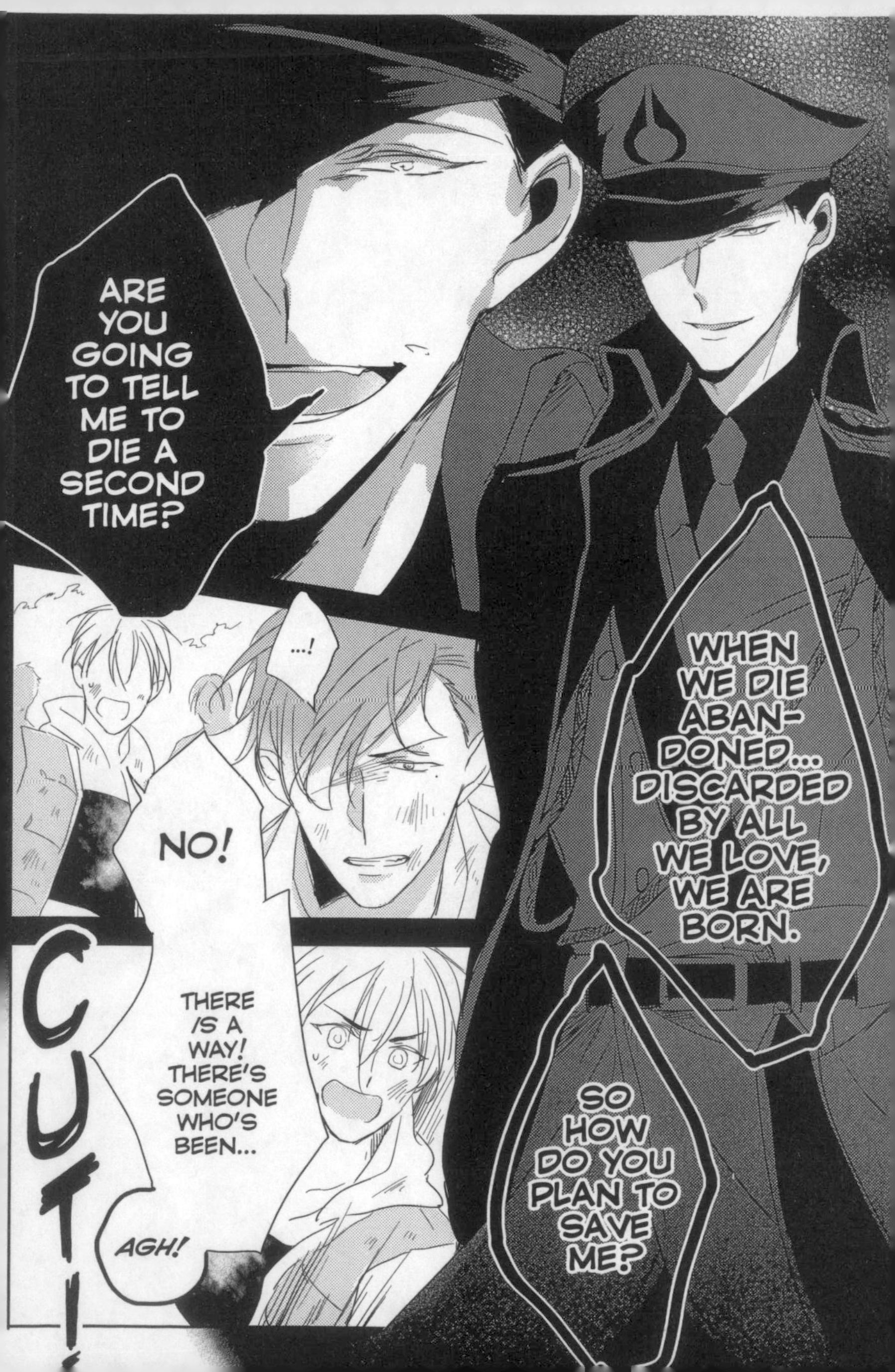

WHEN WE DIE ABAN-DONED... DISCARDED BY ALL WE LOVE, WE ARE BORN.
SO HOW DO YOU PLAN TO SAVE ME?
ARE YOU GOING TO TELL ME TO DIE A SECOND TIME?
...!
NO!
THERE IS A WAY! THERE'S SOMEONE WHO'S BEEN...
AGH!
CUT!

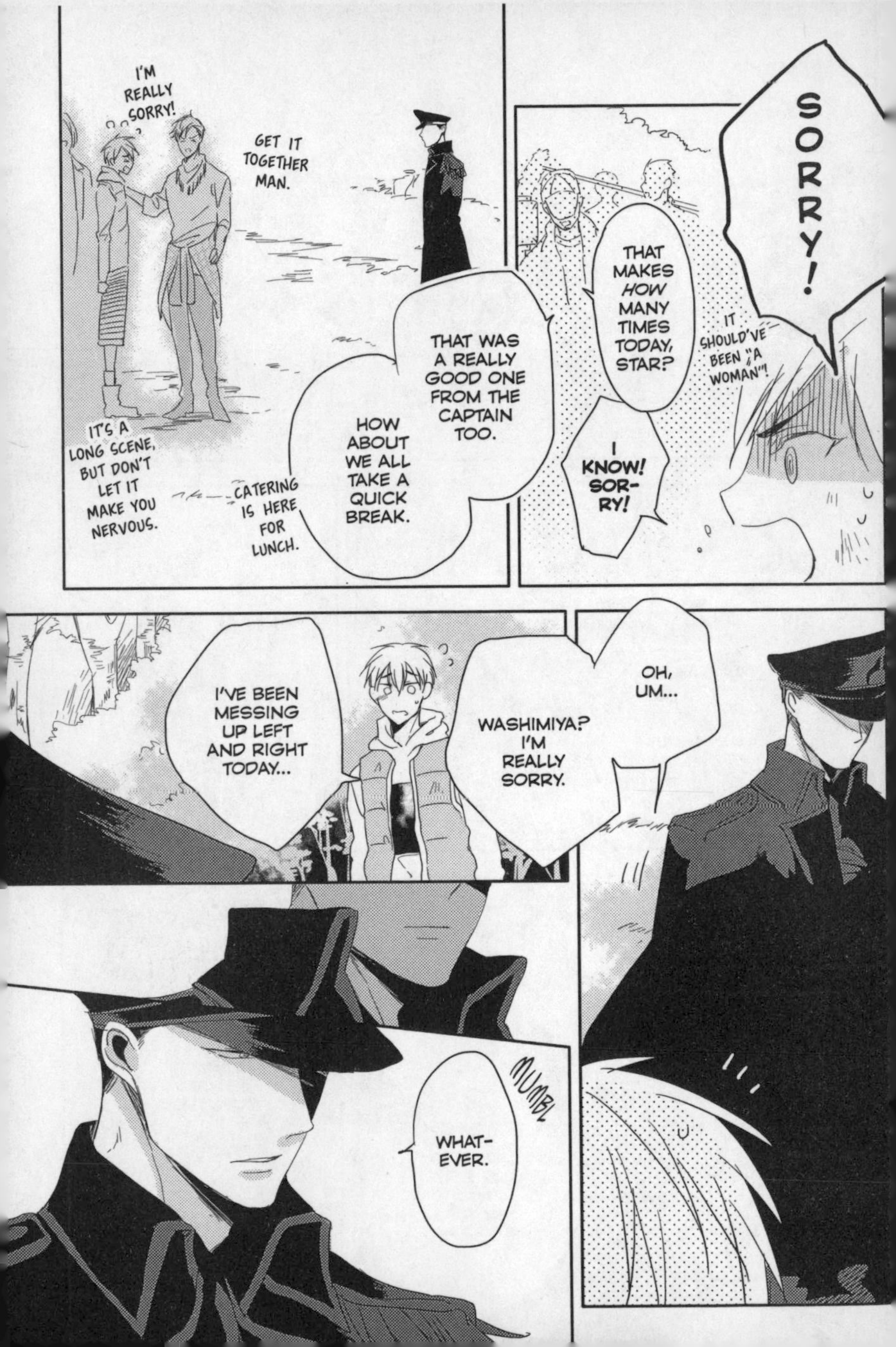
SORRY!
IT SHOULD'VE BEEN "A WOMAN"!
THAT MAKES *HOW* MANY TIMES TODAY, STAR?
I KNOW! SORRY!
THAT WAS A REALLY GOOD ONE FROM THE CAPTAIN TOO.
I'M REALLY SORRY!
GET IT TOGETHER MAN.
HOW ABOUT WE ALL TAKE A QUICK BREAK.
CATERING IS HERE FOR LUNCH.
IT'S A LONG SCENE, BUT DON'T LET IT MAKE YOU NERVOUS.
OH, UM...
WASHIMIYA? I'M REALLY SORRY.
I'VE BEEN MESSING UP LEFT AND RIGHT TODAY...
MUMBL
WHAT-EVER.

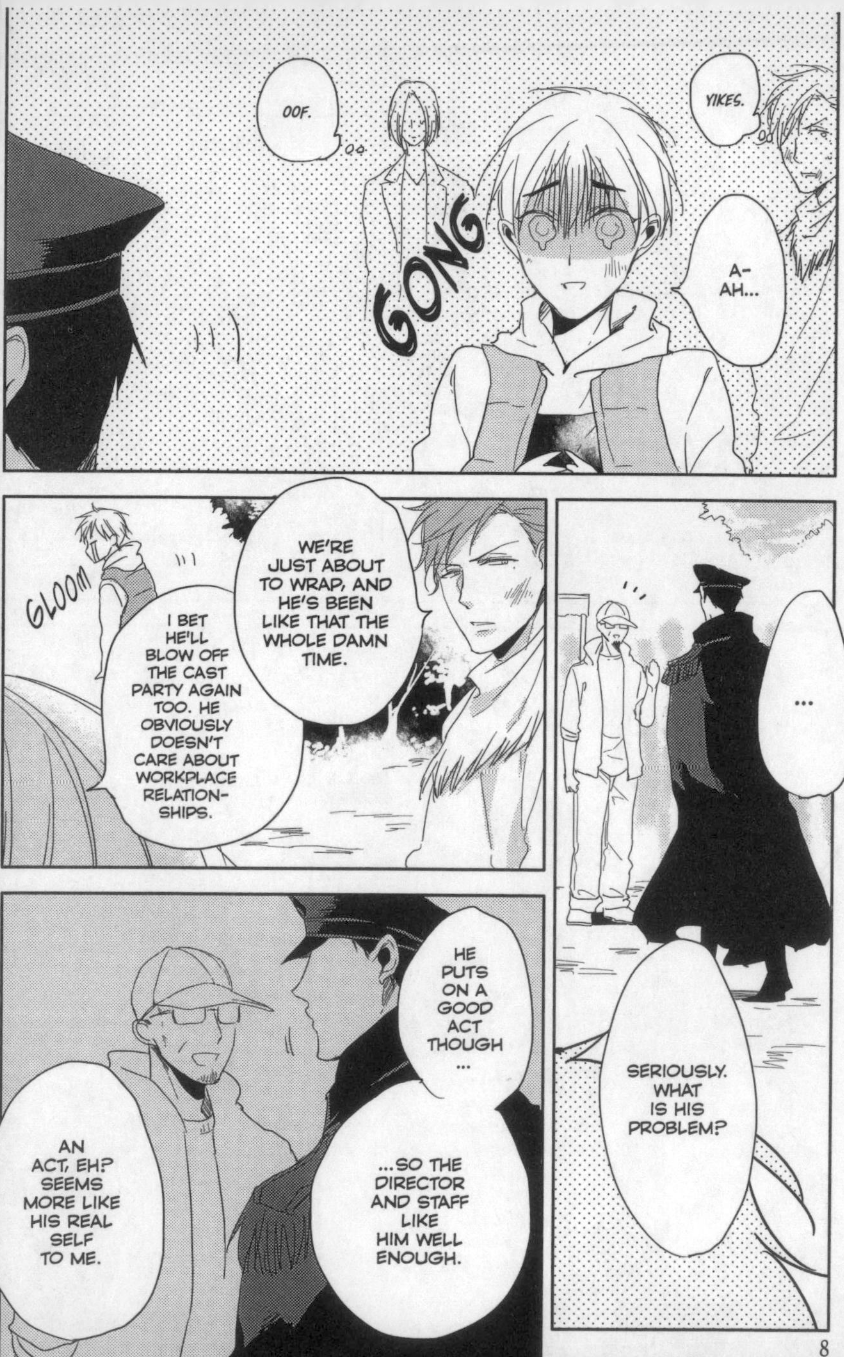
YIKES.
OOF.
GONG
A- AH...
...
SERIOUSLY. WHAT IS HIS PROBLEM?
WE'RE JUST ABOUT TO WRAP, AND HE'S BEEN LIKE THAT THE WHOLE DAMN TIME.
GLOOM
I BET HE'LL BLOW OFF THE CAST PARTY AGAIN TOO. HE OBVIOUSLY DOESN'T CARE ABOUT WORKPLACE RELATION-SHIPS.
HE PUTS ON A GOOD ACT THOUGH ...
...SO THE DIRECTOR AND STAFF LIKE HIM WELL ENOUGH.
AN ACT, EH? SEEMS MORE LIKE HIS REAL SELF TO ME.

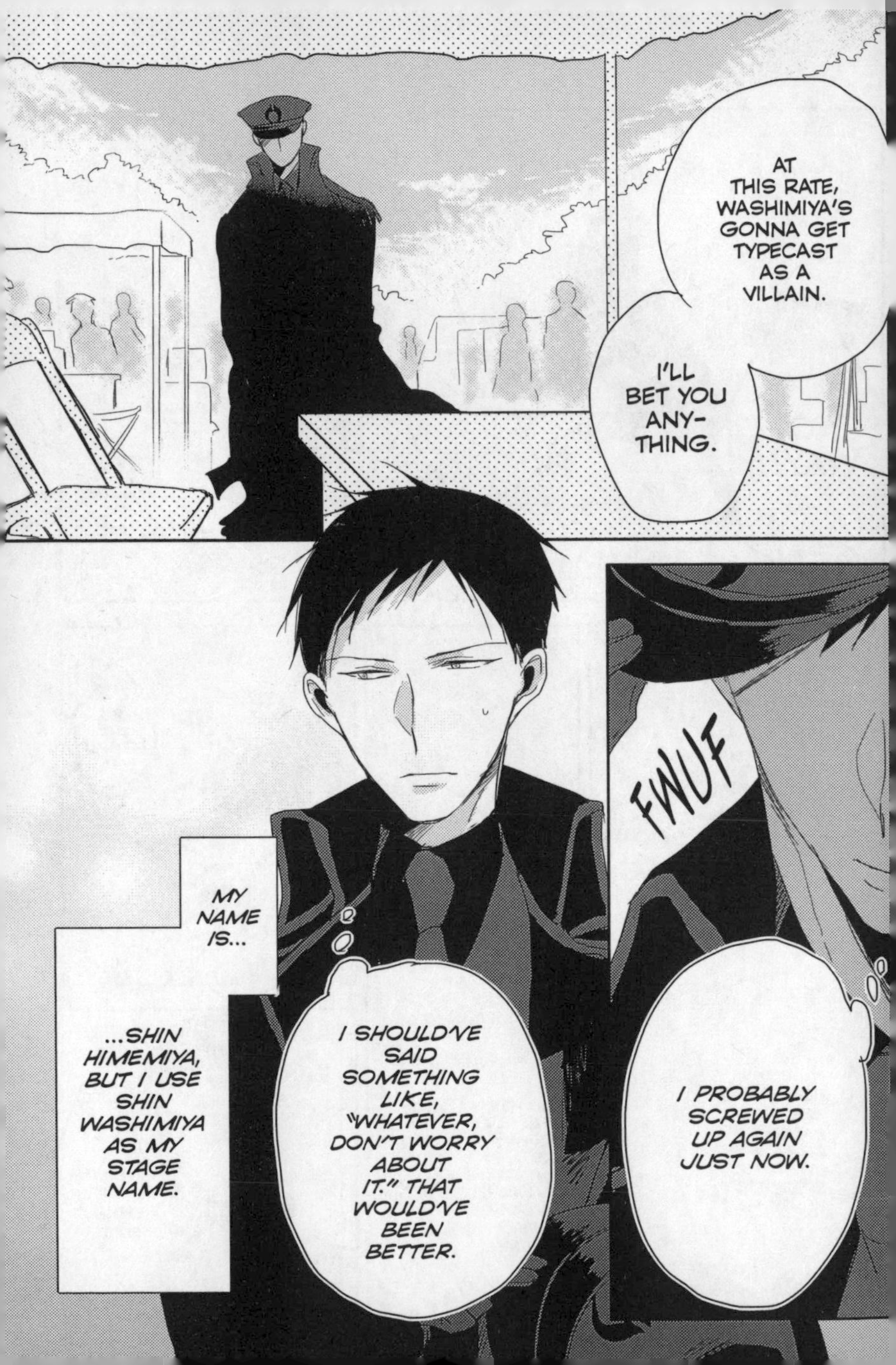
AT THIS RATE, WASHIMIYA'S GONNA GET TYPECAST AS A VILLAIN.
I'LL BET YOU ANY-THING.
FWUF
I PROBABLY SCREWED UP AGAIN JUST NOW.
I SHOULD'VE SAID SOMETHING LIKE, "WHATEVER, DON'T WORRY ABOUT IT." THAT WOULD'VE BEEN BETTER.
MY NAME IS...
...SHIN HIMEMIYA, BUT I USE SHIN WASHIMIYA AS MY STAGE NAME.

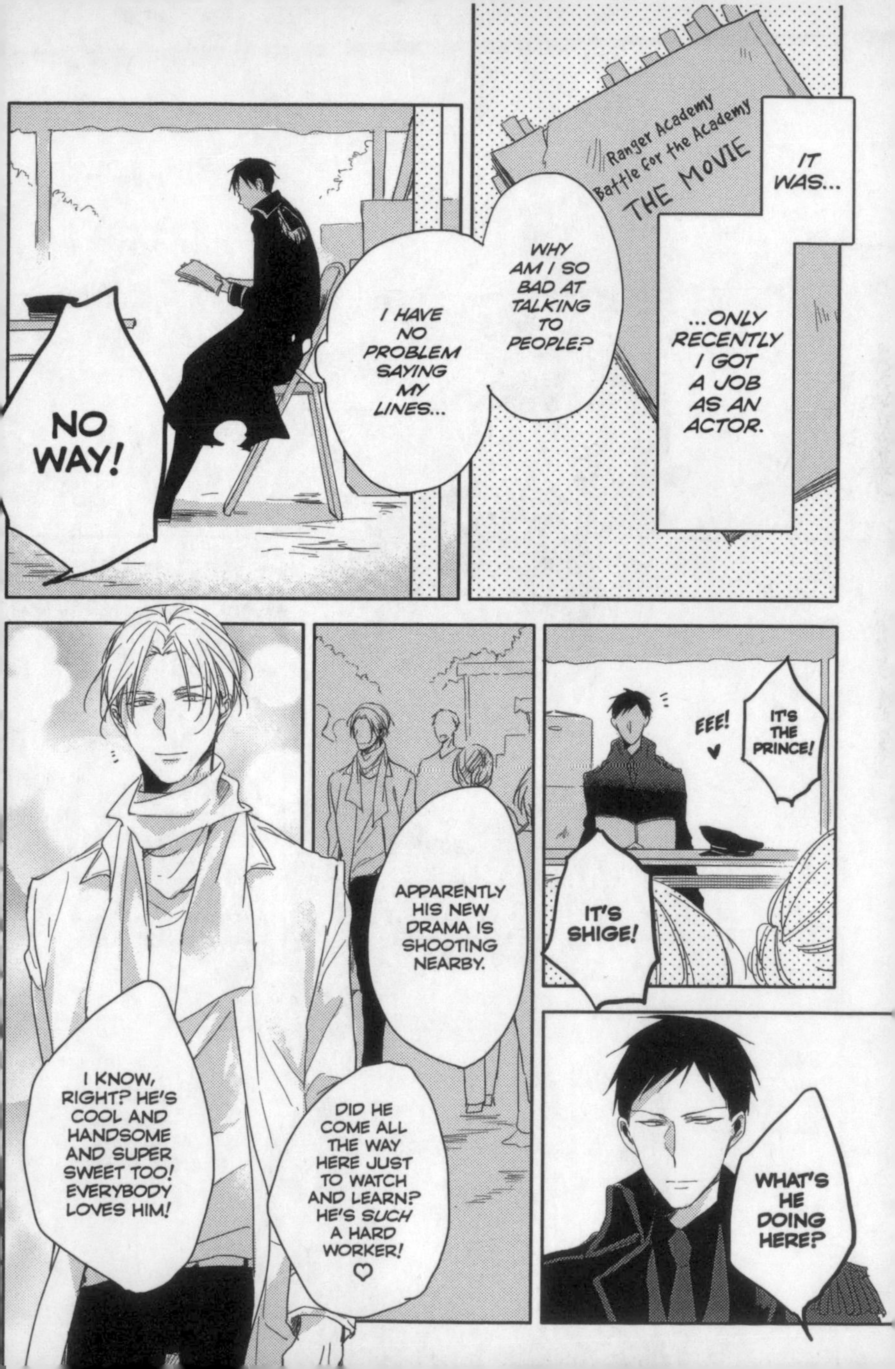
Ranger Academy
Battle for the Academy
THE MOVIE
IT WAS...
...ONLY RECENTLY I GOT A JOB AS AN ACTOR.
WHY AM I SO BAD AT TALKING TO PEOPLE?
I HAVE NO PROBLEM SAYING MY LINES...
NO WAY!
IT'S THE PRINCE!
EEE! ♥
IT'S SHIGE!
WHAT'S HE DOING HERE?
APPARENTLY HIS NEW DRAMA IS SHOOTING NEARBY.
DID HE COME ALL THE WAY HERE JUST TO WATCH AND LEARN? HE'S *SUCH* A HARD WORKER! ♡
I KNOW, RIGHT? HE'S COOL AND HANDSOME AND SUPER SWEET TOO! EVERYBODY LOVES HIM!

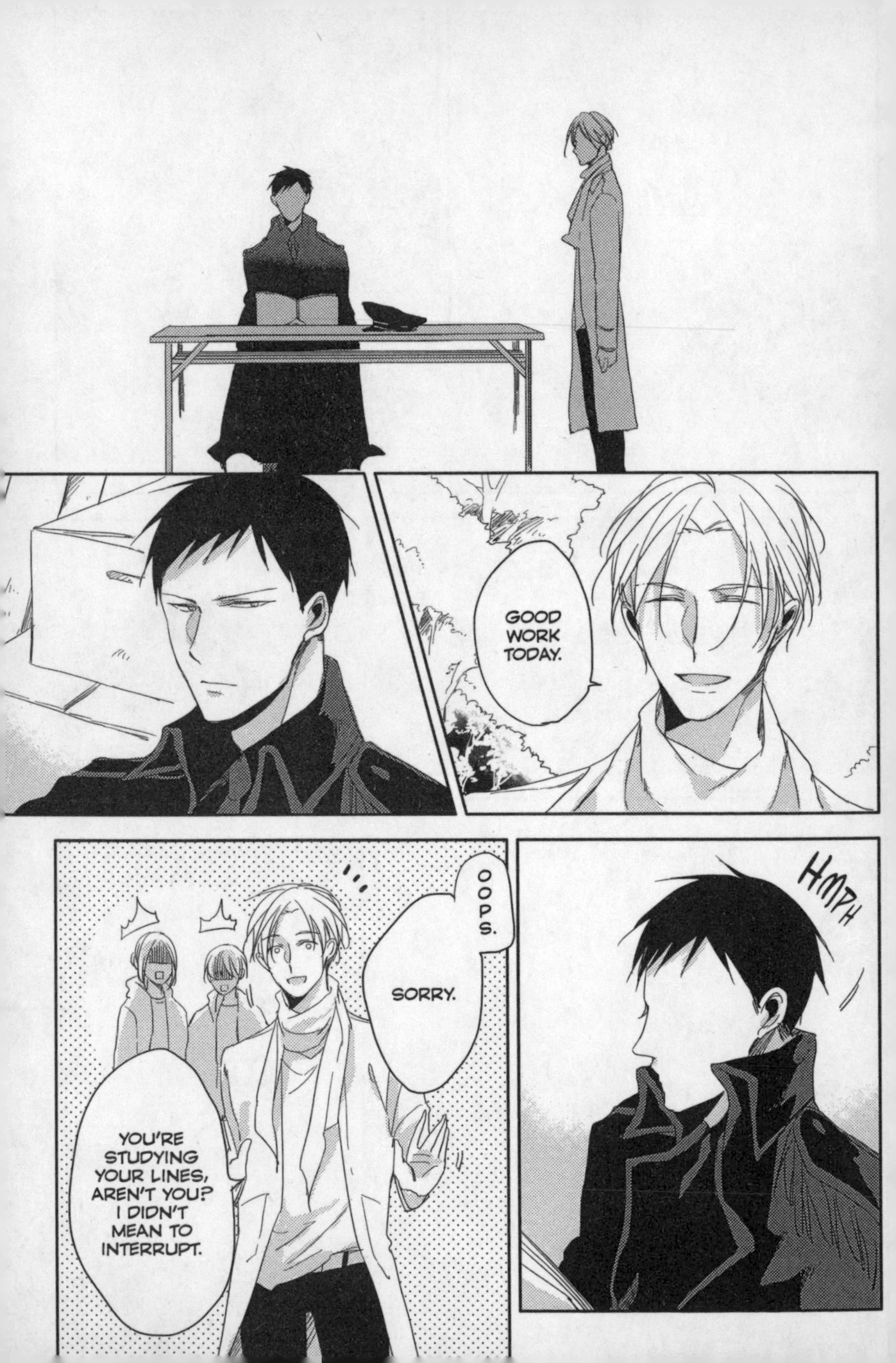
GOOD WORK TODAY.
HMPH
OOPS.
SORRY.
YOU'RE STUDYING YOUR LINES, AREN'T YOU? I DIDN'T MEAN TO INTERRUPT.

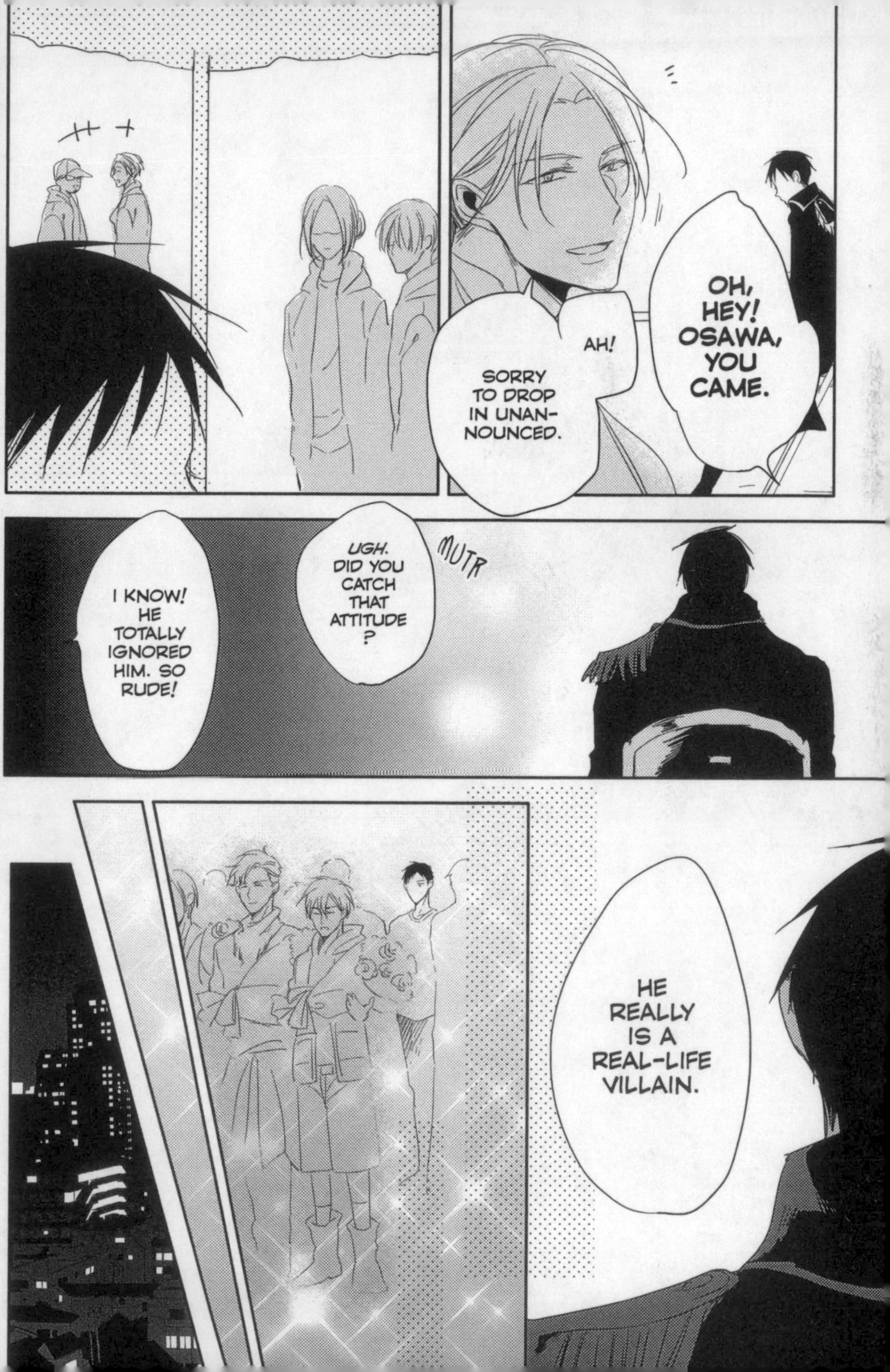
OH, HEY! OSAWA, YOU CAME.
AH!
SORRY TO DROP IN UNAN-NOUNCED.
MUTR
UGH. DID YOU CATCH THAT ATTITUDE?
I KNOW! HE TOTALLY IGNORED HIM. SO RUDE!
HE REALLY IS A REAL-LIFE VILLAIN.

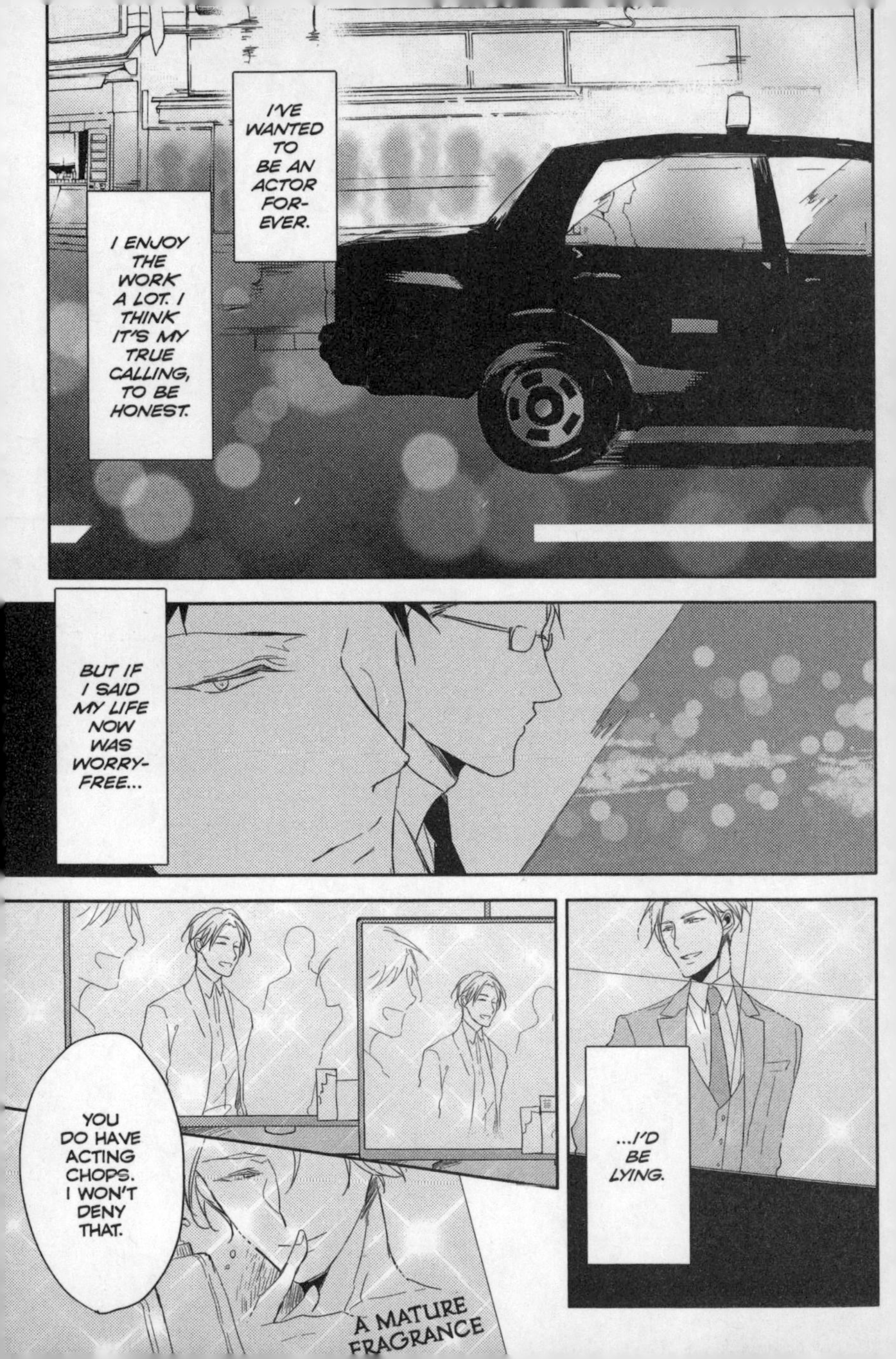
I'VE WANTED TO BE AN ACTOR FOR-EVER.
I ENJOY THE WORK A LOT. I THINK IT'S MY TRUE CALLING, TO BE HONEST.
BUT IF I SAID MY LIFE NOW WAS WORRY-FREE...
...I'D BE LYING.
YOU DO HAVE ACTING CHOPS. I WON'T DENY THAT.
A MATURE FRAGRANCE

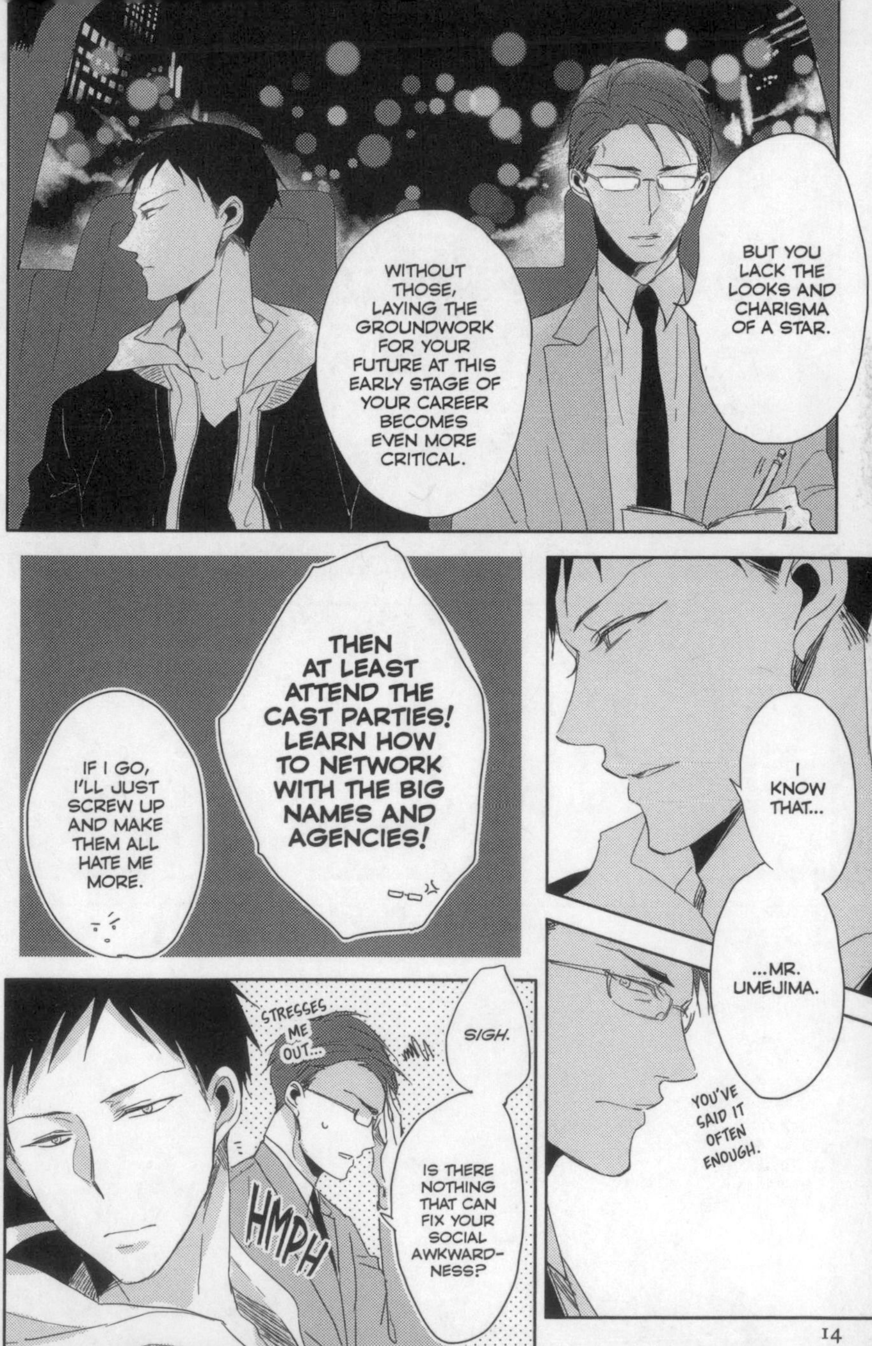
BUT YOU LACK THE LOOKS AND CHARISMA OF A STAR.
WITHOUT THOSE, LAYING THE GROUNDWORK FOR YOUR FUTURE AT THIS EARLY STAGE OF YOUR CAREER BECOMES EVEN MORE CRITICAL.
I KNOW THAT...
...MR. UMEJIMA.
YOU'VE SAID IT OFTEN ENOUGH.
THEN AT LEAST ATTEND THE CAST PARTIES! LEARN HOW TO NETWORK WITH THE BIG NAMES AND AGENCIES!
IF I GO, I'LL JUST SCREW UP AND MAKE THEM ALL HATE ME MORE.
SIGH.
STRESSES ME OUT...
IS THERE NOTHING THAT CAN FIX YOUR SOCIAL AWKWARD-NESS?
HMPH

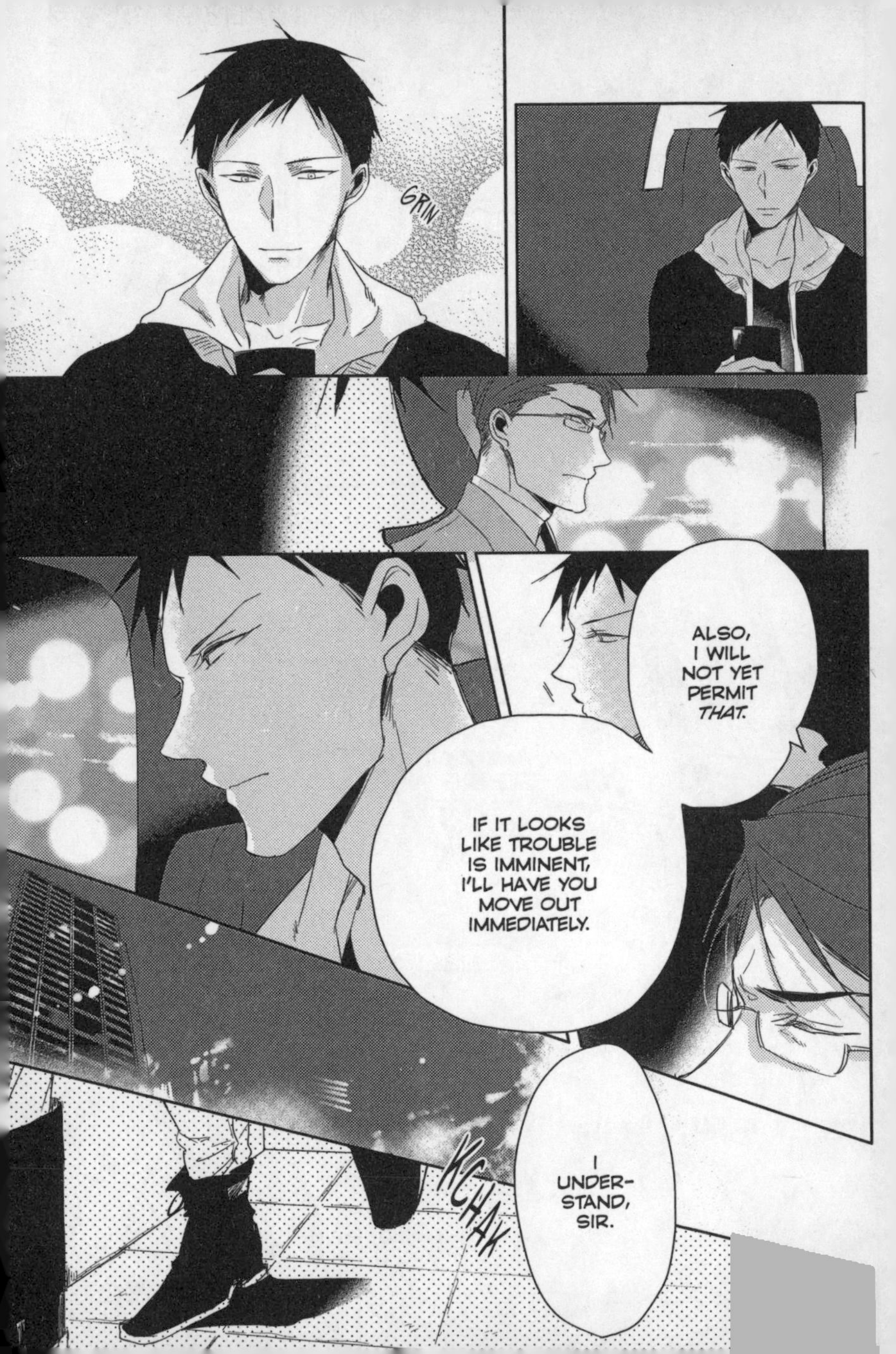
GRIN
ALSO, I WILL NOT YET PERMIT *THAT.*
IF IT LOOKS LIKE TROUBLE IS IMMINENT, I'LL HAVE YOU MOVE OUT IMMEDIATELY.
I UNDER-STAND, SIR.
KCHAK

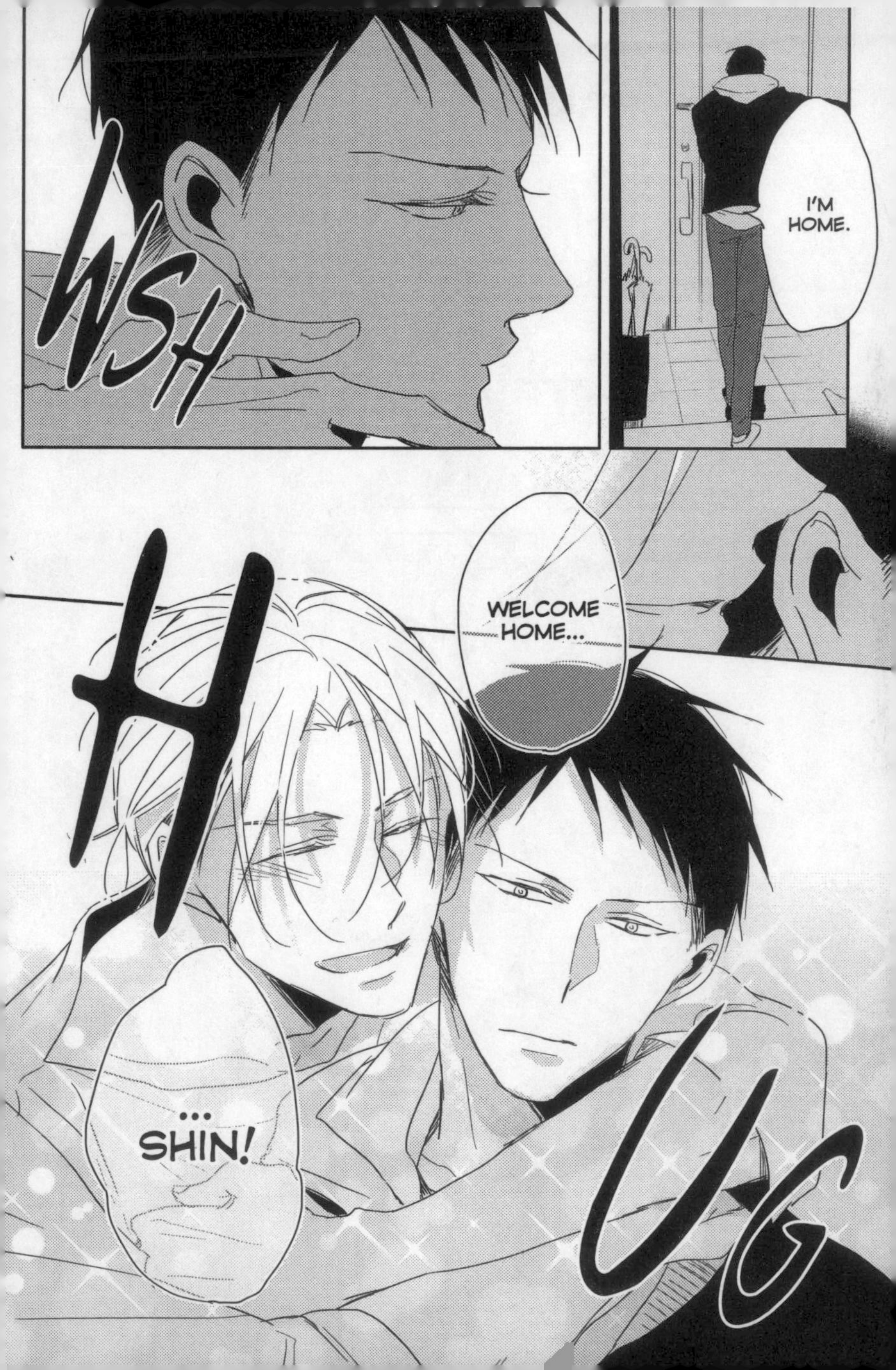
I'M HOME.
WSH
WELCOME HOME...
H
UG
... SHIN!

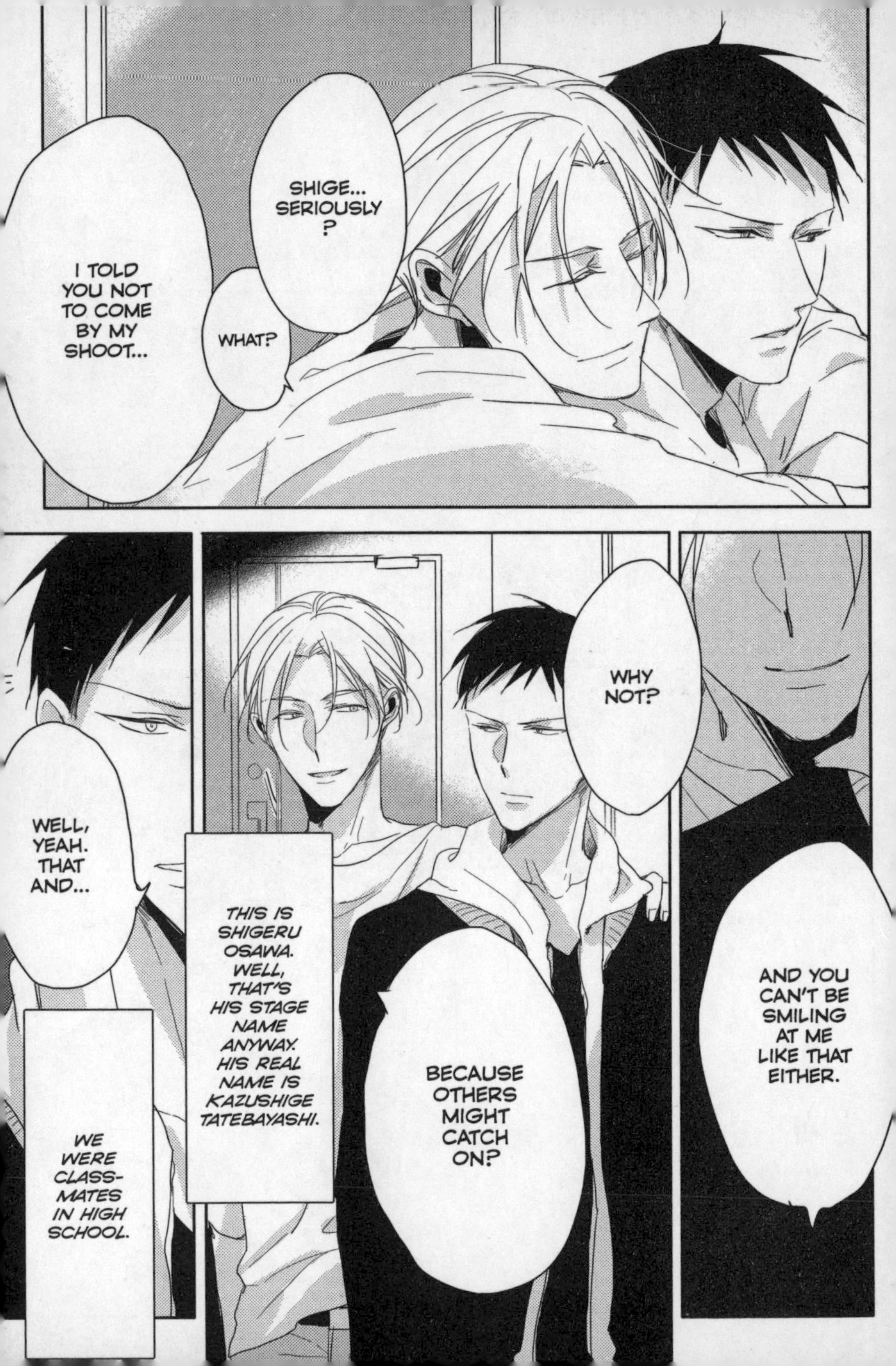
SHIGE... SERIOUSLY?
WHAT?
I TOLD YOU NOT TO COME BY MY SHOOT...
WHY NOT?
AND YOU CAN'T BE SMILING AT ME LIKE THAT EITHER.
THIS IS SHIGERU OSAWA. WELL, THAT'S HIS STAGE NAME ANYWAY. HIS REAL NAME IS KAZUSHIGE TATEBAYASHI.
BECAUSE OTHERS MIGHT CATCH ON?
WELL, YEAH. THAT AND...
WE WERE CLASS-MATES IN HIGH SCHOOL.

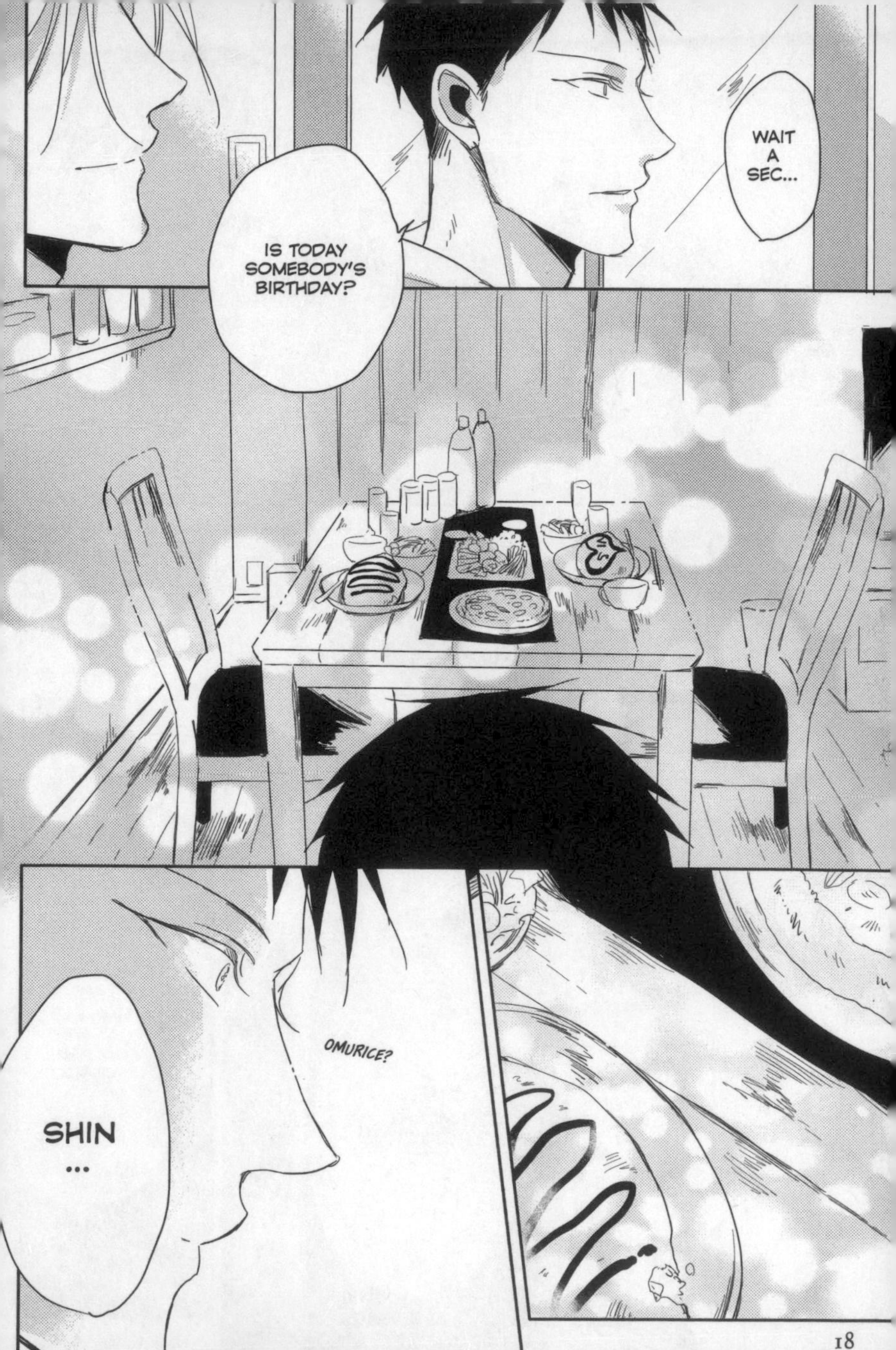
WAIT A SEC...
IS TODAY SOMEBODY'S BIRTHDAY?
OMURICE?
SHIN ...

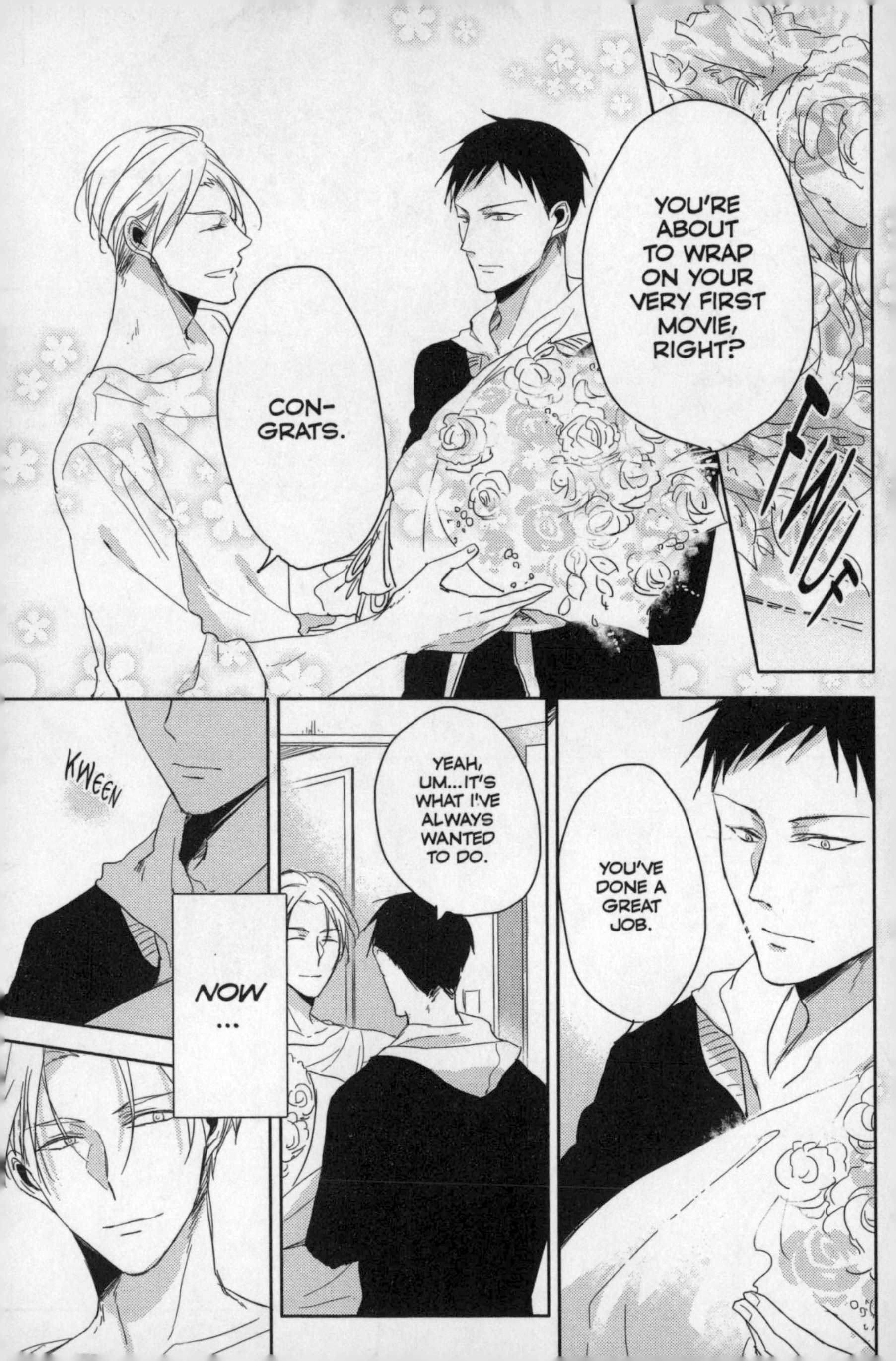
YOU'RE ABOUT TO WRAP ON YOUR VERY FIRST MOVIE, RIGHT?
FWUF
CON-GRATS.
YOU'VE DONE A GREAT JOB.
YEAH, UM...IT'S WHAT I'VE ALWAYS WANTED TO DO.
KWEEN
NOW ...

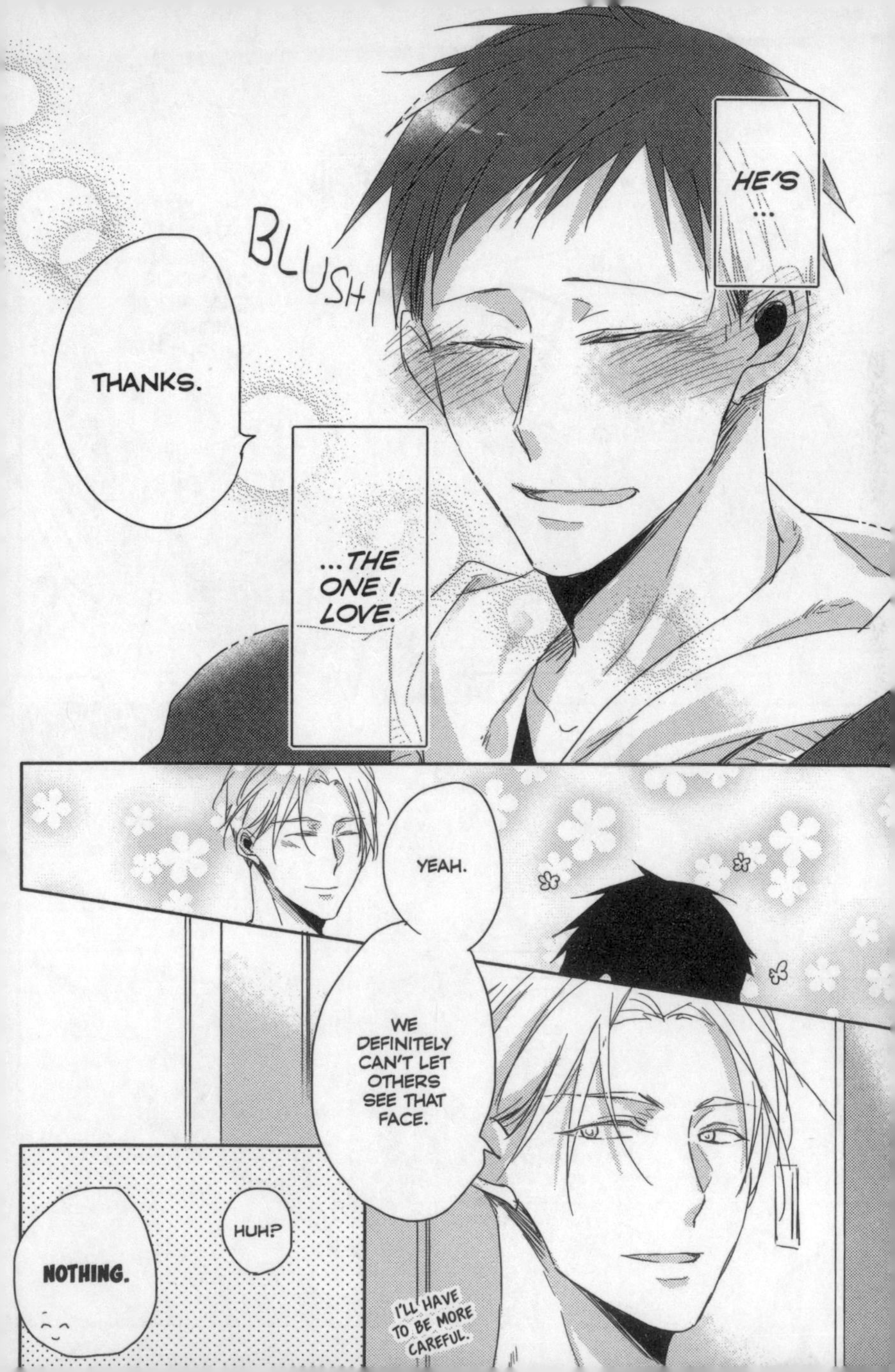
HE'S ...
BLUSH
THANKS.
...THE ONE I LOVE.
YEAH.
WE DEFINITELY CAN'T LET OTHERS SEE THAT FACE.
I'LL HAVE TO BE MORE CAREFUL.
HUH?
NOTHING.

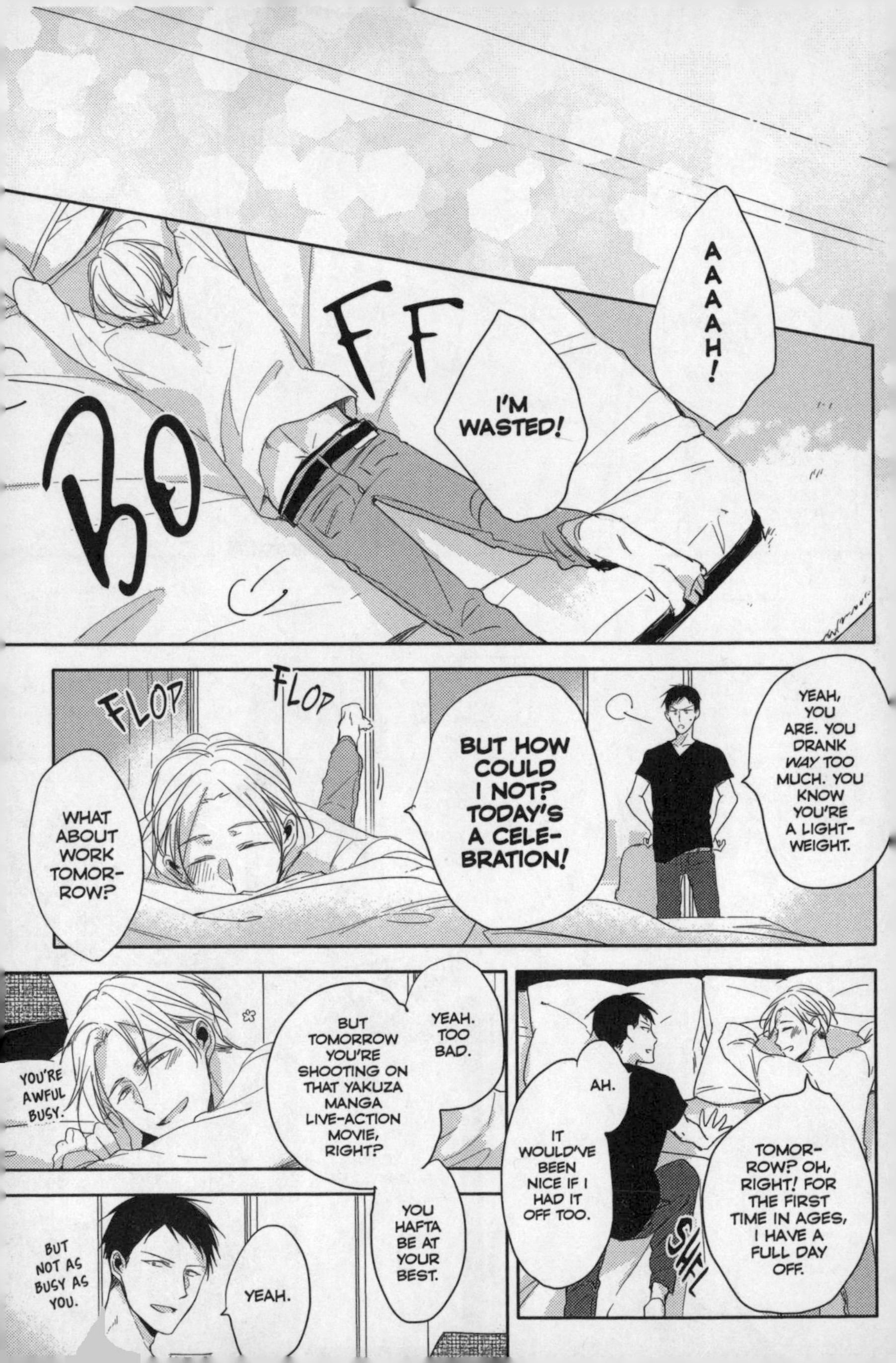

AAAAAH!
I'M WASTED!
BOFF
YEAH, YOU ARE. YOU DRANK WAY TOO MUCH. YOU KNOW YOU'RE A LIGHT-WEIGHT.
BUT HOW COULD I NOT? TODAY'S A CELE-BRATION!
FLOP
FLOP
WHAT ABOUT WORK TOMOR-ROW?
TOMOR-ROW? OH, RIGHT! FOR THE FIRST TIME IN AGES, I HAVE A FULL DAY OFF.
AH.
IT WOULD'VE BEEN NICE IF I HAD IT OFF TOO.
SHFL
YEAH. TOO BAD.
BUT TOMORROW YOU'RE SHOOTING ON THAT YAKUZA MANGA LIVE-ACTION MOVIE, RIGHT?
YOU'RE AWFUL BUSY.
YOU HAFTA BE AT YOUR BEST.
YEAH.
BUT NOT AS BUSY AS YOU.

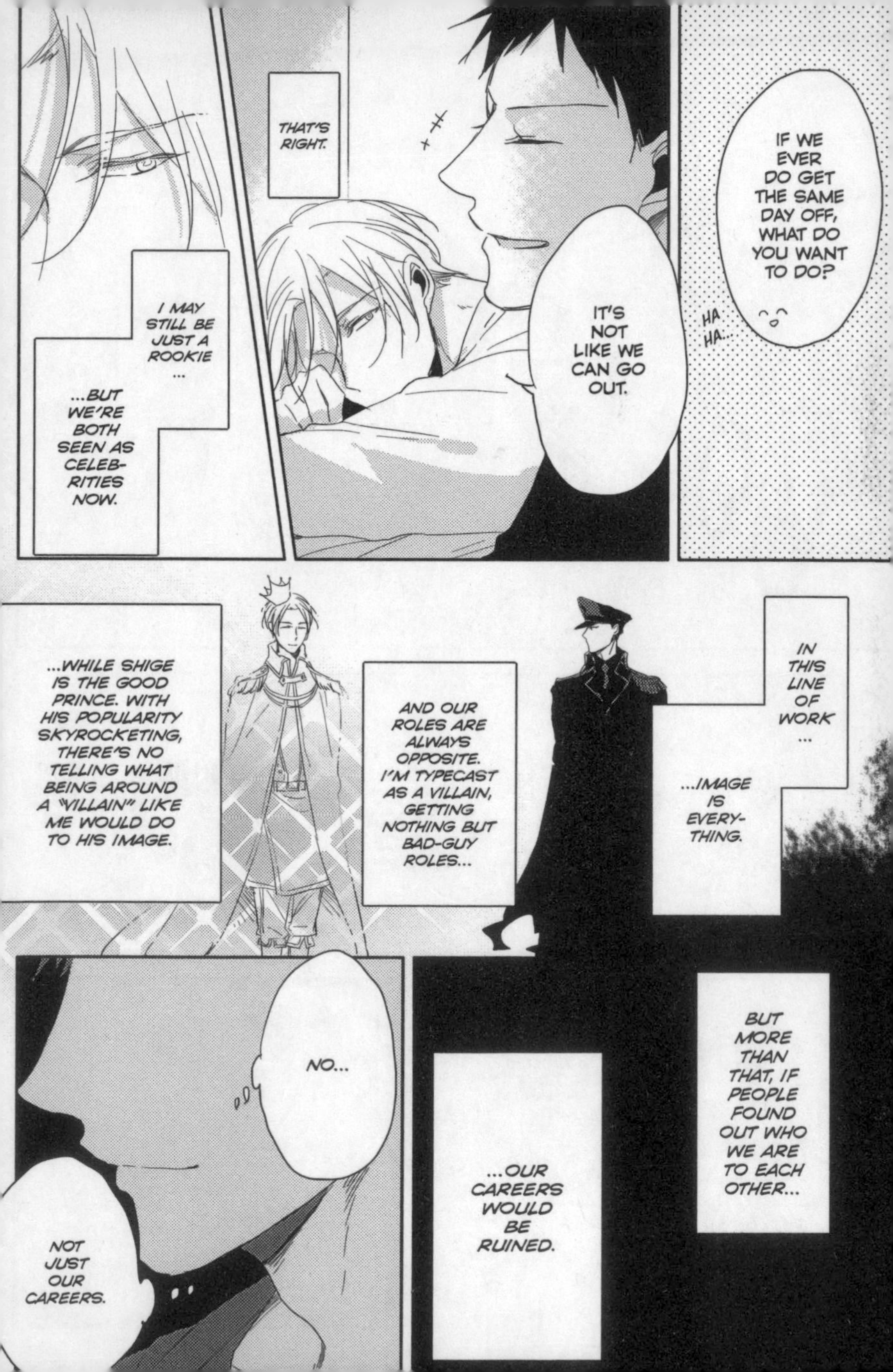

IF WE EVER DO GET THE SAME DAY OFF, WHAT DO YOU WANT TO DO?
HA HA...
IT'S NOT LIKE WE CAN GO OUT.
THAT'S RIGHT.
I MAY STILL BE JUST A ROOKIE...
...BUT WE'RE BOTH SEEN AS CELEB-RITIES NOW.
IN THIS LINE OF WORK...
...IMAGE IS EVERY-THING.
AND OUR ROLES ARE ALWAYS OPPOSITE. I'M TYPECAST AS A VILLAIN, GETTING NOTHING BUT BAD-GUY ROLES...
...WHILE SHIGE IS THE GOOD PRINCE. WITH HIS POPULARITY SKYROCKETING, THERE'S NO TELLING WHAT BEING AROUND A "VILLAIN" LIKE ME WOULD DO TO HIS IMAGE.
BUT MORE THAN THAT, IF PEOPLE FOUND OUT WHO WE ARE TO EACH OTHER...
...OUR CAREERS WOULD BE RUINED.
NO...
NOT JUST OUR CAREERS.

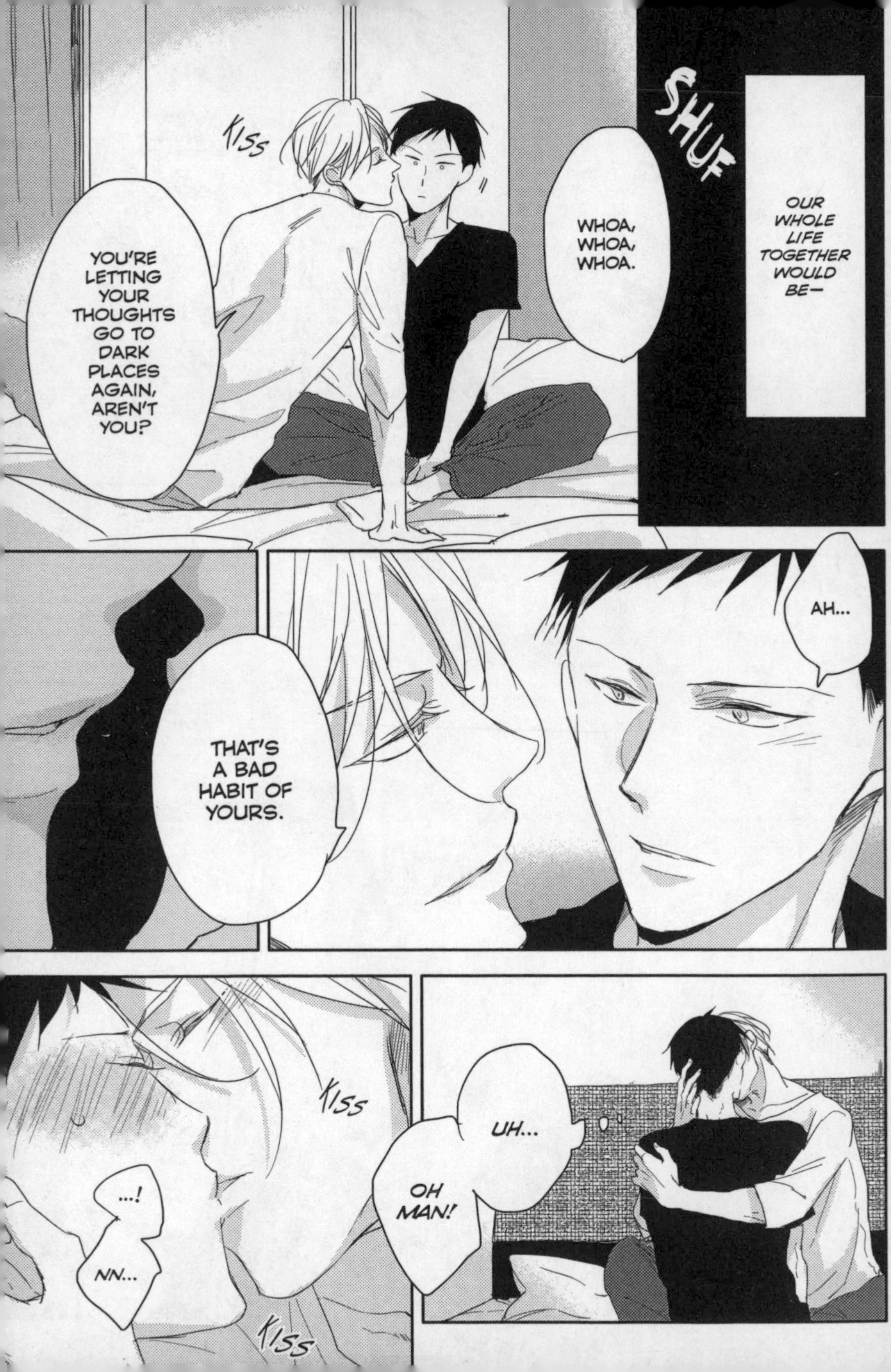
SHUF
OUR WHOLE LIFE TOGETHER WOULD BE—
WHOA, WHOA, WHOA.
KISS
YOU'RE LETTING YOUR THOUGHTS GO TO DARK PLACES AGAIN, AREN'T YOU?
AH...
THAT'S A BAD HABIT OF YOURS.
UH...
OH MAN!
KISS
...!
NN...
KISS

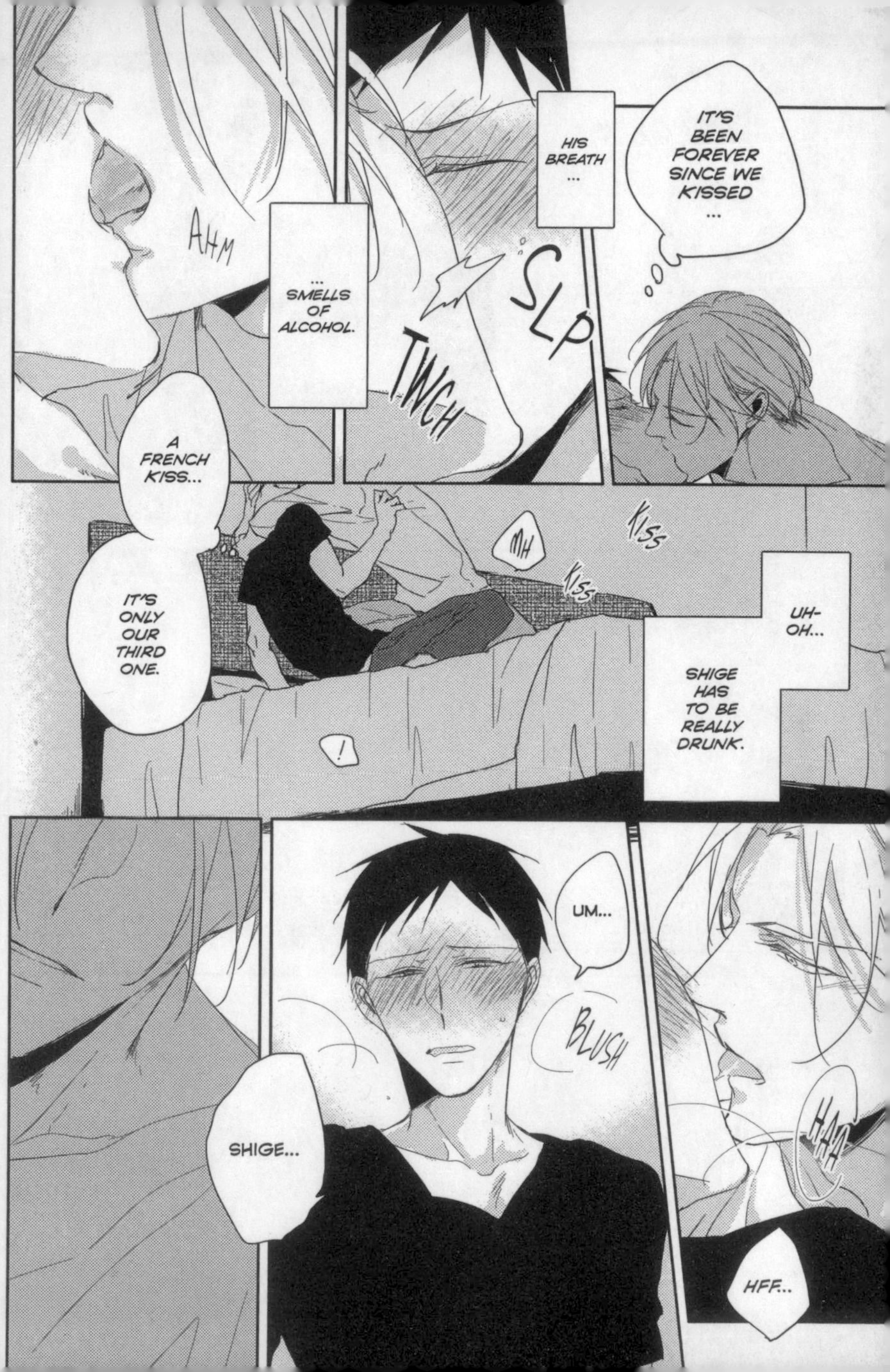
IT'S BEEN FOREVER SINCE WE KISSED ...
HIS BREATH ...
SLP
TWCH
... SMELLS OF ALCOHOL.
AHM
A FRENCH KISS...
UH-OH...
SHIGE HAS TO BE REALLY DRUNK.
KISS
KISS
MH
!
IT'S ONLY OUR THIRD ONE.
HAA
HFF...
UM...
BLUSH
SHIGE...

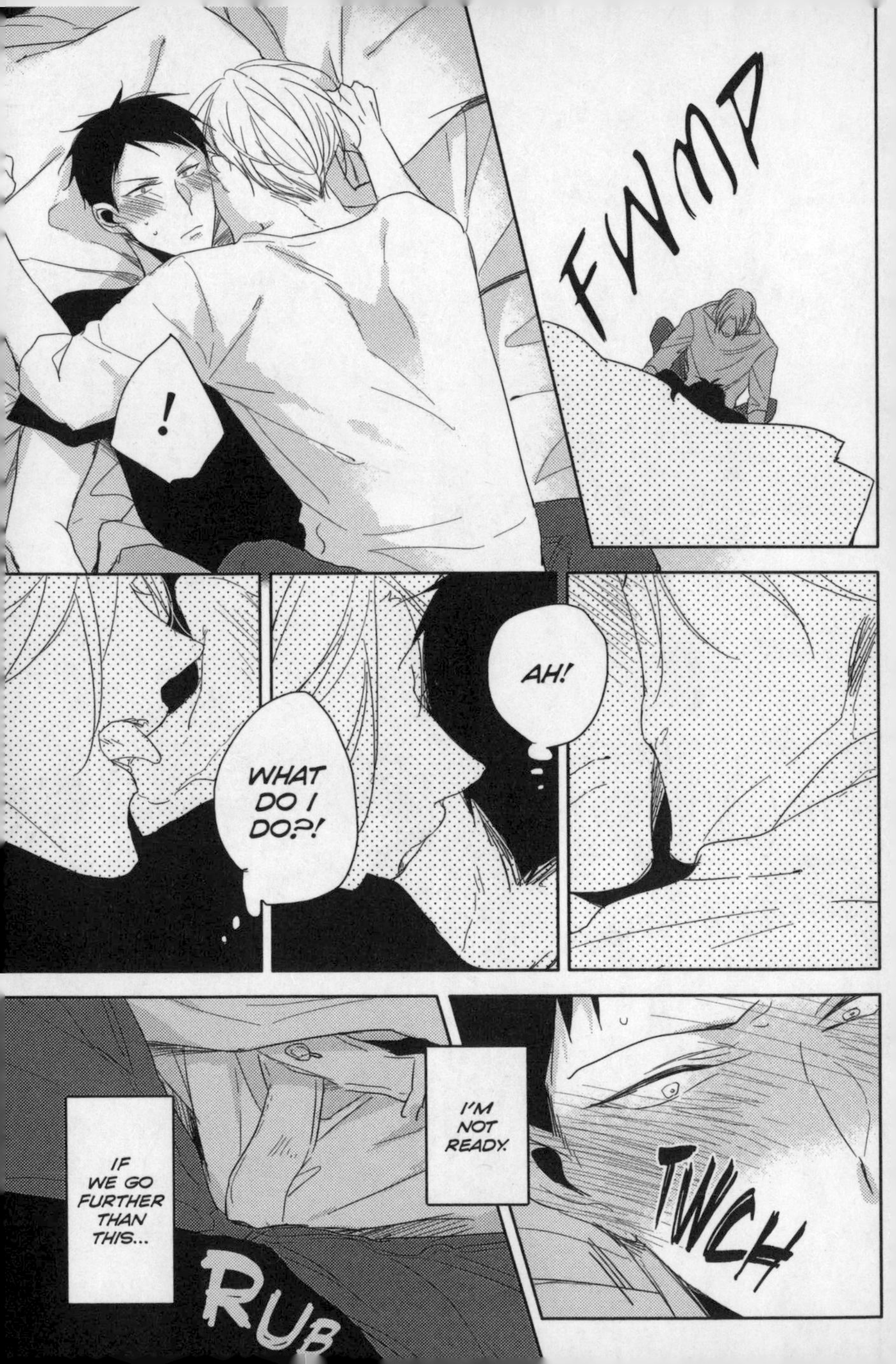
FWMP
!
AH!
WHAT DO I DO?!
TWCH
IF WE GO FURTHER THAN THIS...
I'M NOT READY.
RUB

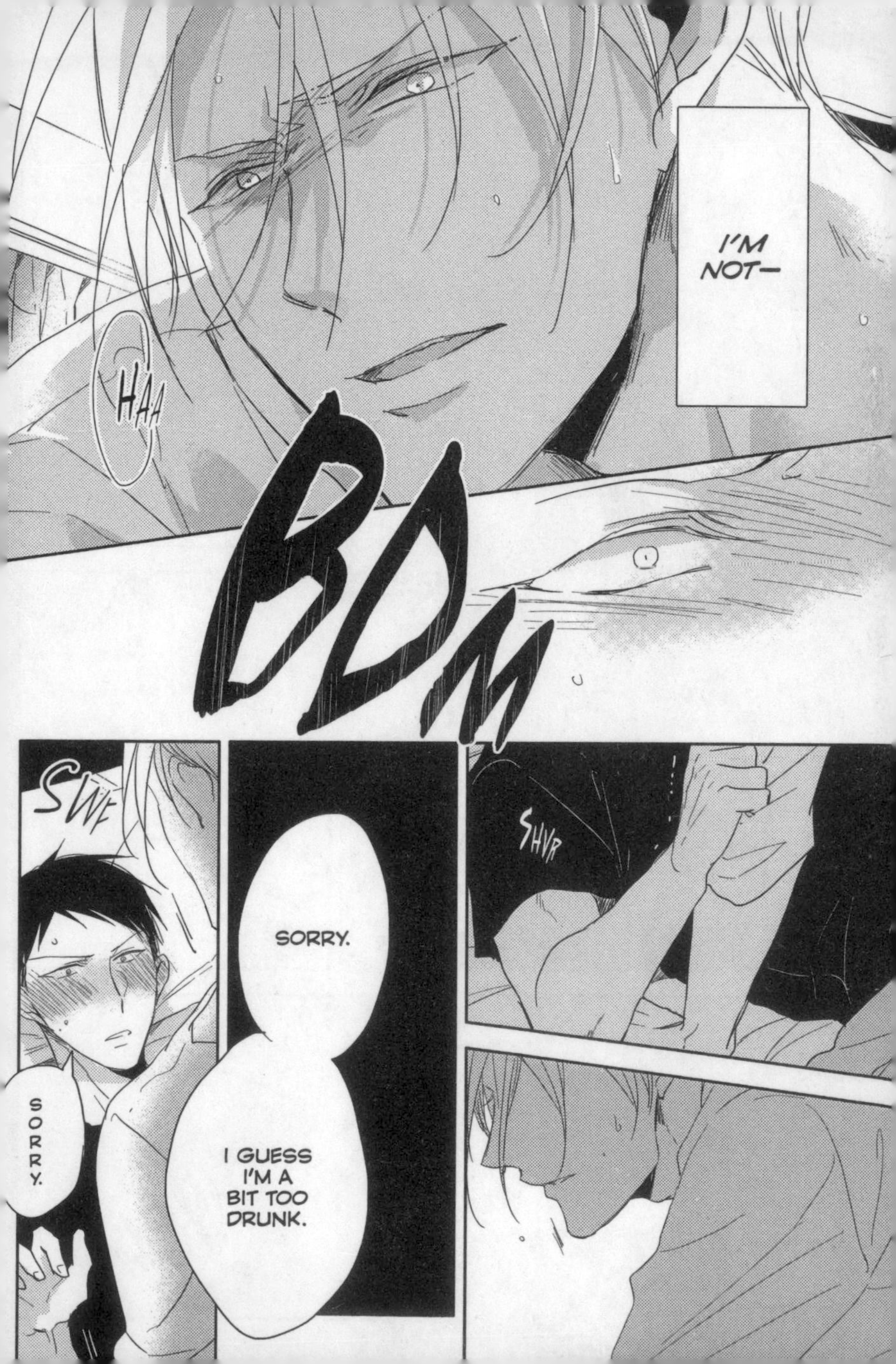
I'M NOT—
HAA
BDM
SHVR
SORRY.
I GUESS I'M A BIT TOO DRUNK.
SWF
SORRY.

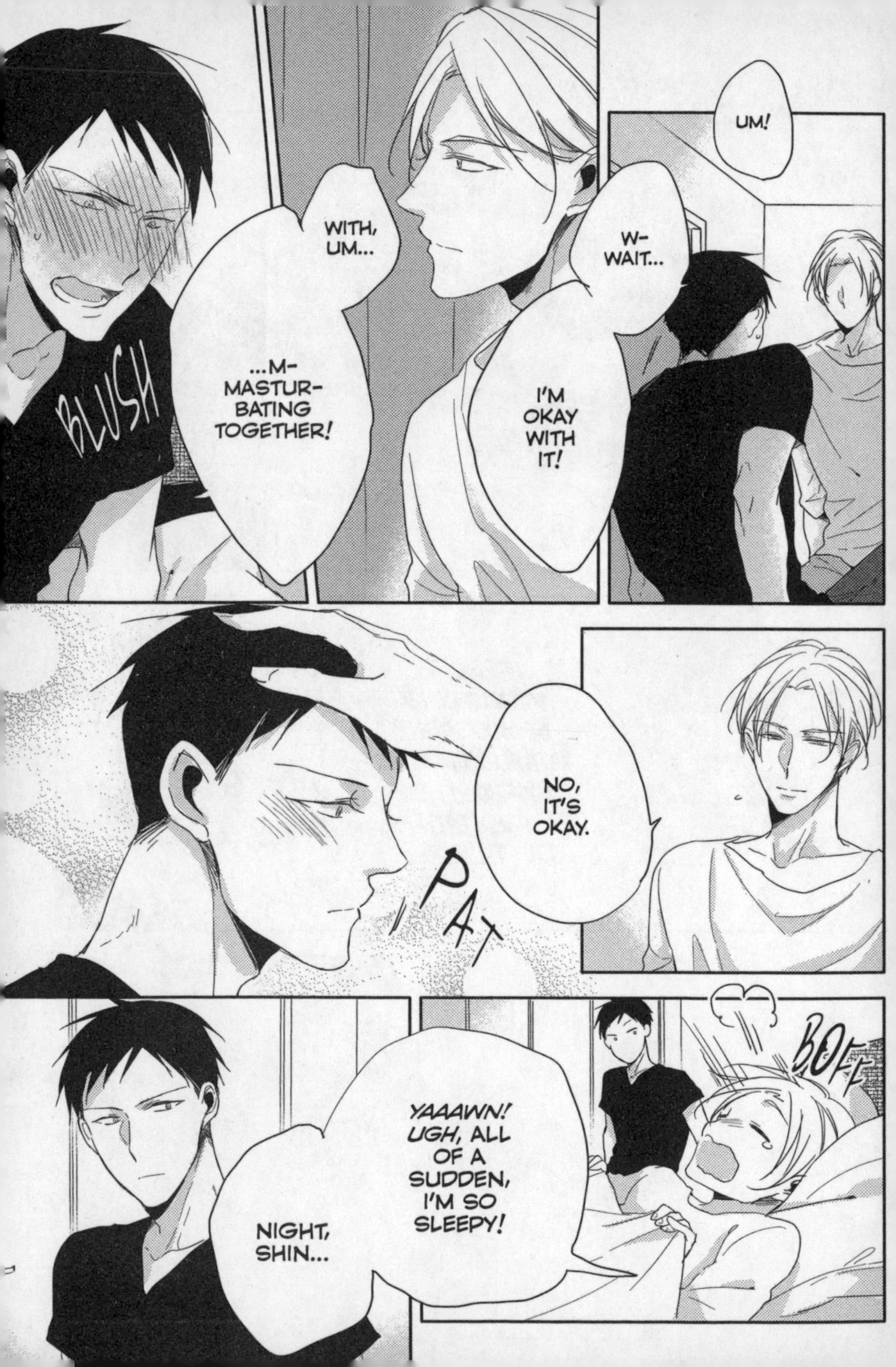
UM!
W-
WAIT...
WITH,
UM...
...M-
MASTUR-
BATING
TOGETHER!
I'M
OKAY
WITH
IT!
BLUSH
NO,
IT'S
OKAY.
PAT
BOFF
YAAAWN!
UGH, ALL
OF A
SUDDEN,
I'M SO
SLEEPY!
NIGHT,
SHIN...

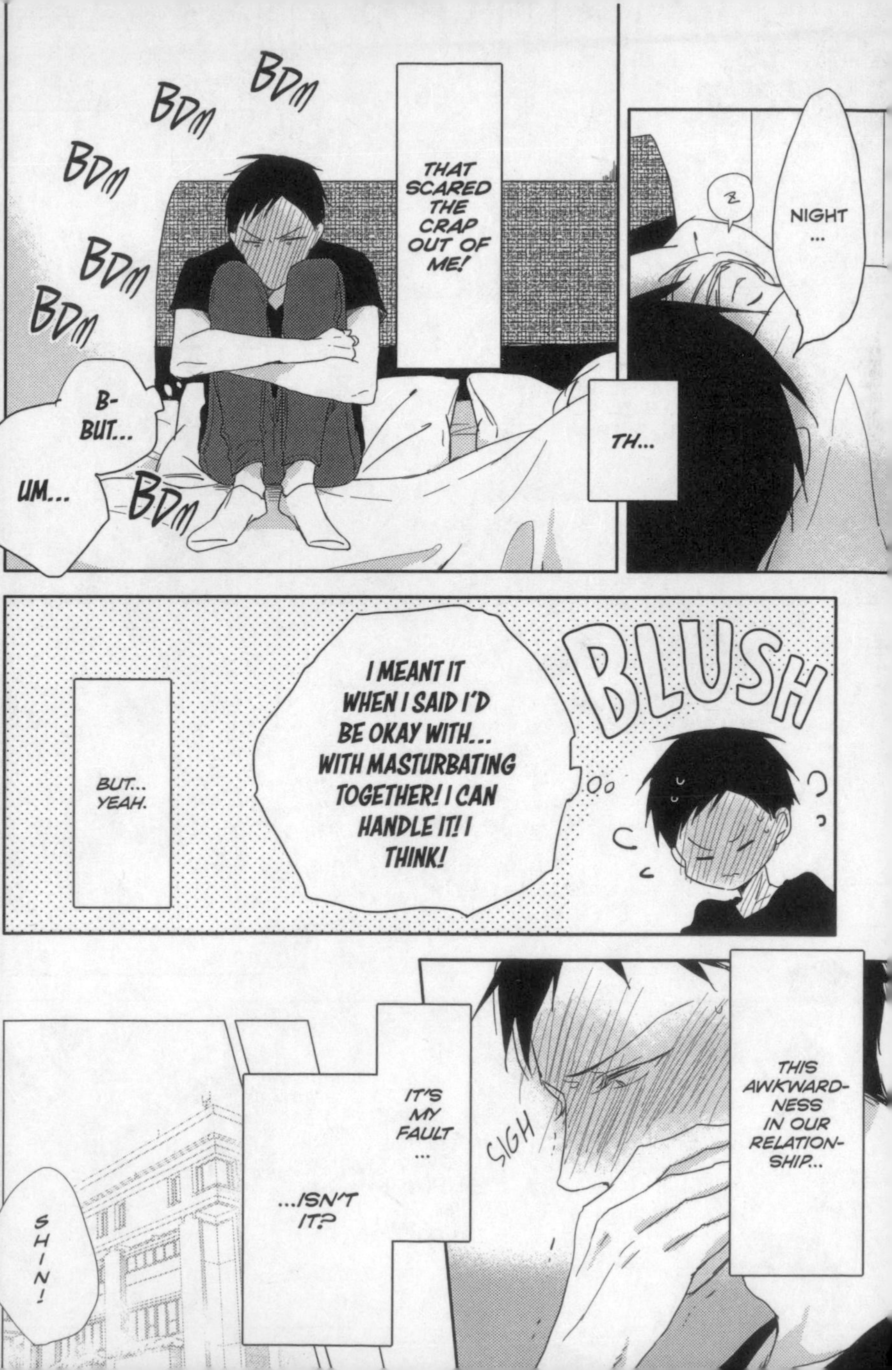
NIGHT ...
z
TH...
THAT SCARED THE CRAP OUT OF ME!
BDM
BDM
BDM
BDM
BDM
B- BUT...
UM...
BDM
BLUSH
I MEANT IT WHEN I SAID I'D BE OKAY WITH... WITH MASTURBATING TOGETHER! I CAN HANDLE IT! I THINK!
BUT... YEAH.
THIS AWKWARDNESS IN OUR RELATIONSHIP...
SIGH
IT'S MY FAULT ...
...ISN'T IT?
SHIN!

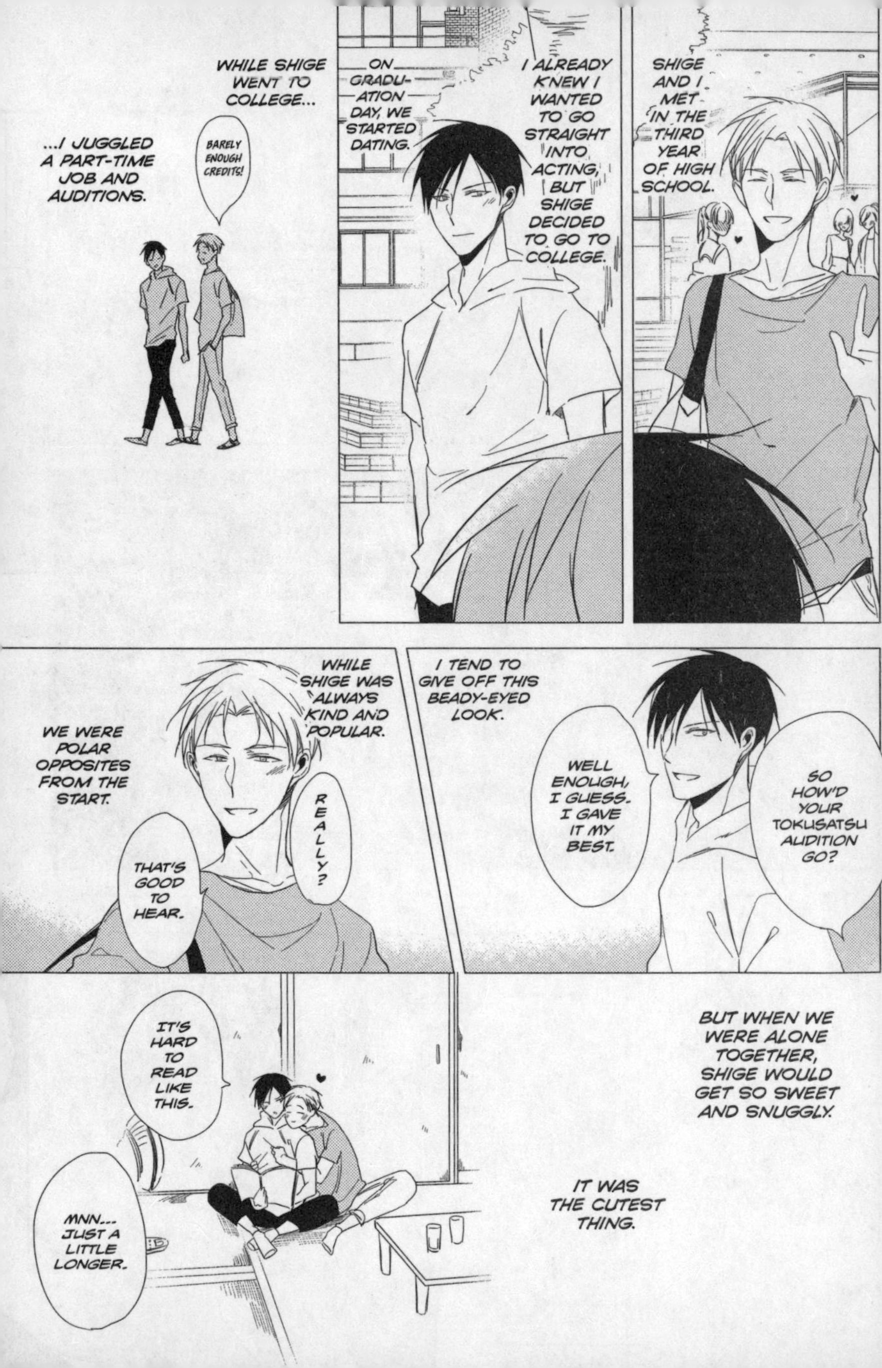
SHIGE AND I MET IN THE THIRD YEAR OF HIGH SCHOOL.
I ALREADY KNEW I WANTED TO GO STRAIGHT INTO ACTING, BUT SHIGE DECIDED TO GO TO COLLEGE.
—ON GRADUATION DAY, WE STARTED DATING.
WHILE SHIGE WENT TO COLLEGE...
BARELY ENOUGH CREDITS!
...I JUGGLED A PART-TIME JOB AND AUDITIONS.
I TEND TO GIVE OFF THIS BEADY-EYED LOOK.
SO HOW'D YOUR TOKUSATSU AUDITION GO?
WELL ENOUGH, I GUESS. I GAVE IT MY BEST.
WHILE SHIGE WAS ALWAYS KIND AND POPULAR.
REALLY?
WE WERE POLAR OPPOSITES FROM THE START.
THAT'S GOOD TO HEAR.
BUT WHEN WE WERE ALONE TOGETHER, SHIGE WOULD GET SO SWEET AND SNUGGLY.
IT WAS THE CUTEST THING.
IT'S HARD TO READ LIKE THIS.
MNN... JUST A LITTLE LONGER.

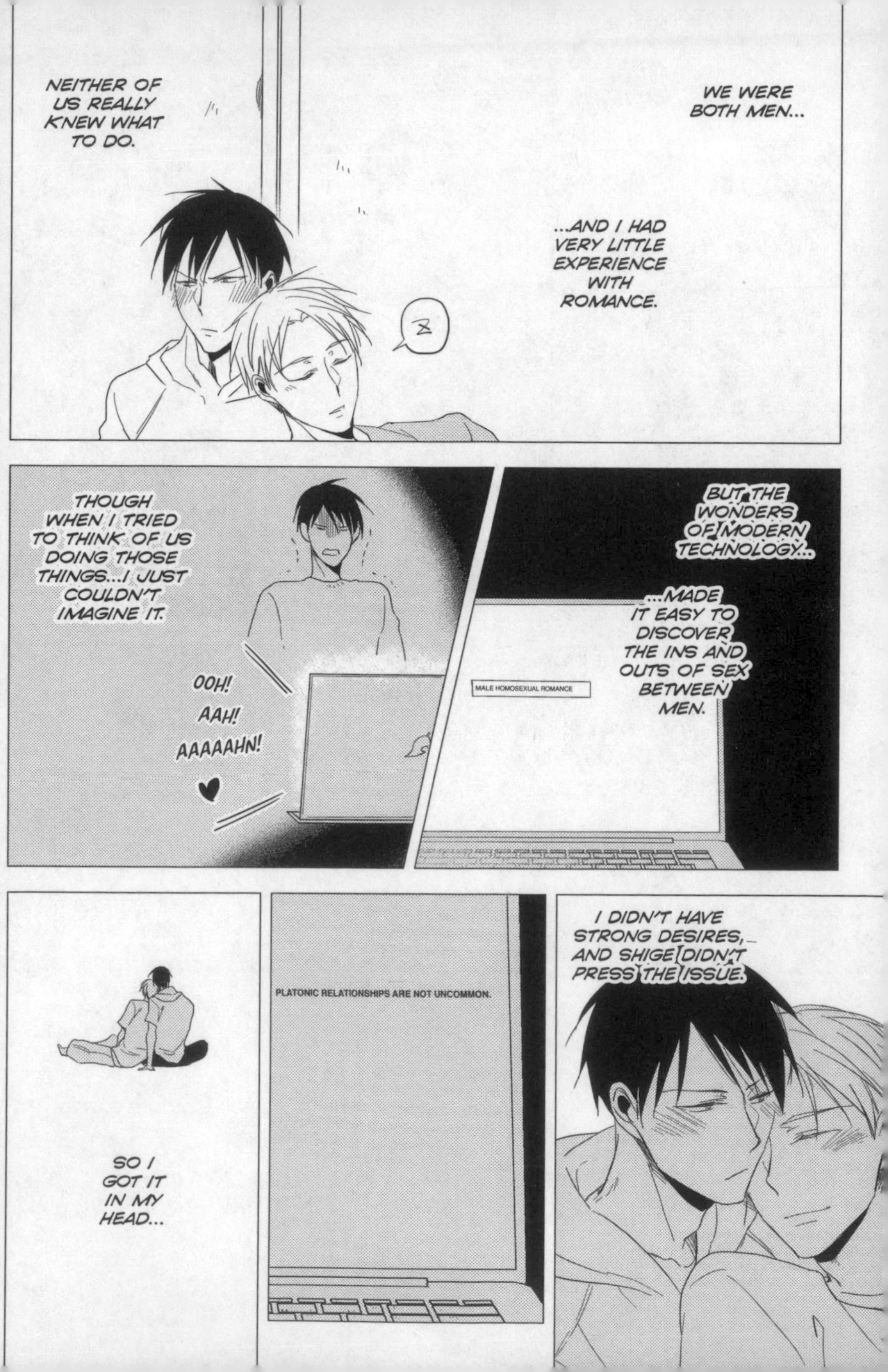
WE WERE BOTH MEN...
...AND I HAD VERY LITTLE EXPERIENCE WITH ROMANCE.
NEITHER OF US REALLY KNEW WHAT TO DO.
Z
BUT THE WONDERS OF MODERN TECHNOLOGY...
...MADE IT EASY TO DISCOVER THE INS AND OUTS OF SEX BETWEEN MEN.
MALE HOMOSEXUAL ROMANCE
THOUGH WHEN I TRIED TO THINK OF US DOING THOSE THINGS...I JUST COULDN'T IMAGINE IT.
OOH!
AAH!
AAAAAHN!
I DIDN'T HAVE STRONG DESIRES, AND SHIGE DIDN'T PRESS THE ISSUE.
PLATONIC RELATIONSHIPS ARE NOT UNCOMMON.
SO I GOT IT IN MY HEAD...

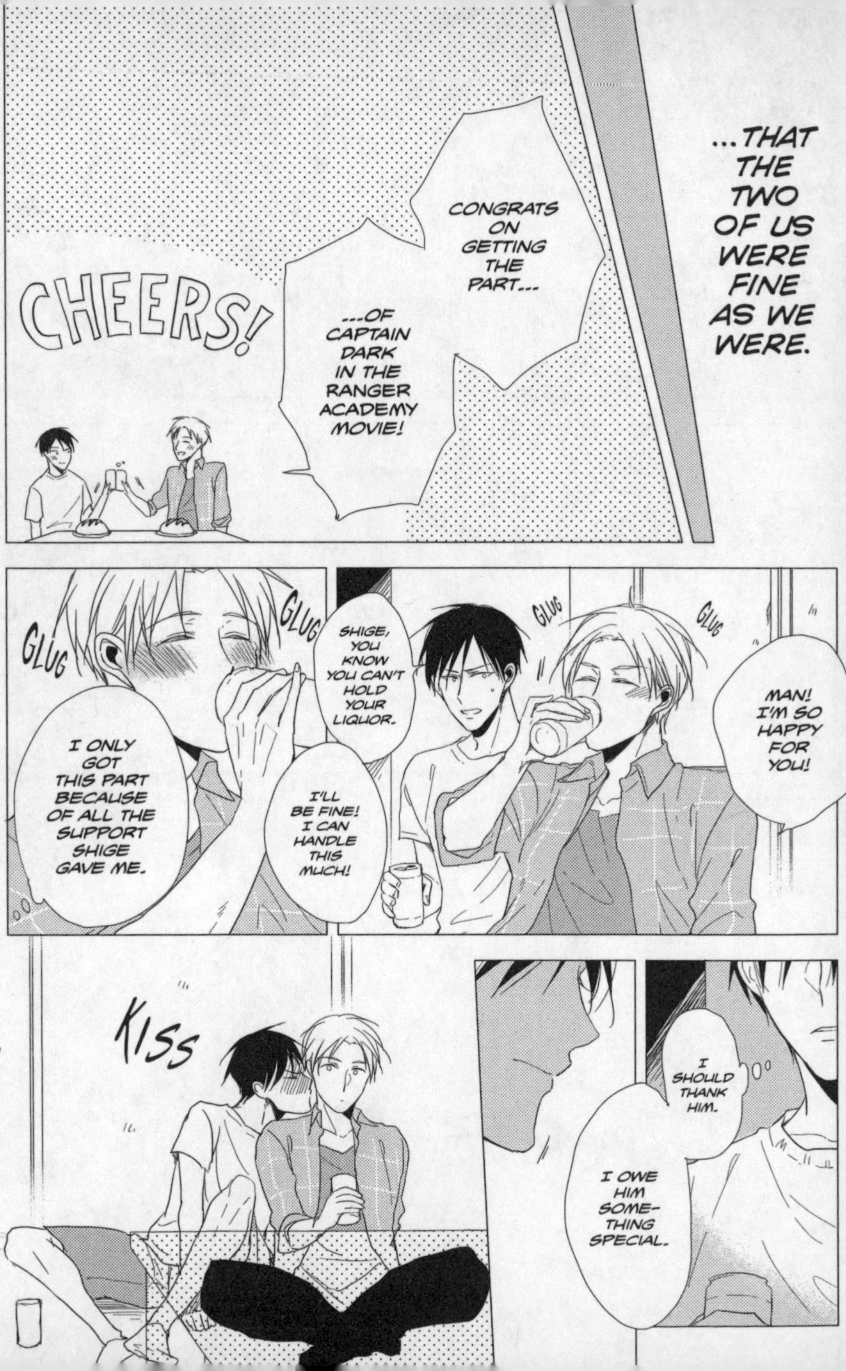
...THAT THE TWO OF US WERE FINE AS WE WERE.
CONGRATS ON GETTING THE PART...
...OF CAPTAIN DARK IN THE RANGER ACADEMY MOVIE!
CHEERS!
GLUG
GLUG
MAN! I'M SO HAPPY FOR YOU!
SHIGE, YOU KNOW YOU CAN'T HOLD YOUR LIQUOR.
I'LL BE FINE! I CAN HANDLE THIS MUCH!
GLUG
GLUG
I ONLY GOT THIS PART BECAUSE OF ALL THE SUPPORT SHIGE GAVE ME.
I SHOULD THANK HIM.
I OWE HIM SOMETHING SPECIAL.
KISS

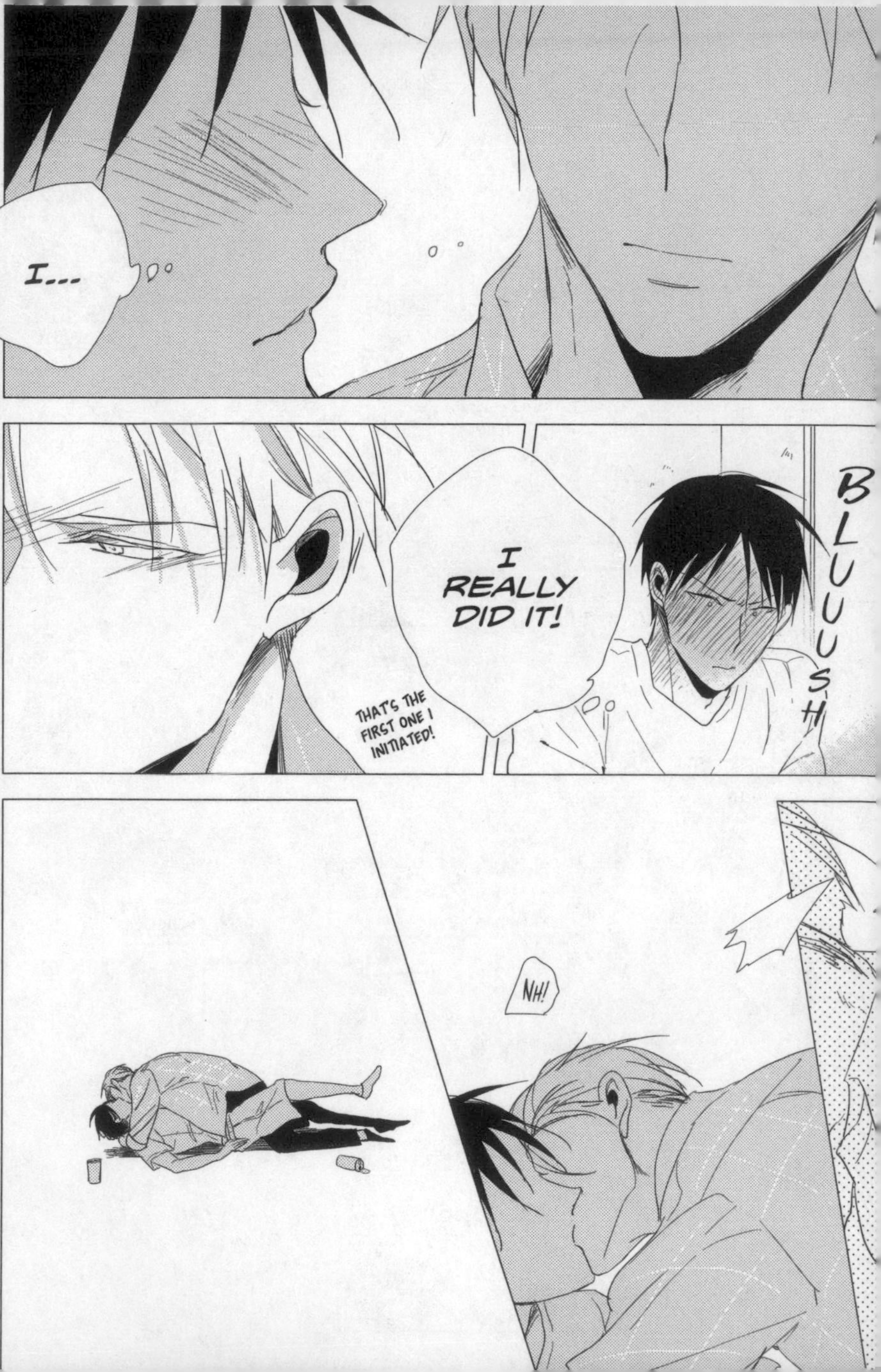
I...
BLUUUUSH
I REALLY DID IT!
THAT'S THE FIRST ONE I INITIATED!
NH!

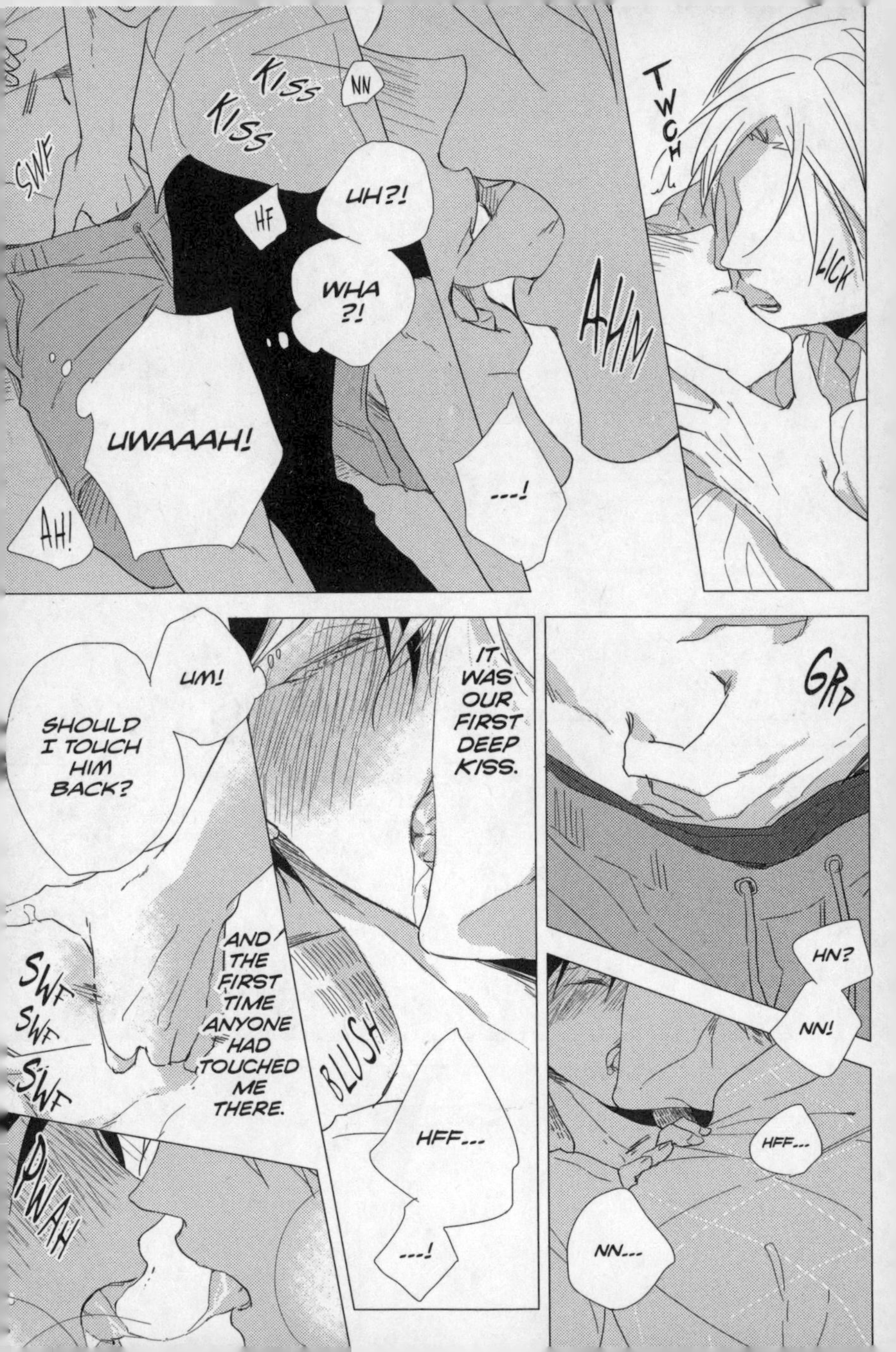
TWCH
LICK
AHN
NN
KISS
KISS
UH?!
HF
WHA ?!
SWF
---!
UWAAAH!
AH!
GRP
HN?
NN!
HFF...
NN...
IT WAS OUR FIRST DEEP KISS.
BLUSH
HFF...
---!
UM!
SHOULD I TOUCH HIM BACK?
AND THE FIRST TIME ANYONE HAD TOUCHED ME THERE.
SWF
SWF
SWF
PWAH

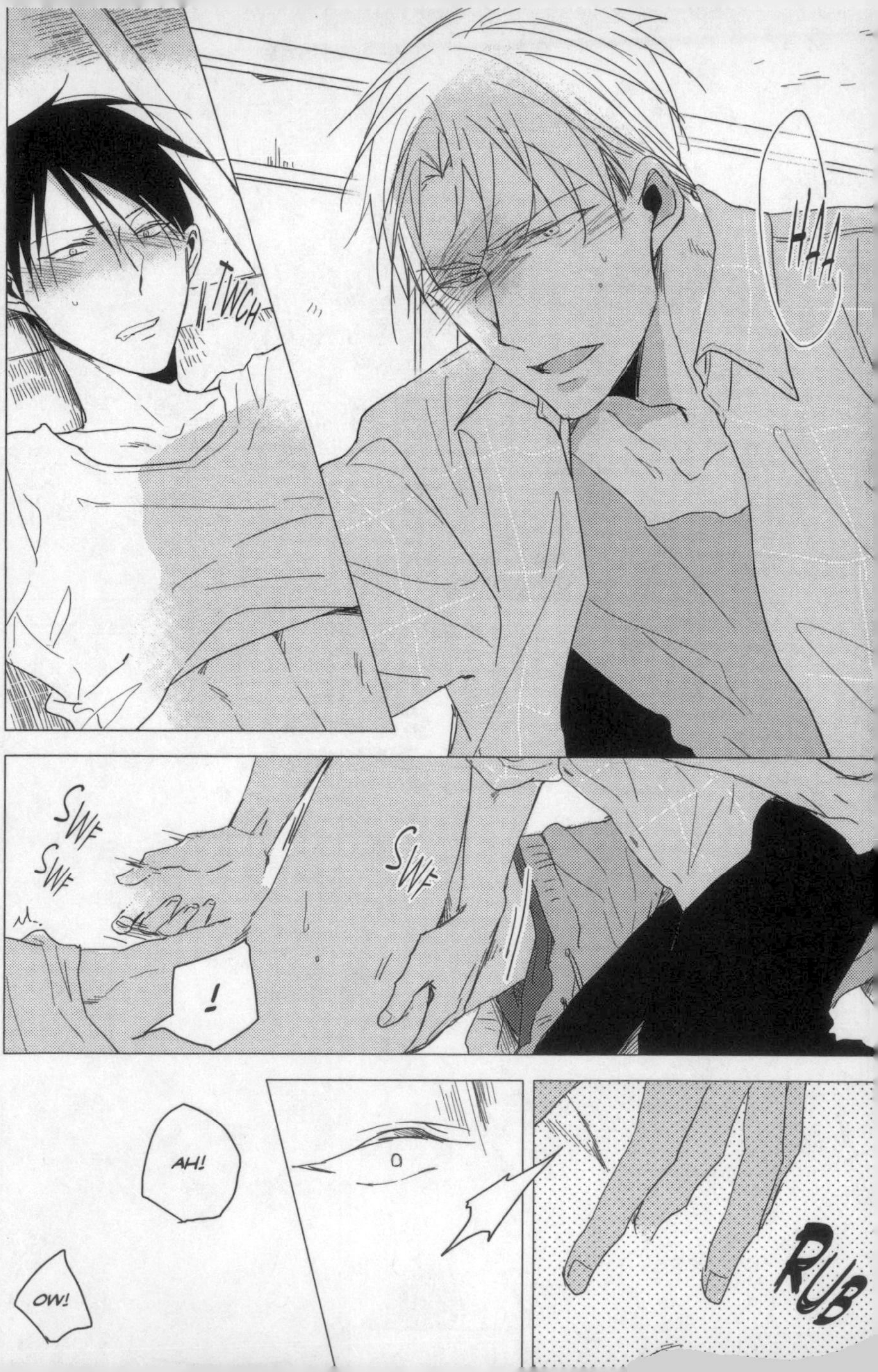
HAA
TWCH
SWF
SWF
SWF
!
RUB
AH!
OW!

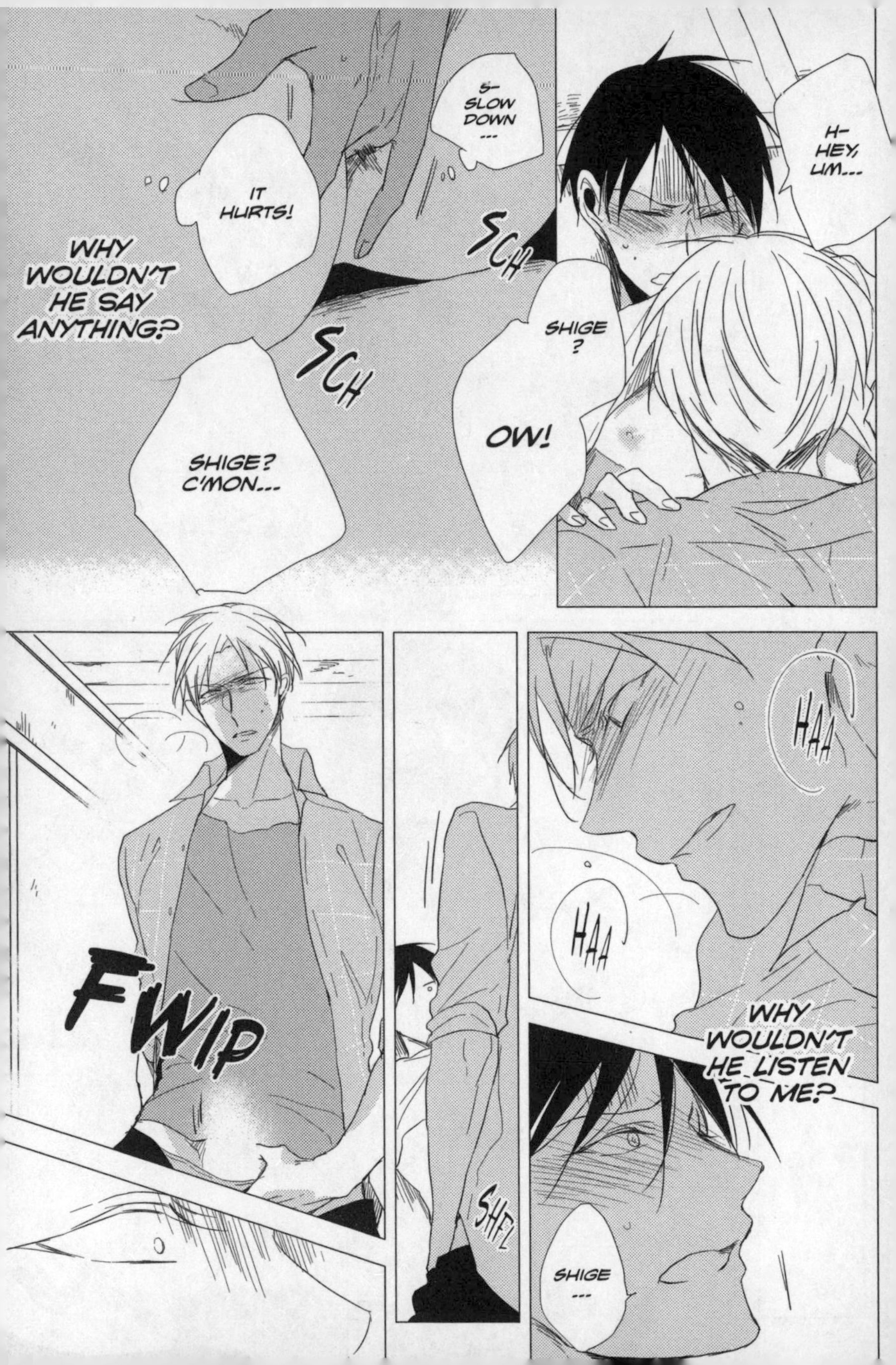
H-HEY, UM...
SHIGE?
OW!
S-SLOW DOWN...
SCH
IT HURTS!
WHY WOULDN'T HE SAY ANYTHING?
SCH
SHIGE? C'MON...
HAA
HAA
WHY WOULDN'T HE LISTEN TO ME?
SHIGE...
SHFL
FWIP

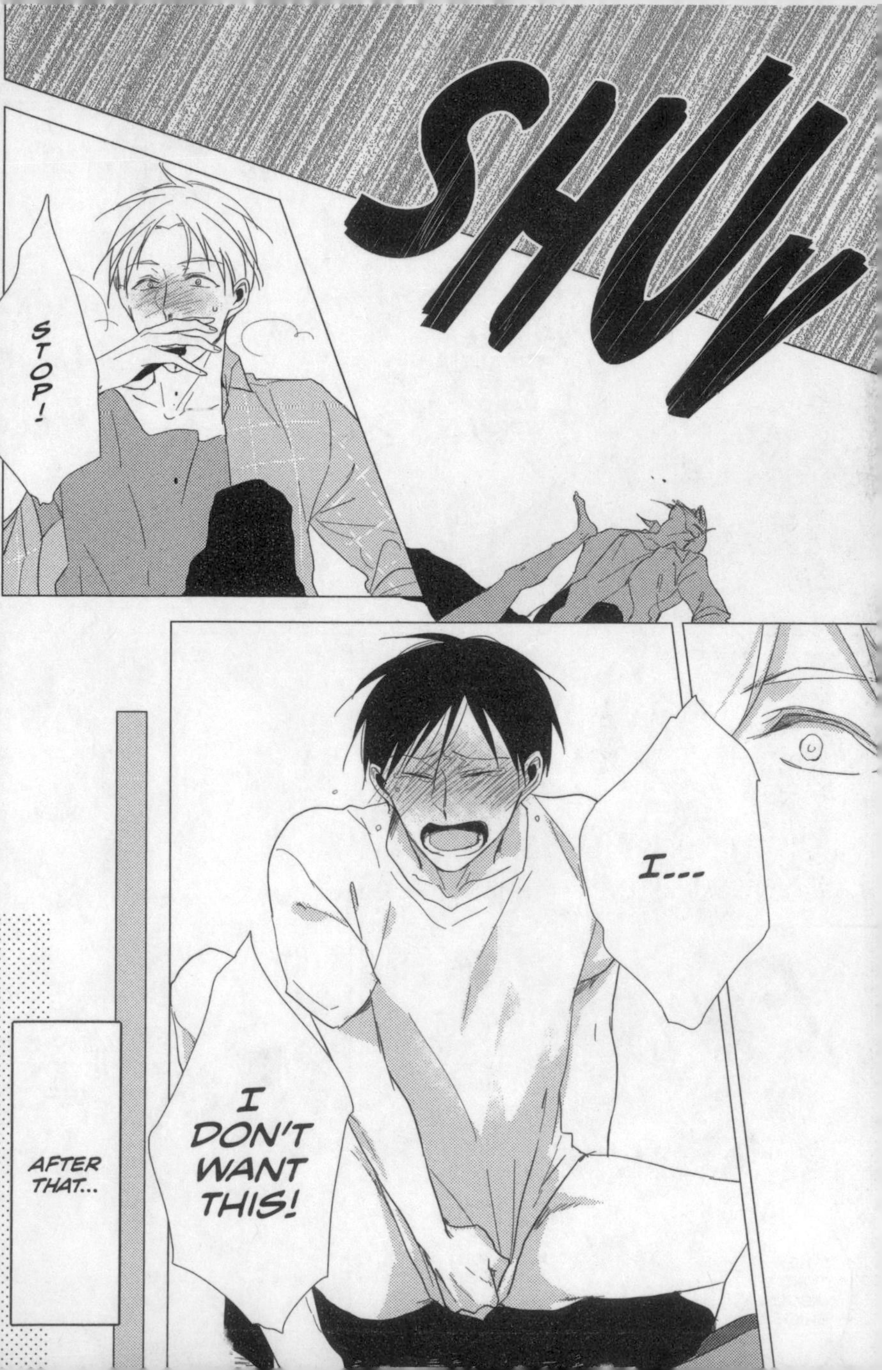
SHUV
STOP!
I...
I DON'T WANT THIS!
AFTER THAT...

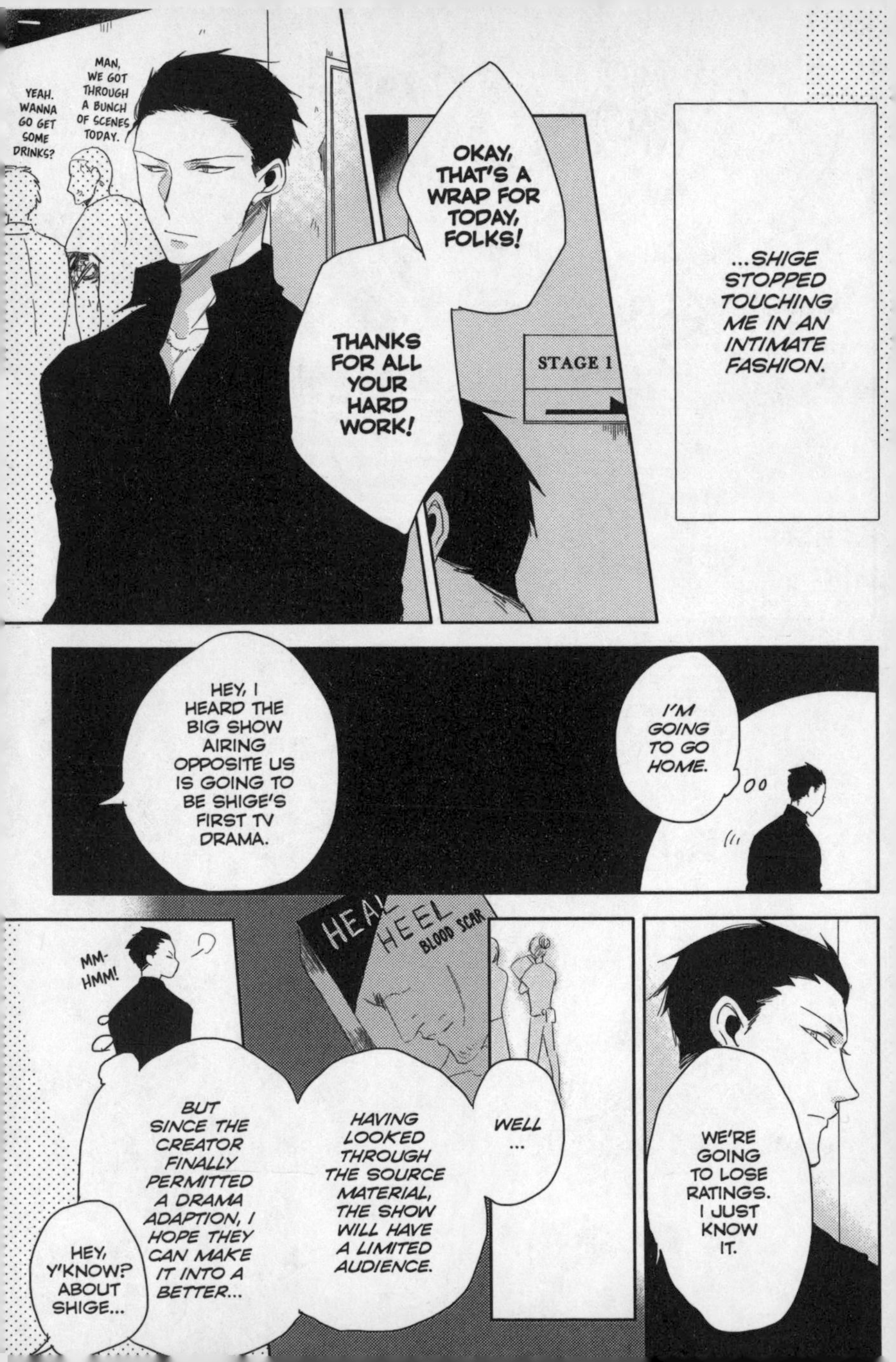
...SHIGE STOPPED TOUCHING ME IN AN INTIMATE FASHION.
STAGE 1
OKAY, THAT'S A WRAP FOR TODAY, FOLKS!
THANKS FOR ALL YOUR HARD WORK!
MAN, WE GOT THROUGH A BUNCH OF SCENES TODAY.
YEAH. WANNA GO GET SOME DRINKS?
I'M GOING TO GO HOME.
HEY, I HEARD THE BIG SHOW AIRING OPPOSITE US IS GOING TO BE SHIGE'S FIRST TV DRAMA.
WE'RE GOING TO LOSE RATINGS. I JUST KNOW IT.
HEAL
HEEL
BLOOD SCAR
WELL...
HAVING LOOKED THROUGH THE SOURCE MATERIAL, THE SHOW WILL HAVE A LIMITED AUDIENCE.
BUT SINCE THE CREATOR FINALLY PERMITTED A DRAMA ADAPTION, I HOPE THEY CAN MAKE IT INTO A BETTER...
MM-HMM!
HEY, Y'KNOW? ABOUT SHIGE...

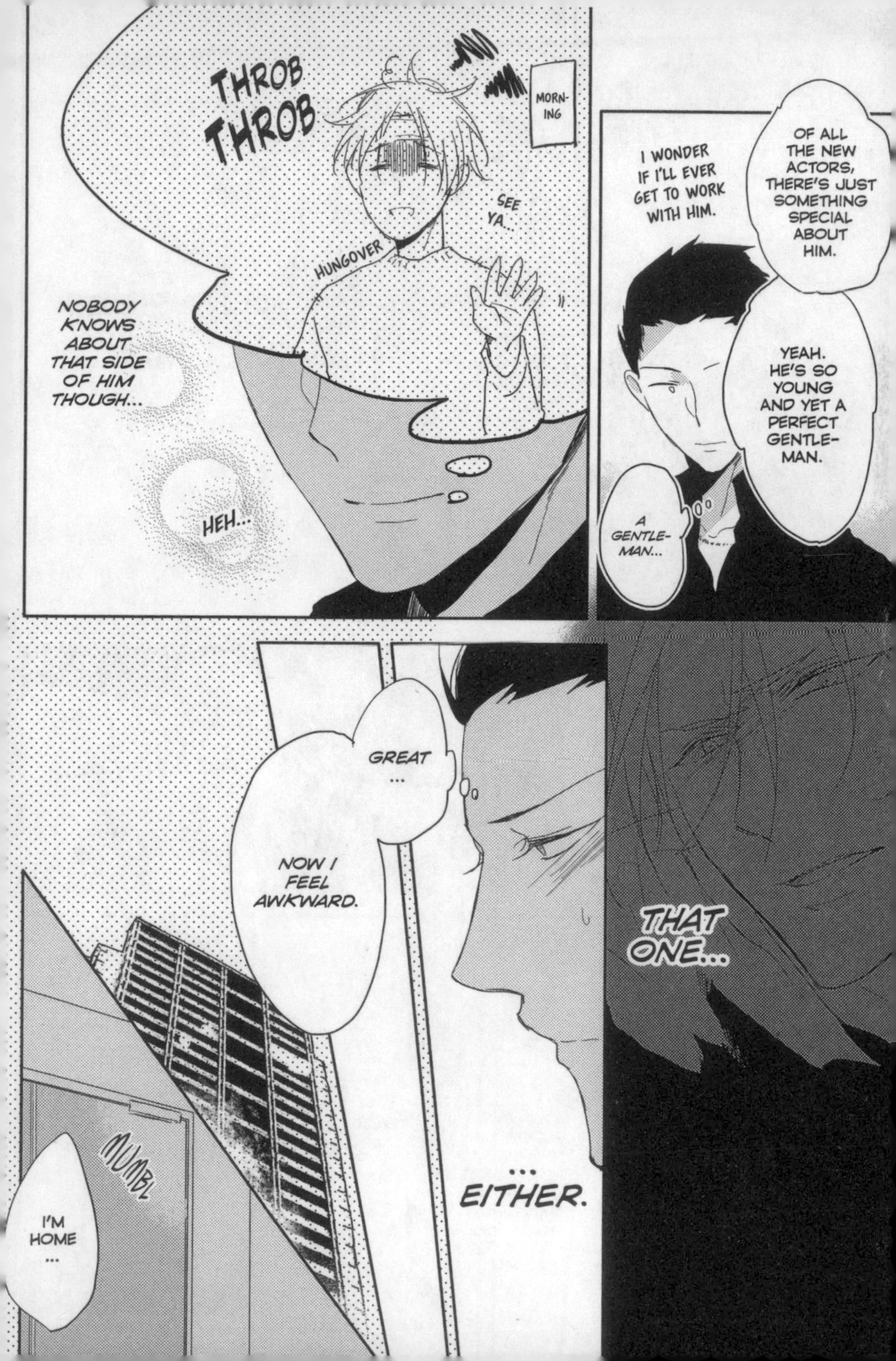
OF ALL THE NEW ACTORS, THERE'S JUST SOMETHING SPECIAL ABOUT HIM.
I WONDER IF I'LL EVER GET TO WORK WITH HIM.
YEAH. HE'S SO YOUNG AND YET A PERFECT GENTLE-MAN.
A GENTLE-MAN...
MORN-ING
THROB THROB
SEE YA...
HUNGOVER
NOBODY KNOWS ABOUT THAT SIDE OF HIM THOUGH...
HEH...
THAT ONE...
GREAT...
NOW I FEEL AWKWARD.
...EITHER.
MUMBL
I'M HOME...

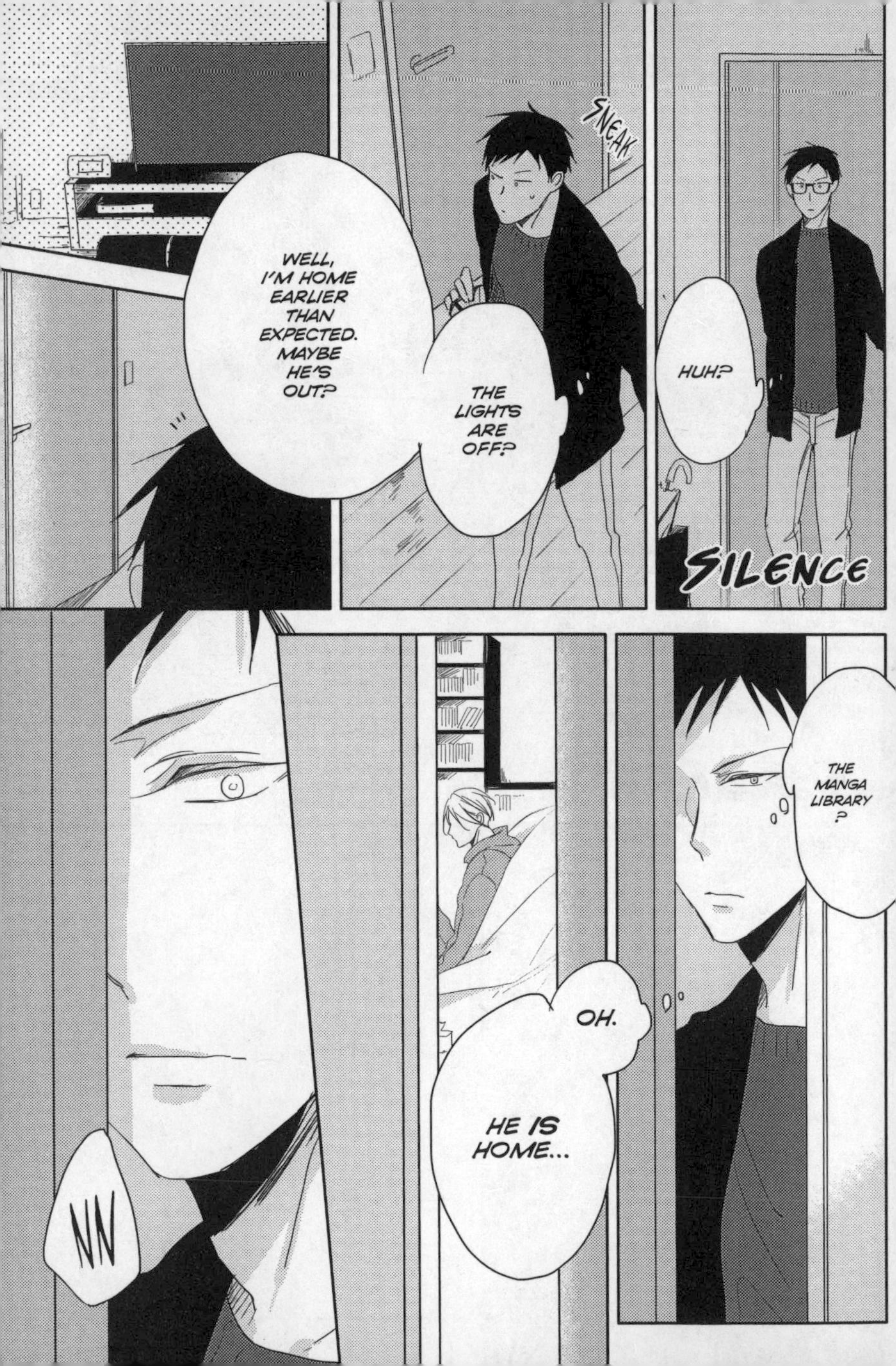
HUH?
SILENCE
SNEAK
THE LIGHTS ARE OFF?
WELL, I'M HOME EARLIER THAN EXPECTED. MAYBE HE'S OUT?
THE MANGA LIBRARY?
OH.
HE IS HOME...
NN

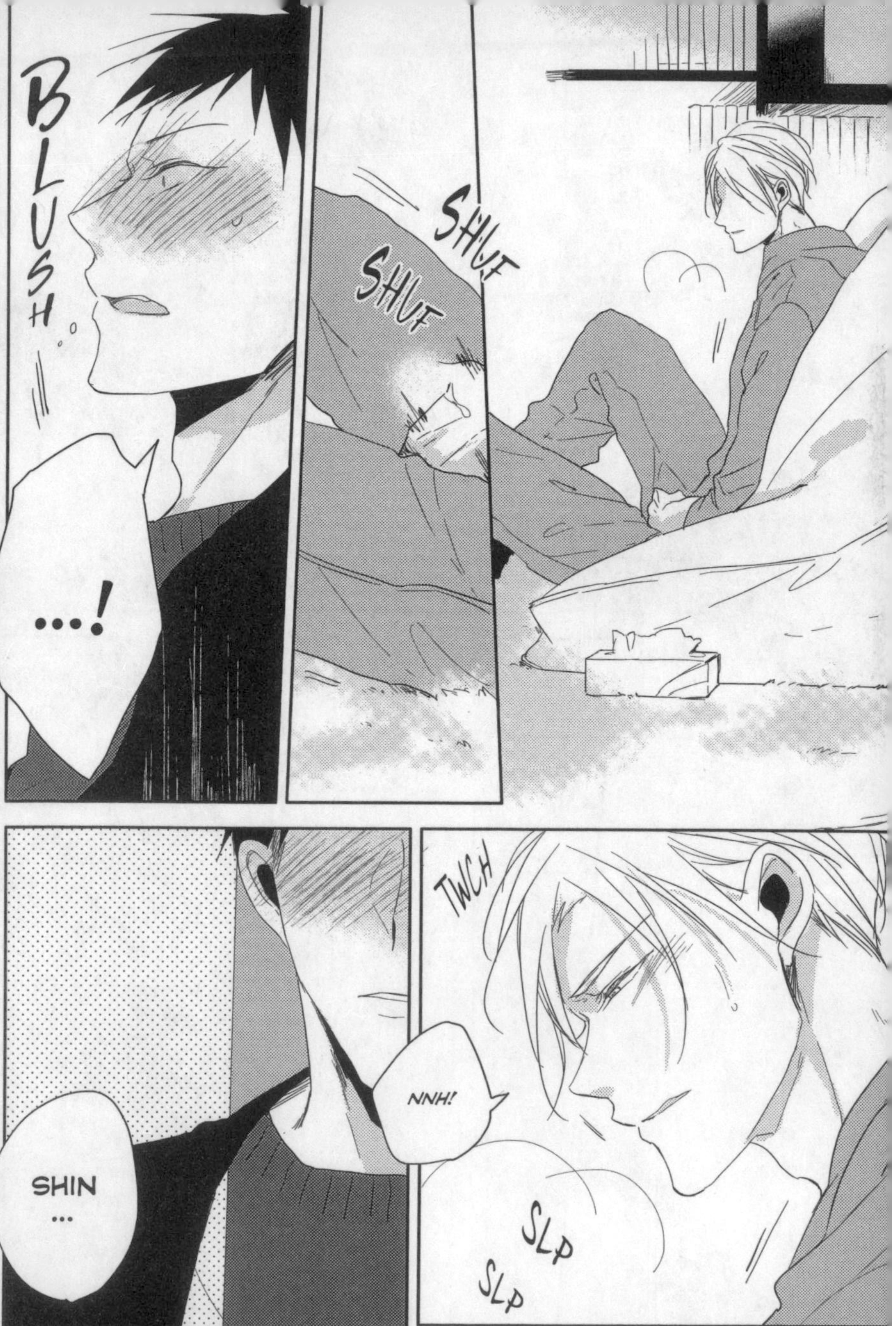
SHUF
SHUF
BLUSH
...!
TWCH
SLP
SLP
NNH!
SHIN
...

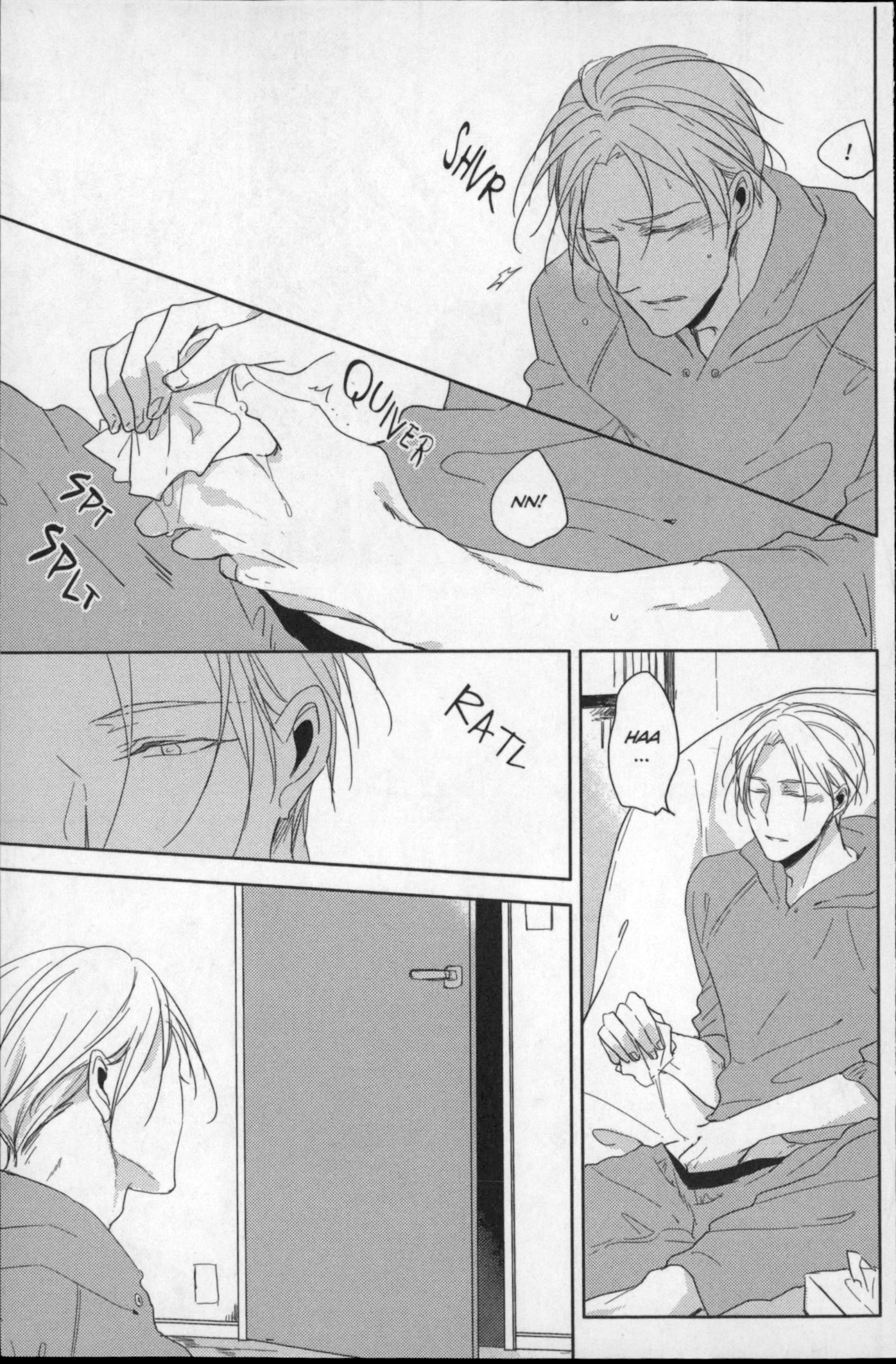
!
SHVR
NN!
QUIVER
SPT
SPLT
HAA ...
RATL

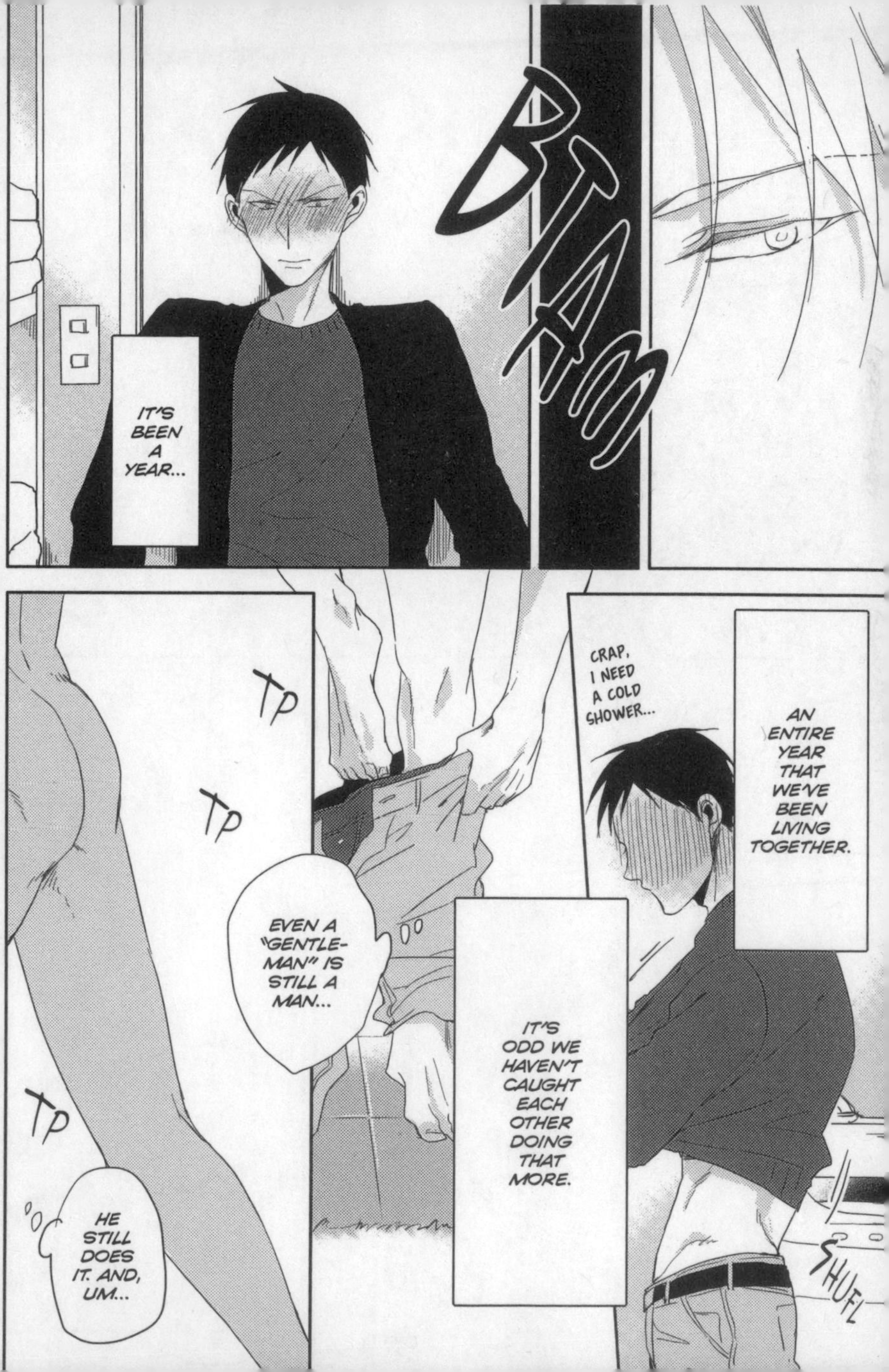
BLAM
IT'S BEEN A YEAR...
AN ENTIRE YEAR THAT WE'VE BEEN LIVING TOGETHER.
CRAP, I NEED A COLD SHOWER...
SHUFL
IT'S ODD WE HAVEN'T CAUGHT EACH OTHER DOING THAT MORE.
EVEN A "GENTLE-MAN" IS STILL A MAN...
TP
TP
TP
HE STILL DOES IT. AND, UM...

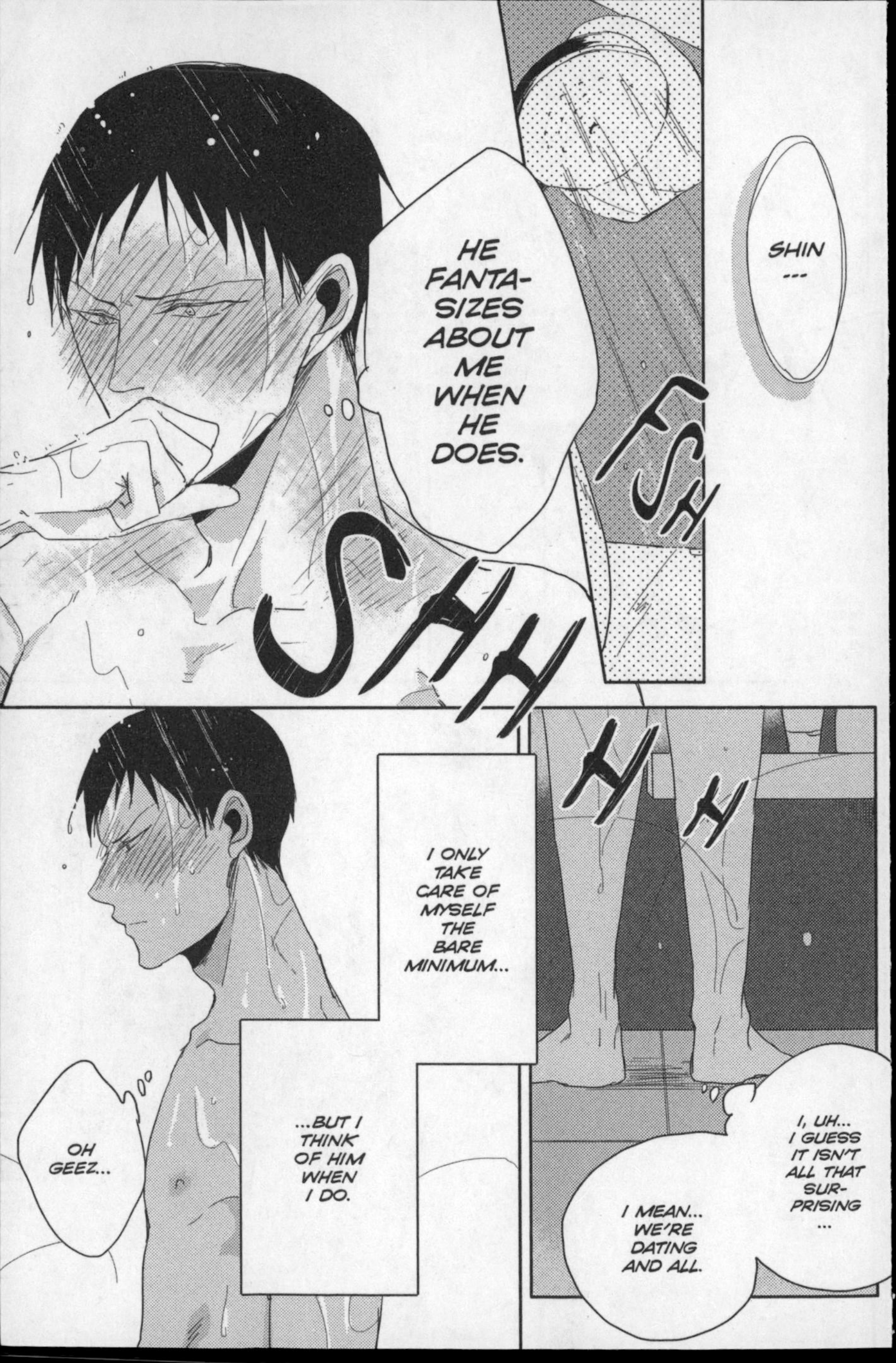
SHIN ---
FSH
HE FANTA-SIZES ABOUT ME WHEN HE DOES.
SHHHH
I, UH... I GUESS IT ISN'T ALL THAT SUR-PRISING ...
I MEAN... WE'RE DATING AND ALL.
I ONLY TAKE CARE OF MYSELF THE BARE MINIMUM...
...BUT I THINK OF HIM WHEN I DO.
OH GEEZ...

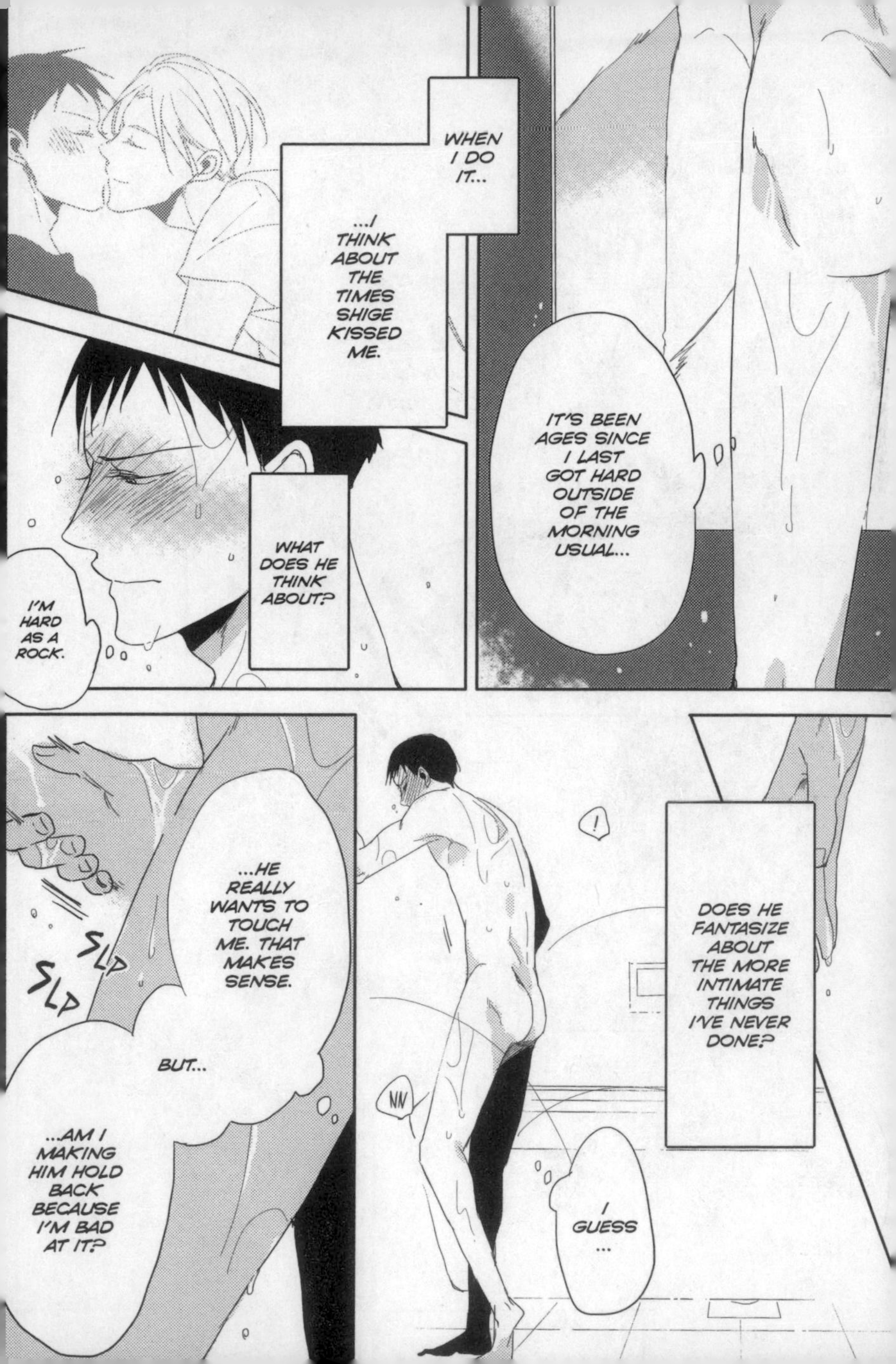
IT'S BEEN AGES SINCE I LAST GOT HARD OUTSIDE OF THE MORNING USUAL...
WHEN I DO IT...
...I THINK ABOUT THE TIMES SHIGE KISSED ME.
WHAT DOES HE THINK ABOUT?
I'M HARD AS A ROCK.
DOES HE FANTASIZE ABOUT THE MORE INTIMATE THINGS I'VE NEVER DONE?
!
NN
I GUESS ...
...HE REALLY WANTS TO TOUCH ME. THAT MAKES SENSE.
SLP
SLP
BUT...
...AM I MAKING HIM HOLD BACK BECAUSE I'M BAD AT IT?

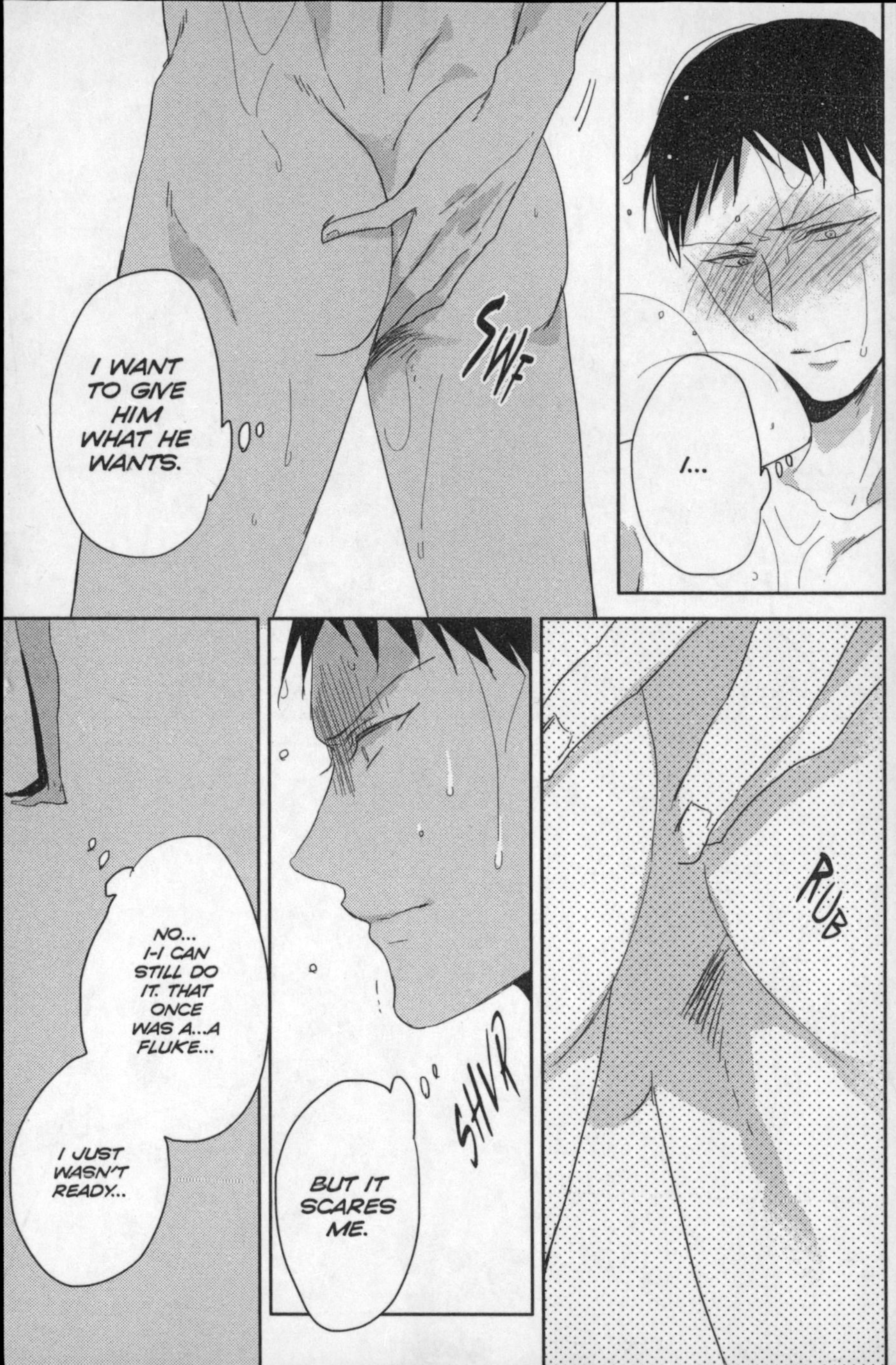
I...
SWF
I WANT TO GIVE HIM WHAT HE WANTS.
RUB
SHVR
BUT IT SCARES ME.
NO... I-I CAN STILL DO IT. THAT ONCE WAS A...A FLUKE...
I JUST WASN'T READY...

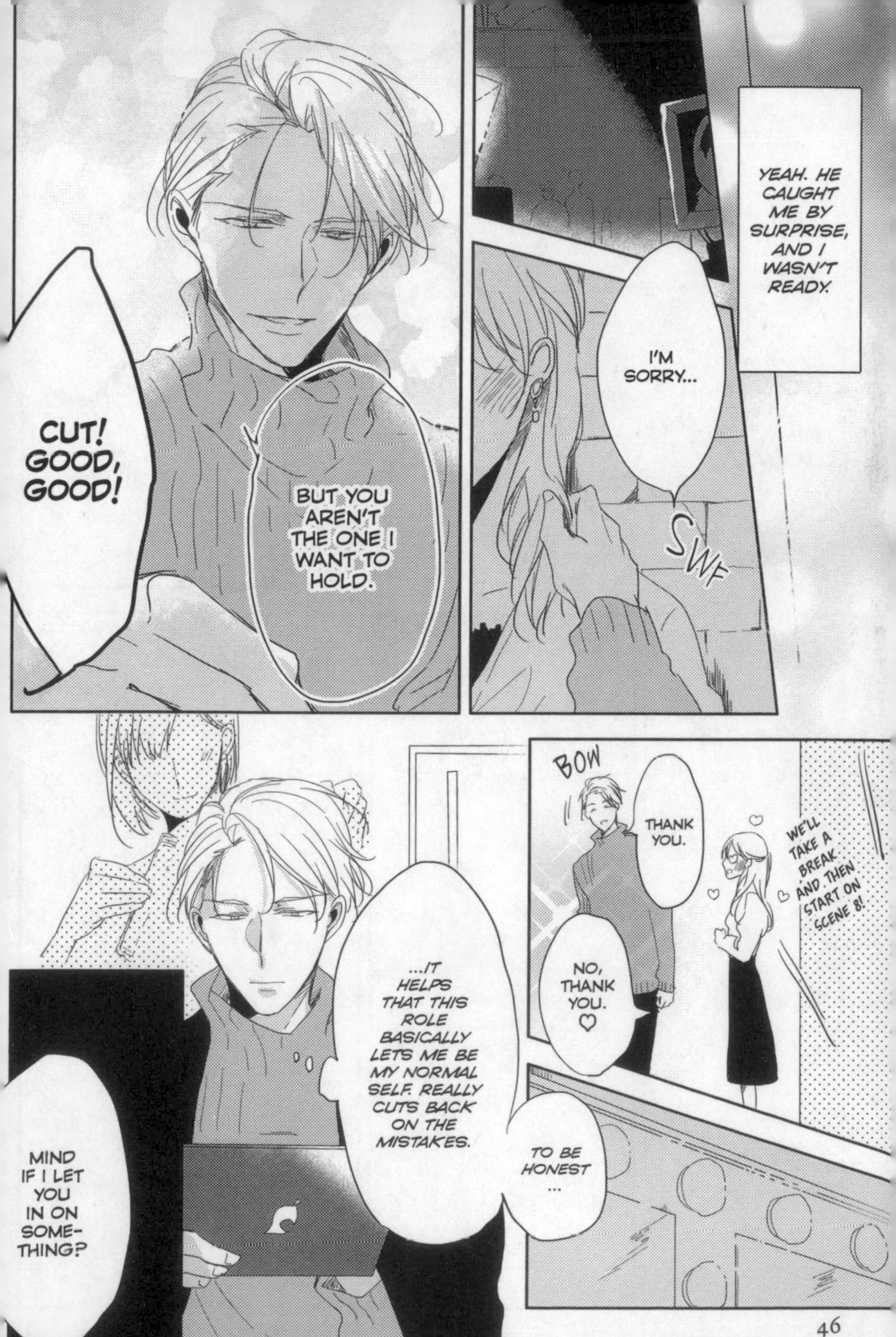
YEAH. HE CAUGHT ME BY SURPRISE, AND I WASN'T READY.
I'M SORRY...
SWF
BUT YOU AREN'T THE ONE I WANT TO HOLD.
CUT! GOOD, GOOD!
WE'LL TAKE A BREAK AND THEN START ON SCENE 8!
BOW
THANK YOU.
NO, THANK YOU. ♡
TO BE HONEST...
...IT HELPS THAT THIS ROLE BASICALLY LETS ME BE MY NORMAL SELF. REALLY CUTS BACK ON THE MISTAKES.
MIND IF I LET YOU IN ON SOMETHING?

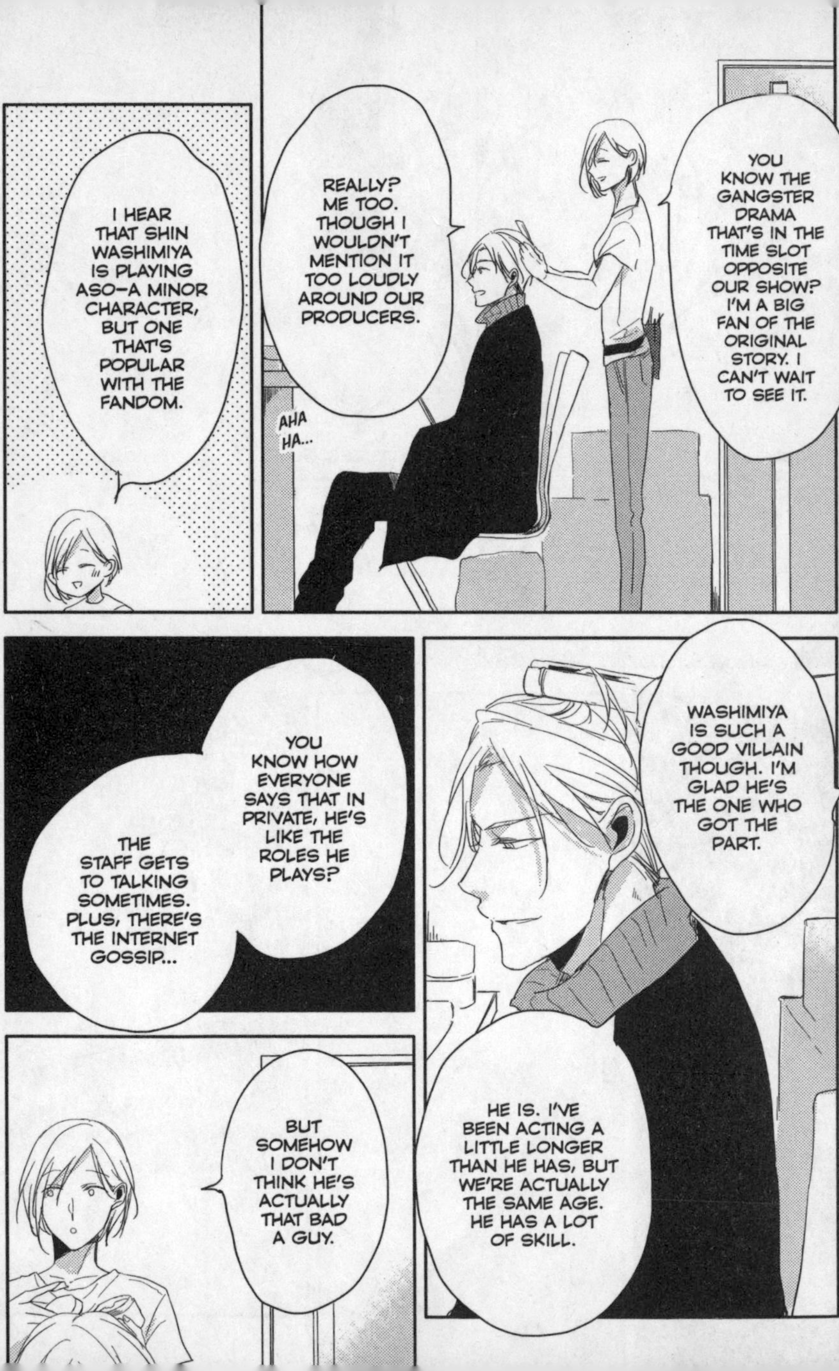
YOU KNOW THE GANGSTER DRAMA THAT'S IN THE TIME SLOT OPPOSITE OUR SHOW? I'M A BIG FAN OF THE ORIGINAL STORY. I CAN'T WAIT TO SEE IT.
REALLY? ME TOO. THOUGH I WOULDN'T MENTION IT TOO LOUDLY AROUND OUR PRODUCERS.
AHA HA...
I HEAR THAT SHIN WASHIMIYA IS PLAYING ASO—A MINOR CHARACTER, BUT ONE THAT'S POPULAR WITH THE FANDOM.
WASHIMIYA IS SUCH A GOOD VILLAIN THOUGH. I'M GLAD HE'S THE ONE WHO GOT THE PART.
HE IS. I'VE BEEN ACTING A LITTLE LONGER THAN HE HAS, BUT WE'RE ACTUALLY THE SAME AGE. HE HAS A LOT OF SKILL.
YOU KNOW HOW EVERYONE SAYS THAT IN PRIVATE, HE'S LIKE THE ROLES HE PLAYS?
THE STAFF GETS TO TALKING SOMETIMES. PLUS, THERE'S THE INTERNET GOSSIP...
BUT SOMEHOW I DON'T THINK HE'S ACTUALLY THAT BAD A GUY.

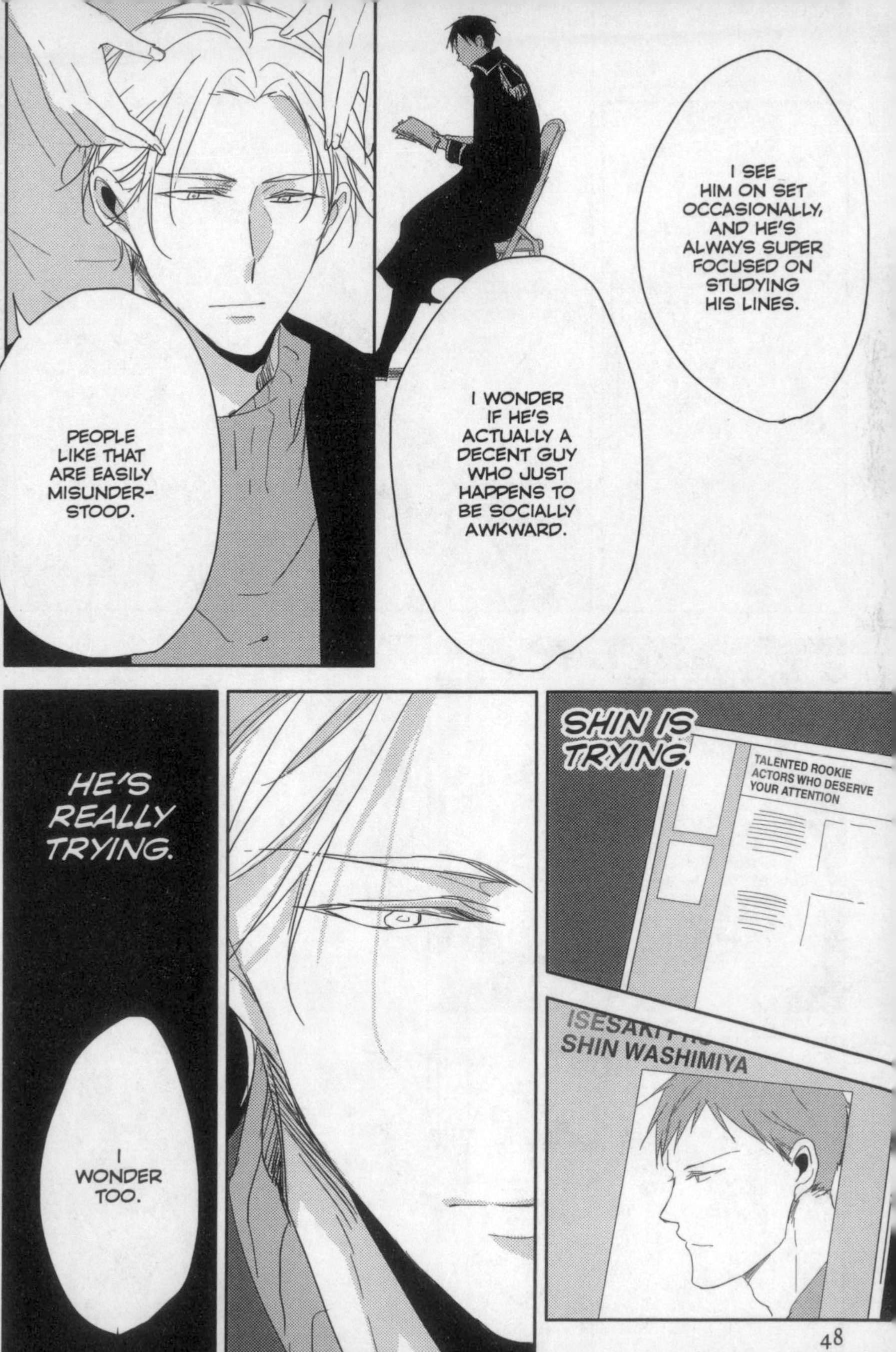
I SEE HIM ON SET OCCASIONALLY, AND HE'S ALWAYS SUPER FOCUSED ON STUDYING HIS LINES.
I WONDER IF HE'S ACTUALLY A DECENT GUY WHO JUST HAPPENS TO BE SOCIALLY AWKWARD.
PEOPLE LIKE THAT ARE EASILY MISUNDER-STOOD.
SHIN IS TRYING.
TALENTED ROOKIE ACTORS WHO DESERVE YOUR ATTENTION
ISESAKI
SHIN WASHIMIYA
HE'S REALLY TRYING.
I WONDER TOO.

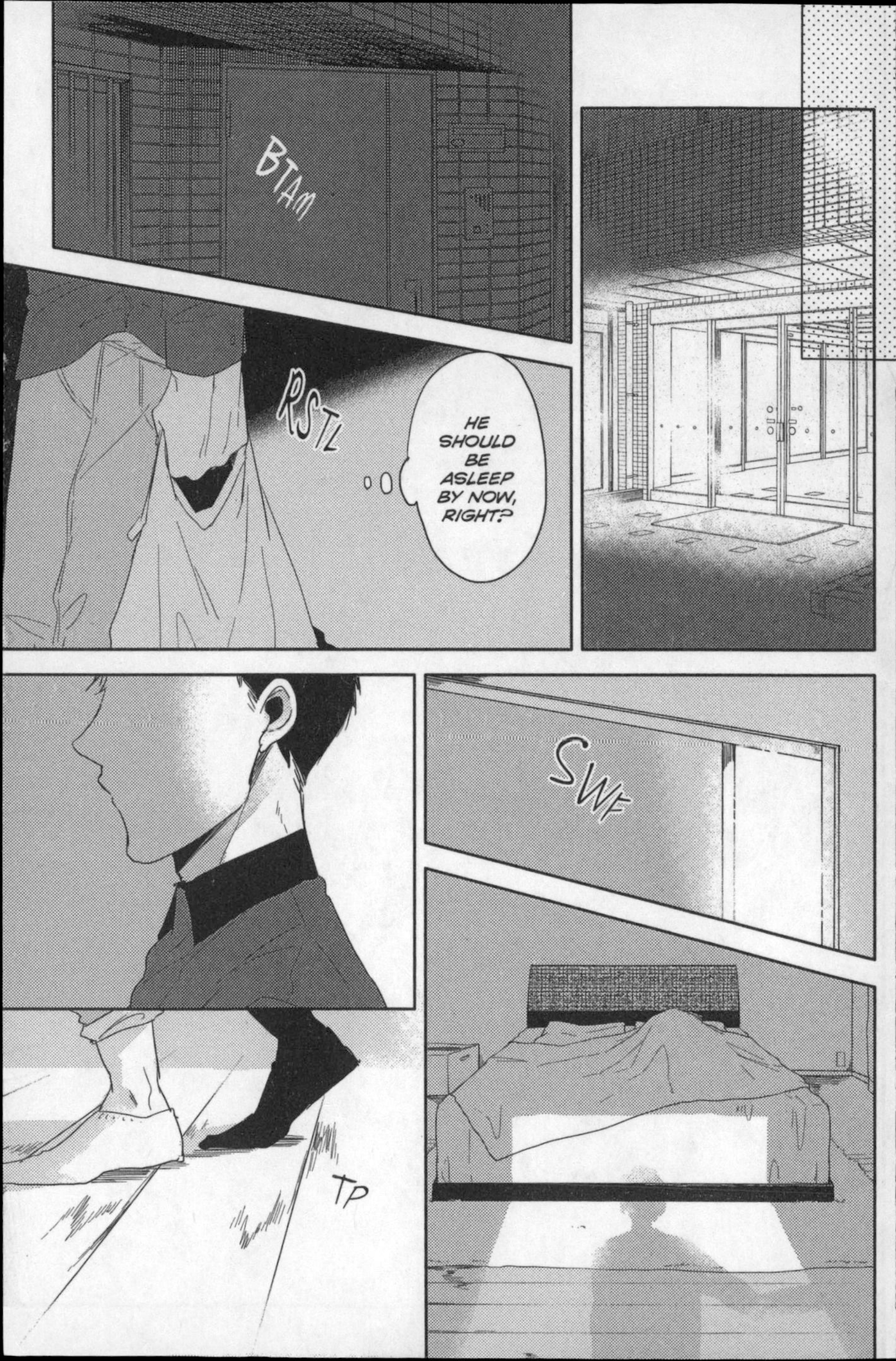
BTAM
RSTL
HE SHOULD BE ASLEEP BY NOW, RIGHT?
SWF
TP

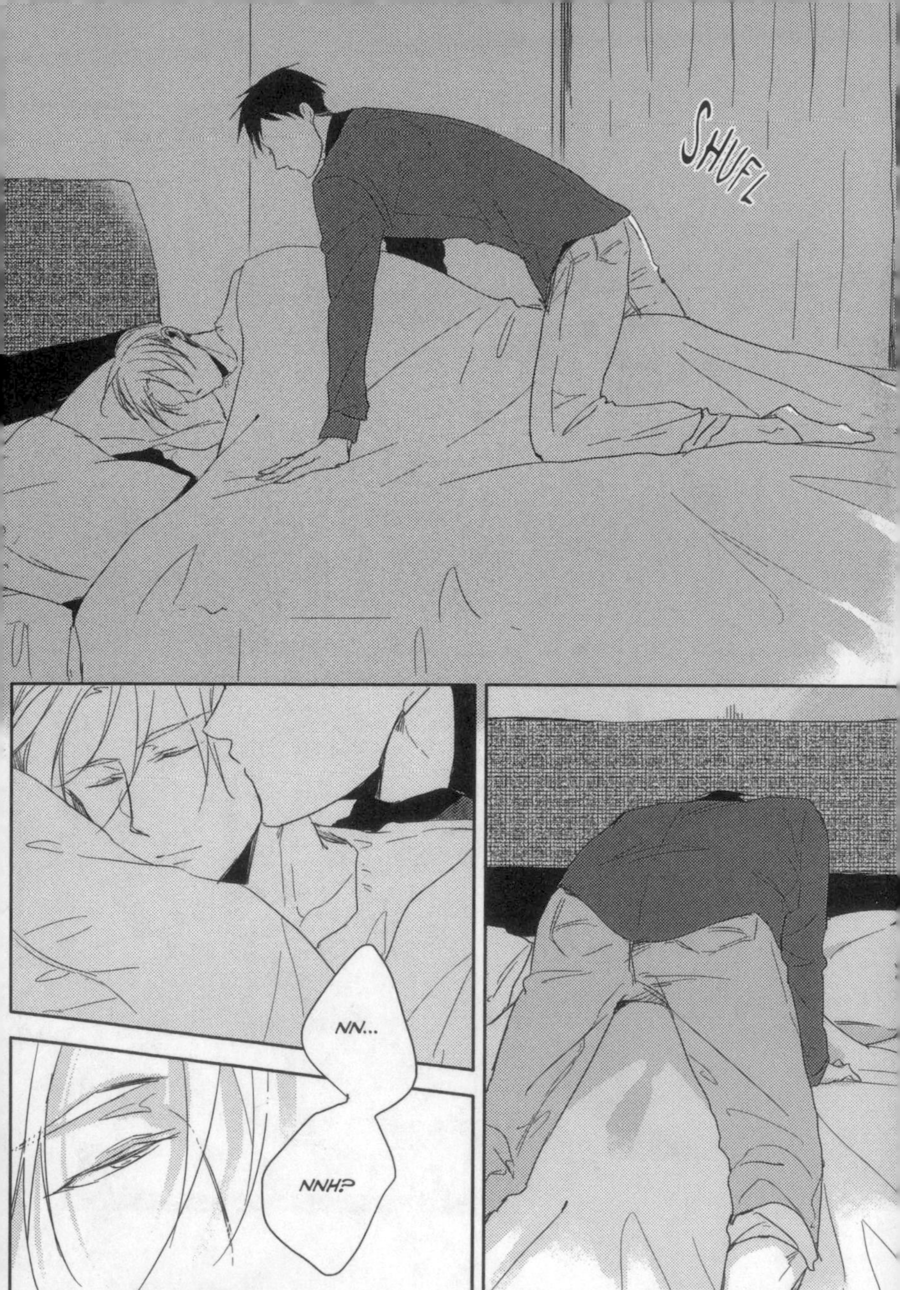
SHUFL
NN...
NNH?

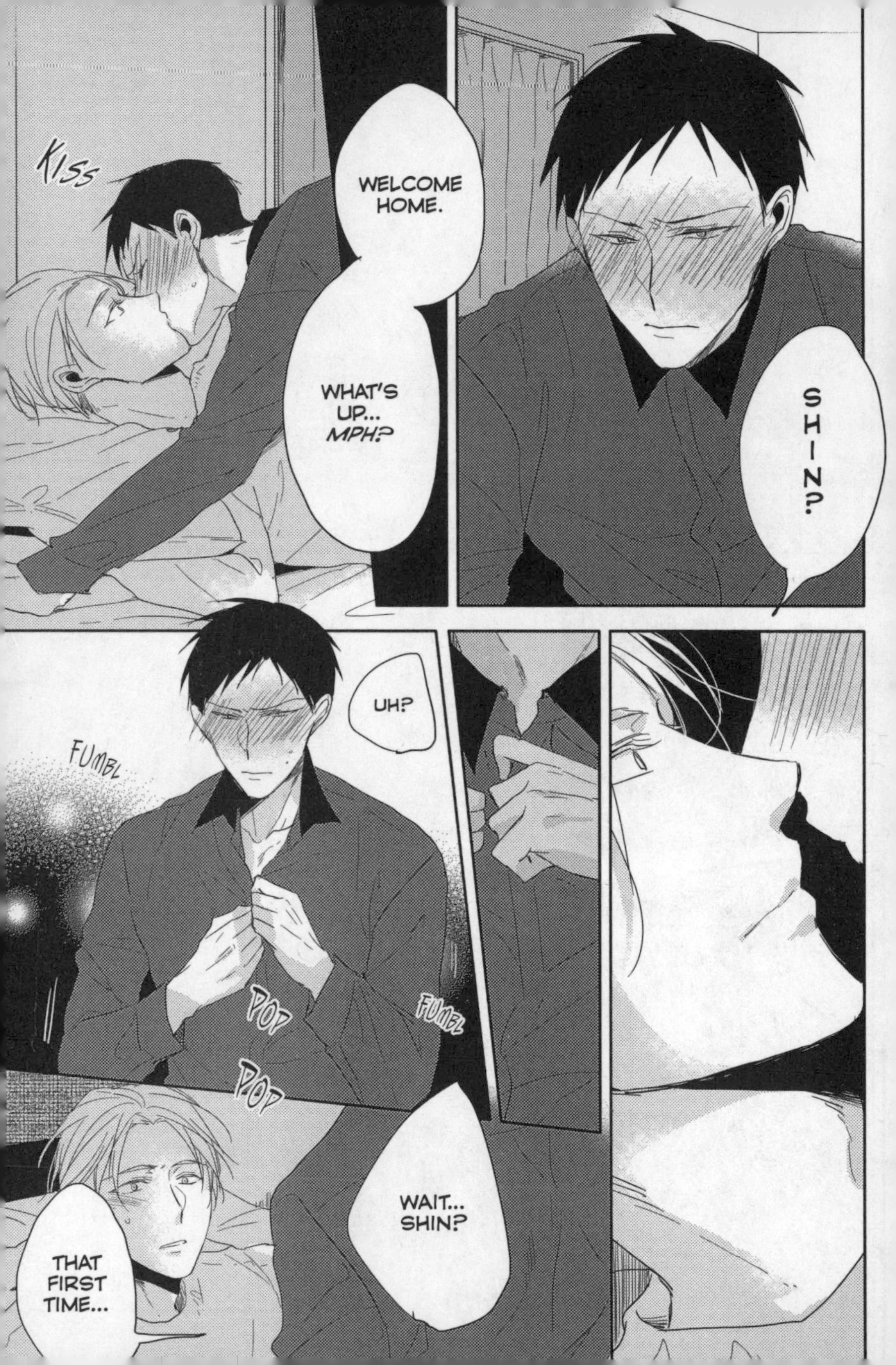
S H I N ?
WELCOME HOME.
WHAT'S UP... MPH?
KISS
UH?
FUMBL
FUMBL
POP
FUMBL
POP
WAIT... SHIN?
THAT FIRST TIME...

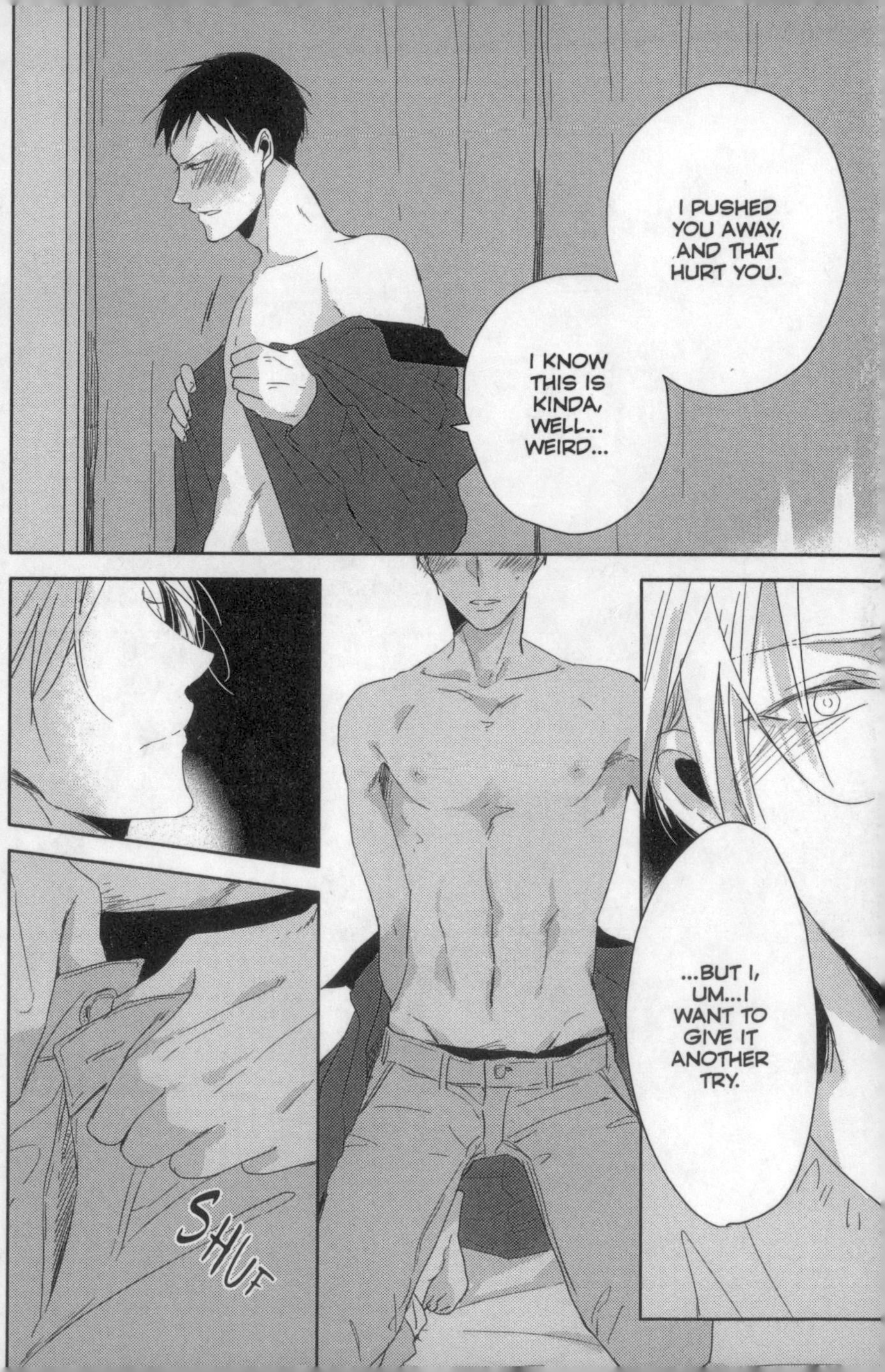
I PUSHED YOU AWAY, AND THAT HURT YOU.
I KNOW THIS IS KINDA, WELL... WEIRD...
...BUT I, UM...I WANT TO GIVE IT ANOTHER TRY.
SHUF

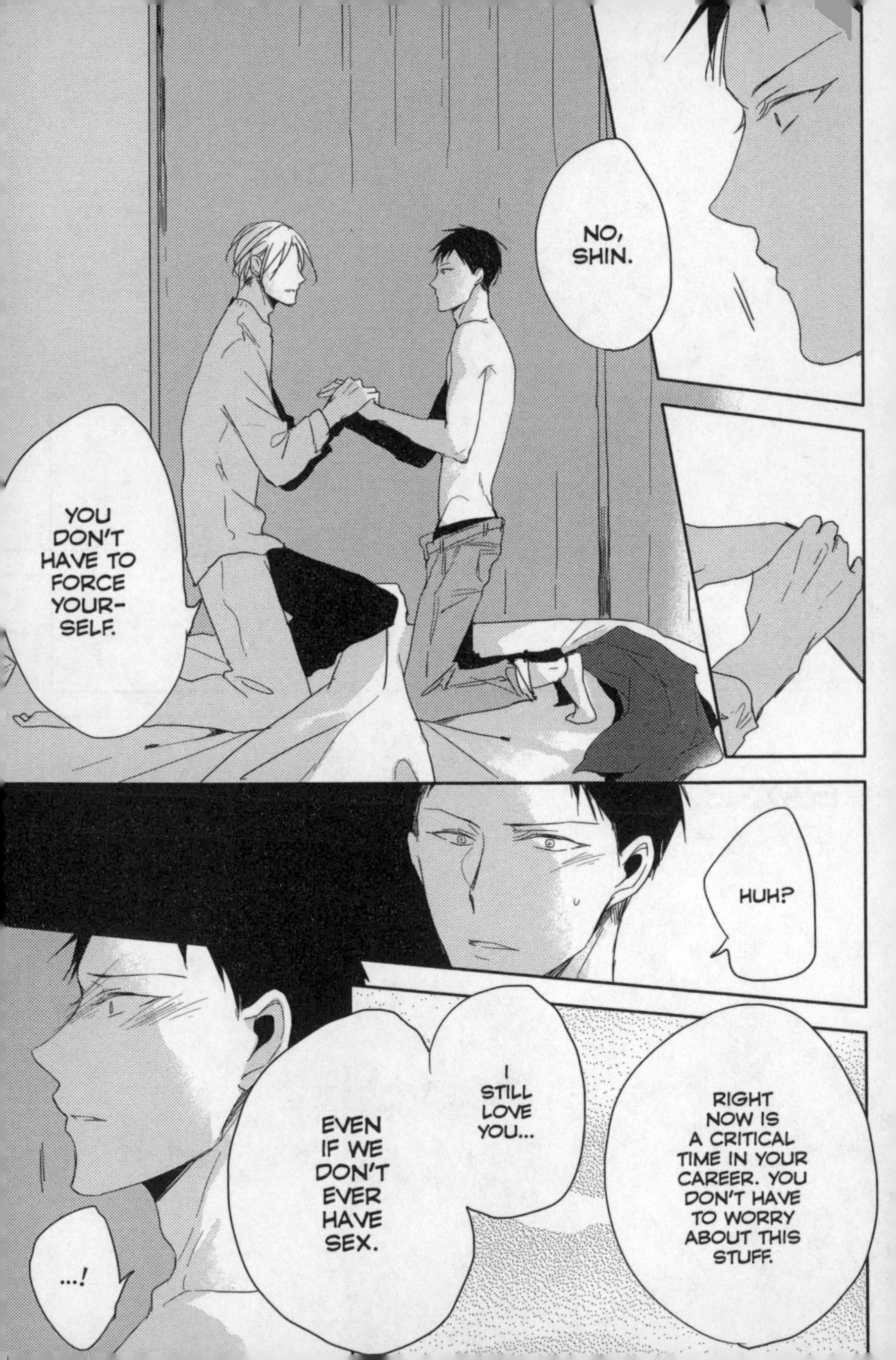
NO, SHIN.
YOU DON'T HAVE TO FORCE YOUR-SELF.
HUH?
RIGHT NOW IS A CRITICAL TIME IN YOUR CAREER. YOU DON'T HAVE TO WORRY ABOUT THIS STUFF.
I STILL LOVE YOU...
EVEN IF WE DON'T EVER HAVE SEX.
...!

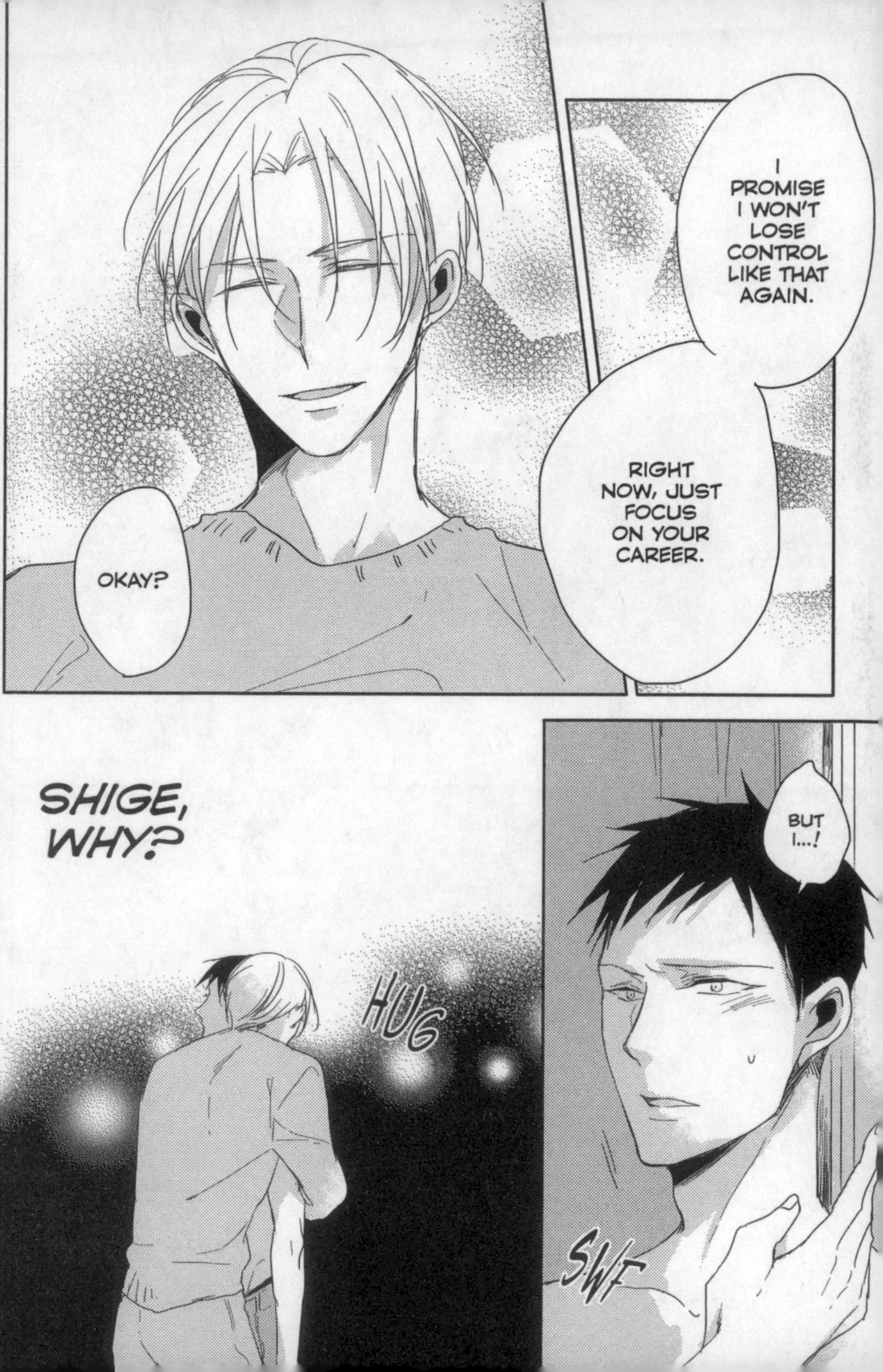
I PROMISE I WON'T LOSE CONTROL LIKE THAT AGAIN.
RIGHT NOW, JUST FOCUS ON YOUR CAREER.
OKAY?
BUT I...!
SWF
SHIGE, WHY?
HUG

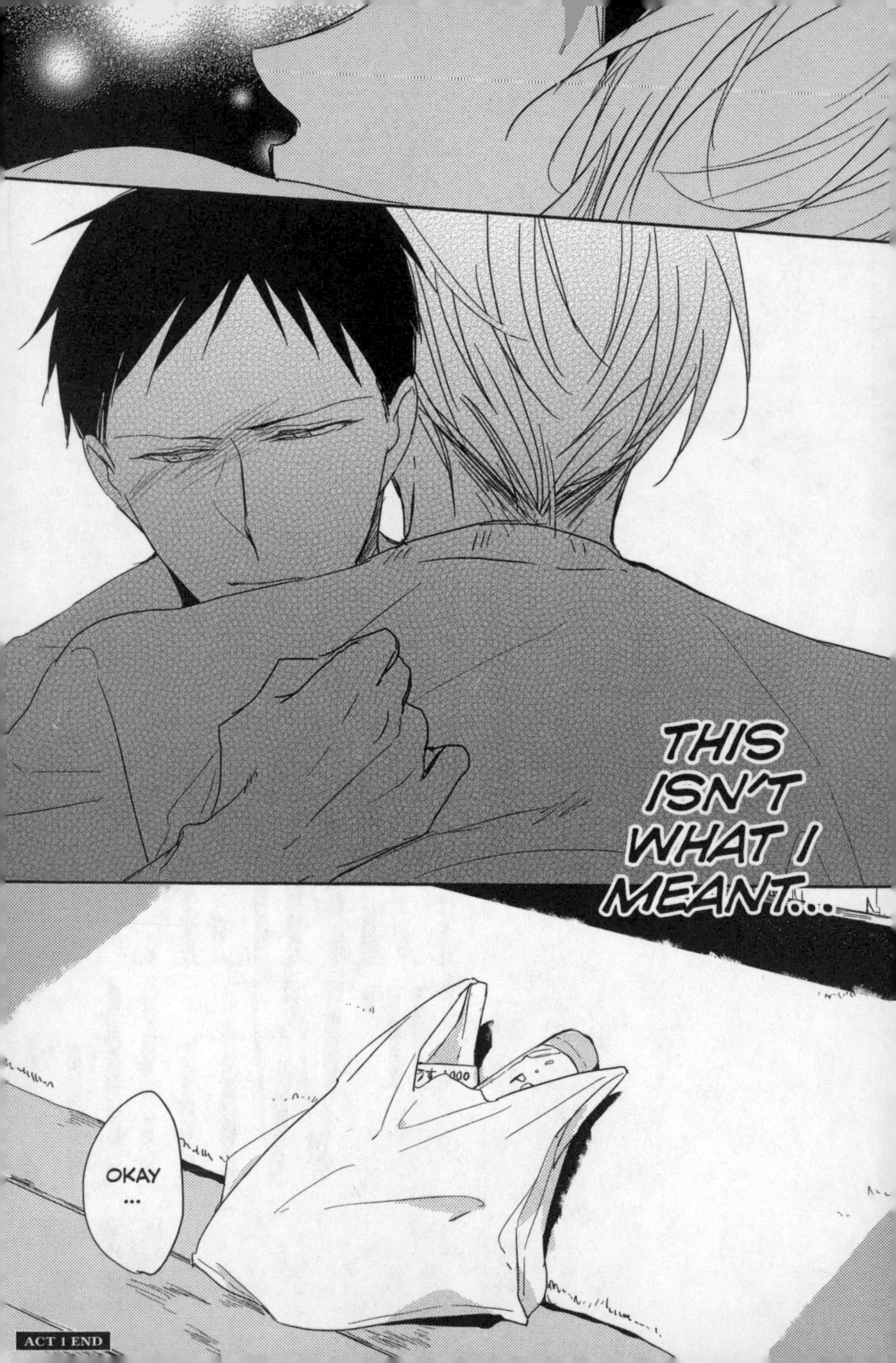
THIS ISN'T WHAT I MEANT...
OKAY ...
ACT 1 END

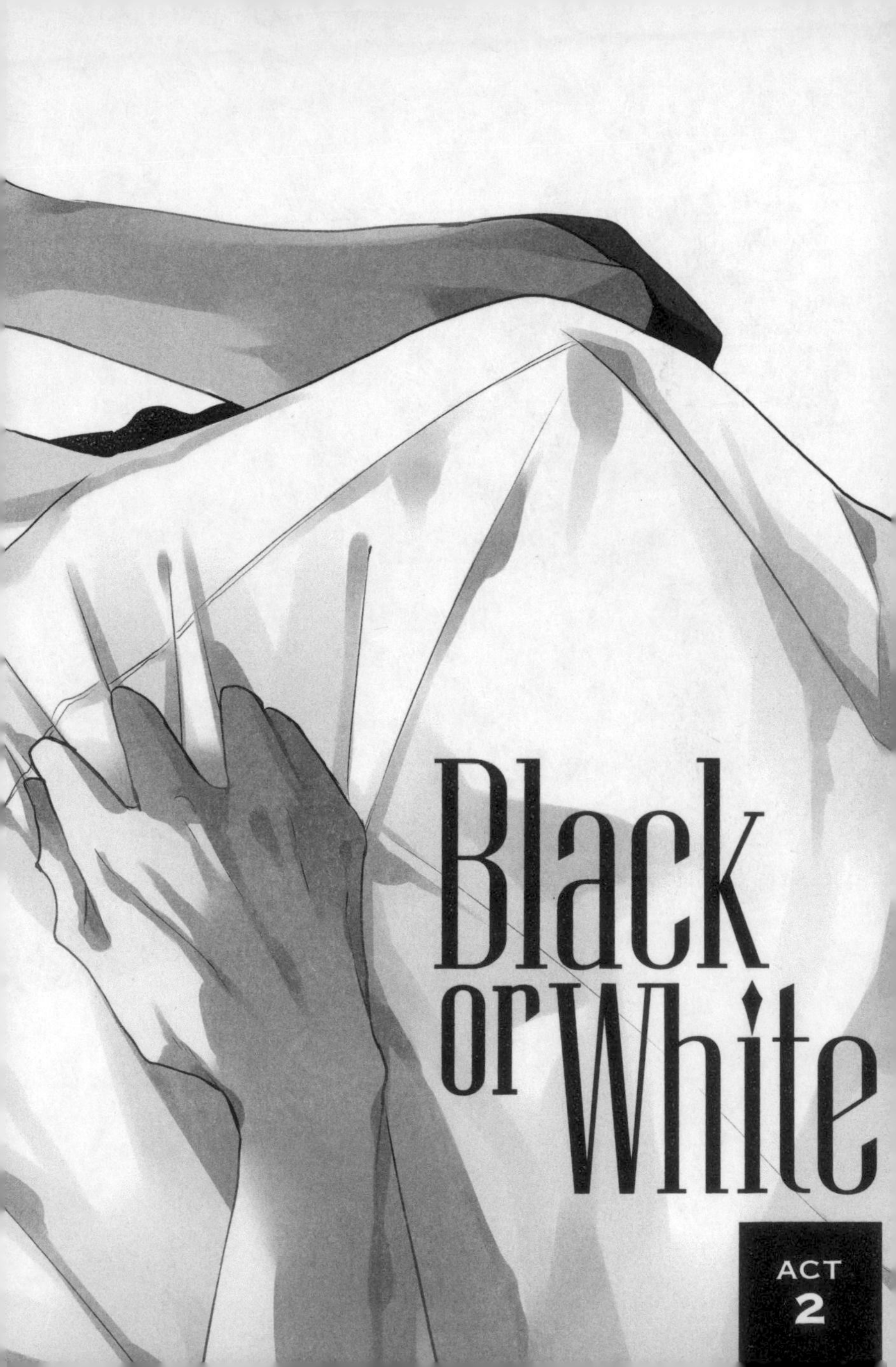
Black or White
ACT 2

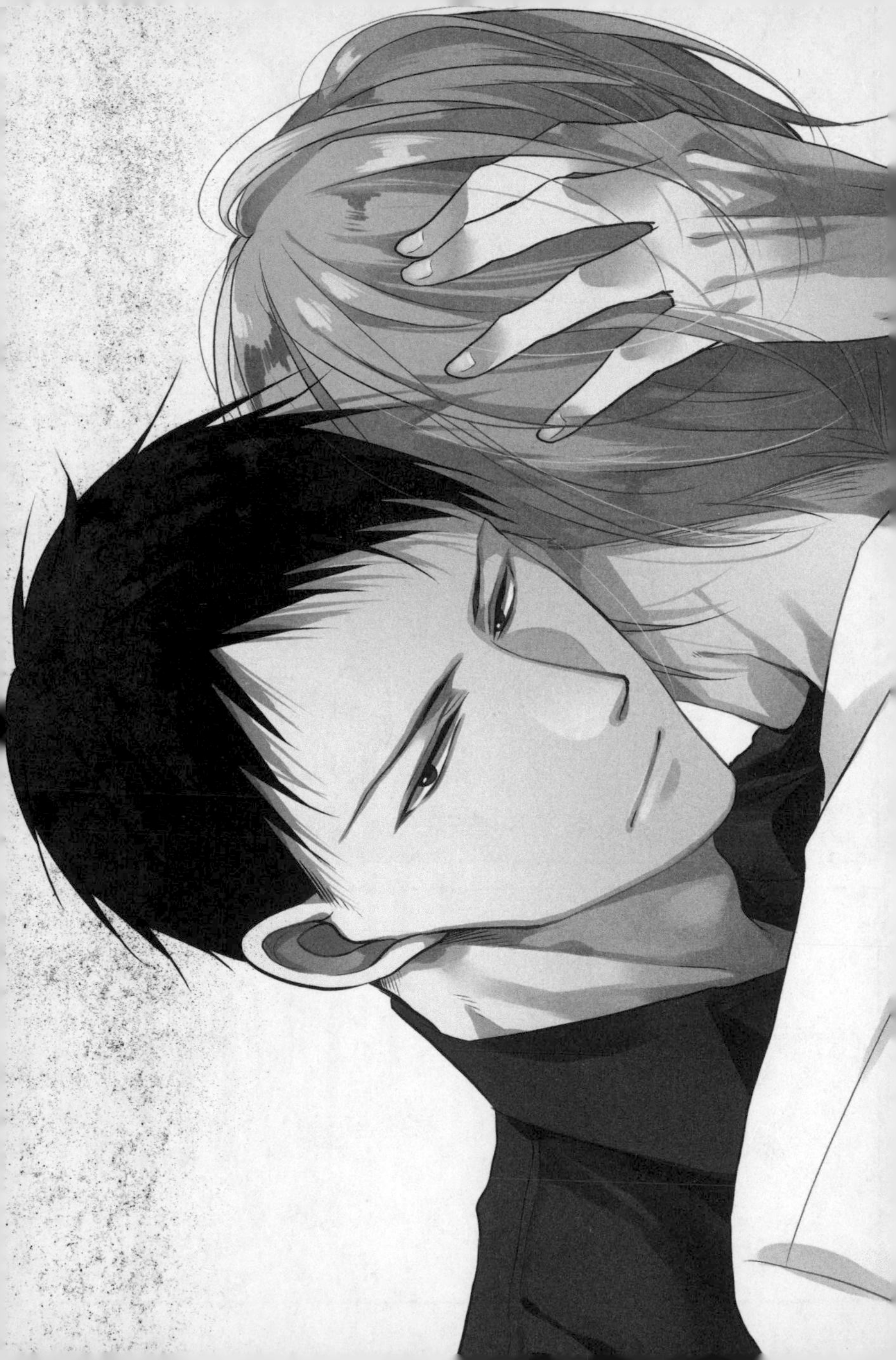

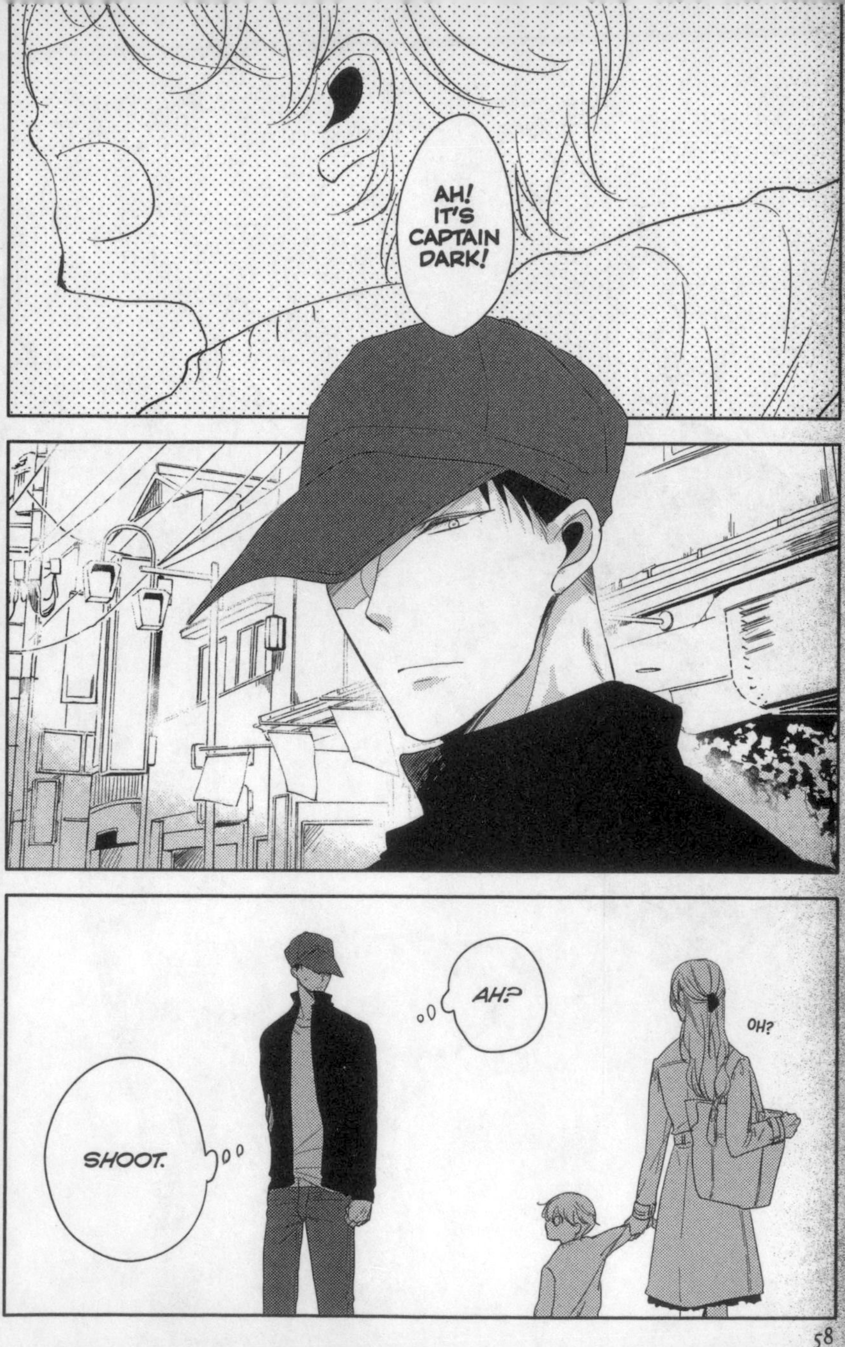
AH! IT'S CAPTAIN DARK!
OH?
AH?
SHOOT.

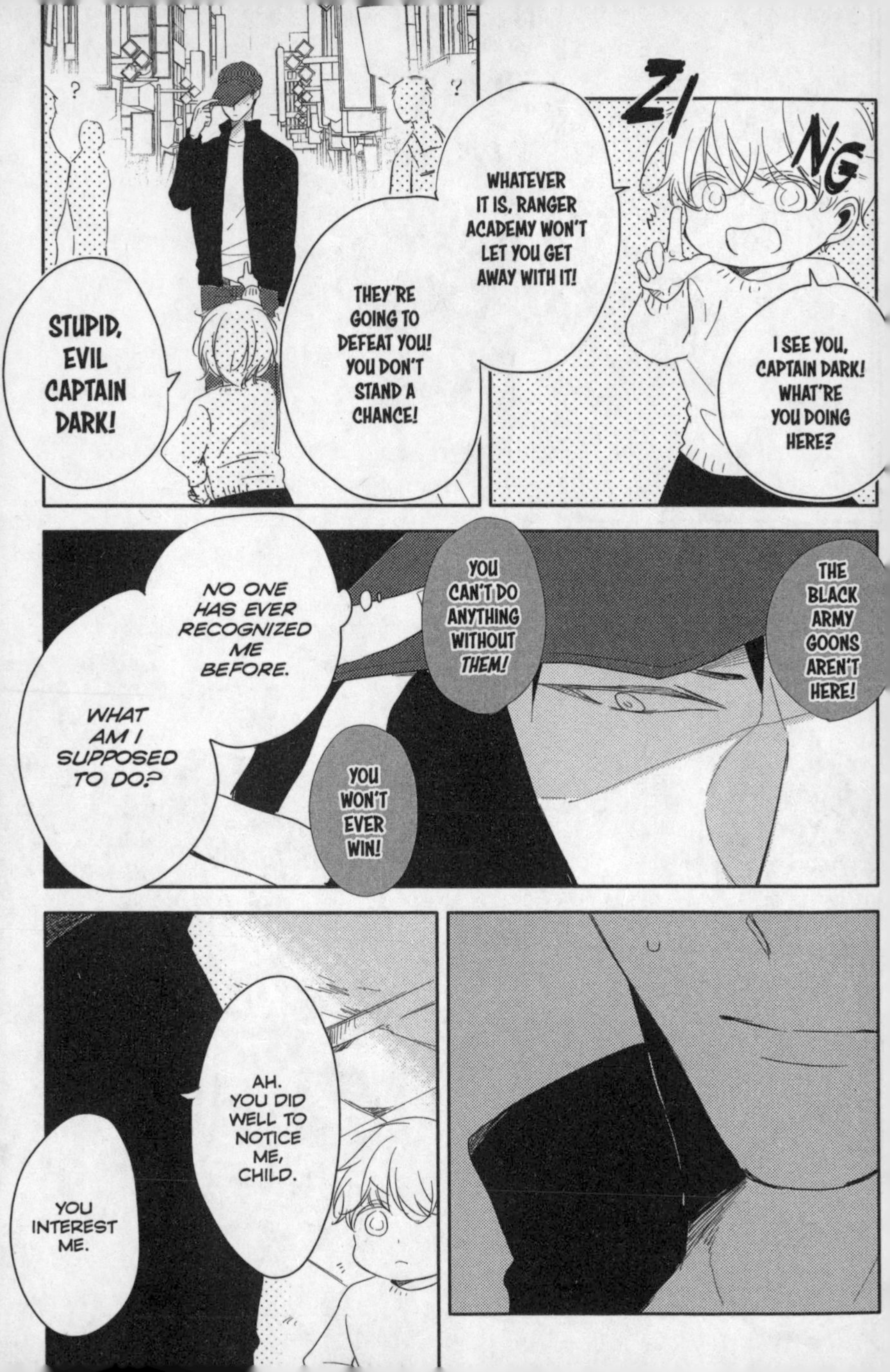
ZING
I SEE YOU, CAPTAIN DARK! WHAT'RE YOU DOING HERE?
WHATEVER IT IS, RANGER ACADEMY WON'T LET YOU GET AWAY WITH IT!
THEY'RE GOING TO DEFEAT YOU! YOU DON'T STAND A CHANCE!
STUPID, EVIL CAPTAIN DARK!
THE BLACK ARMY GOONS AREN'T HERE!
YOU CAN'T DO ANYTHING WITHOUT *THEM!*
YOU WON'T EVER WIN!
NO ONE HAS EVER RECOGNIZED ME BEFORE.
WHAT AM I SUPPOSED TO DO?
AH. YOU DID WELL TO NOTICE ME, CHILD.
YOU INTEREST ME.

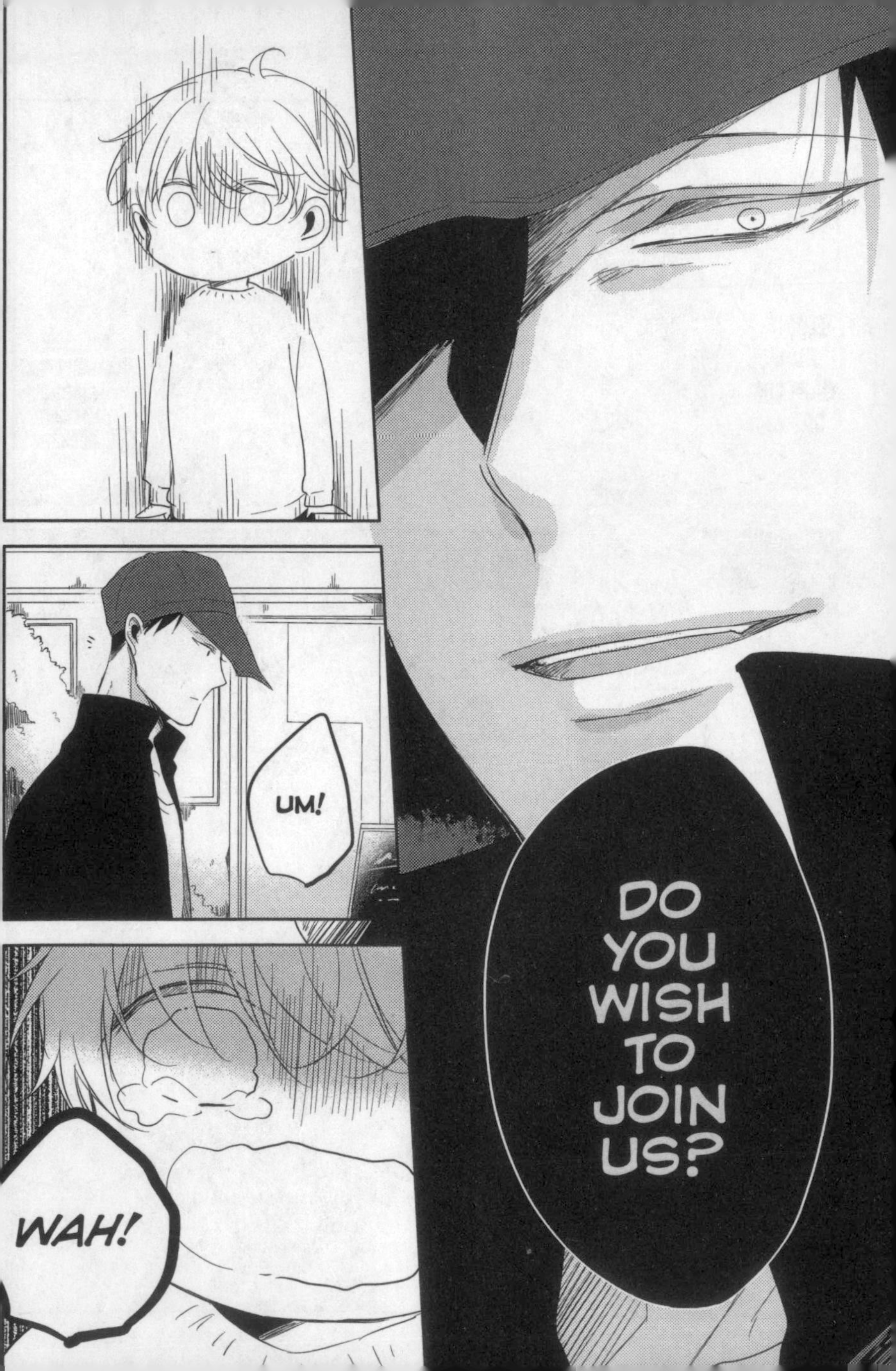
DO YOU WISH TO JOIN US?
UM!
WAH!

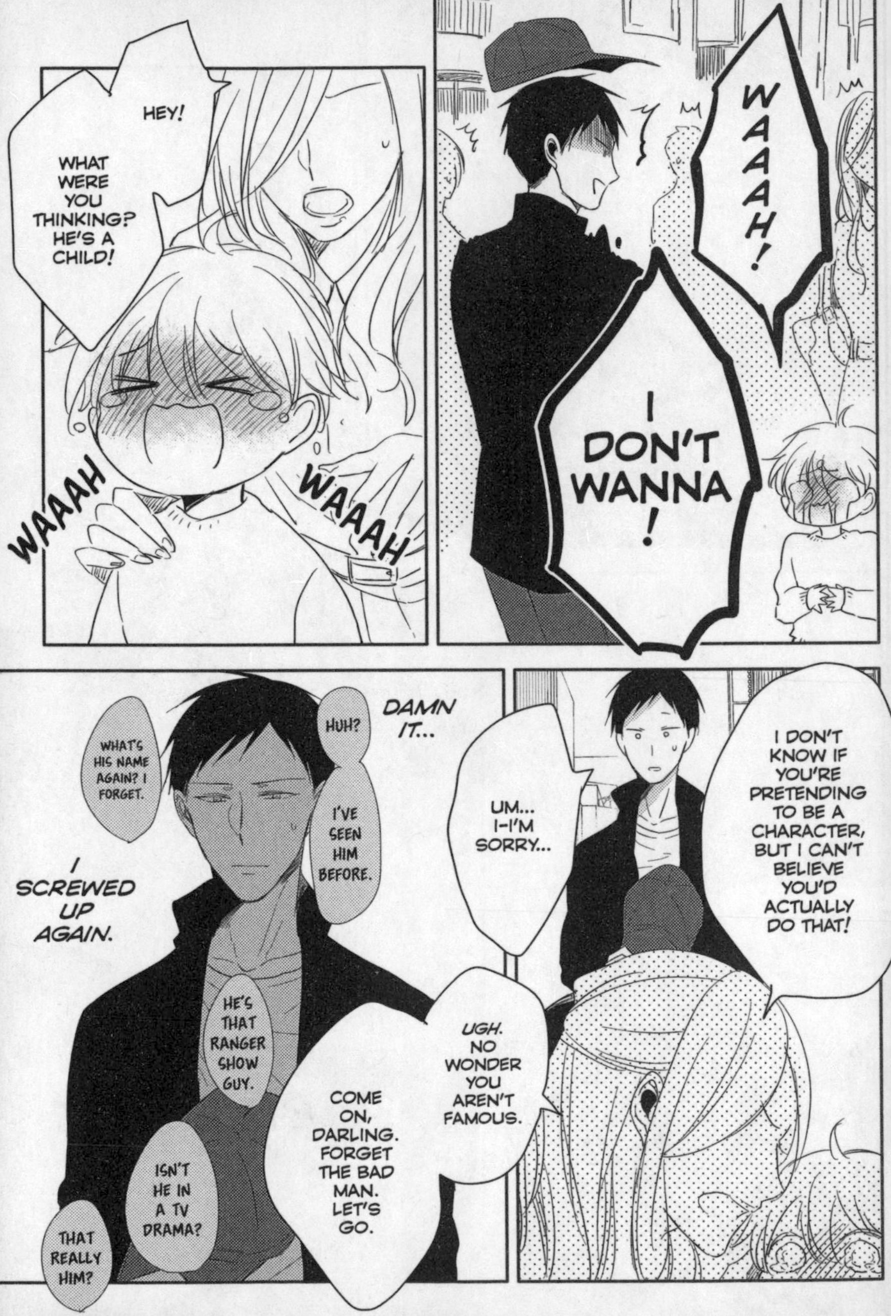

WAAAAH!
I DON'T WANNA!
HEY!
WHAT WERE YOU THINKING? HE'S A CHILD!
WAAAH
WAAAH
I DON'T KNOW IF YOU'RE PRETENDING TO BE A CHARACTER, BUT I CAN'T BELIEVE YOU'D ACTUALLY DO THAT!
UM... I-I'M SORRY...
UGH. NO WONDER YOU AREN'T FAMOUS.
COME ON, DARLING. FORGET THE BAD MAN. LET'S GO.
DAMN IT...
HUH?
I'VE SEEN HIM BEFORE.
WHAT'S HIS NAME AGAIN? I FORGET.
I SCREWED UP AGAIN.
HE'S THAT RANGER SHOW GUY.
ISN'T HE IN A TV DRAMA?
THAT REALLY HIM?

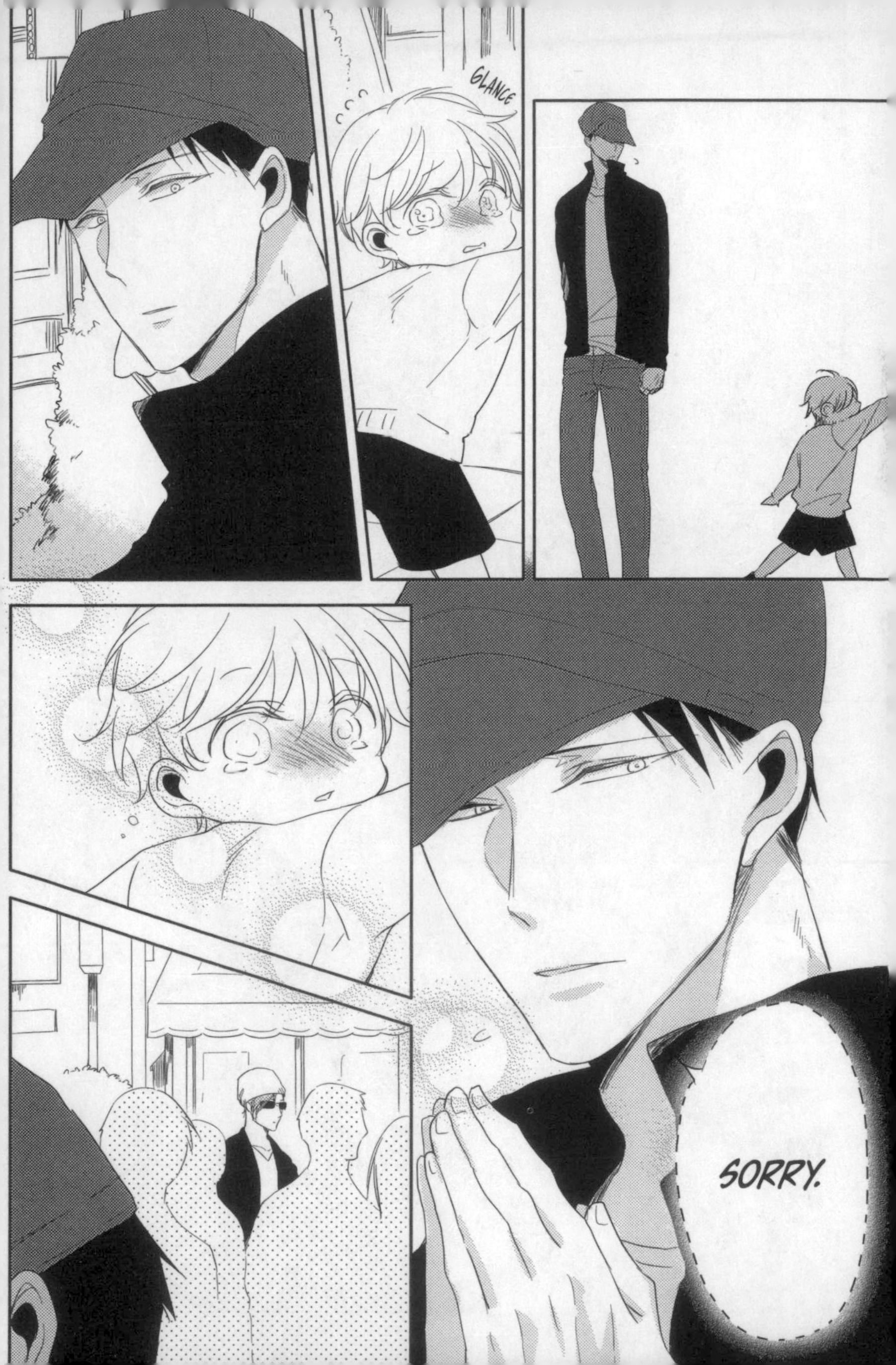
GLANCE
SORRY.

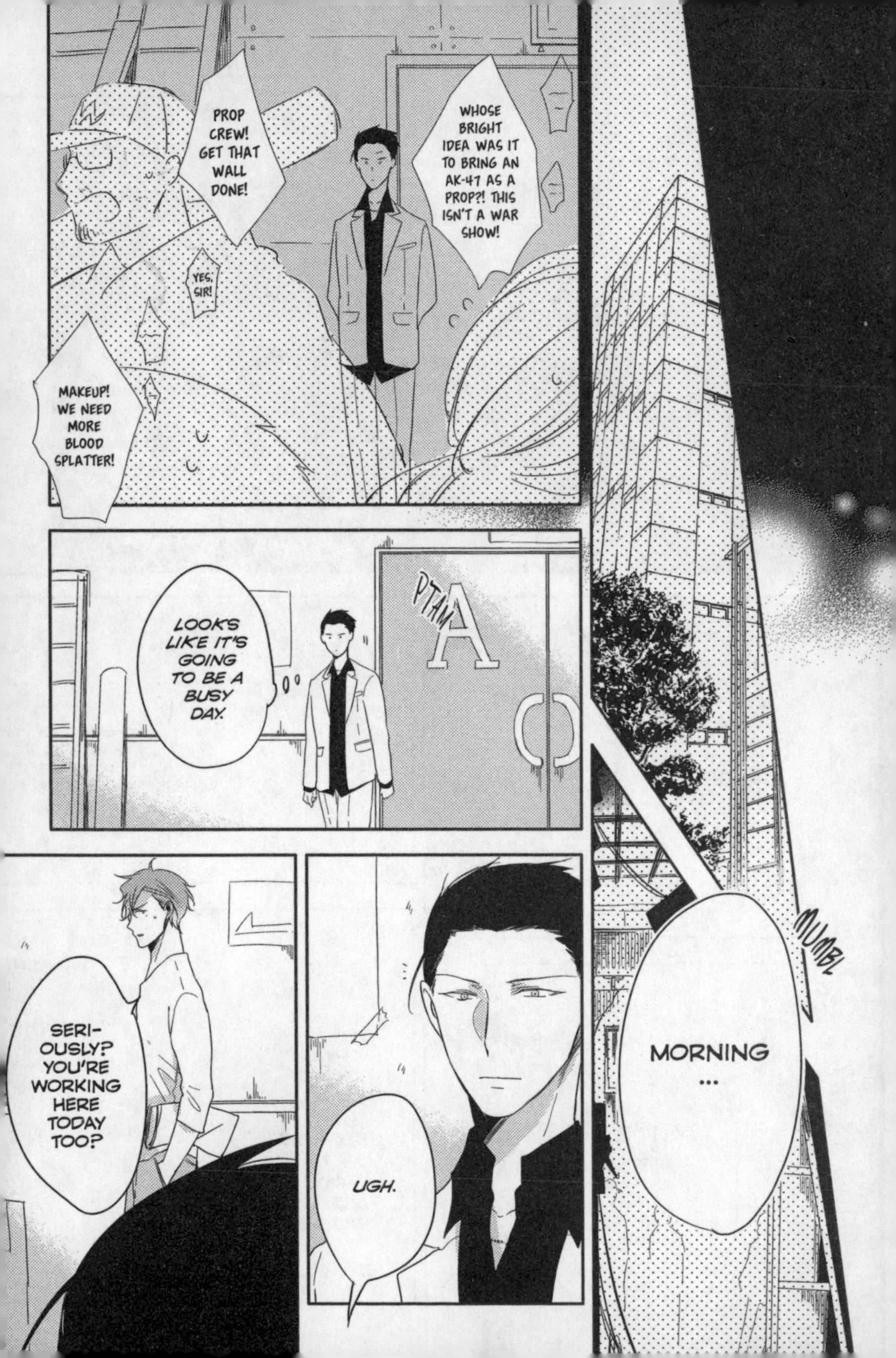
MUMBL
MORNING...
WHOSE BRIGHT IDEA WAS IT TO BRING AN AK-47 AS A PROP?! THIS ISN'T A WAR SHOW!
PROP CREW! GET THAT WALL DONE!
YES, SIR!
MAKEUP! WE NEED MORE BLOOD SPLATTER!
PTAM
LOOKS LIKE IT'S GOING TO BE A BUSY DAY.
UGH.
SERI-OUSLY? YOU'RE WORKING HERE TODAY TOO?

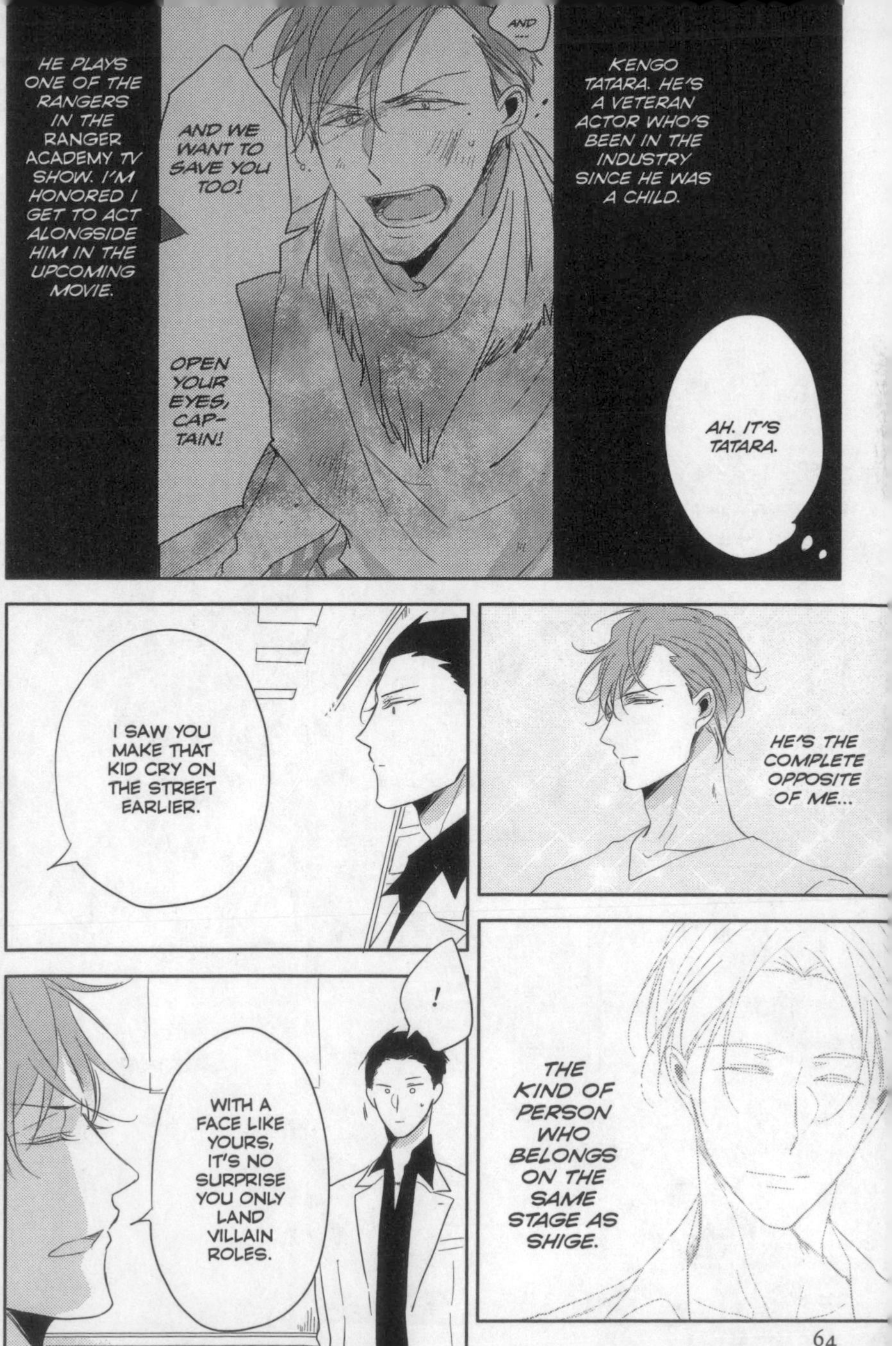
AND ---
KENGO TATARA. HE'S A VETERAN ACTOR WHO'S BEEN IN THE INDUSTRY SINCE HE WAS A CHILD.
HE PLAYS ONE OF THE RANGERS IN THE RANGER ACADEMY TV SHOW. I'M HONORED I GET TO ACT ALONGSIDE HIM IN THE UPCOMING MOVIE.
AND WE WANT TO SAVE YOU TOO!
OPEN YOUR EYES, CAP-TAIN!
AH. IT'S TATARA.
HE'S THE COMPLETE OPPOSITE OF ME...
I SAW YOU MAKE THAT KID CRY ON THE STREET EARLIER.
THE KIND OF PERSON WHO BELONGS ON THE SAME STAGE AS SHIGE.
!
WITH A FACE LIKE YOURS, IT'S NO SURPRISE YOU ONLY LAND VILLAIN ROLES.

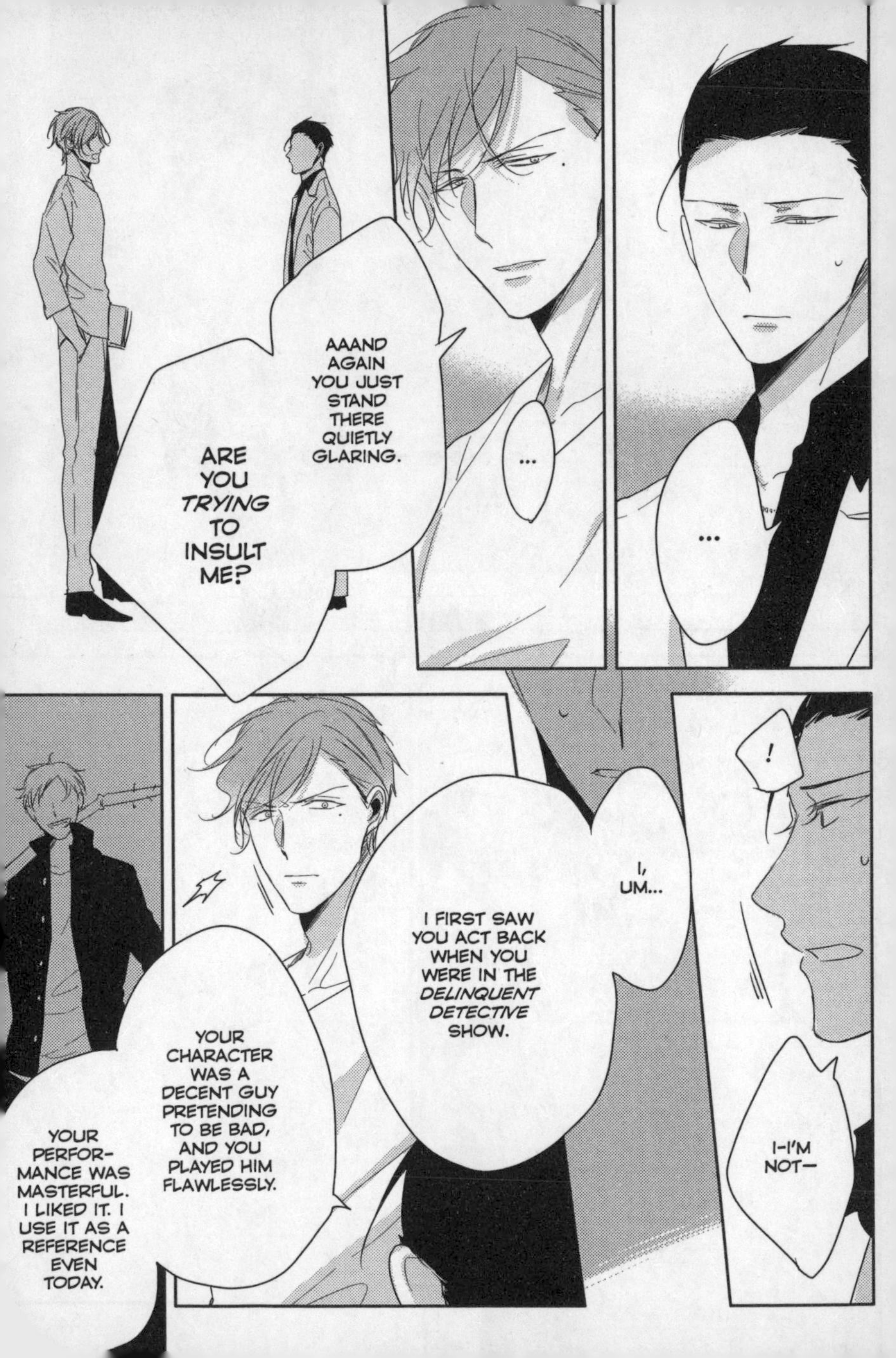
...
...
AAAND AGAIN YOU JUST STAND THERE QUIETLY GLARING.
ARE YOU *TRYING* TO INSULT ME?
!
I-I'M NOT—
I, UM...
I FIRST SAW YOU ACT BACK WHEN YOU WERE IN THE *DELINQUENT DETECTIVE* SHOW.
YOUR CHARACTER WAS A DECENT GUY PRETENDING TO BE BAD, AND YOU PLAYED HIM FLAWLESSLY.
YOUR PERFOR-MANCE WAS MASTERFUL. I LIKED IT. I USE IT AS A REFERENCE EVEN TODAY.

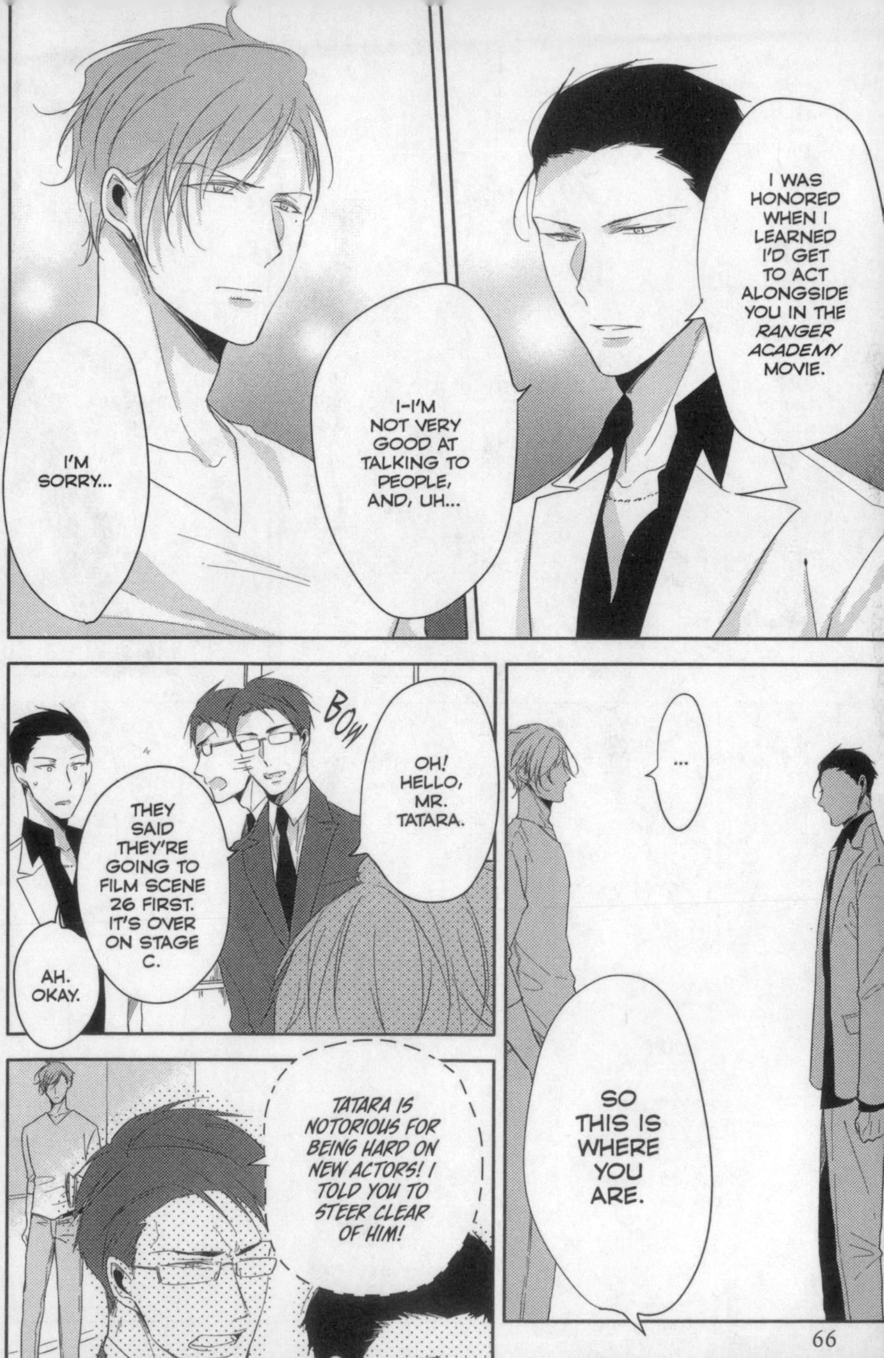
I WAS HONORED WHEN I LEARNED I'D GET TO ACT ALONGSIDE YOU IN THE *RANGER ACADEMY* MOVIE.
I-I'M NOT VERY GOOD AT TALKING TO PEOPLE, AND, UH...
I'M SORRY...
...
SO THIS IS WHERE YOU ARE.
BOW
OH! HELLO, MR. TATARA.
THEY SAID THEY'RE GOING TO FILM SCENE 26 FIRST. IT'S OVER ON STAGE C.
AH. OKAY.
TATARA IS NOTORIOUS FOR BEING HARD ON NEW ACTORS! I TOLD YOU TO STEER CLEAR OF HIM!

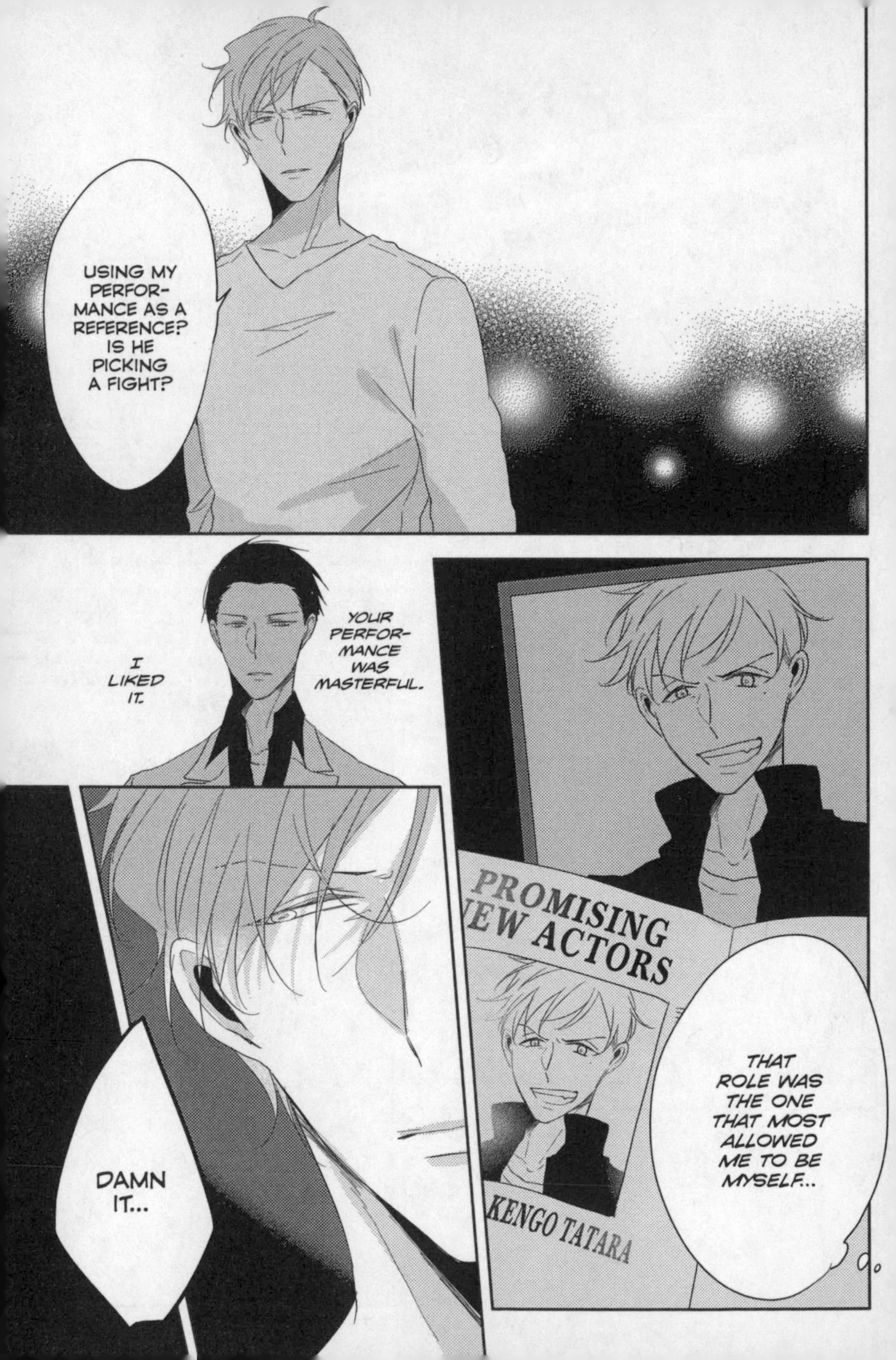
USING MY PERFORMANCE AS A REFERENCE? IS HE PICKING A FIGHT?
PROMISING NEW ACTORS
KENGO TATARA
THAT ROLE WAS THE ONE THAT MOST ALLOWED ME TO BE MYSELF...
YOUR PERFORMANCE WAS MASTERFUL.
I LIKED IT.
DAMN IT...

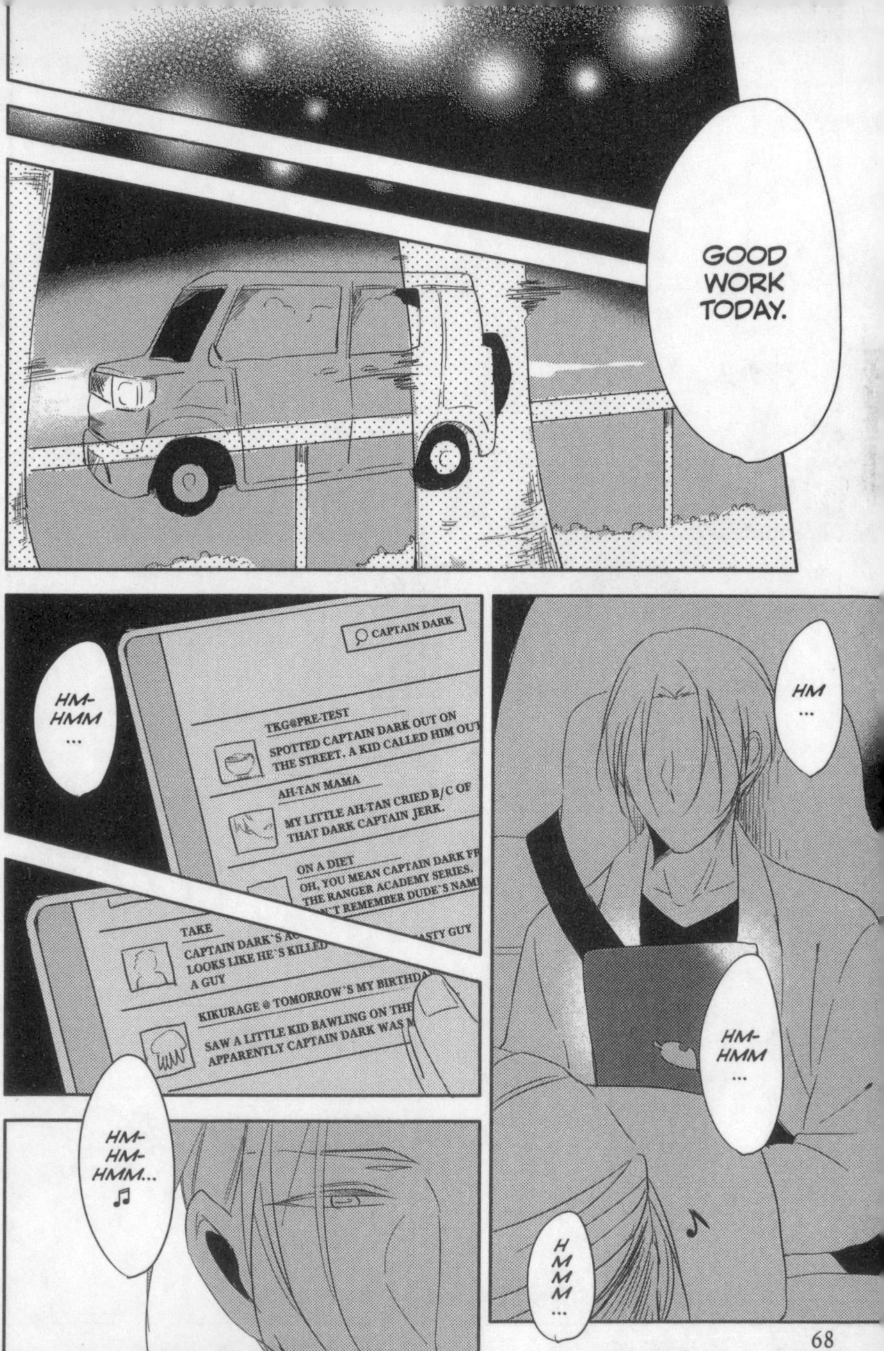
GOOD WORK TODAY.
HM ...
HM-HMM ...
HMMM ...
HM-HMM ...
CAPTAIN DARK
TKG@PRE-TEST
SPOTTED CAPTAIN DARK OUT ON THE STREET. A KID CALLED HIM OU
AH-TAN MAMA
MY LITTLE AH-TAN CRIED B/C OF THAT DARK CAPTAIN JERK.
ON A DIET
OH, YOU MEAN CAPTAIN DARK FR THE RANGER ACADEMY SERIES.
TAKE
CAPTAIN DARK'S A LOOKS LIKE HE'S KILLED A GUY
ASTY GUY
KIKURAGE @ TOMORROW'S MY BIRTHDA
SAW A LITTLE KID BAWLING ON THE APPARENTLY CAPTAIN DARK WAS
HM-HM-HMM... ♫

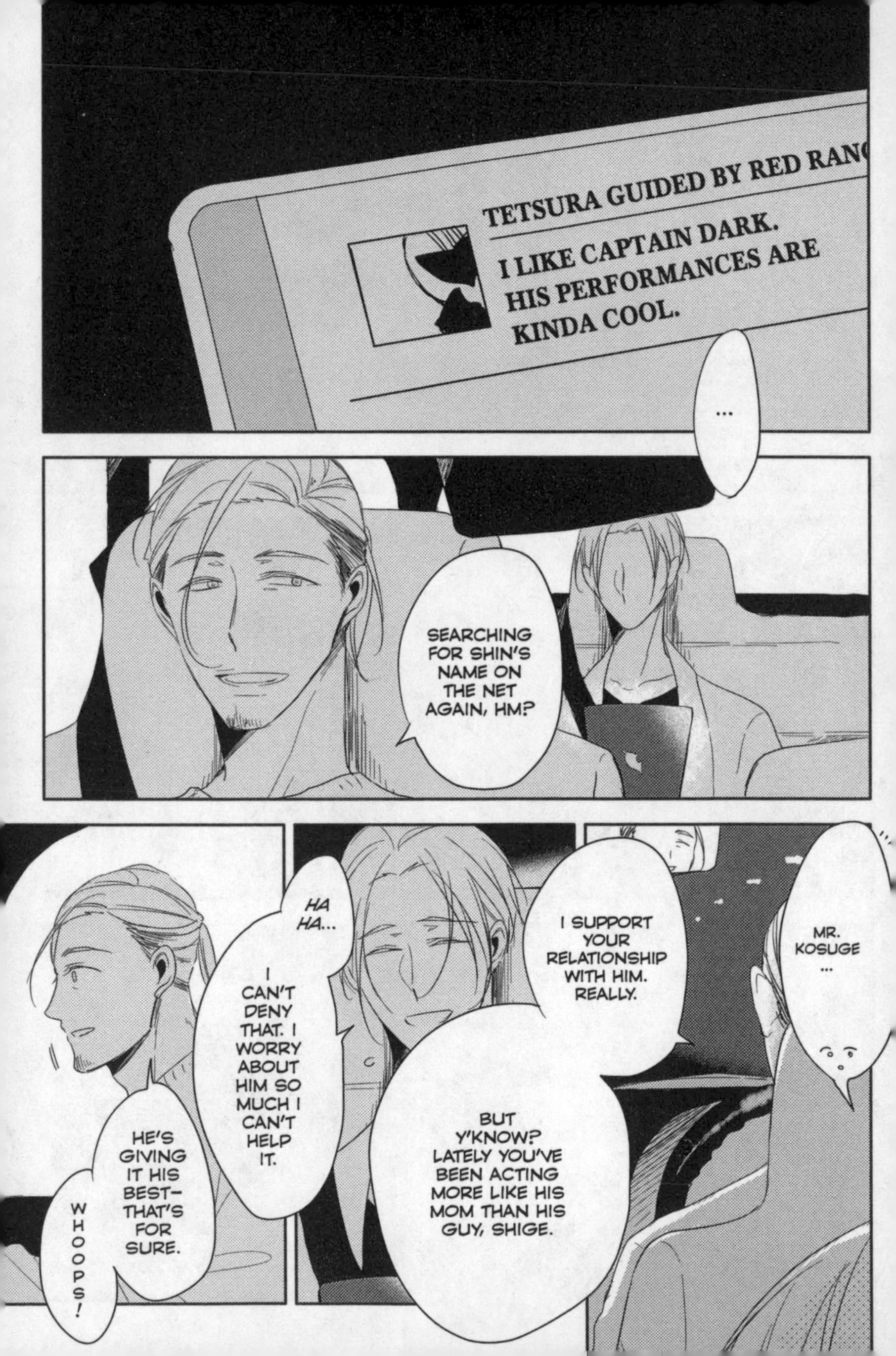
TETSURA GUIDED BY RED RAN
I LIKE CAPTAIN DARK. HIS PERFORMANCES ARE KINDA COOL.
...
SEARCHING FOR SHIN'S NAME ON THE NET AGAIN, HM?
MR. KOSUGE ...
I SUPPORT YOUR RELATIONSHIP WITH HIM. REALLY.
BUT Y'KNOW? LATELY YOU'VE BEEN ACTING MORE LIKE HIS MOM THAN HIS GUY, SHIGE.
HA HA...
I CAN'T DENY THAT. I WORRY ABOUT HIM SO MUCH I CAN'T HELP IT.
HE'S GIVING IT HIS BEST—THAT'S FOR SURE.
WHOOPS!

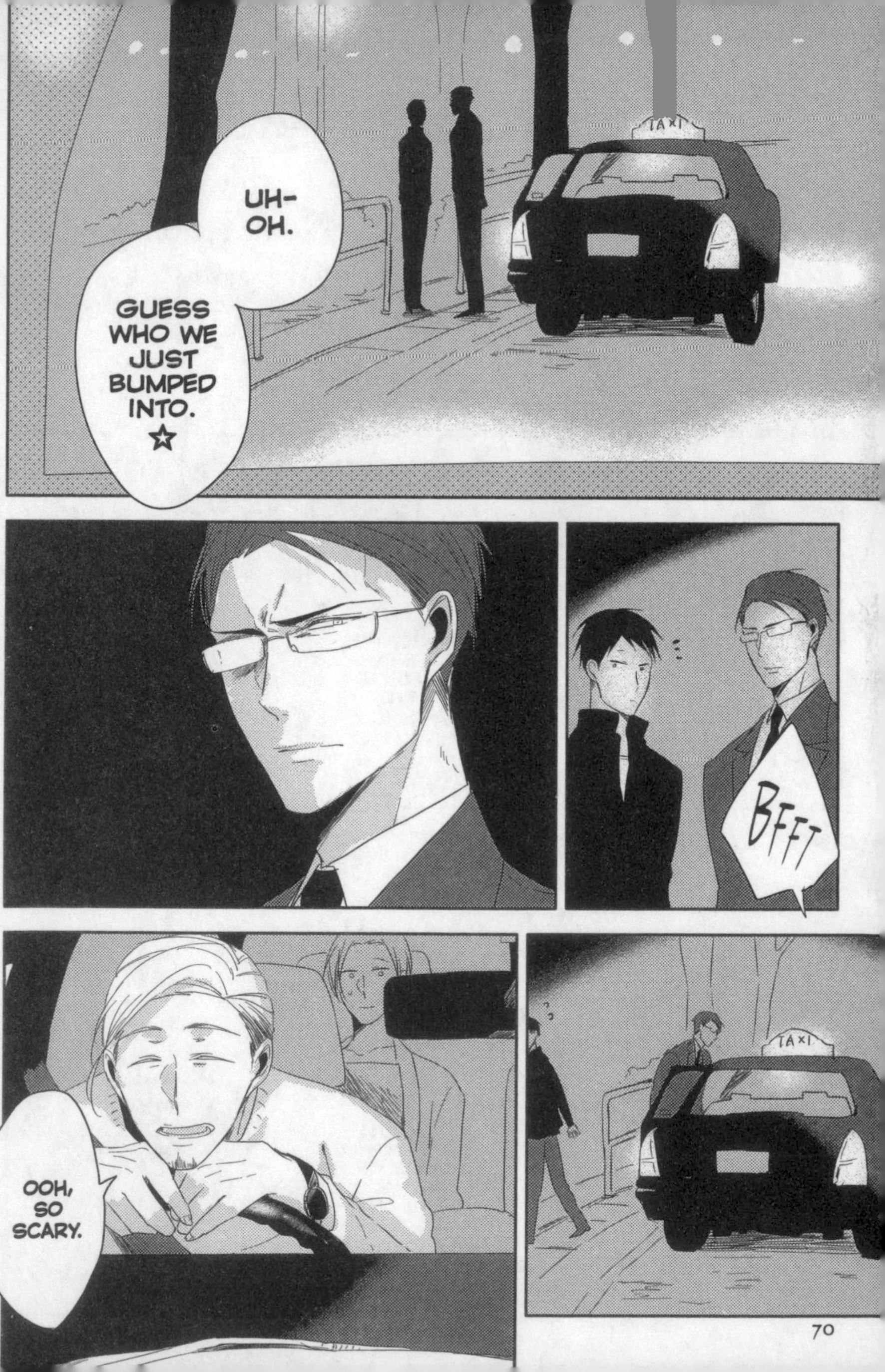
UH-OH.
GUESS WHO WE JUST BUMPED INTO. ☆
BFFT
OOH, SO SCARY.

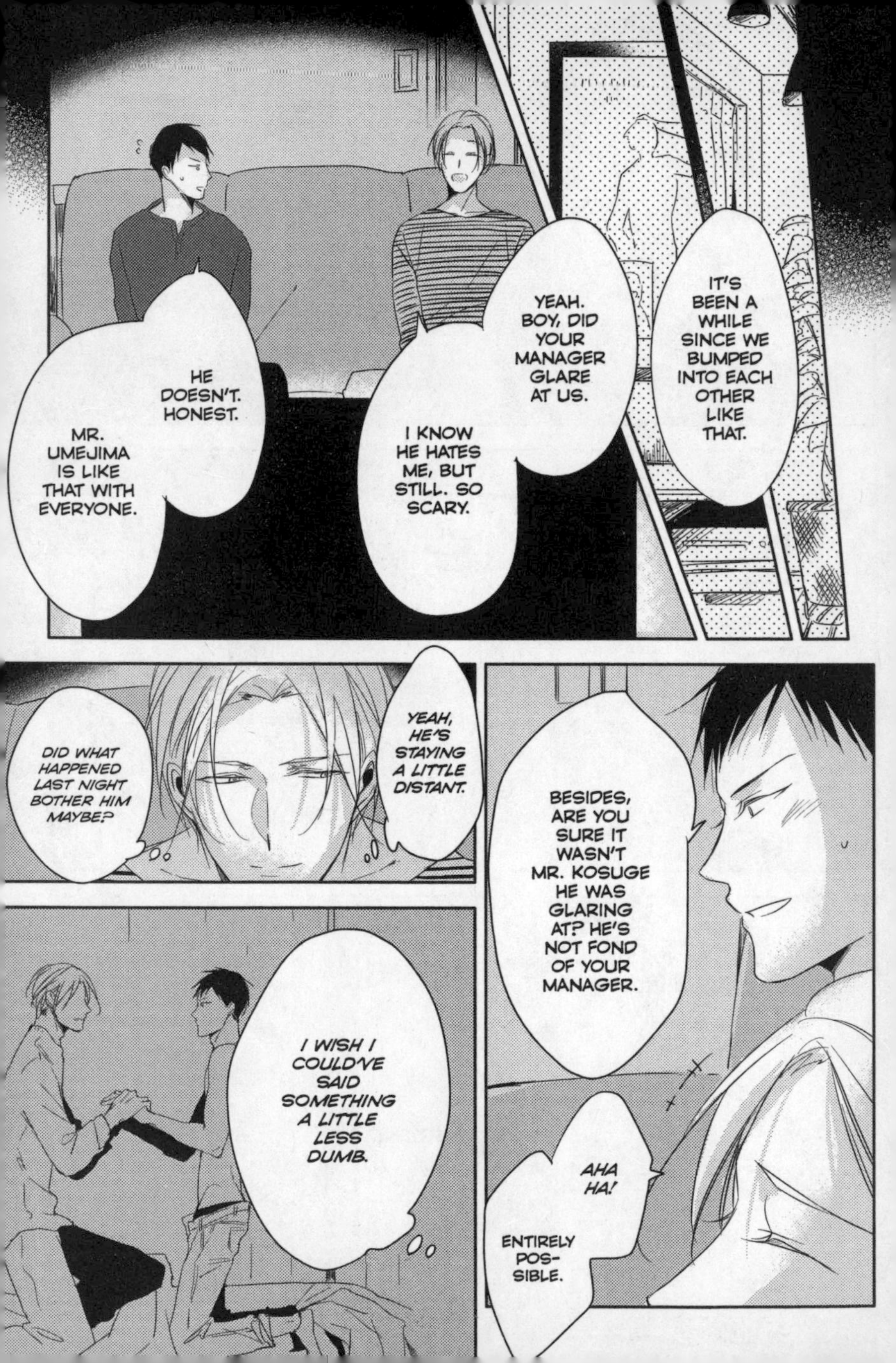
IT'S BEEN A WHILE SINCE WE BUMPED INTO EACH OTHER LIKE THAT.
YEAH. BOY, DID YOUR MANAGER GLARE AT US.
I KNOW HE HATES ME, BUT STILL. SO SCARY.
HE DOESN'T. HONEST.
MR. UMEJIMA IS LIKE THAT WITH EVERYONE.
BESIDES, ARE YOU SURE IT WASN'T MR. KOSUGE HE WAS GLARING AT? HE'S NOT FOND OF YOUR MANAGER.
AHA HA!
ENTIRELY POS-SIBLE.
YEAH, HE'S STAYING A LITTLE DISTANT.
DID WHAT HAPPENED LAST NIGHT BOTHER HIM MAYBE?
I WISH I COULD'VE SAID SOMETHING A LITTLE LESS DUMB.

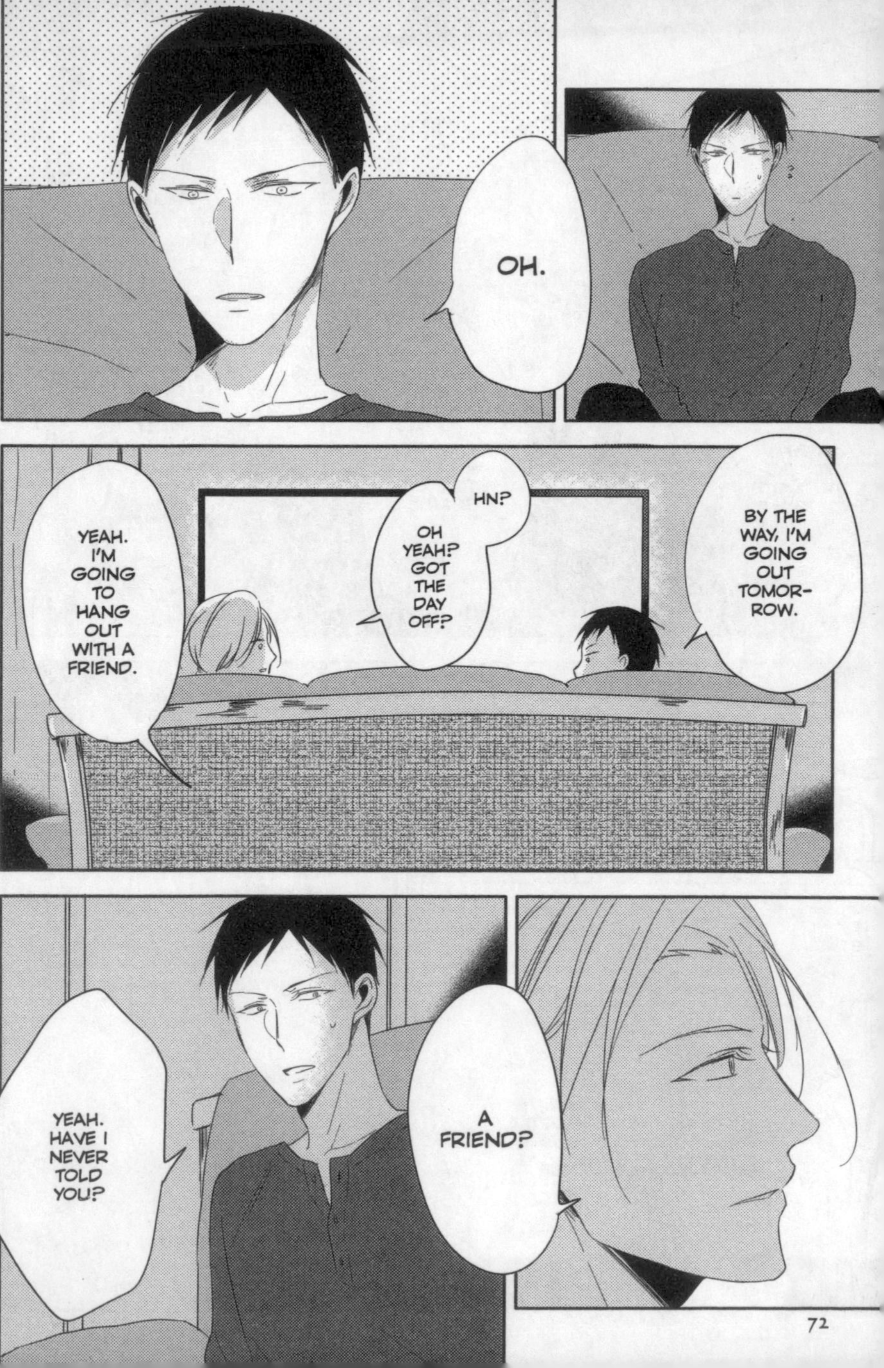
OH.
BY THE WAY, I'M GOING OUT TOMORROW.
HN?
OH YEAH? GOT THE DAY OFF?
YEAH. I'M GOING TO HANG OUT WITH A FRIEND.
A FRIEND?
YEAH. HAVE I NEVER TOLD YOU?

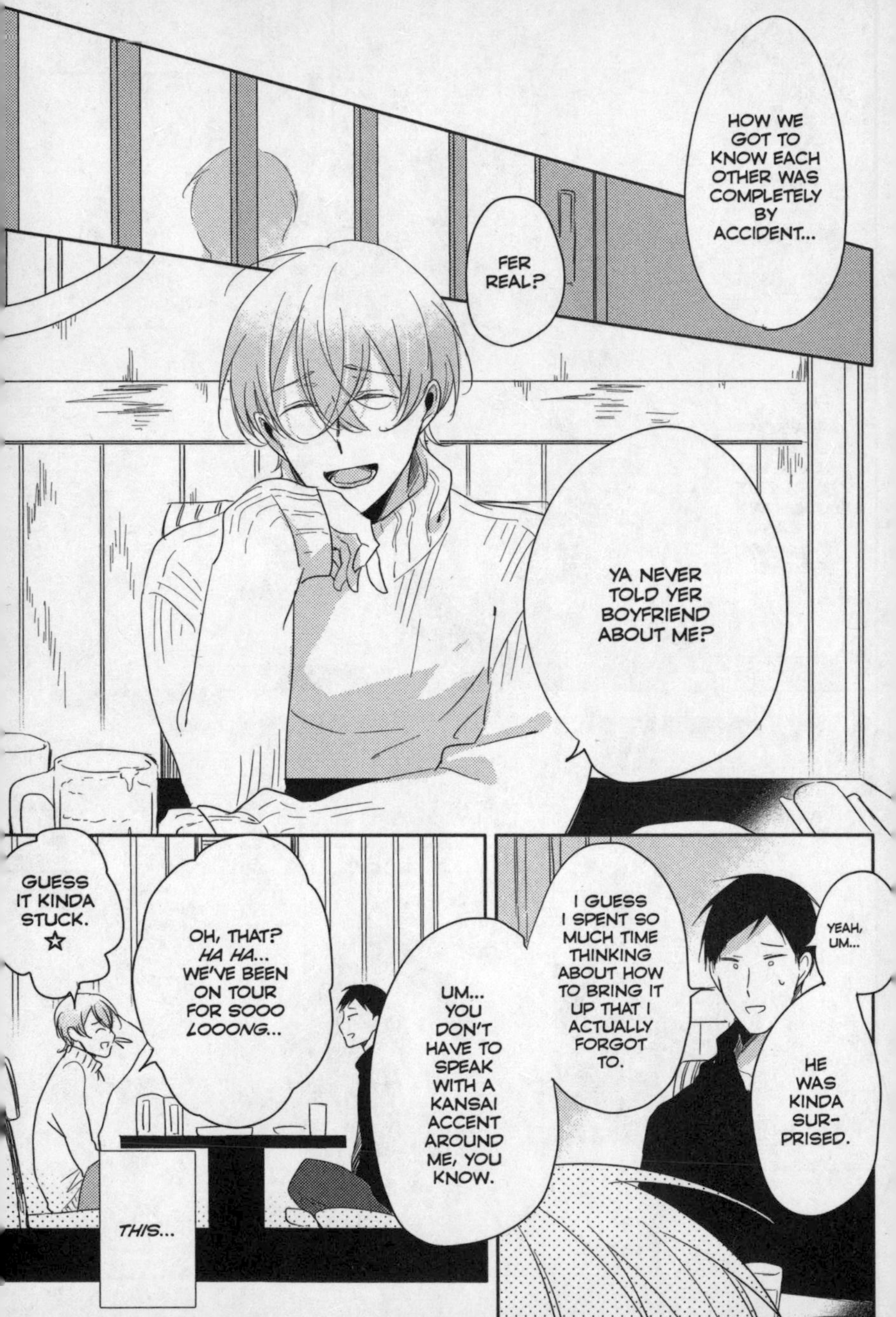
HOW WE GOT TO KNOW EACH OTHER WAS COMPLETELY BY ACCIDENT...
FER REAL?
YA NEVER TOLD YER BOYFRIEND ABOUT ME?
YEAH, UM...
HE WAS KINDA SUR-PRISED.
I GUESS I SPENT SO MUCH TIME THINKING ABOUT HOW TO BRING IT UP THAT I ACTUALLY FORGOT TO.
UM... YOU DON'T HAVE TO SPEAK WITH A KANSAI ACCENT AROUND ME, YOU KNOW.
OH, THAT? *HA HA*... WE'VE BEEN ON TOUR FOR SOOO *LOOONG*...
GUESS IT KINDA STUCK. ☆
THIS...

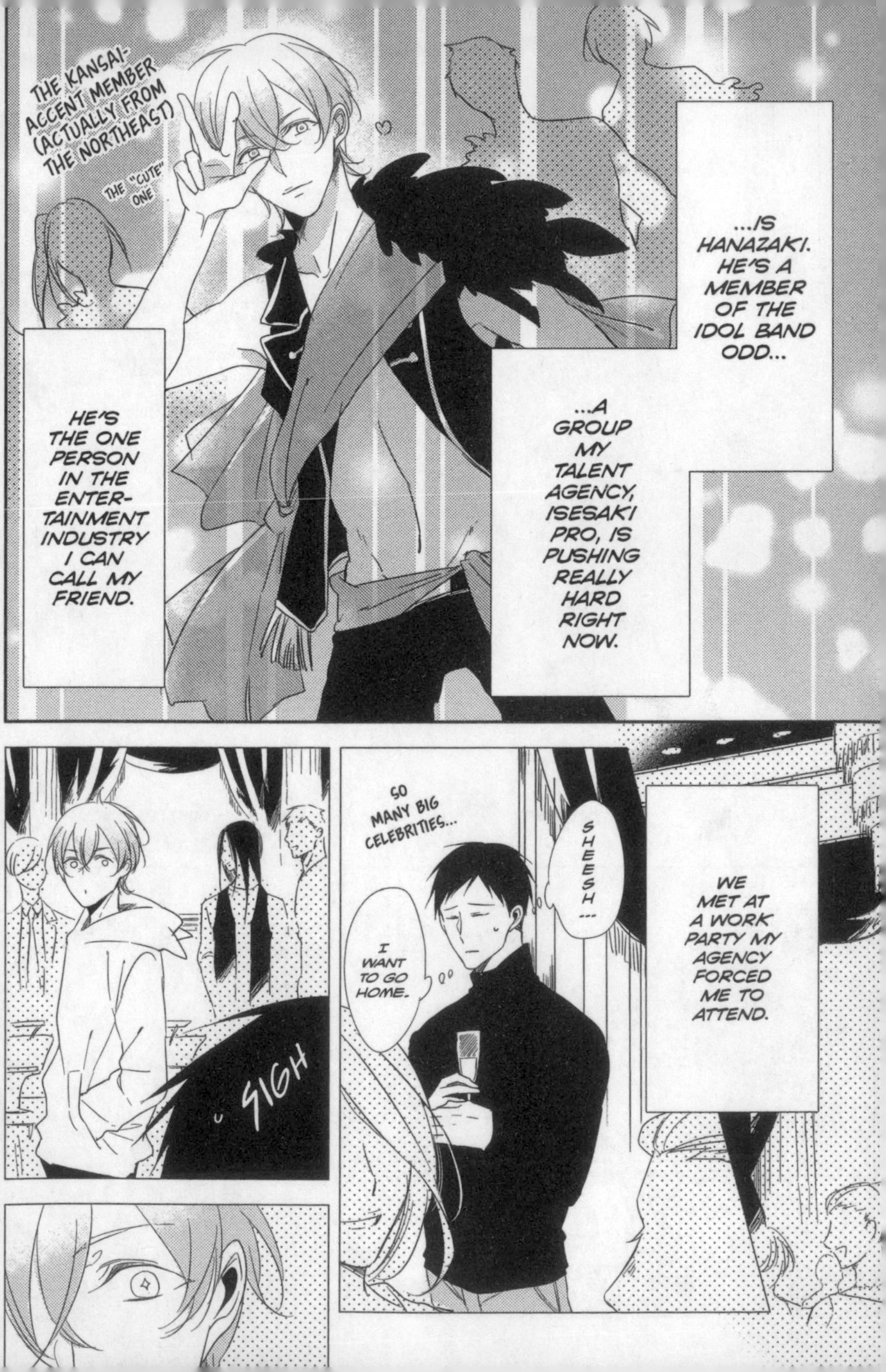
...IS HANAZAKI. HE'S A MEMBER OF THE IDOL BAND ODD...
...A GROUP MY TALENT AGENCY, ISESAKI PRO, IS PUSHING REALLY HARD RIGHT NOW.
THE KANSAI-ACCENT MEMBER (ACTUALLY FROM THE NORTHEAST)
THE "CUTE" ONE
HE'S THE ONE PERSON IN THE ENTERTAINMENT INDUSTRY I CAN CALL MY FRIEND.
WE MET AT A WORK PARTY MY AGENCY FORCED ME TO ATTEND.
SHEESH...
SO MANY BIG CELEBRITIES...
I WANT TO GO HOME.
SIGH

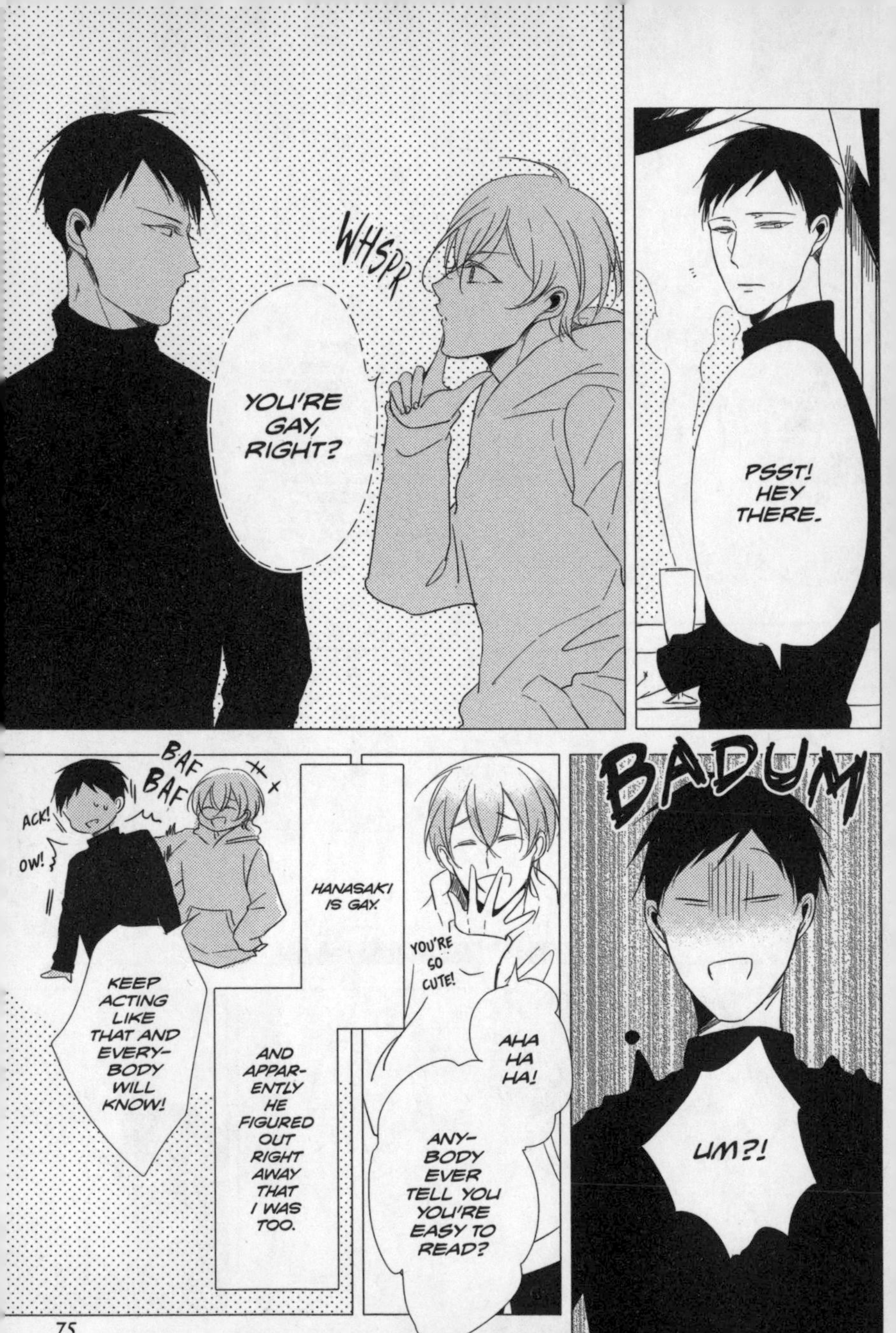
PSST! HEY THERE.
WHSPR
YOU'RE GAY, RIGHT?
BADUM
UM?!
YOU'RE SO CUTE!
AHA HA HA!
ANY-BODY EVER TELL YOU YOU'RE EASY TO READ?
HANASAKI IS GAY.
AND APPARENTLY HE FIGURED OUT RIGHT AWAY THAT I WAS TOO.
BAF BAF
ACK!
OW!
KEEP ACTING LIKE THAT AND EVERY-BODY WILL KNOW!

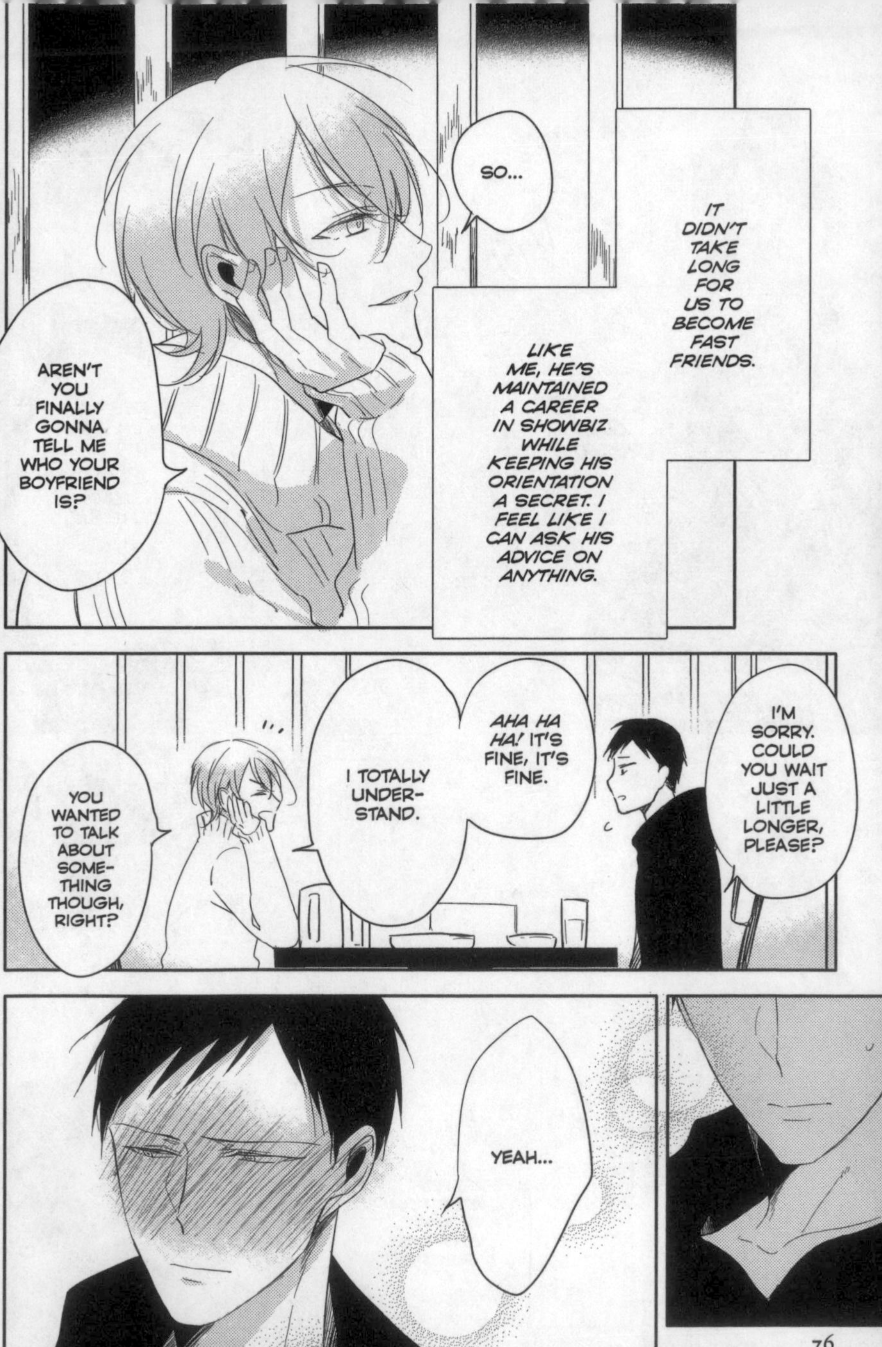
IT DIDN'T TAKE LONG FOR US TO BECOME FAST FRIENDS.
SO...
LIKE ME, HE'S MAINTAINED A CAREER IN SHOWBIZ WHILE KEEPING HIS ORIENTATION A SECRET. I FEEL LIKE I CAN ASK HIS ADVICE ON ANYTHING.
AREN'T YOU FINALLY GONNA TELL ME WHO YOUR BOYFRIEND IS?
I'M SORRY. COULD YOU WAIT JUST A LITTLE LONGER, PLEASE?
AHA HA HA! IT'S FINE, IT'S FINE.
I TOTALLY UNDER-STAND.
YOU WANTED TO TALK ABOUT SOME-THING THOUGH, RIGHT?
YEAH...

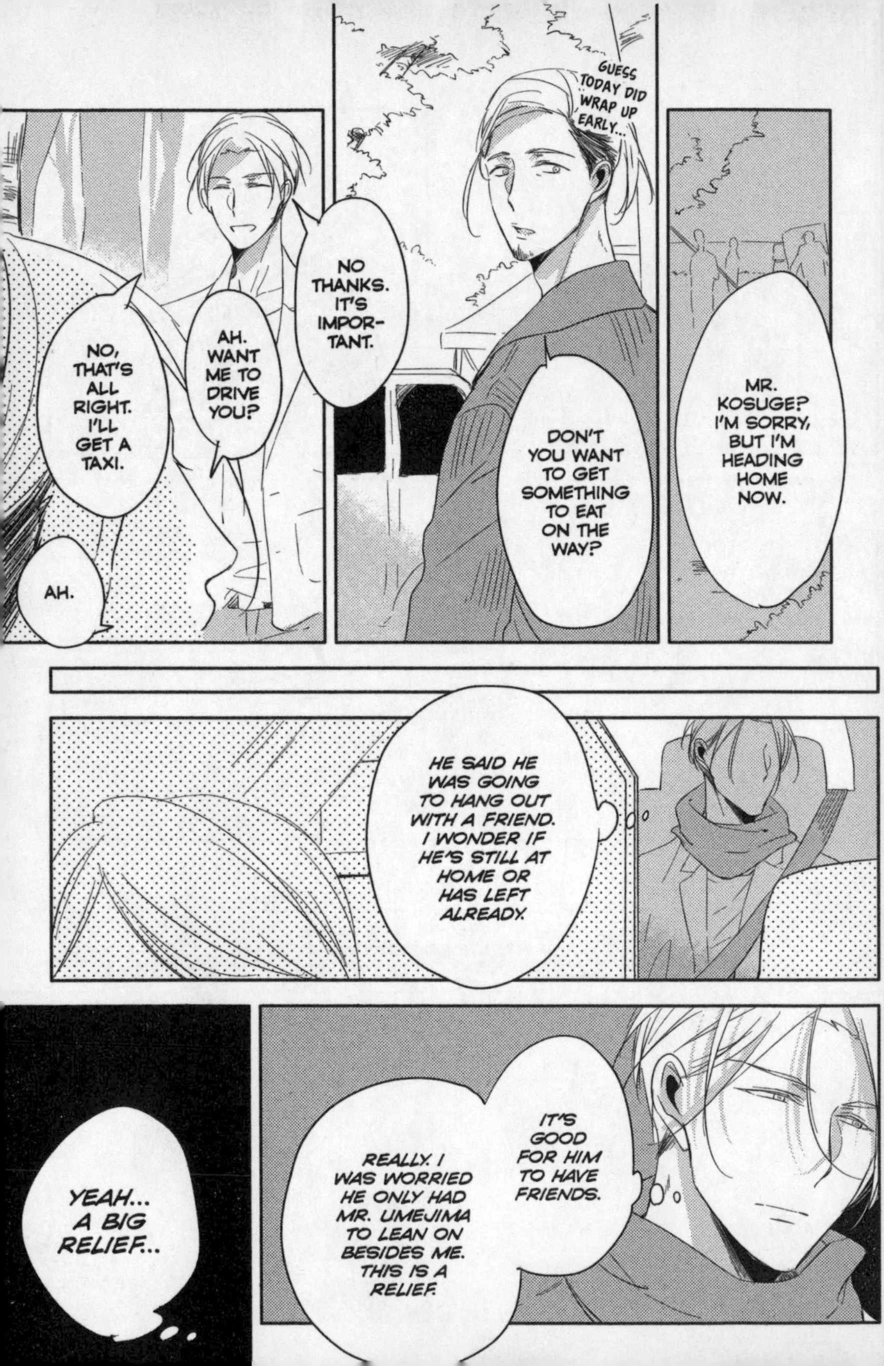
MR. KOSUGE? I'M SORRY, BUT I'M HEADING HOME NOW.
GUESS TODAY DID WRAP UP EARLY...
DON'T YOU WANT TO GET SOMETHING TO EAT ON THE WAY?
NO THANKS. IT'S IMPOR-TANT.
AH. WANT ME TO DRIVE YOU?
NO, THAT'S ALL RIGHT. I'LL GET A TAXI.
AH.
HE SAID HE WAS GOING TO HANG OUT WITH A FRIEND. I WONDER IF HE'S STILL AT HOME OR HAS LEFT ALREADY.
IT'S GOOD FOR HIM TO HAVE FRIENDS.
REALLY. I WAS WORRIED HE ONLY HAD MR. UMEJIMA TO LEAN ON BESIDES ME. THIS IS A RELIEF.
YEAH... A BIG RELIEF...

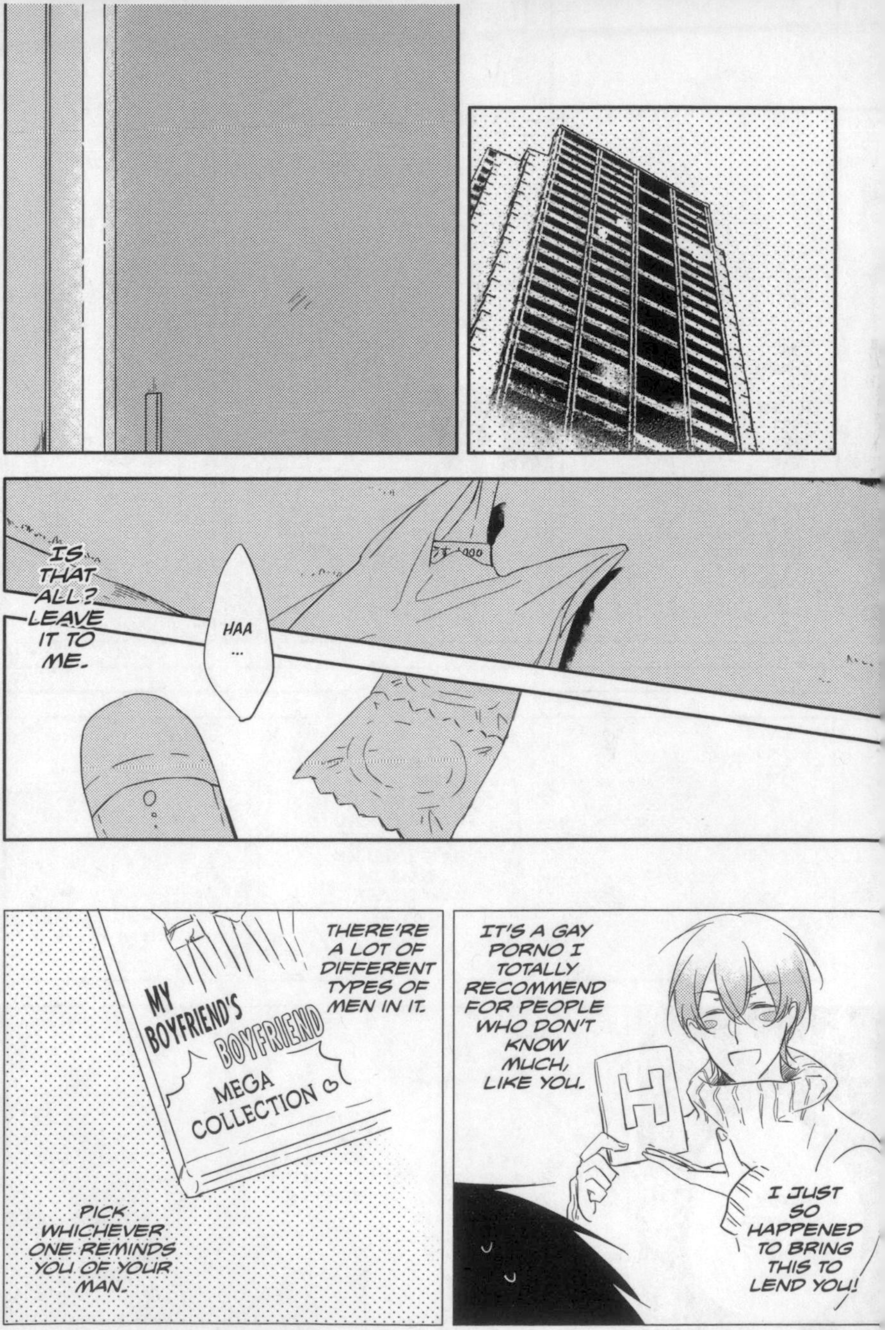
IS THAT ALL? LEAVE IT TO ME.
HAA...
IT'S A GAY PORNO I TOTALLY RECOMMEND FOR PEOPLE WHO DON'T KNOW MUCH, LIKE YOU.
H
I JUST SO HAPPENED TO BRING THIS TO LEND YOU!
THERE'RE A LOT OF DIFFERENT TYPES OF MEN IN IT.
MY BOYFRIEND'S BOYFRIEND MEGA COLLECTION
PICK WHICHEVER ONE REMINDS YOU OF YOUR MAN.

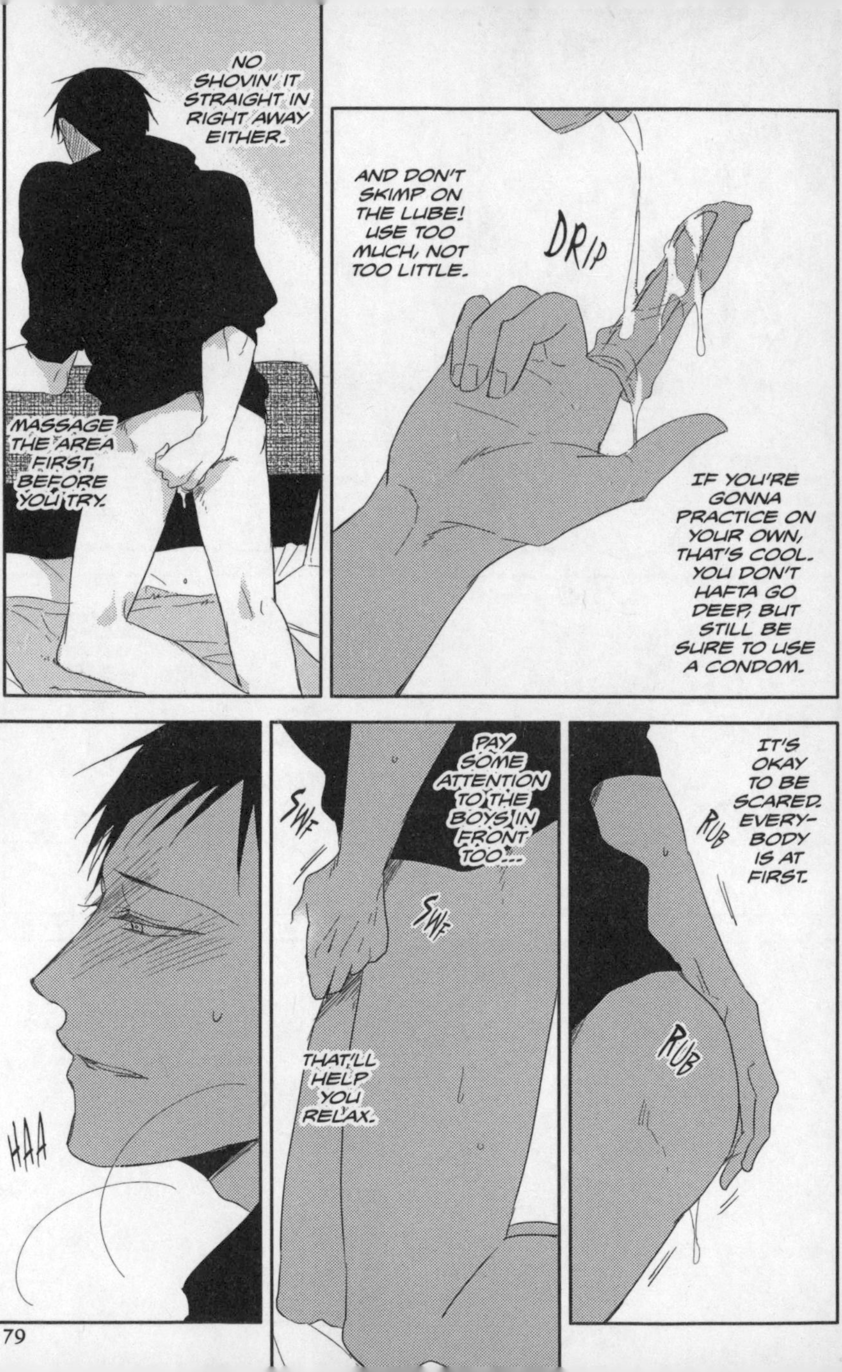
AND DON'T SKIMP ON THE LUBE! USE TOO MUCH, NOT TOO LITTLE.
DRIP
IF YOU'RE GONNA PRACTICE ON YOUR OWN, THAT'S COOL. YOU DON'T HAFTA GO DEEP, BUT STILL BE SURE TO USE A CONDOM.
NO SHOVIN' IT STRAIGHT IN RIGHT AWAY EITHER.
MASSAGE THE AREA FIRST, BEFORE YOU TRY.
IT'S OKAY TO BE SCARED. EVERY-BODY IS AT FIRST.
RUB
RUB
PAY SOME ATTENTION TO THE BOYS IN FRONT TOO...
SWF
SWF
THAT'LL HELP YOU RELAX.
HAA

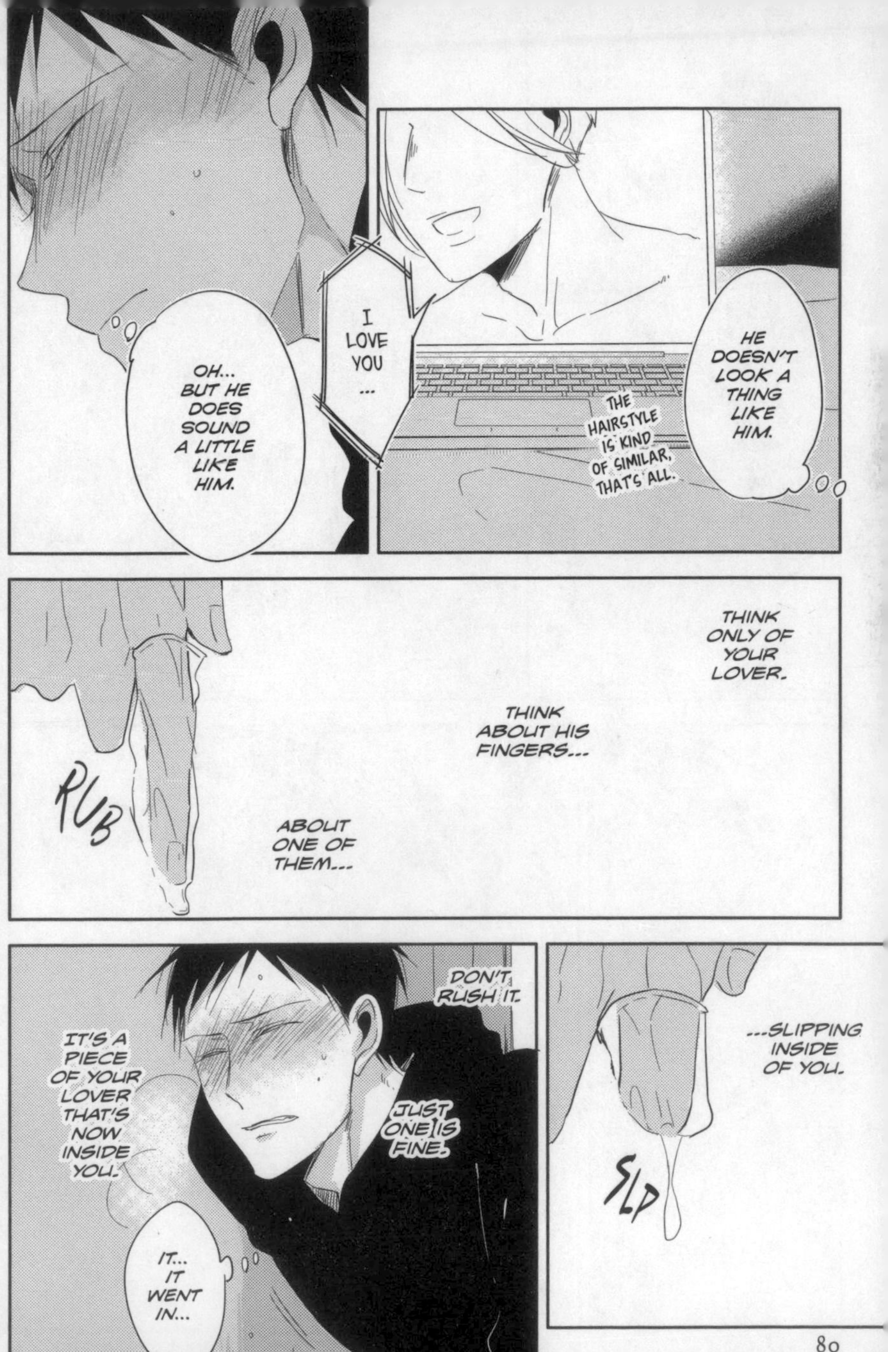
HE DOESN'T LOOK A THING LIKE HIM.
THE HAIRSTYLE IS KIND OF SIMILAR, THAT'S ALL.
I LOVE YOU ...
OH... BUT HE DOES SOUND A LITTLE LIKE HIM.
THINK ONLY OF YOUR LOVER.
THINK ABOUT HIS FINGERS...
ABOUT ONE OF THEM...
RUB
...SLIPPING INSIDE OF YOU.
SLP
DON'T RUSH IT.
JUST ONE IS FINE.
IT'S A PIECE OF YOUR LOVER THAT'S NOW INSIDE YOU.
IT... IT WENT IN...

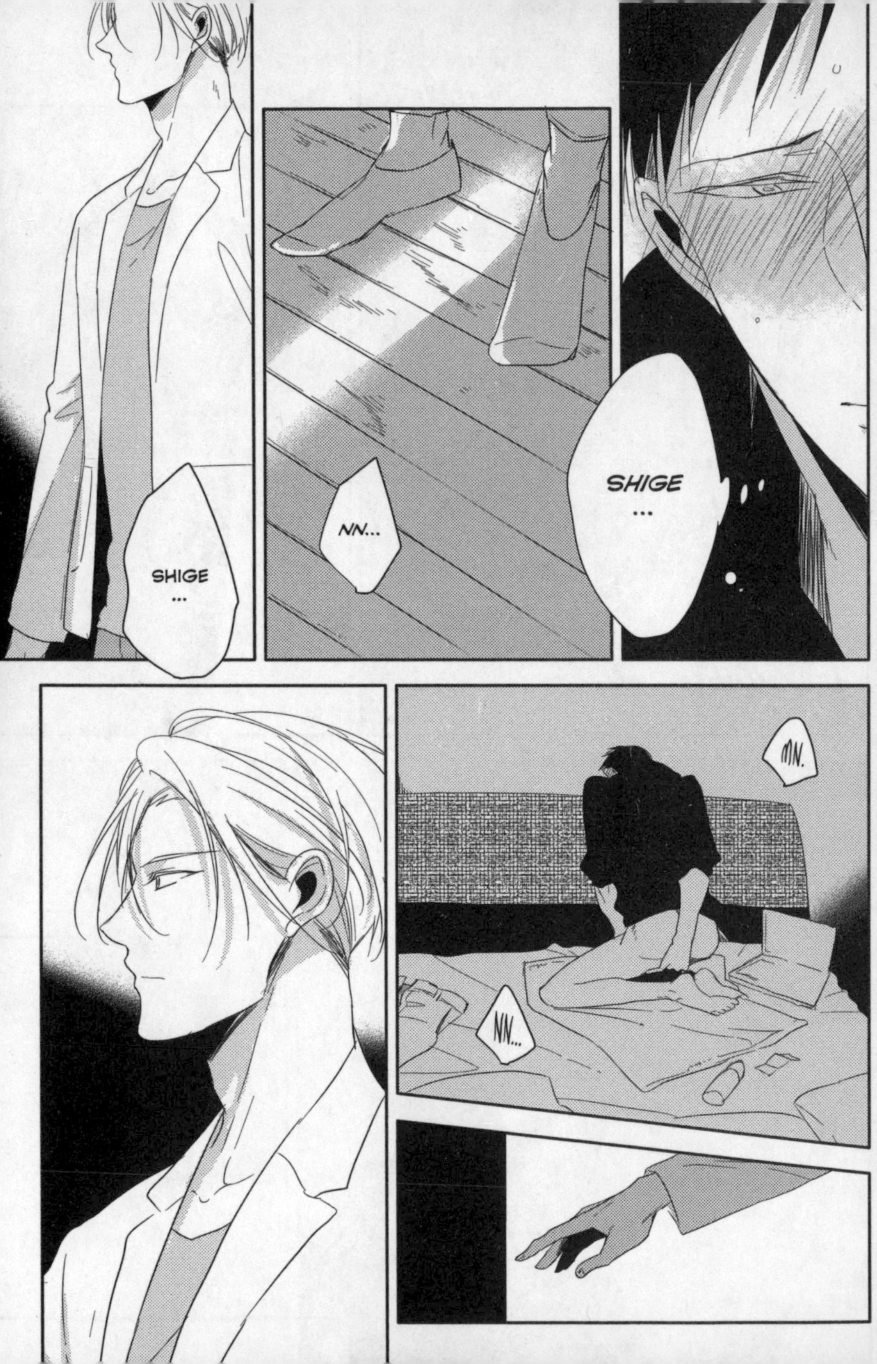
SHIGE
...
NN...
SHIGE
...
MN.
NN...

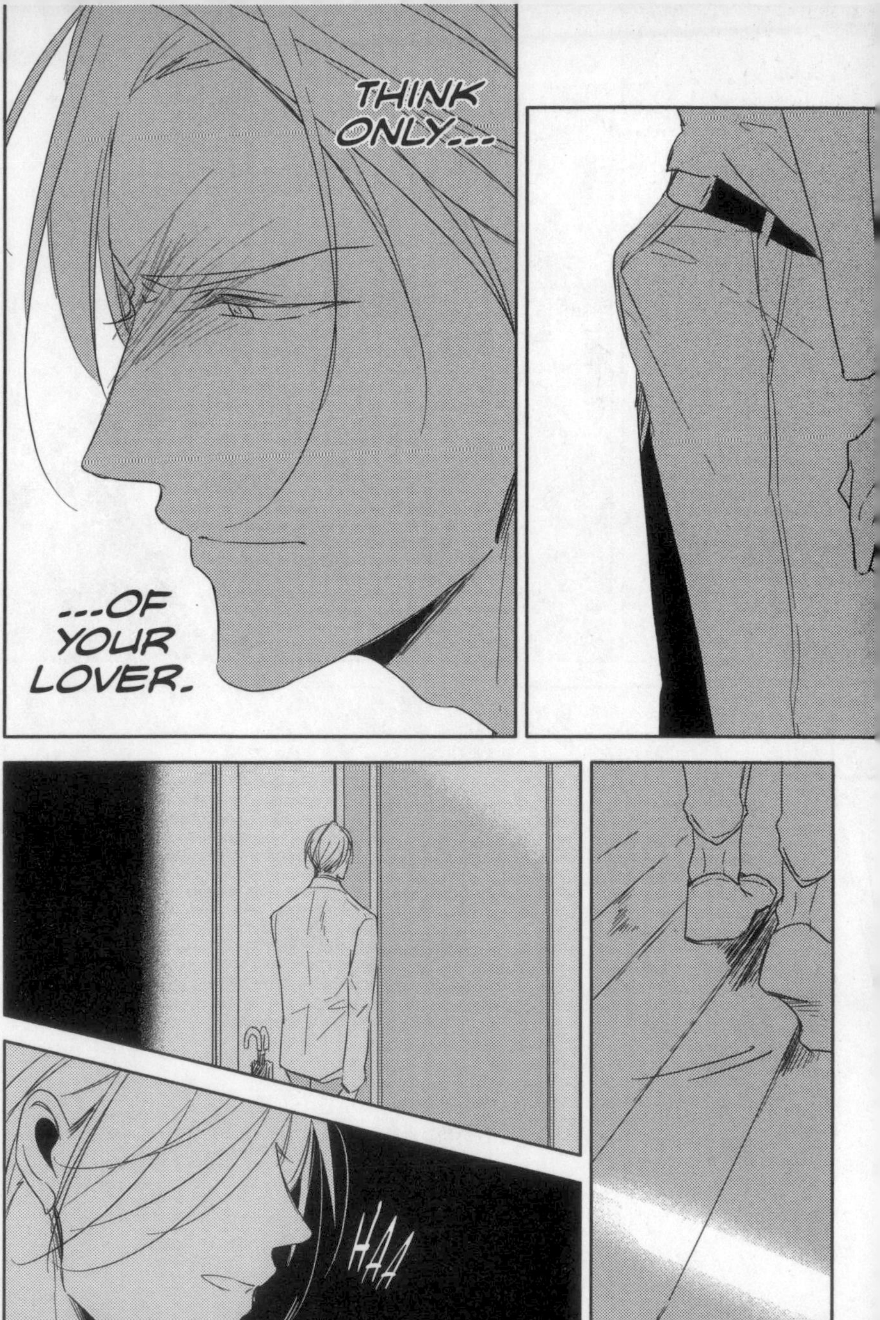
THINK ONLY...
...OF YOUR LOVER.
HAA

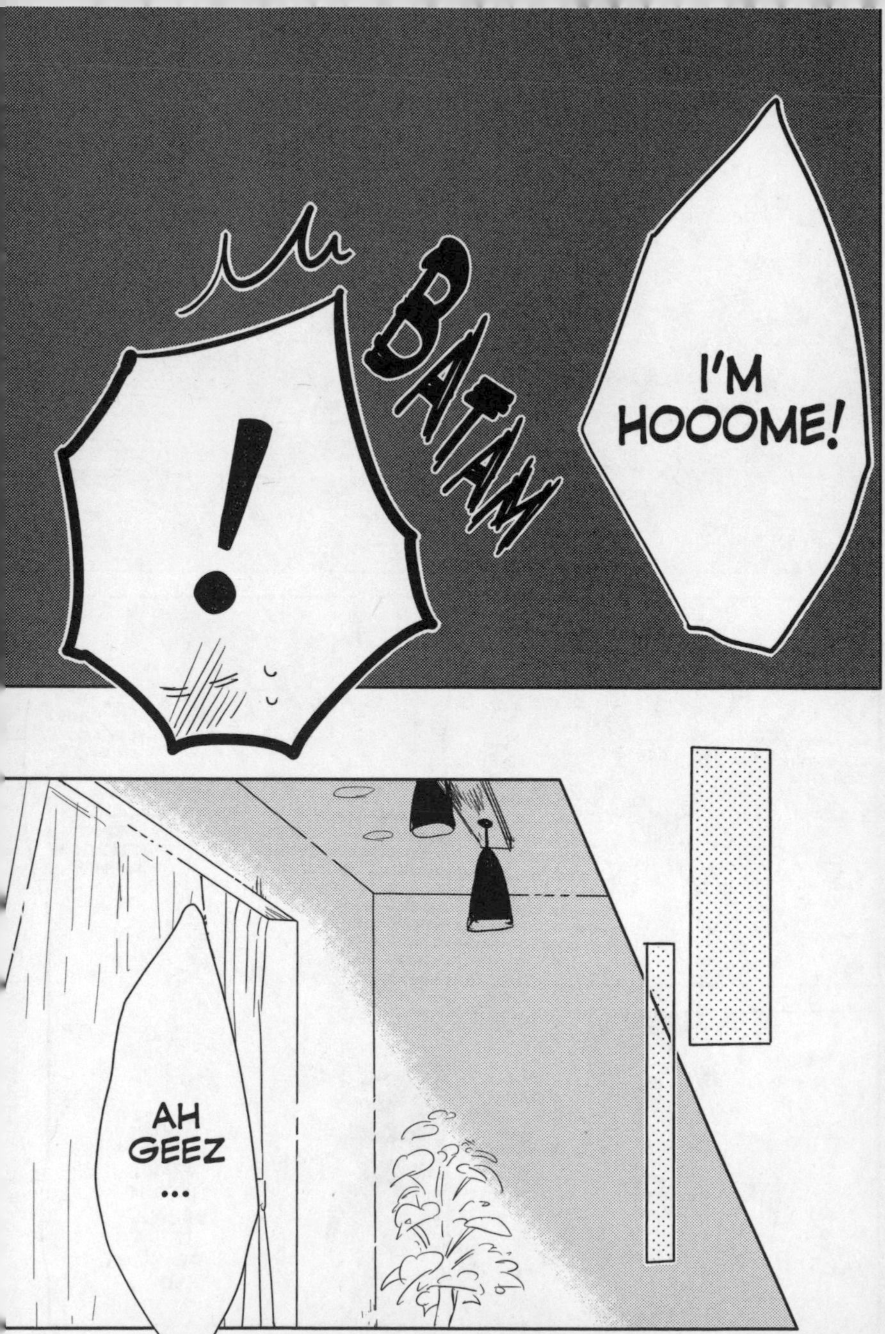
I'M HOOOME!
BATAM
!
AH GEEZ ...

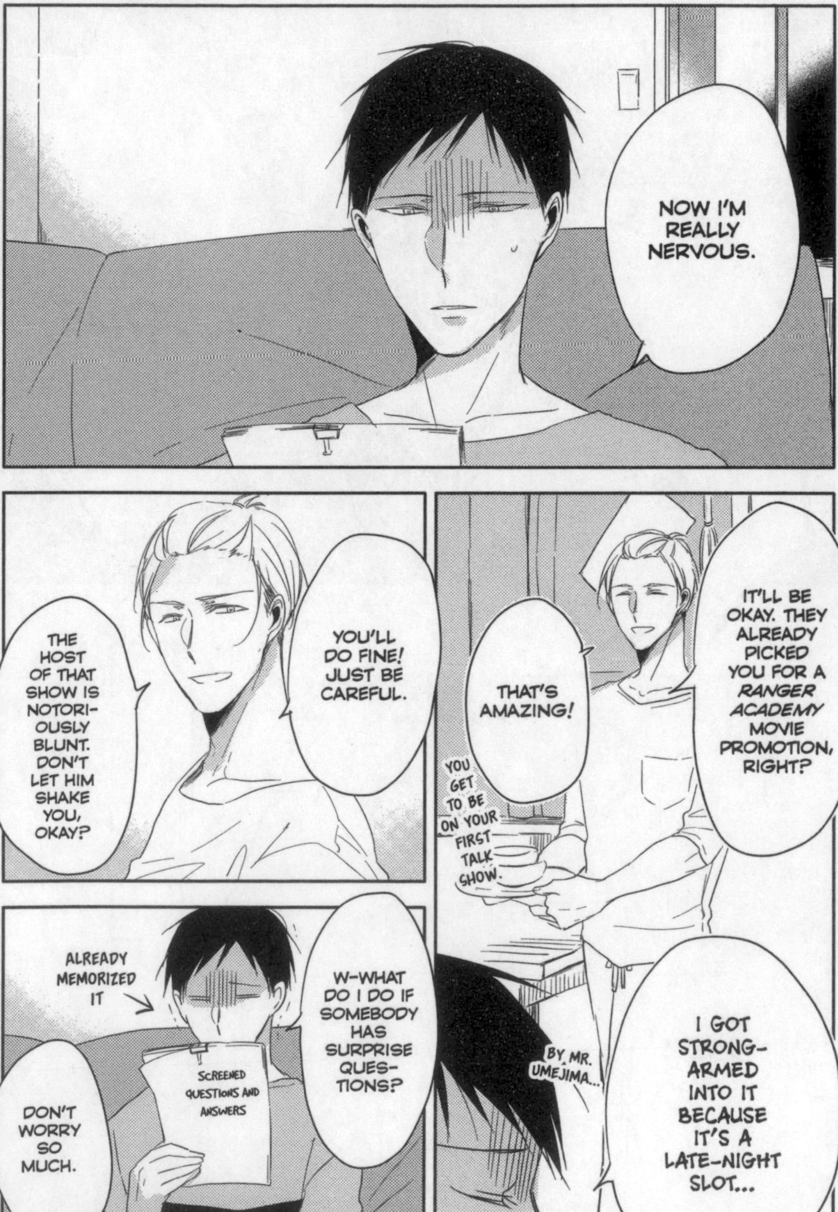
NOW I'M REALLY NERVOUS.
IT'LL BE OKAY. THEY ALREADY PICKED YOU FOR A *RANGER ACADEMY* MOVIE PROMOTION, RIGHT?
THAT'S AMAZING!
YOU GET TO BE ON YOUR FIRST TALK SHOW.
I GOT STRONG-ARMED INTO IT BECAUSE IT'S A LATE-NIGHT SLOT...
BY MR. UMEJIMA...
YOU'LL DO FINE! JUST BE CAREFUL.
THE HOST OF THAT SHOW IS NOTORIOUSLY BLUNT. DON'T LET HIM SHAKE YOU, OKAY?
W-WHAT DO I DO IF SOMEBODY HAS SURPRISE QUES-TIONS?
ALREADY MEMORIZED IT
SCREENED QUESTIONS AND ANSWERS
DON'T WORRY SO MUCH.

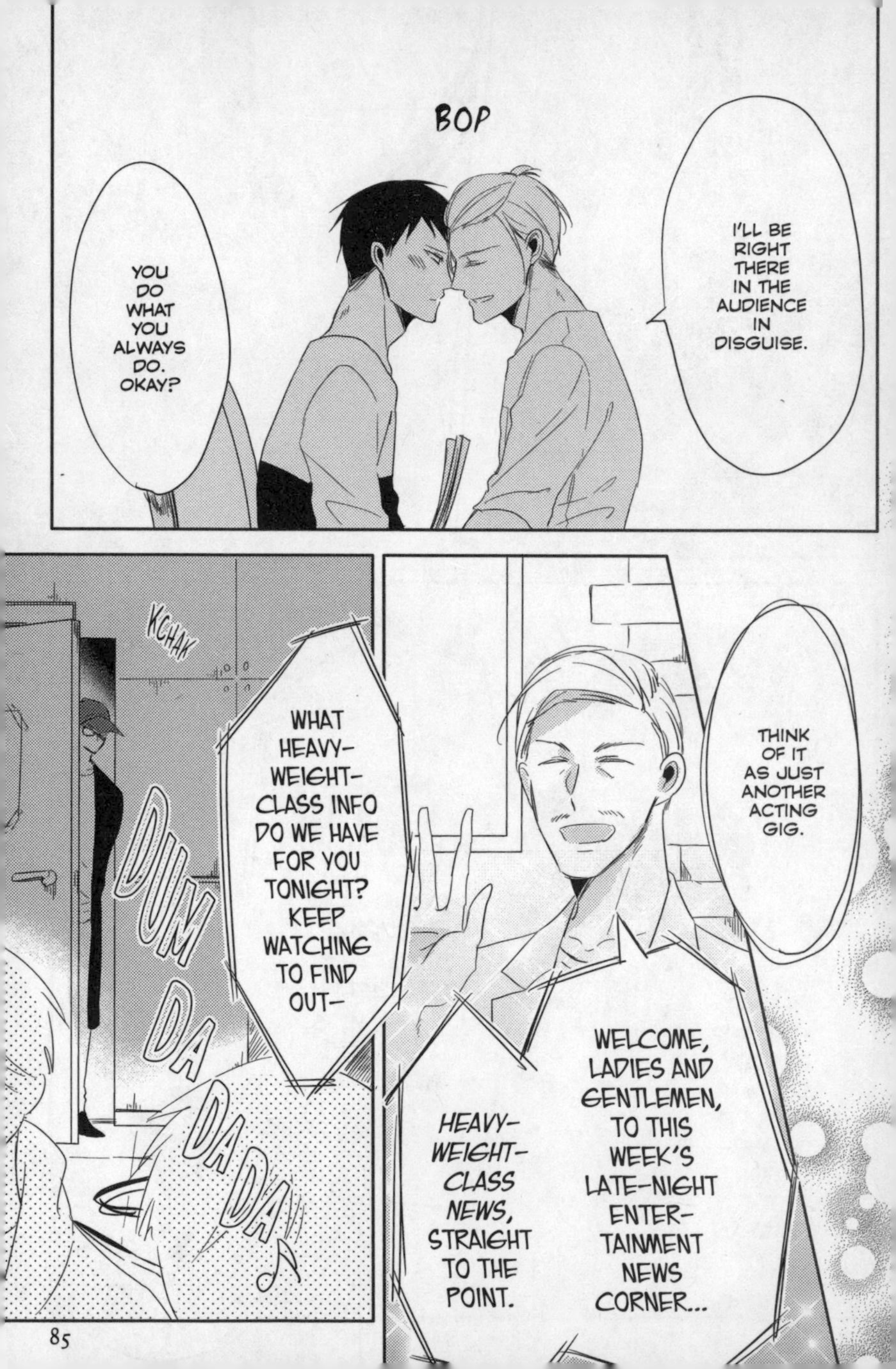
I'LL BE RIGHT THERE IN THE AUDIENCE IN DISGUISE.
BOP
YOU DO WHAT YOU ALWAYS DO. OKAY?
THINK OF IT AS JUST ANOTHER ACTING GIG.
WELCOME, LADIES AND GENTLEMEN, TO THIS WEEK'S LATE-NIGHT ENTER-TAINMENT NEWS CORNER...
HEAVY-WEIGHT-CLASS NEWS, STRAIGHT TO THE POINT.
KCHAK
WHAT HEAVY-WEIGHT-CLASS INFO DO WE HAVE FOR YOU TONIGHT? KEEP WATCHING TO FIND OUT–
DUM DA DA DA♪

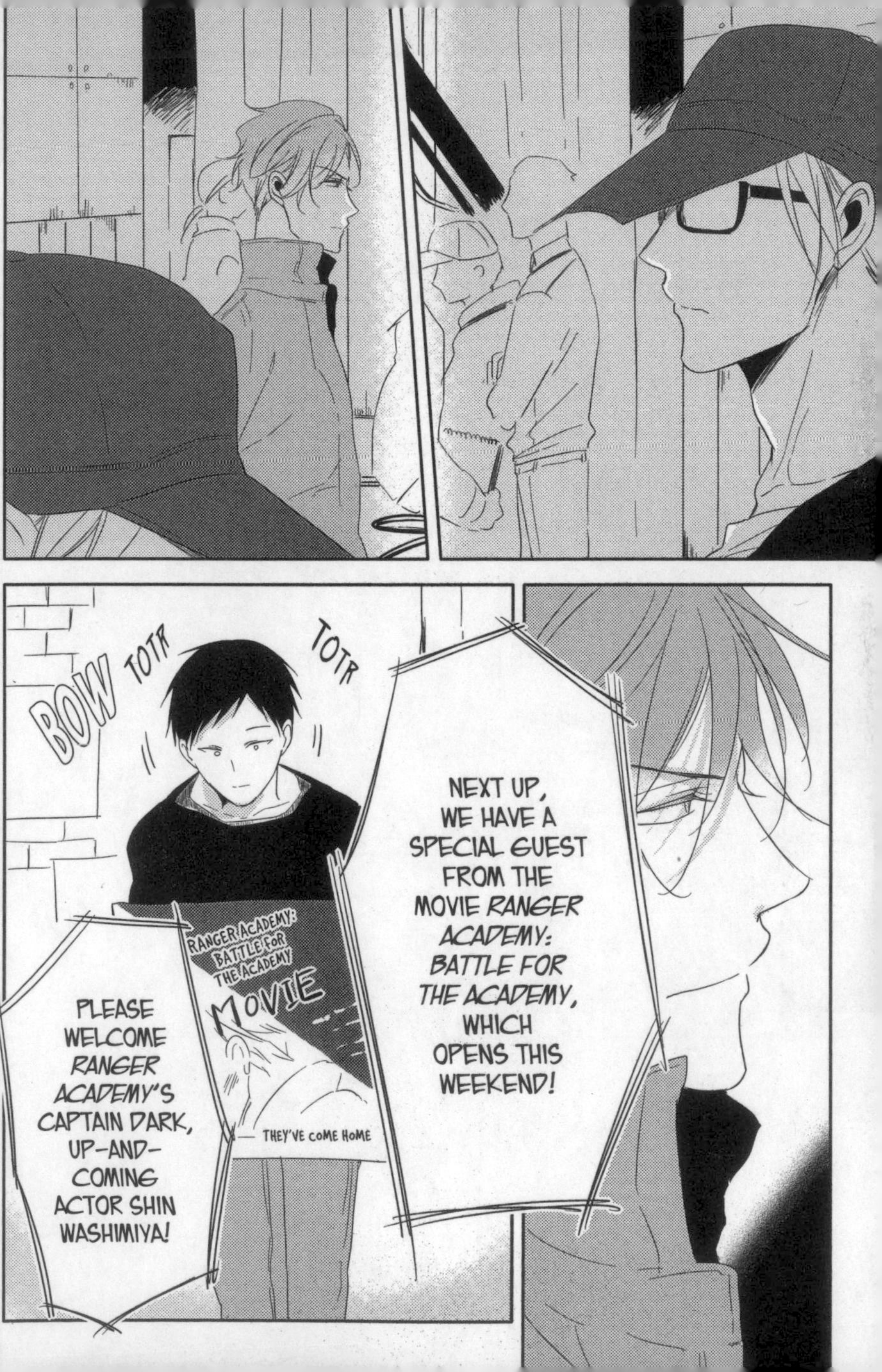
NEXT UP, WE HAVE A SPECIAL GUEST FROM THE MOVIE *RANGER ACADEMY: BATTLE FOR THE ACADEMY*, WHICH OPENS THIS WEEKEND!
TOTR
TOTR
BOW
RANGER ACADEMY: BATTLE FOR THE ACADEMY
MOVIE
— THEY'VE COME HOME
PLEASE WELCOME *RANGER ACADEMY*'S CAPTAIN DARK, UP-AND-COMING ACTOR SHIN WASHIMIYA!

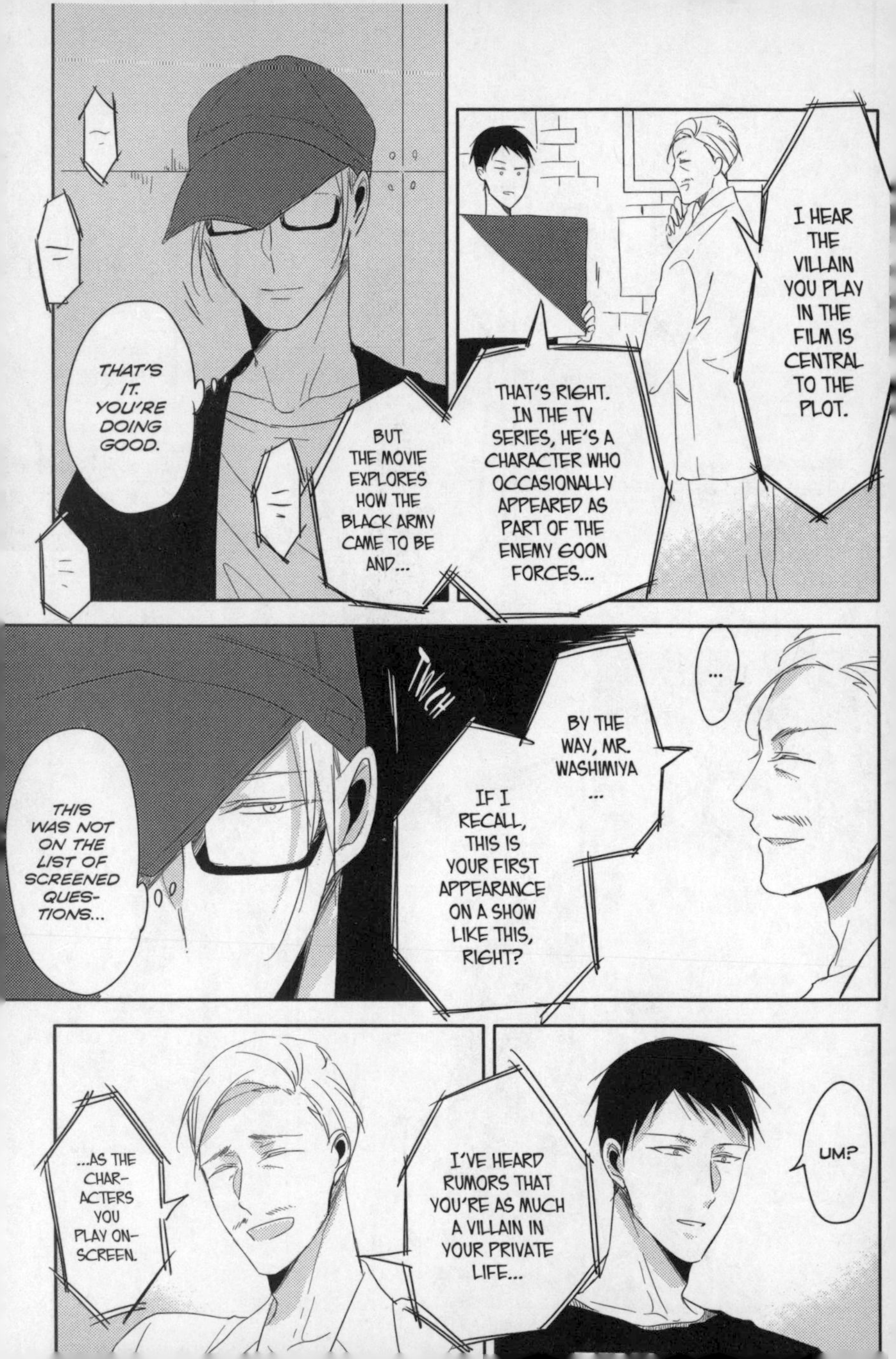
I HEAR THE VILLAIN YOU PLAY IN THE FILM IS CENTRAL TO THE PLOT.
THAT'S RIGHT. IN THE TV SERIES, HE'S A CHARACTER WHO OCCASIONALLY APPEARED AS PART OF THE ENEMY GOON FORCES...
BUT THE MOVIE EXPLORES HOW THE BLACK ARMY CAME TO BE AND...
THAT'S IT. YOU'RE DOING GOOD.
...
BY THE WAY, MR. WASHIMIYA...
IF I RECALL, THIS IS YOUR FIRST APPEARANCE ON A SHOW LIKE THIS, RIGHT?
TWCH
THIS WAS NOT ON THE LIST OF SCREENED QUESTIONS...
UM?
I'VE HEARD RUMORS THAT YOU'RE AS MUCH A VILLAIN IN YOUR PRIVATE LIFE...
...AS THE CHARACTERS YOU PLAY ON-SCREEN.

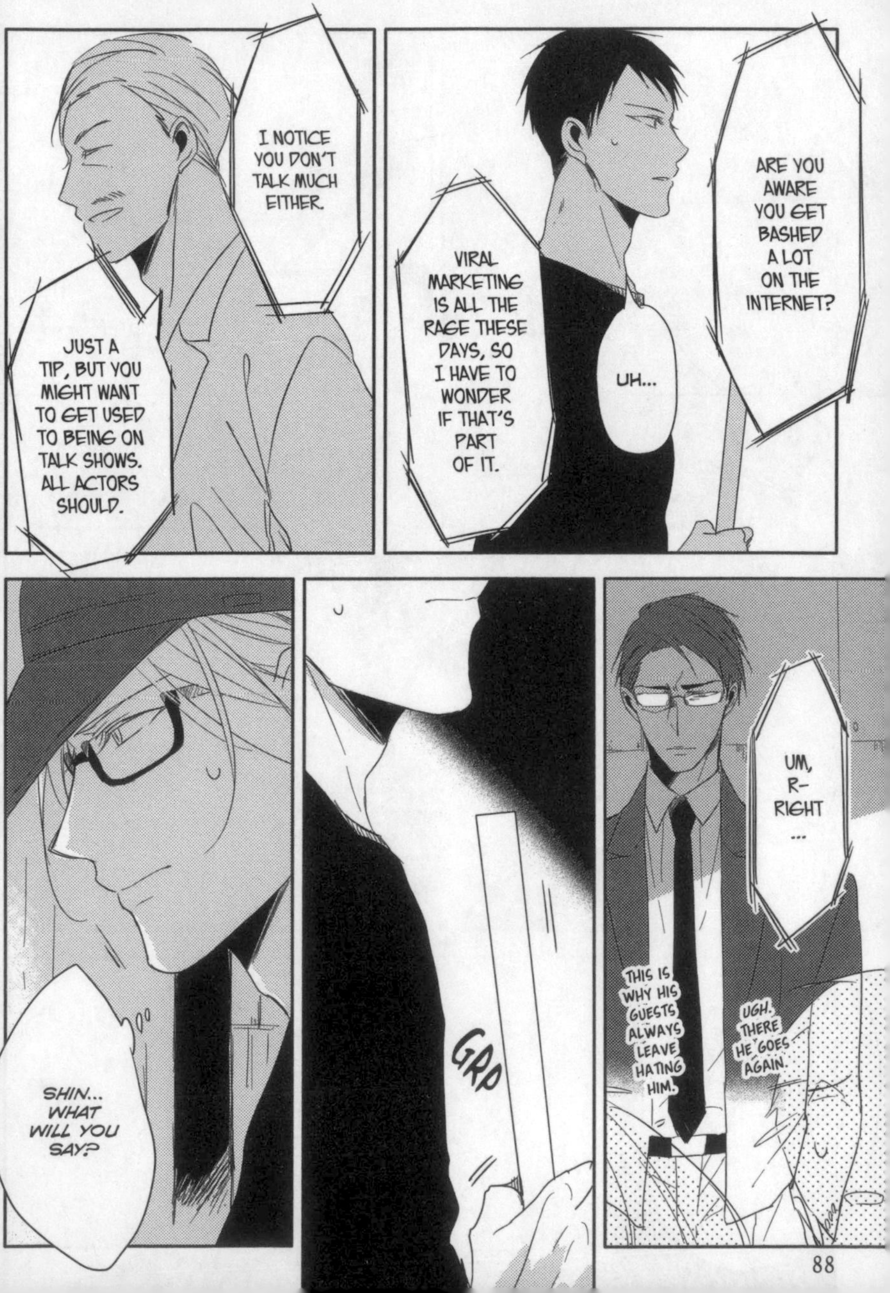
ARE YOU AWARE YOU GET BASHED A LOT ON THE INTERNET?
UH...
VIRAL MARKETING IS ALL THE RAGE THESE DAYS, SO I HAVE TO WONDER IF THAT'S PART OF IT.
I NOTICE YOU DON'T TALK MUCH EITHER.
JUST A TIP, BUT YOU MIGHT WANT TO GET USED TO BEING ON TALK SHOWS. ALL ACTORS SHOULD.
UM, R-RIGHT...
UGH. THERE HE GOES AGAIN.
THIS IS WHY HIS GUESTS ALWAYS LEAVE HATING HIM.
GRIP
SHIN... WHAT WILL YOU SAY?

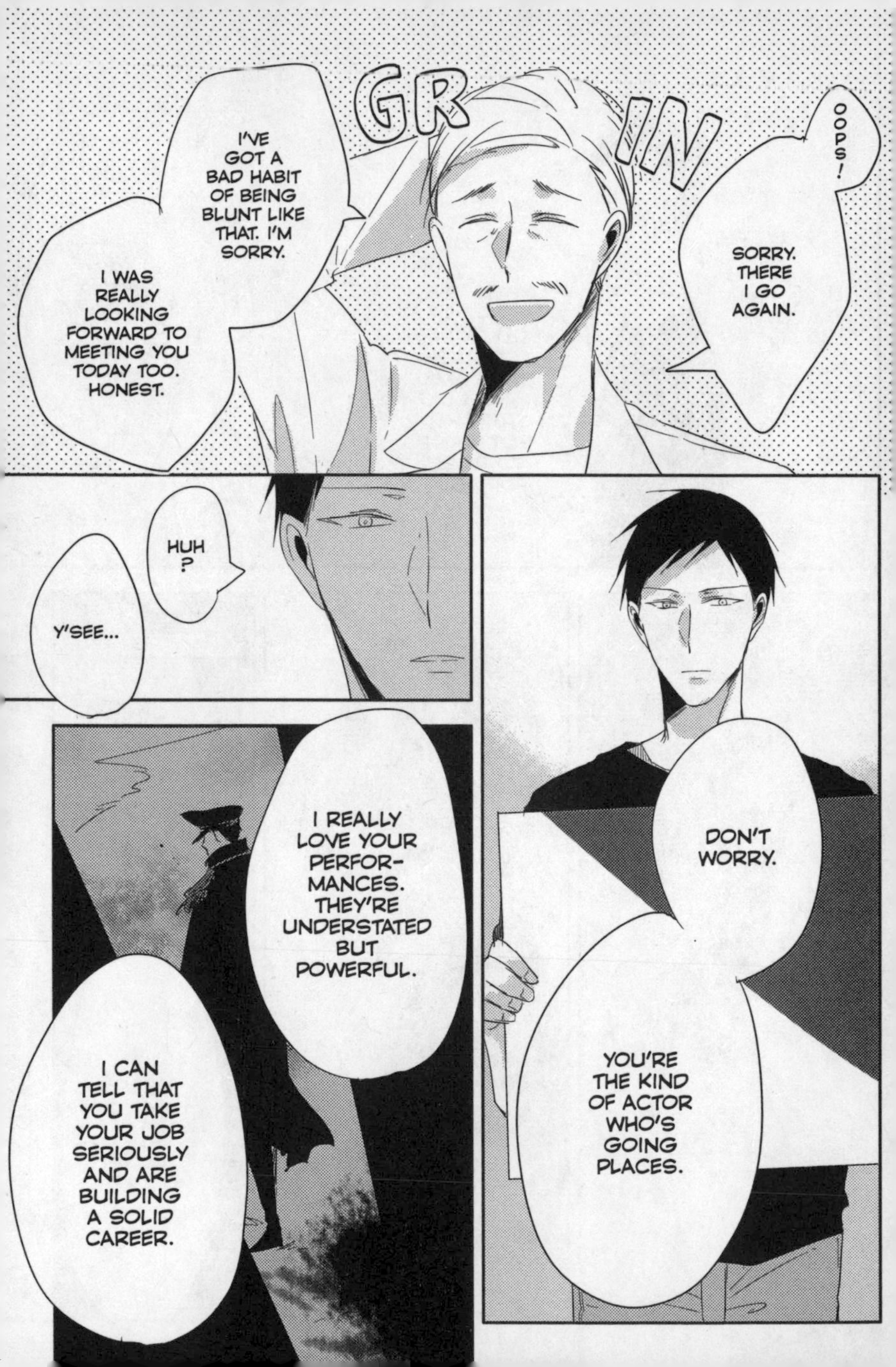
OOPS!
SORRY. THERE I GO AGAIN.
GRIN
I'VE GOT A BAD HABIT OF BEING BLUNT LIKE THAT. I'M SORRY.
I WAS REALLY LOOKING FORWARD TO MEETING YOU TODAY TOO. HONEST.
DON'T WORRY.
YOU'RE THE KIND OF ACTOR WHO'S GOING PLACES.
HUH?
Y'SEE...
I REALLY LOVE YOUR PERFOR-MANCES. THEY'RE UNDERSTATED BUT POWERFUL.
I CAN TELL THAT YOU TAKE YOUR JOB SERIOUSLY AND ARE BUILDING A SOLID CAREER.

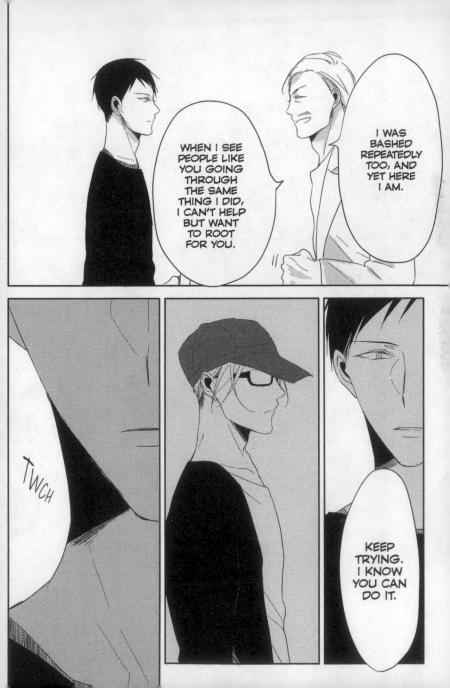

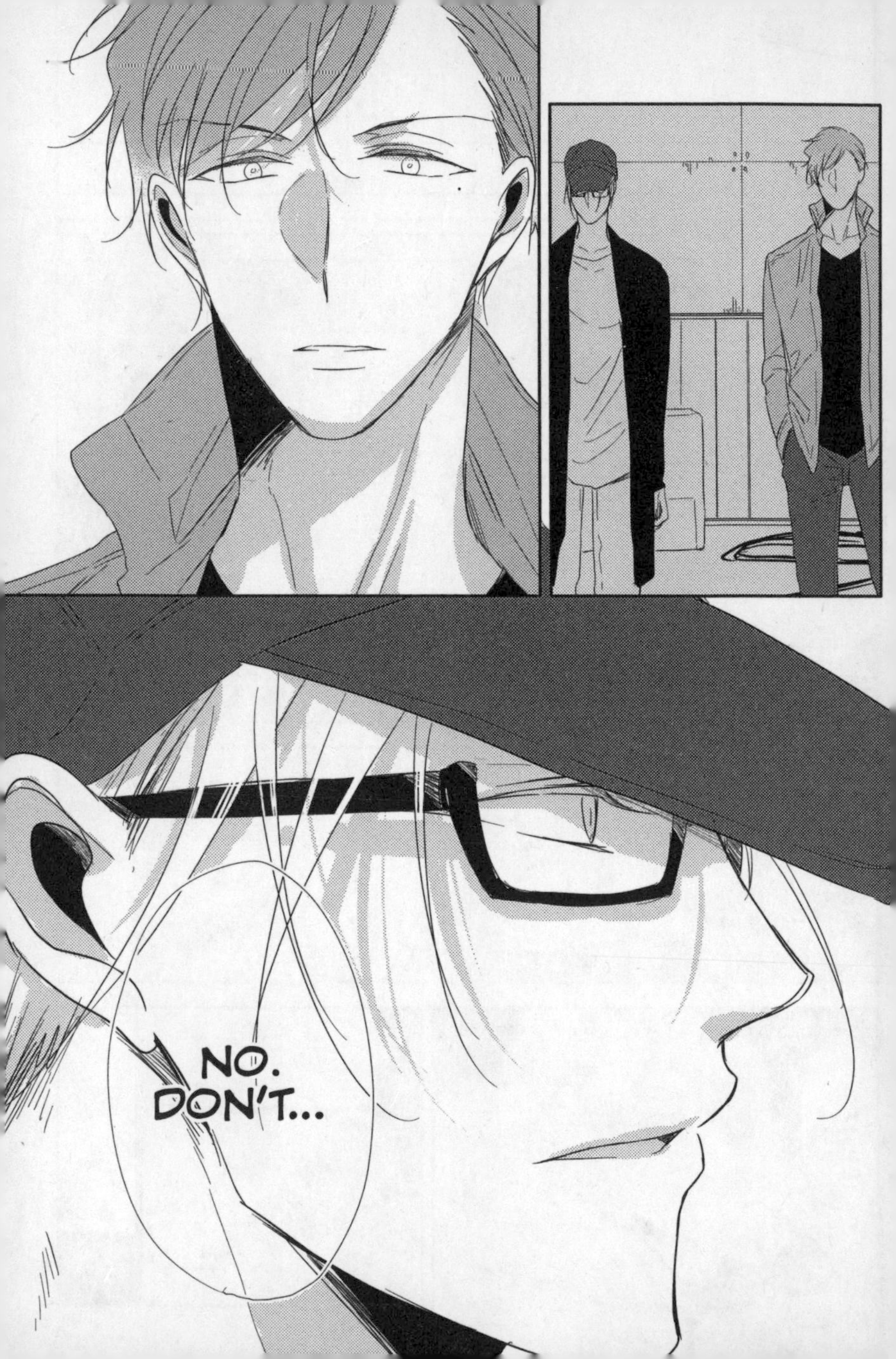
NO.
DON'T...

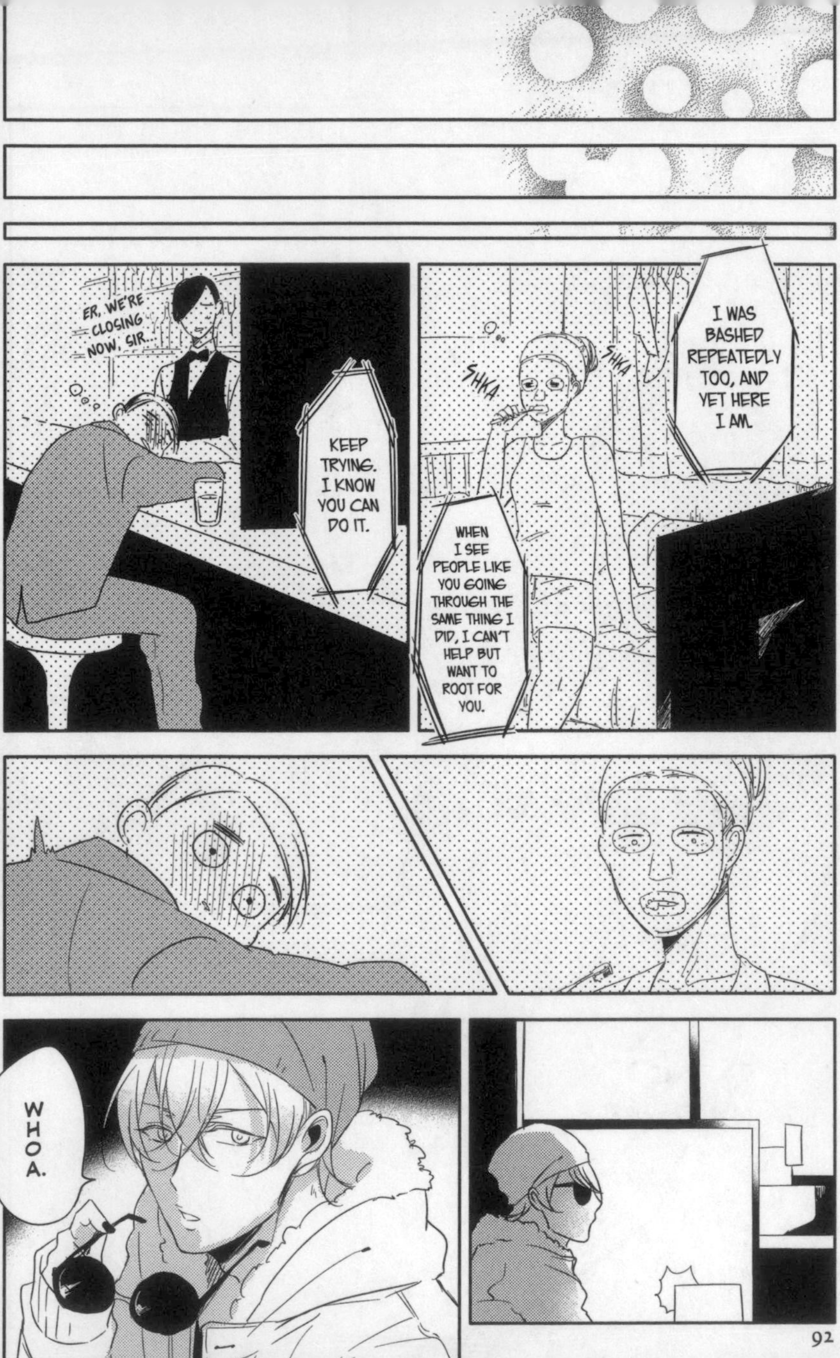
SHKA
SHKA
I WAS BASHED REPEATEDLY TOO, AND YET HERE I AM.
WHEN I SEE PEOPLE LIKE YOU GOING THROUGH THE SAME THING I DID, I CAN'T HELP BUT WANT TO ROOT FOR YOU.
KEEP TRYING. I KNOW YOU CAN DO IT.
ER, WE'RE CLOSING NOW, SIR...
WHOA.

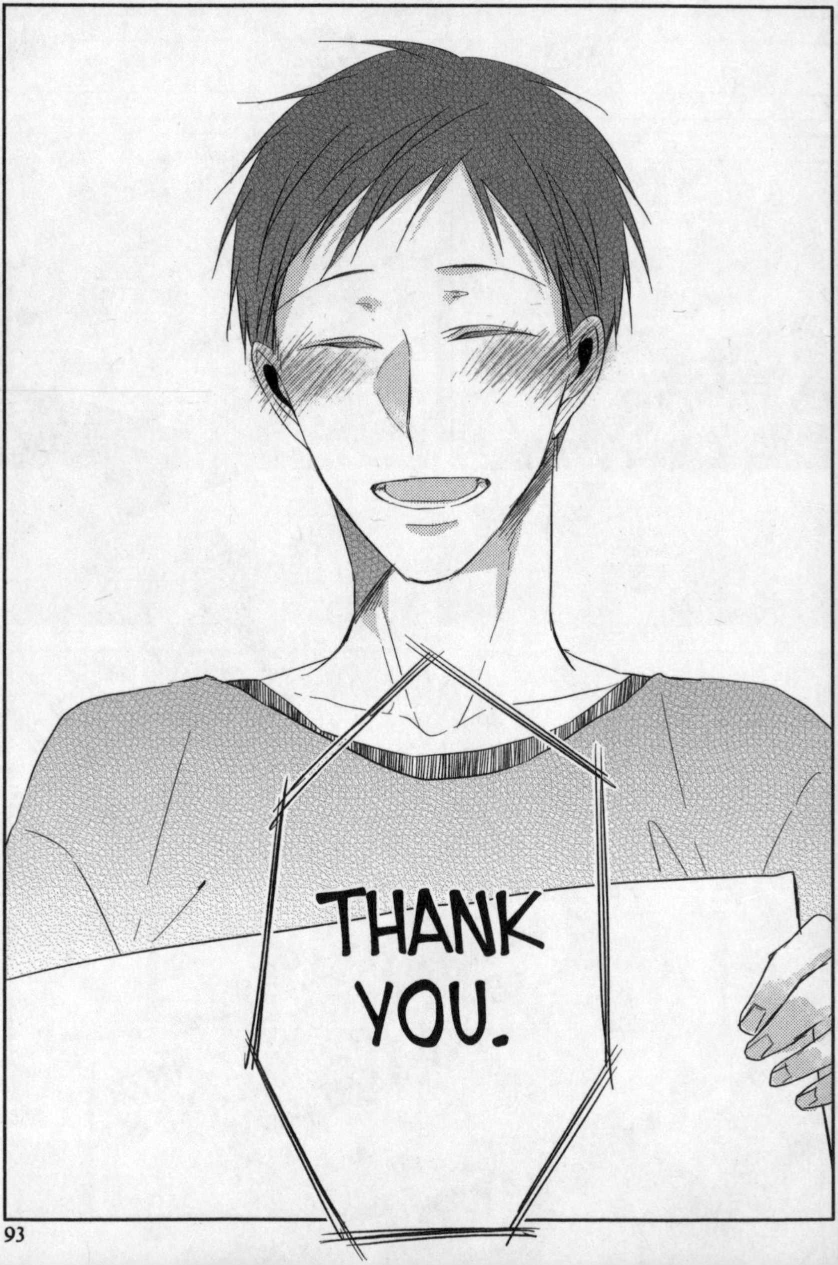
THANK YOU.

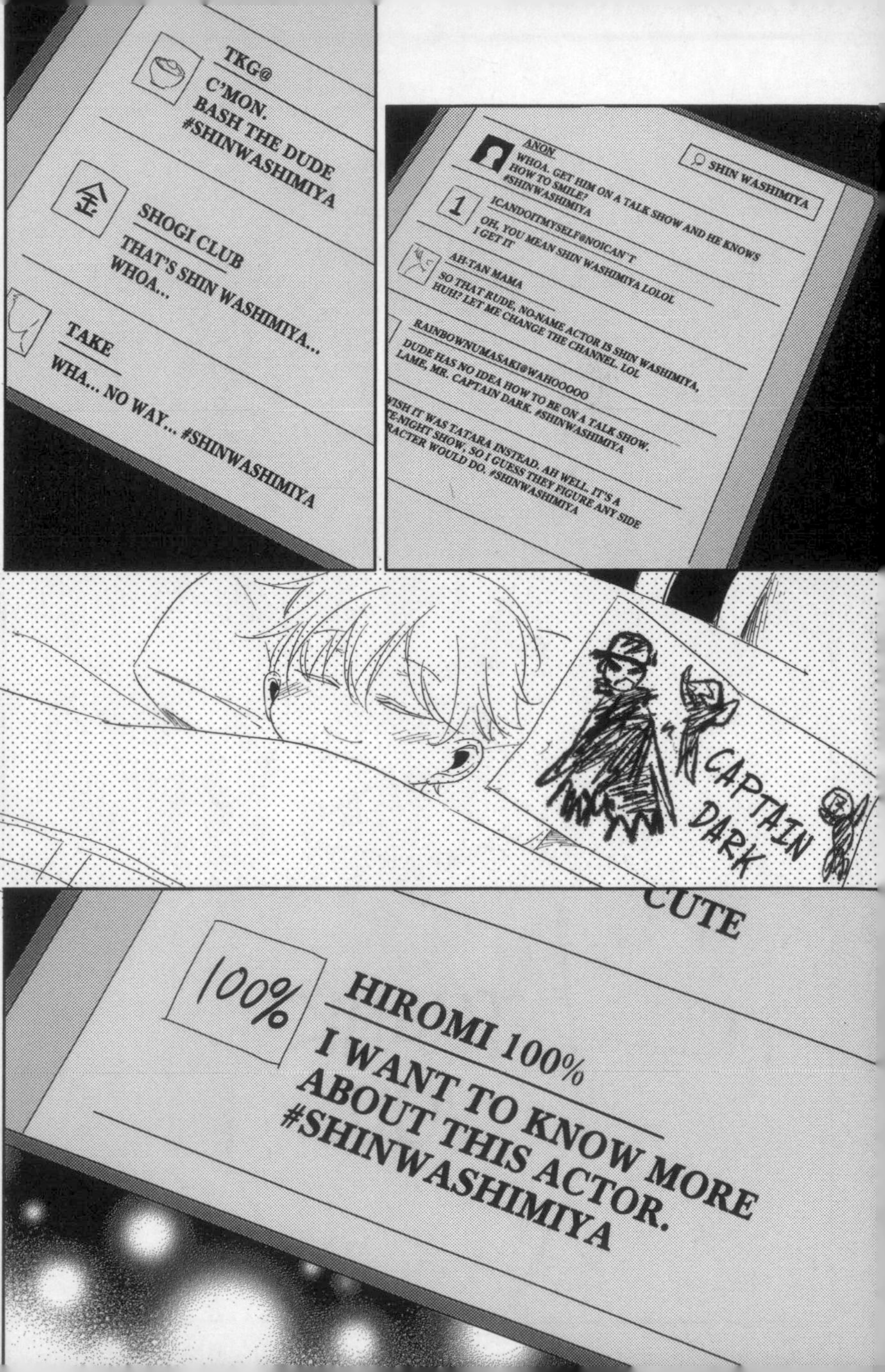
SHIN WASHIMIYA
ANON
WHOA. GET HIM ON A TALK SHOW AND HE KNOWS HOW TO SMILE? #SHINWASHIMIYA
ICANDOITMYSELF@NOICAN'T
OH, YOU MEAN SHIN WASHIMIYA LOLOL I GET IT
AH-TAN MAMA
SO THAT RUDE, NO-NAME ACTOR IS SHIN WASHIMIYA, HUH? LET ME CHANGE THE CHANNEL. LOL
RAINBOWNUMASAKI@WAHOOOOO
DUDE HAS NO IDEA HOW TO BE ON A TALK SHOW. LAME, MR. CAPTAIN DARK. #SHINWASHIMIYA
ISH IT WAS TATARA INSTEAD. AH WELL, IT'S A
E-NIGHT SHOW, SO I GUESS THEY FIGURE ANY SIDE
RACTER WOULD DO. #SHINWASHIMIYA
TKG@
C'MON. BASH THE DUDE #SHINWASHIMIYA
SHOGI CLUB
THAT'S SHIN WASHIMIYA... WHOA...
TAKE
WHA... NO WAY... #SHINWASHIMIYA
CAPTAIN DARK
CUTE
100%
HIROMI 100%
I WANT TO KNOW MORE ABOUT THIS ACTOR. #SHINWASHIMIYA

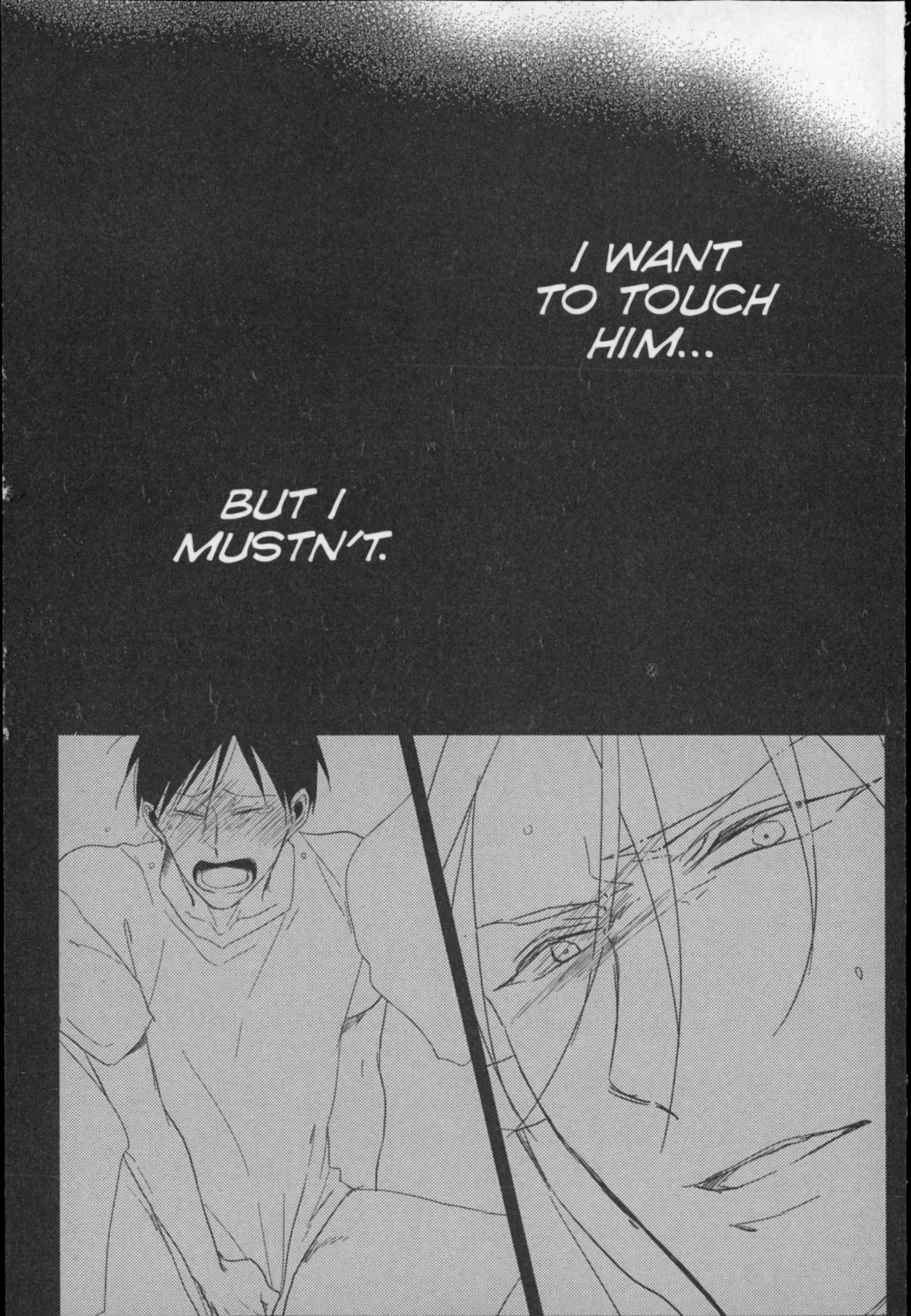
I WANT TO TOUCH HIM...
BUT I MUSTN'T.

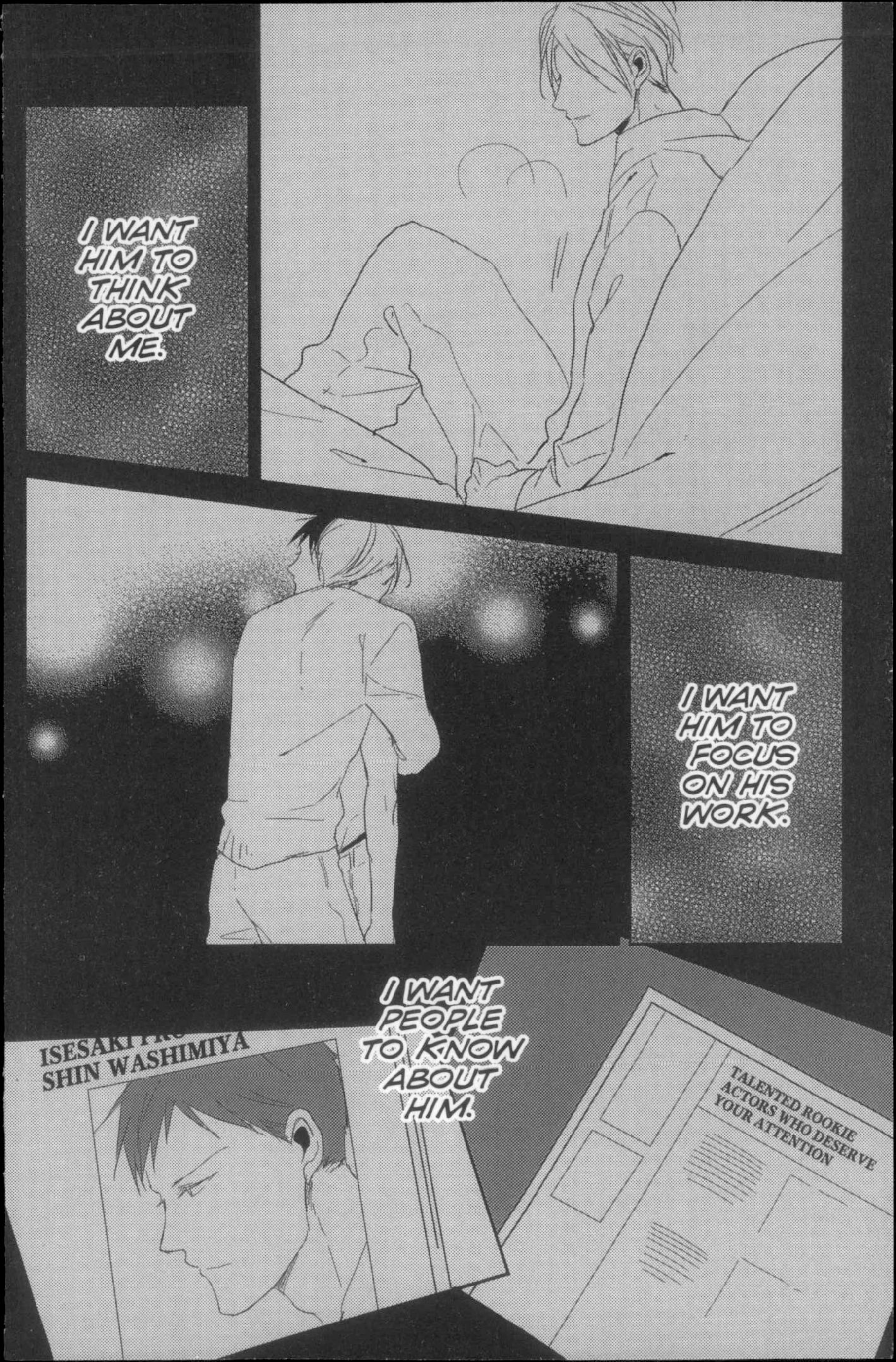
I WANT HIM TO THINK ABOUT ME.
I WANT HIM TO FOCUS ON HIS WORK.
I WANT PEOPLE TO KNOW ABOUT HIM.
TALENTED ROOKIE ACTORS WHO DESERVE YOUR ATTENTION
ISESAKI PRO
SHIN WASHIMIYA

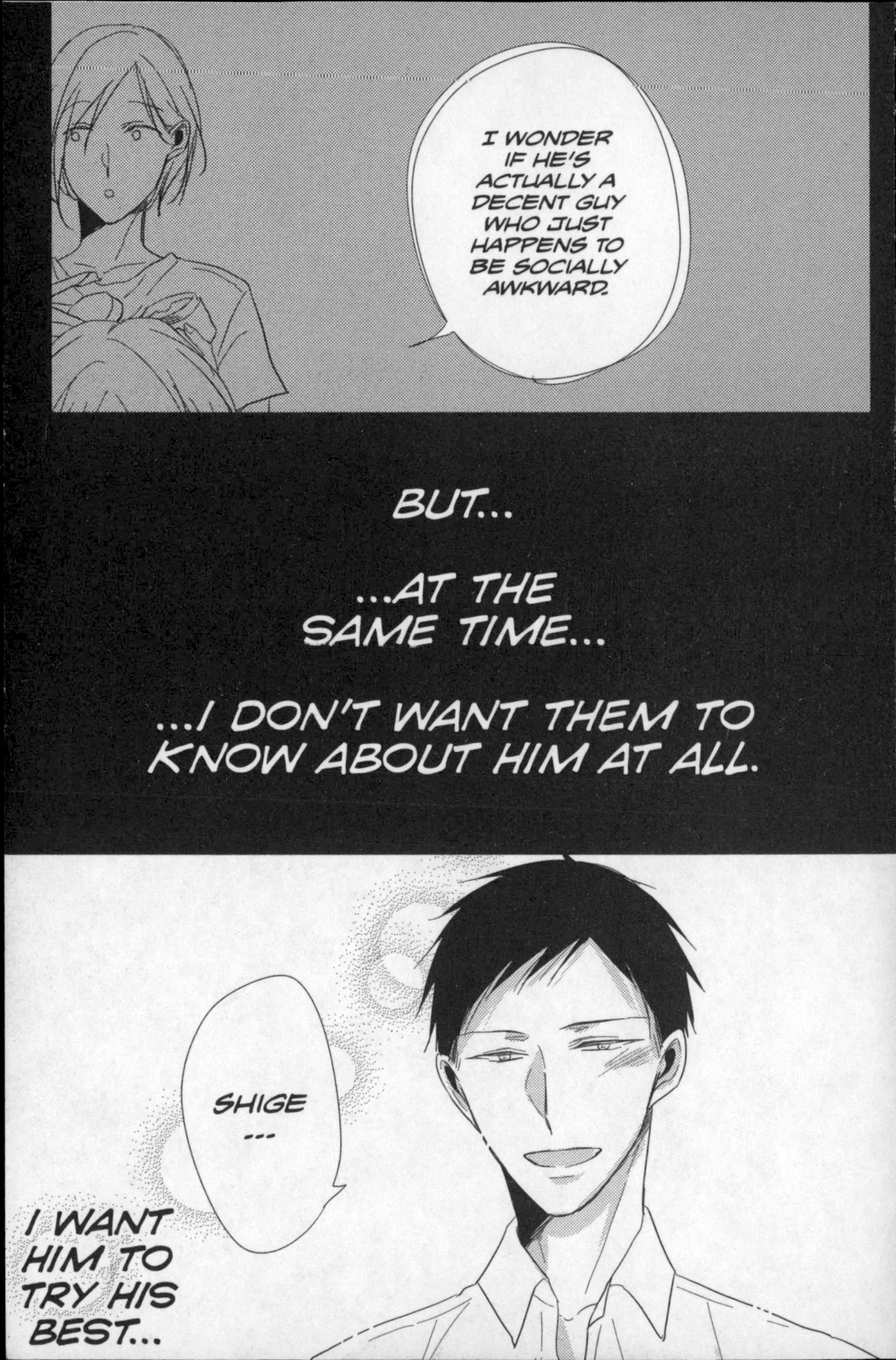
I WONDER IF HE'S ACTUALLY A DECENT GUY WHO JUST HAPPENS TO BE SOCIALLY AWKWARD.
BUT...
...AT THE SAME TIME...
...I DON'T WANT THEM TO KNOW ABOUT HIM AT ALL.
SHIGE ...
I WANT HIM TO TRY HIS BEST...

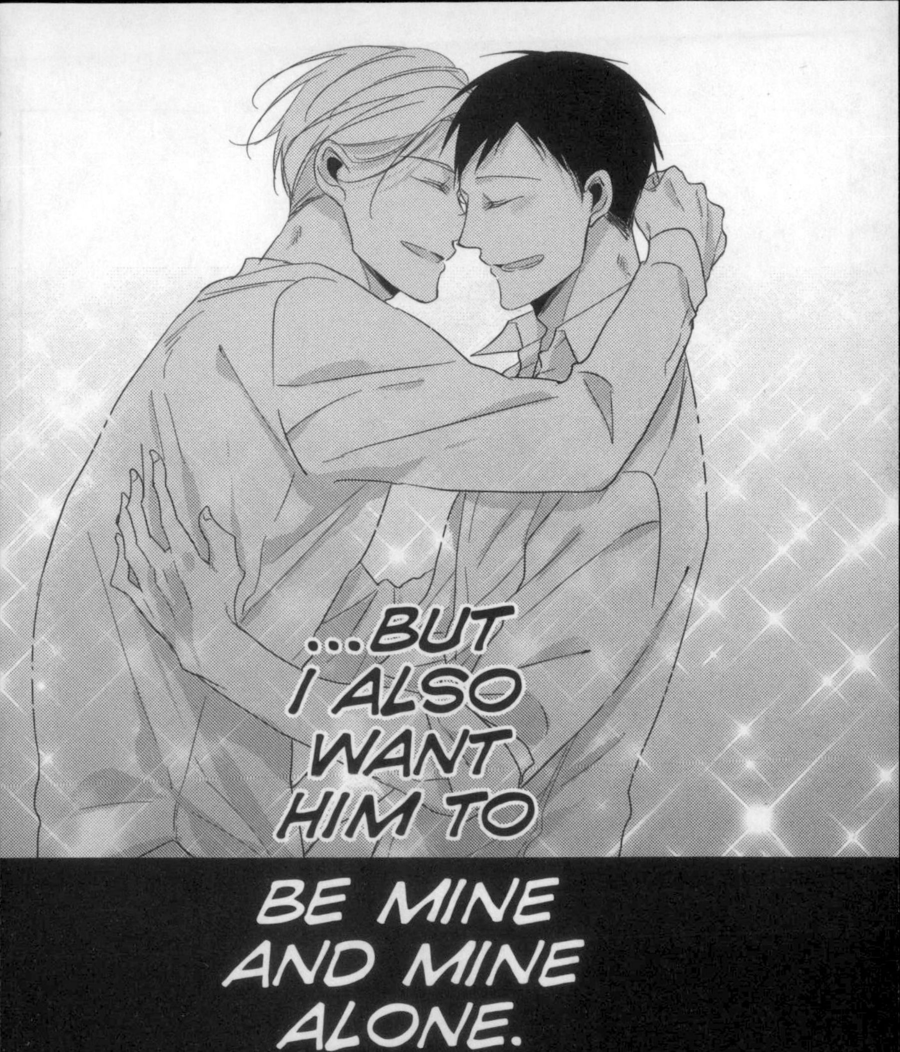
...BUT I ALSO WANT HIM TO
BE MINE AND MINE ALONE.

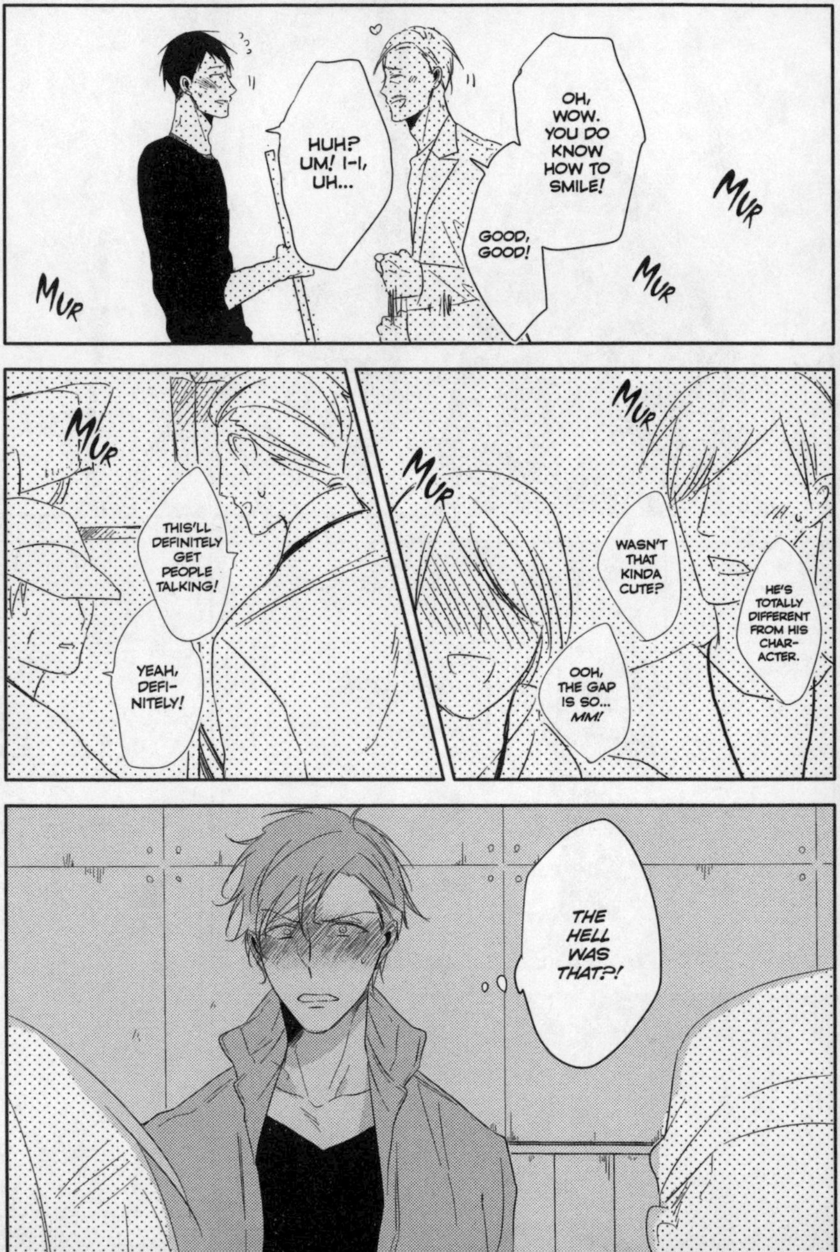
MUR
MUR
OH, WOW. YOU DO KNOW HOW TO SMILE!
GOOD, GOOD!
HUH? UM! I-I, UH...
MUR
MUR
MUR
HE'S TOTALLY DIFFERENT FROM HIS CHARACTER.
WASN'T THAT KINDA CUTE?
OOH, THE GAP IS SO... MM!
MUR
THIS'LL DEFINITELY GET PEOPLE TALKING!
YEAH, DEFINITELY!
THE HELL WAS THAT?!

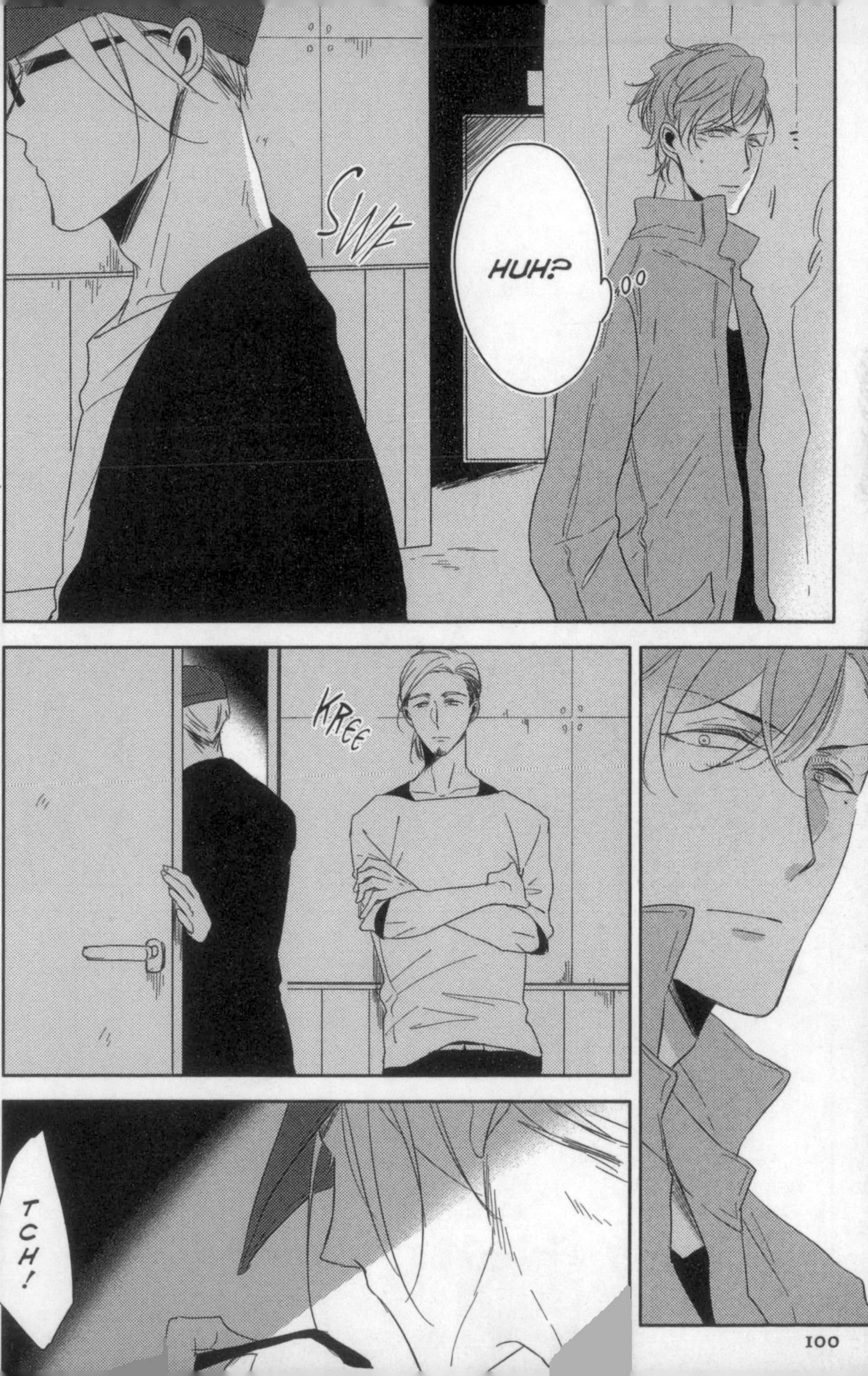
HUH?
SWF
KREE
TCH!

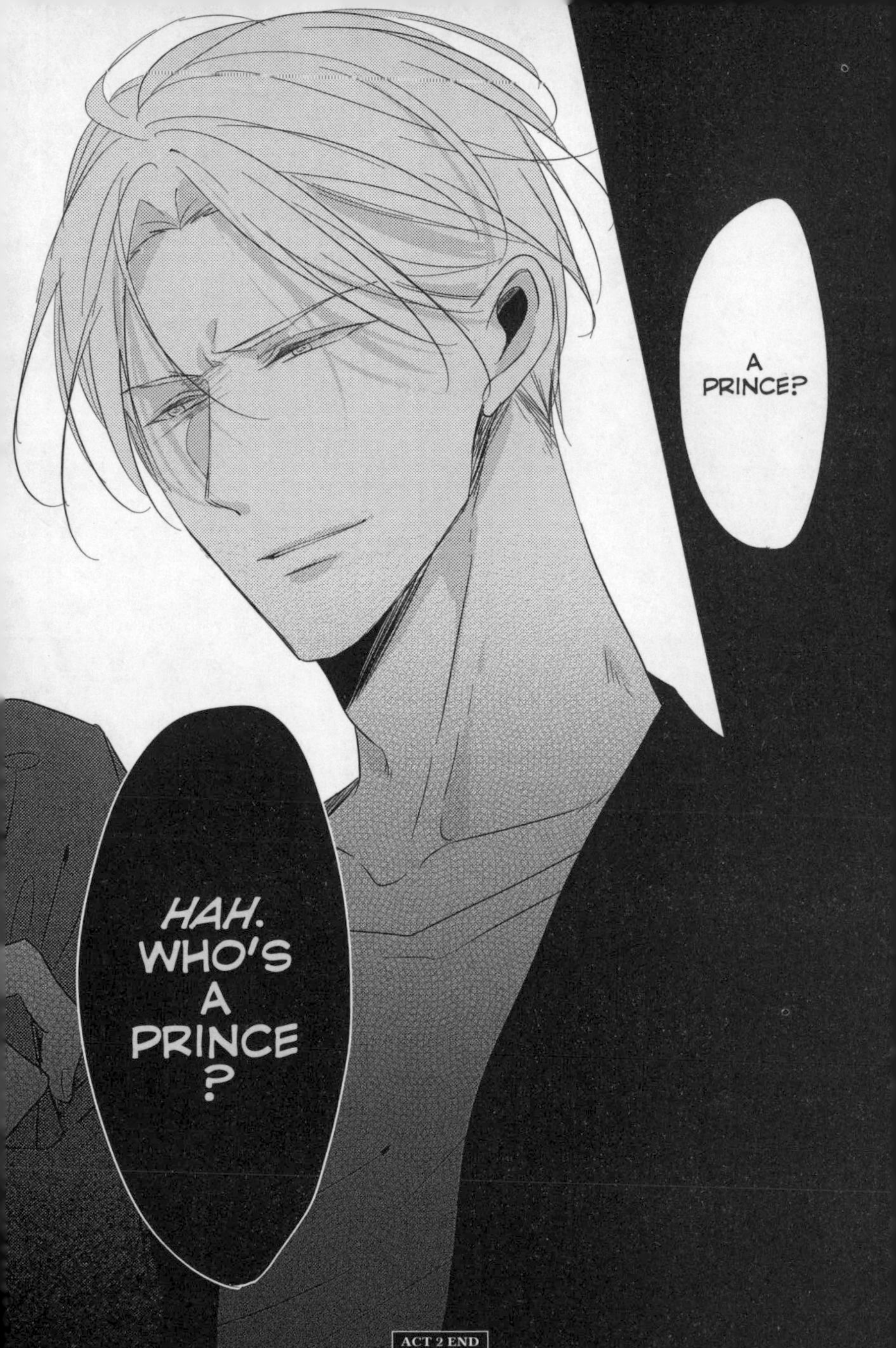
A PRINCE?
HAH. WHO'S A PRINCE?

ACT 2 END

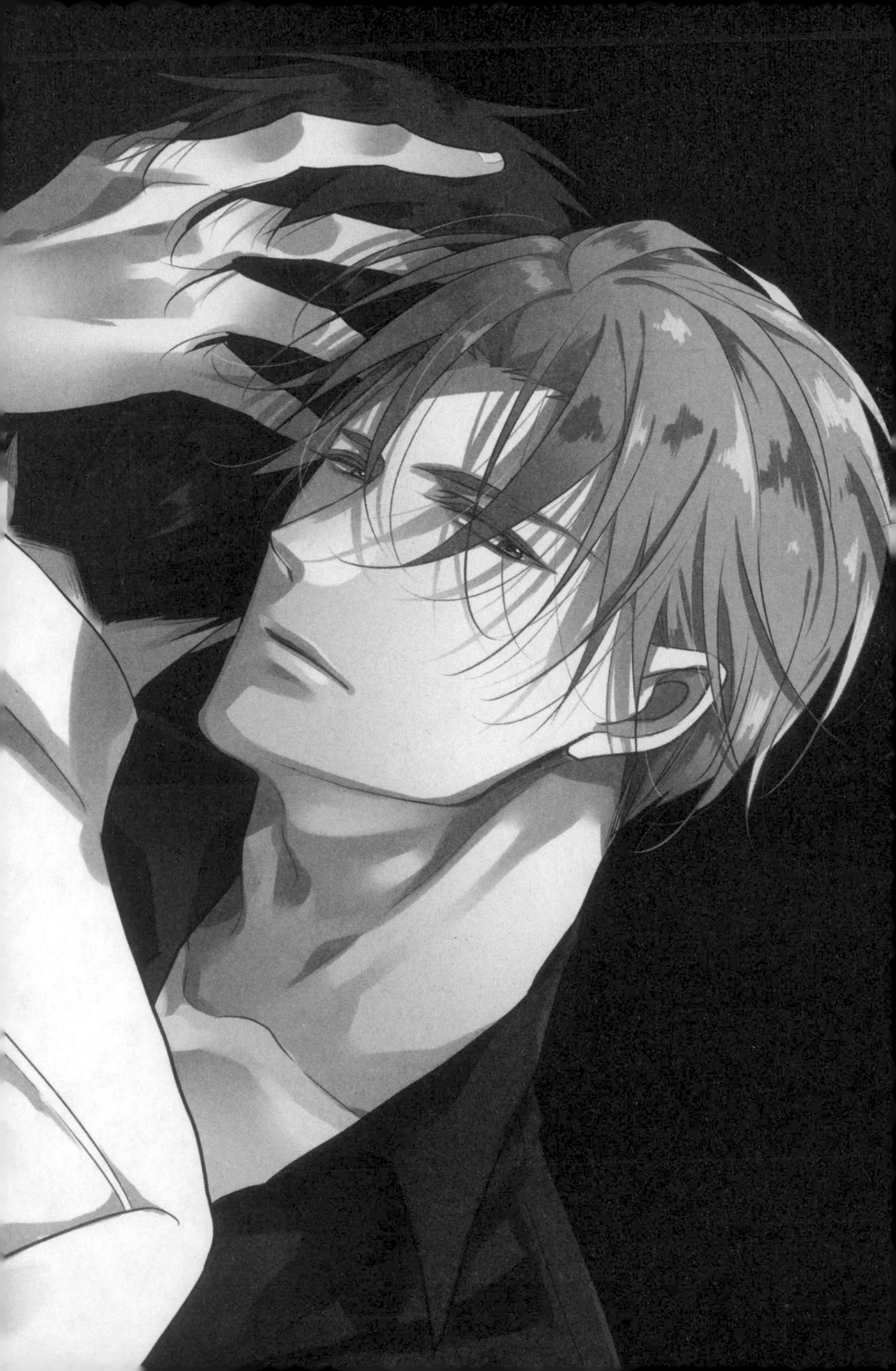

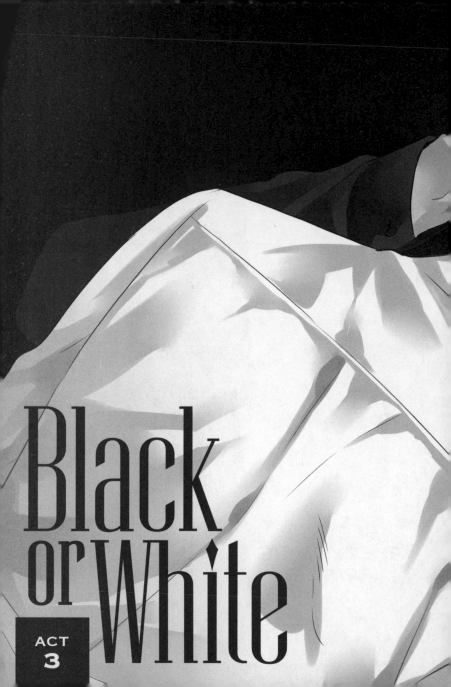

Black
or White

ACT
3

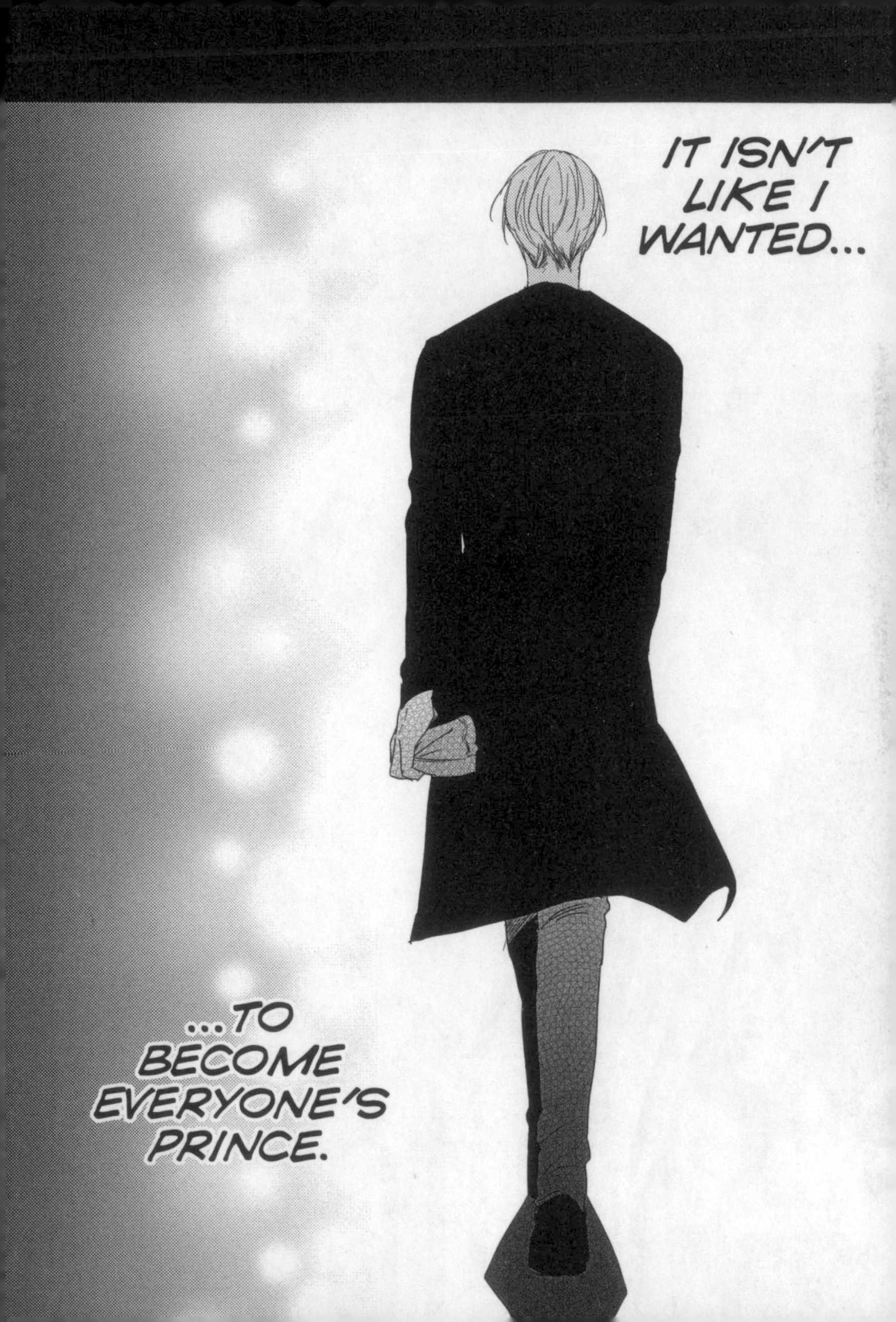
IT ISN'T LIKE I WANTED...
...TO BECOME EVERYONE'S PRINCE.

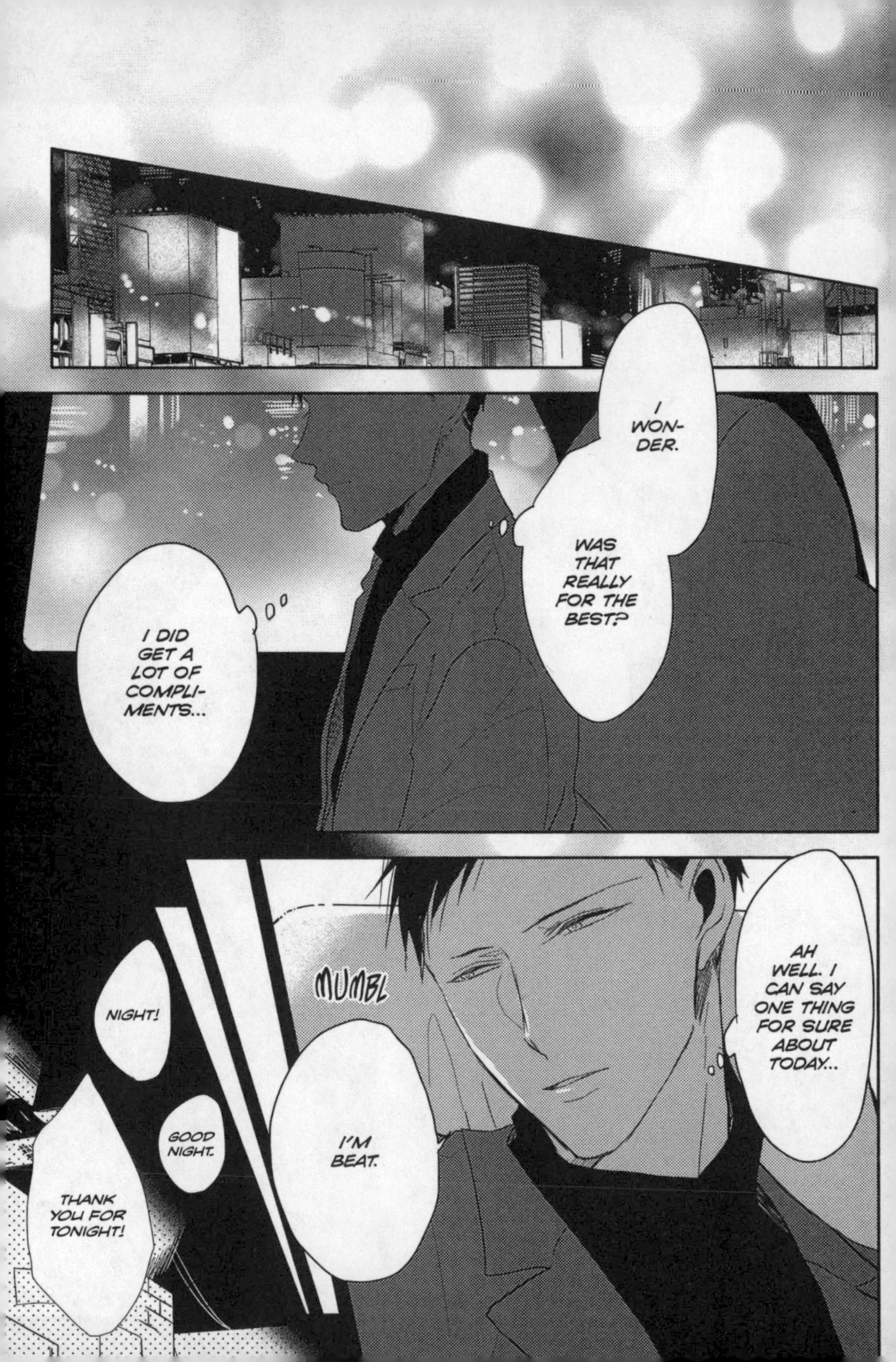

I WONDER.
WAS THAT REALLY FOR THE BEST?
I DID GET A LOT OF COMPLIMENTS...
AH WELL. I CAN SAY ONE THING FOR SURE ABOUT TODAY...
MUMBL
I'M BEAT.
NIGHT!
GOOD NIGHT.
THANK YOU FOR TONIGHT!

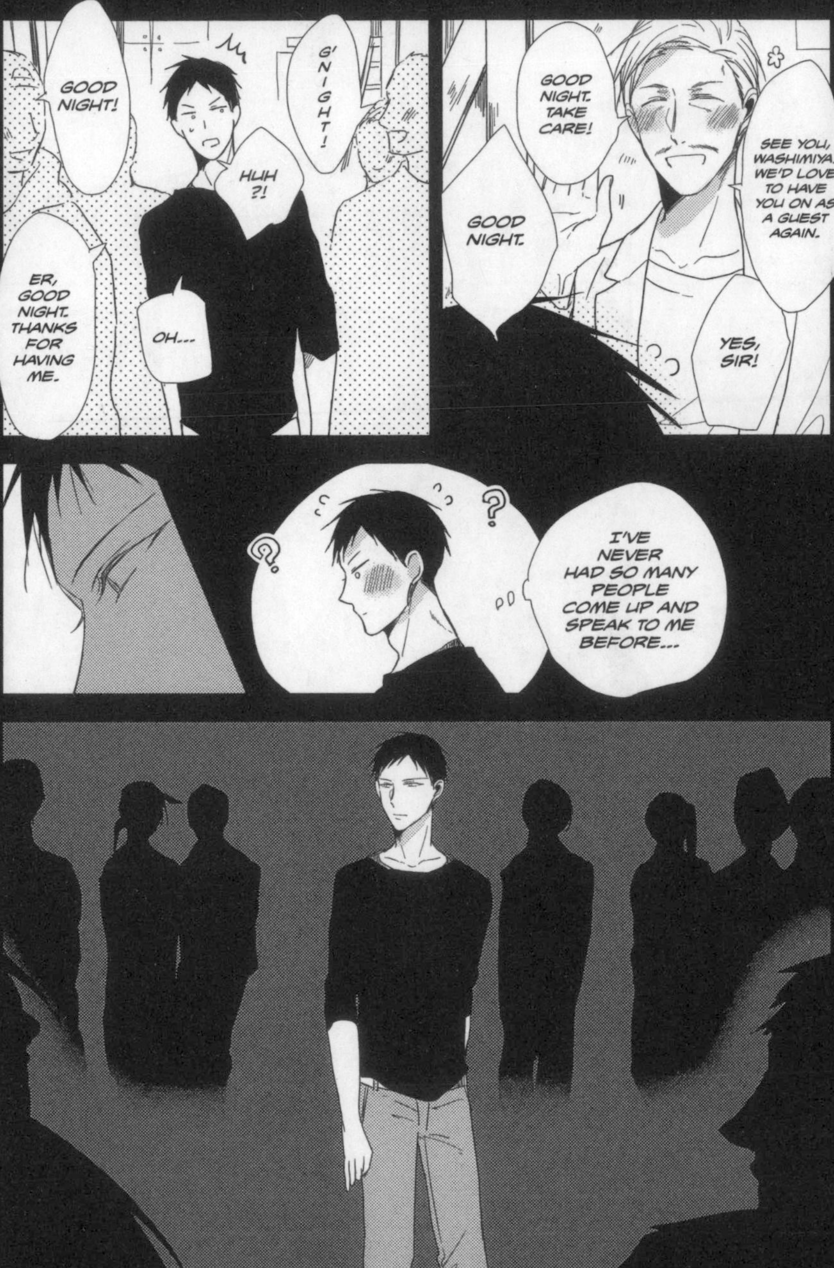
SEE YOU, WASHIMIYA. WE'D LOVE TO HAVE YOU ON AS A GUEST AGAIN.
GOOD NIGHT. TAKE CARE!
YES, SIR!
GOOD NIGHT.
G'NIGHT!
GOOD NIGHT!
HUH?!
ER, GOOD NIGHT. THANKS FOR HAVING ME.
OH...
I'VE NEVER HAD SO MANY PEOPLE COME UP AND SPEAK TO ME BEFORE...

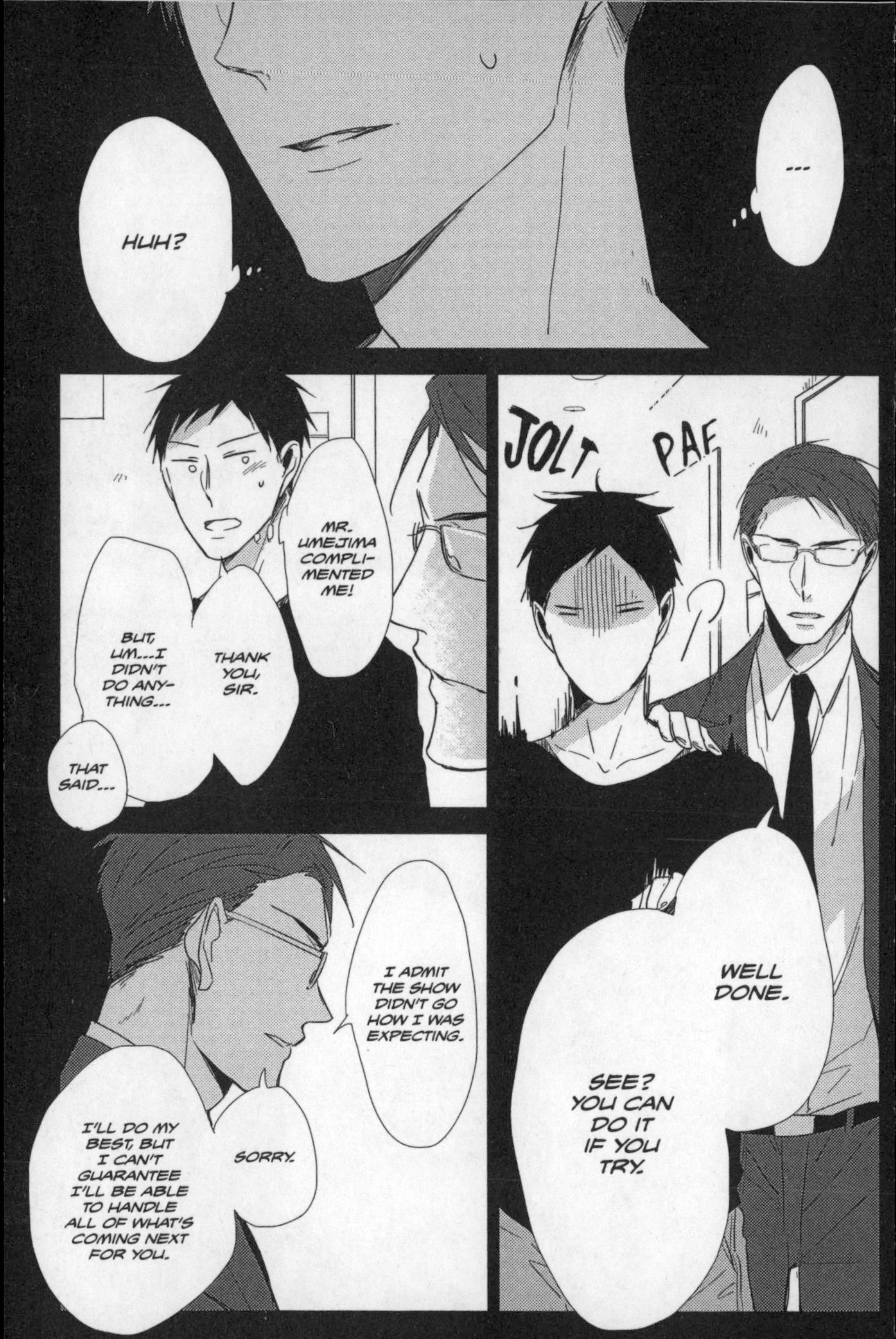
...
HUH?
JOLT
PAF
WELL DONE.
SEE? YOU CAN DO IT IF YOU TRY.
MR. UMEJIMA COMPLIMENTED ME!
THANK YOU, SIR.
BUT, UM...I DIDN'T DO ANYTHING...
THAT SAID...
I ADMIT THE SHOW DIDN'T GO HOW I WAS EXPECTING.
SORRY.
I'LL DO MY BEST, BUT I CAN'T GUARANTEE I'LL BE ABLE TO HANDLE ALL OF WHAT'S COMING NEXT FOR YOU.

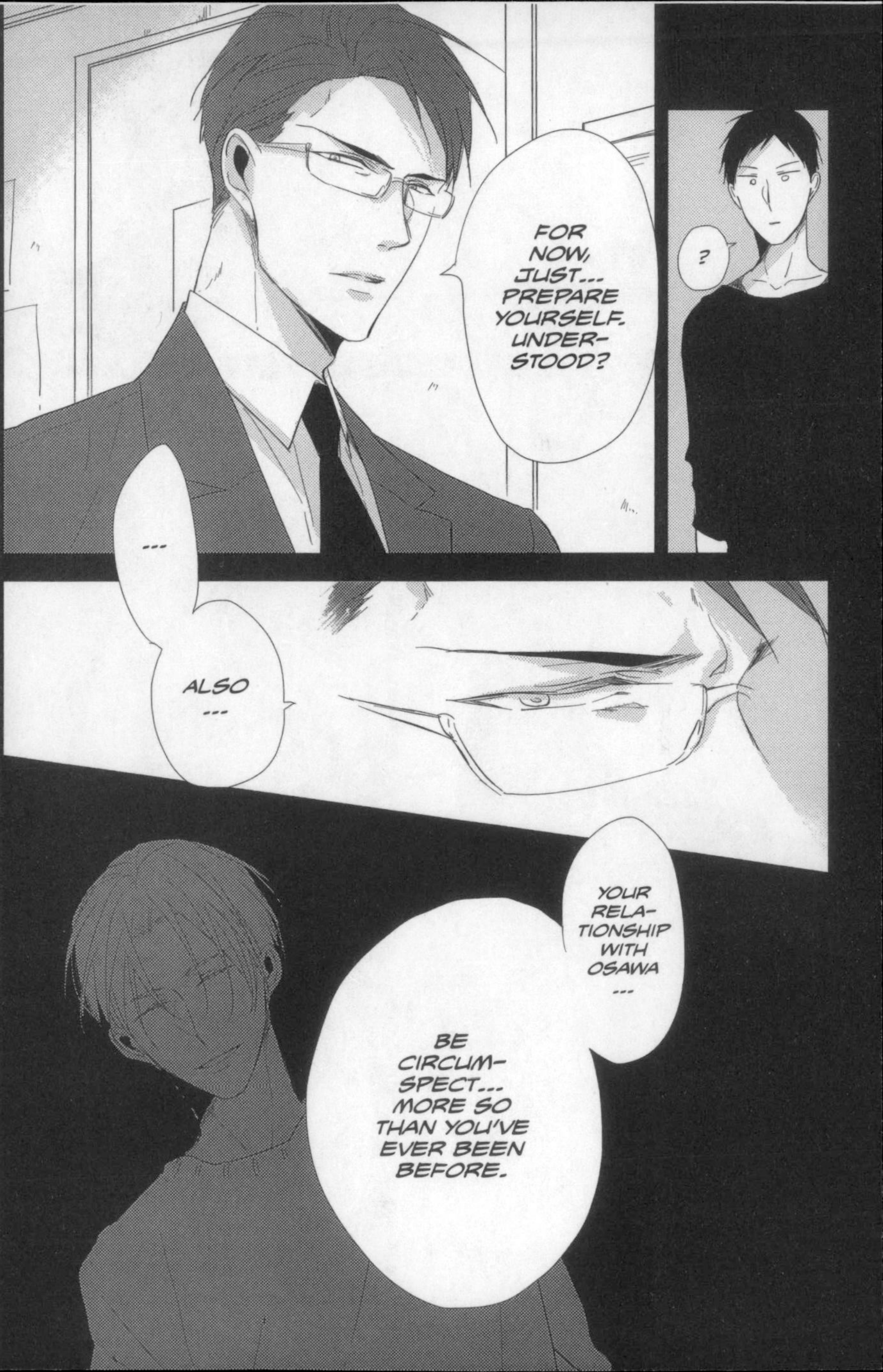
?
FOR NOW, JUST... PREPARE YOURSELF. UNDER-STOOD?

ALSO ---
YOUR RELA-TIONSHIP WITH OSAWA ---
BE CIRCUM-SPECT... MORE SO THAN YOU'VE EVER BEEN BEFORE.

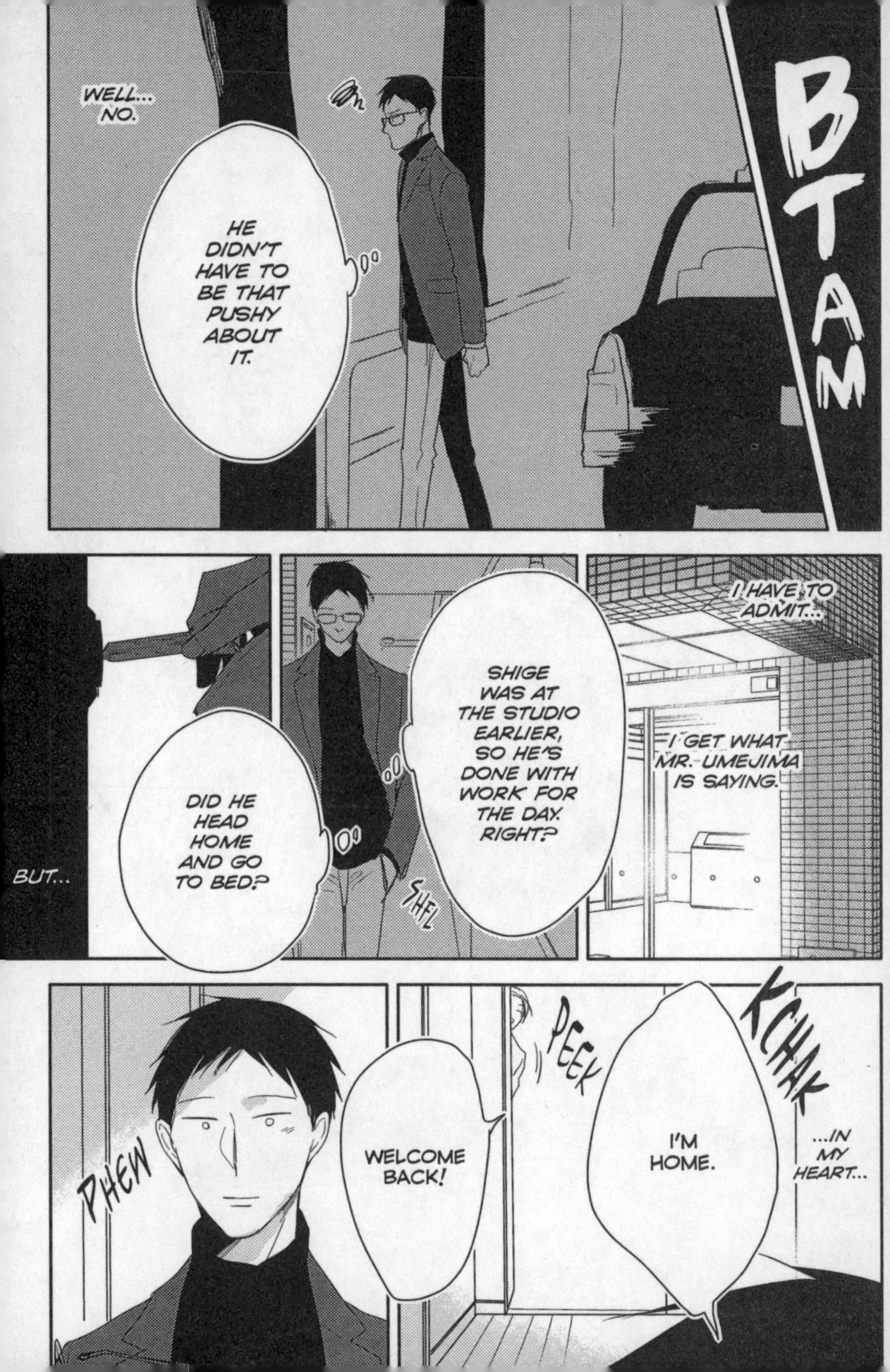
BTAM
WELL... NO.
HE DIDN'T HAVE TO BE THAT PUSHY ABOUT IT.
I HAVE TO ADMIT...
I GET WHAT MR. UMEJIMA IS SAYING.
SHIGE WAS AT THE STUDIO EARLIER, SO HE'S DONE WITH WORK FOR THE DAY. RIGHT?
DID HE HEAD HOME AND GO TO BED?
SHFL
BUT...
KCHAK
...IN MY HEART...
I'M HOME.
PEEK
WELCOME BACK!
PHEW

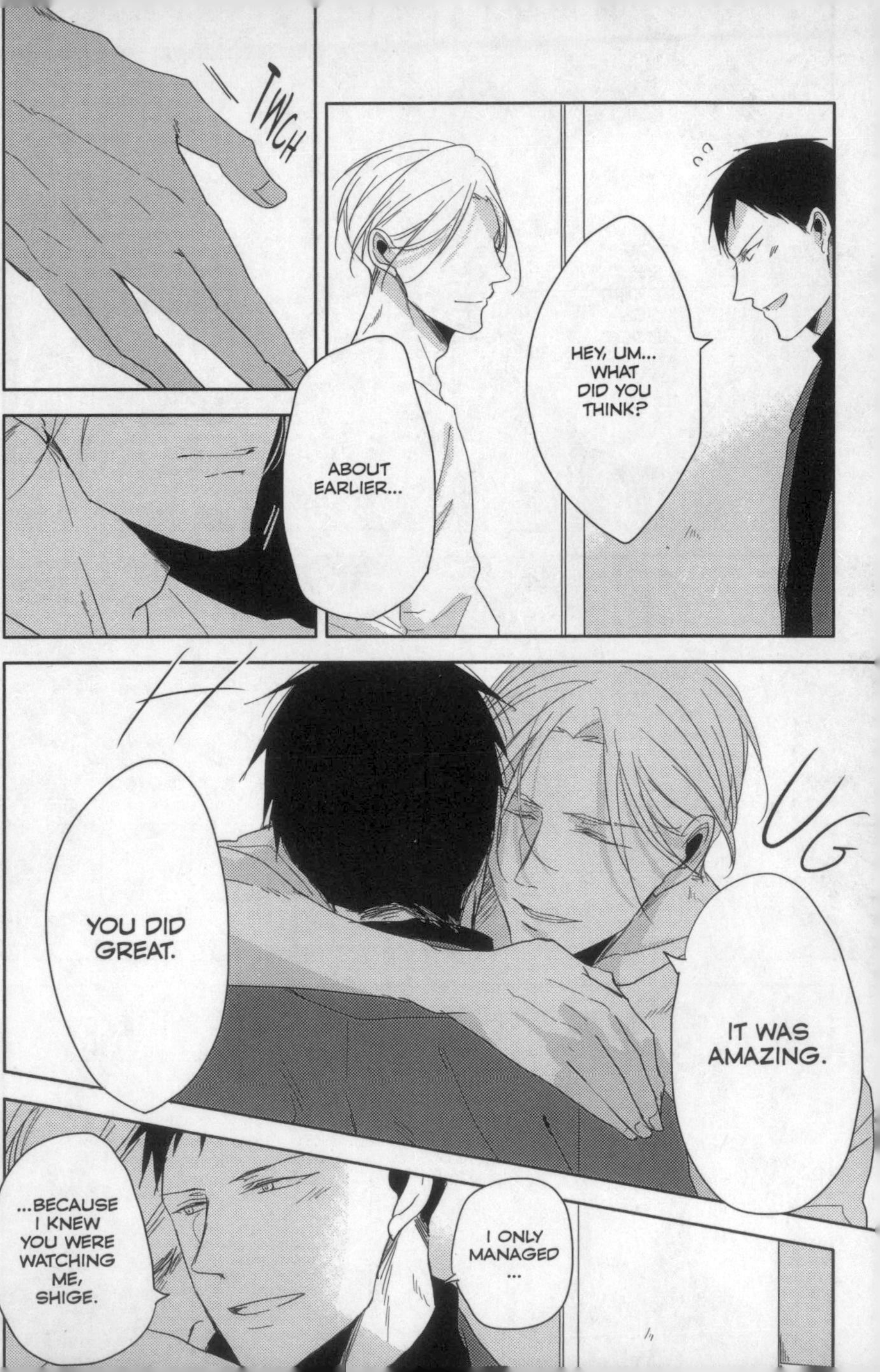
HEY, UM... WHAT DID YOU THINK?
ABOUT EARLIER...
TWCH
HUG
IT WAS AMAZING.
YOU DID GREAT.
I ONLY MANAGED ...
...BECAUSE I KNEW YOU WERE WATCHING ME, SHIGE.

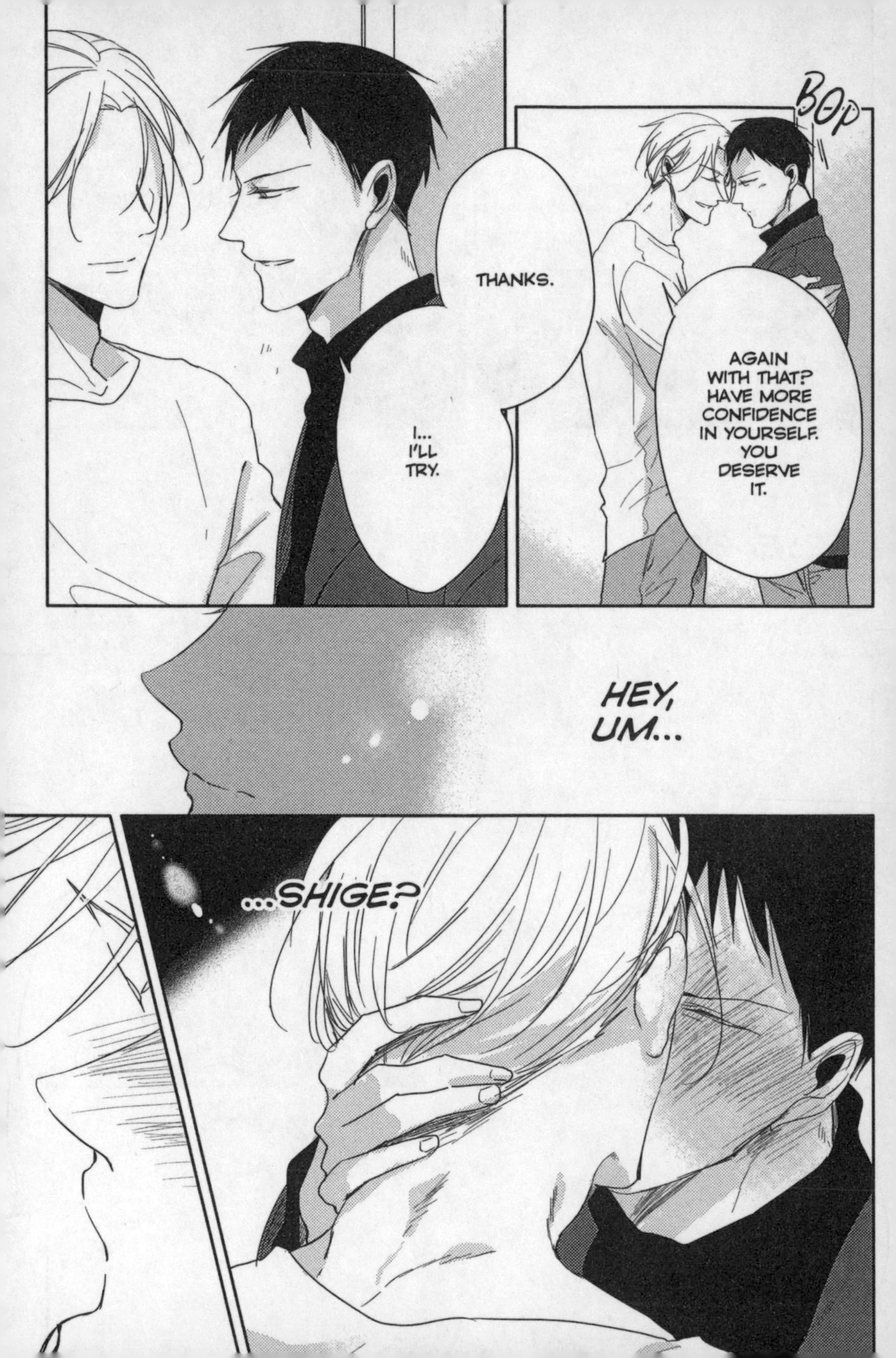
BOP
AGAIN WITH THAT? HAVE MORE CONFIDENCE IN YOURSELF. YOU DESERVE IT.
THANKS.
I... I'LL TRY.
HEY, UM...
...SHIGE?

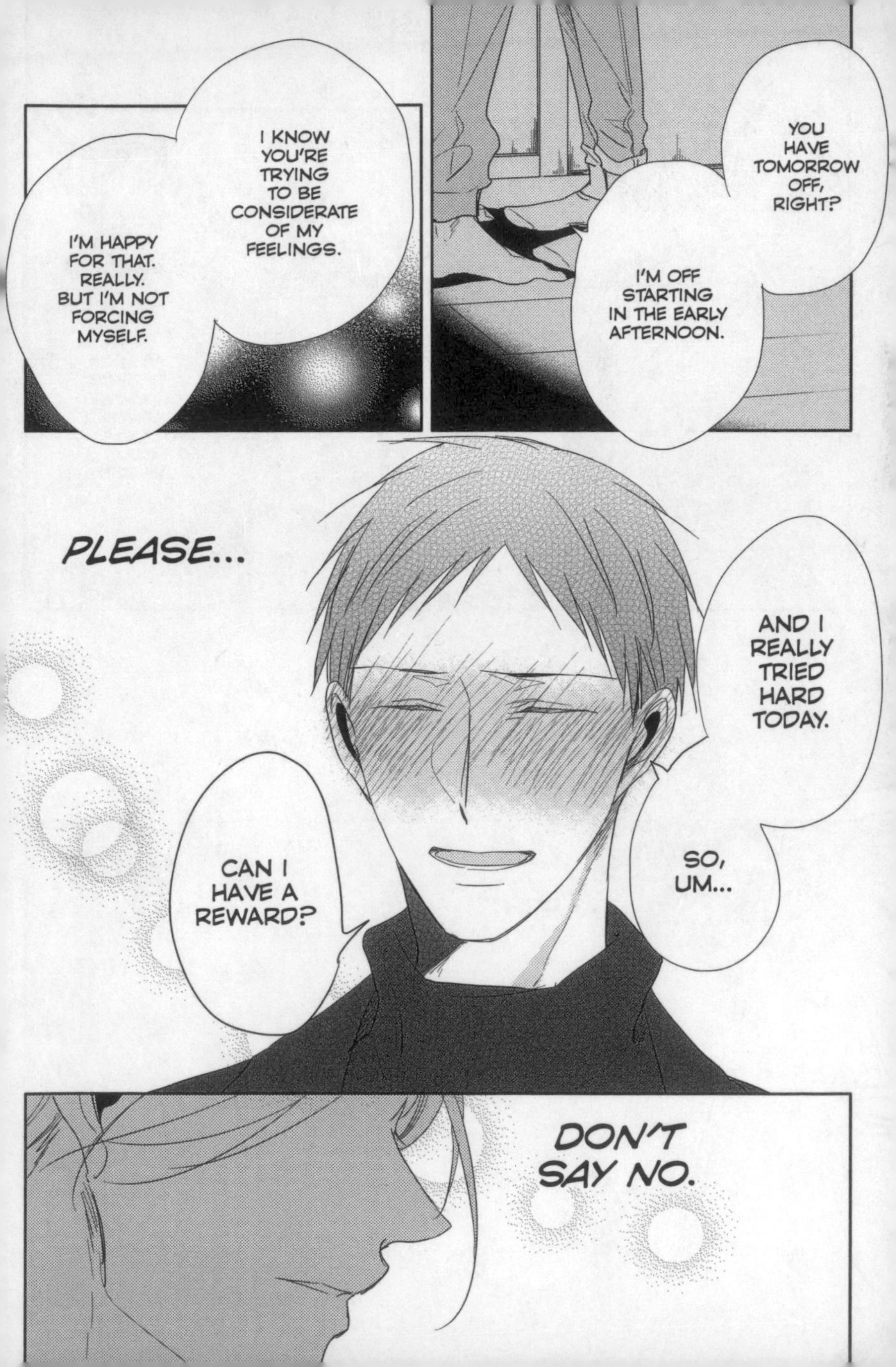
YOU HAVE TOMORROW OFF, RIGHT?
I'M OFF STARTING IN THE EARLY AFTERNOON.
I KNOW YOU'RE TRYING TO BE CONSIDERATE OF MY FEELINGS.
I'M HAPPY FOR THAT. REALLY. BUT I'M NOT FORCING MYSELF.
AND I REALLY TRIED HARD TODAY.
SO, UM...
CAN I HAVE A REWARD?
PLEASE...
DON'T SAY NO.

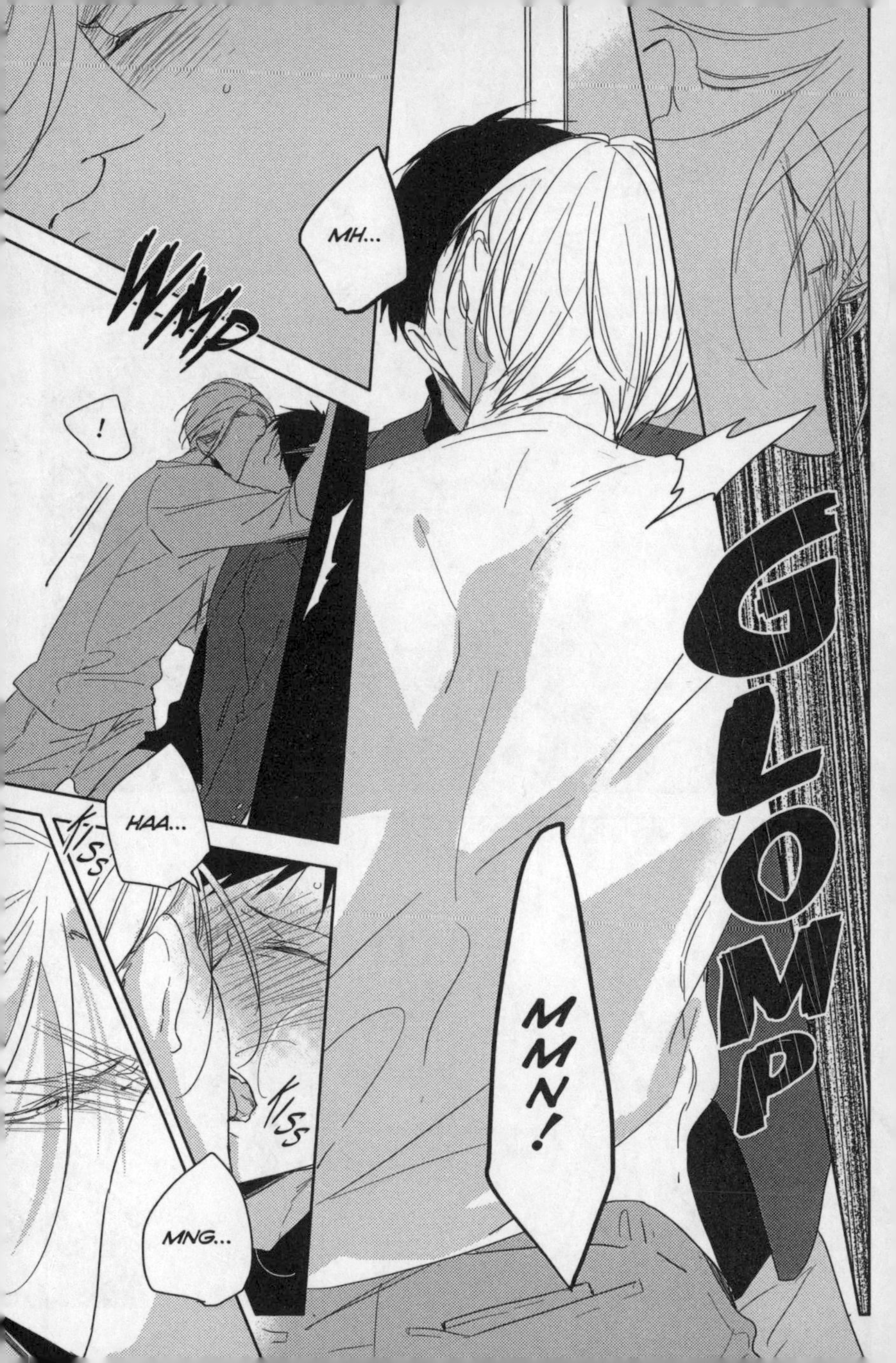
MH...
GLOMP
MMN!
WMP
!
HAA...
KISS
KISS
MNG...

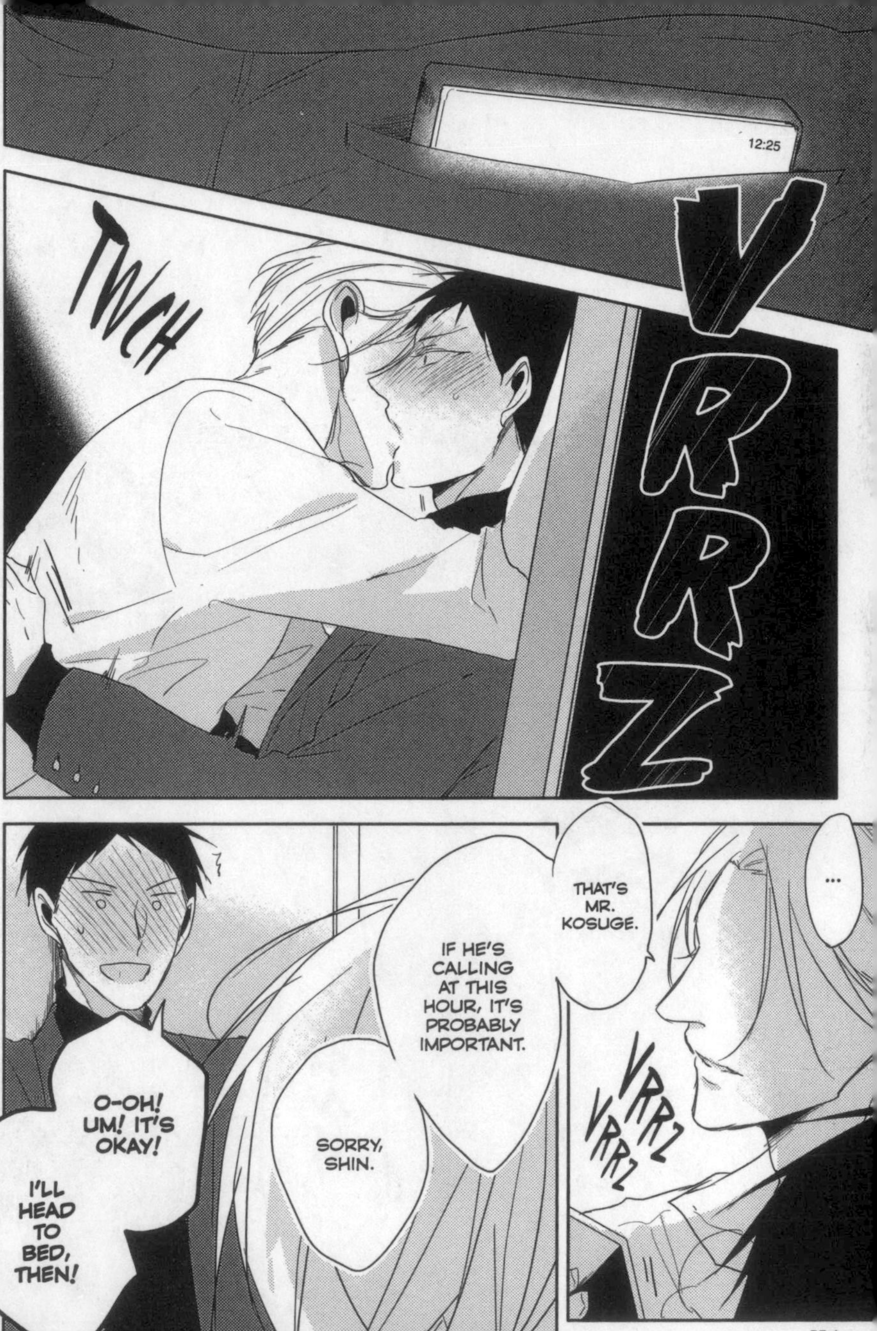
12:25
VRRRZ
TWCH
...
VRRZ VRRZ
THAT'S MR. KOSUGE.
IF HE'S CALLING AT THIS HOUR, IT'S PROBABLY IMPORTANT.
SORRY, SHIN.
O-OH! UM! IT'S OKAY!
I'LL HEAD TO BED, THEN!

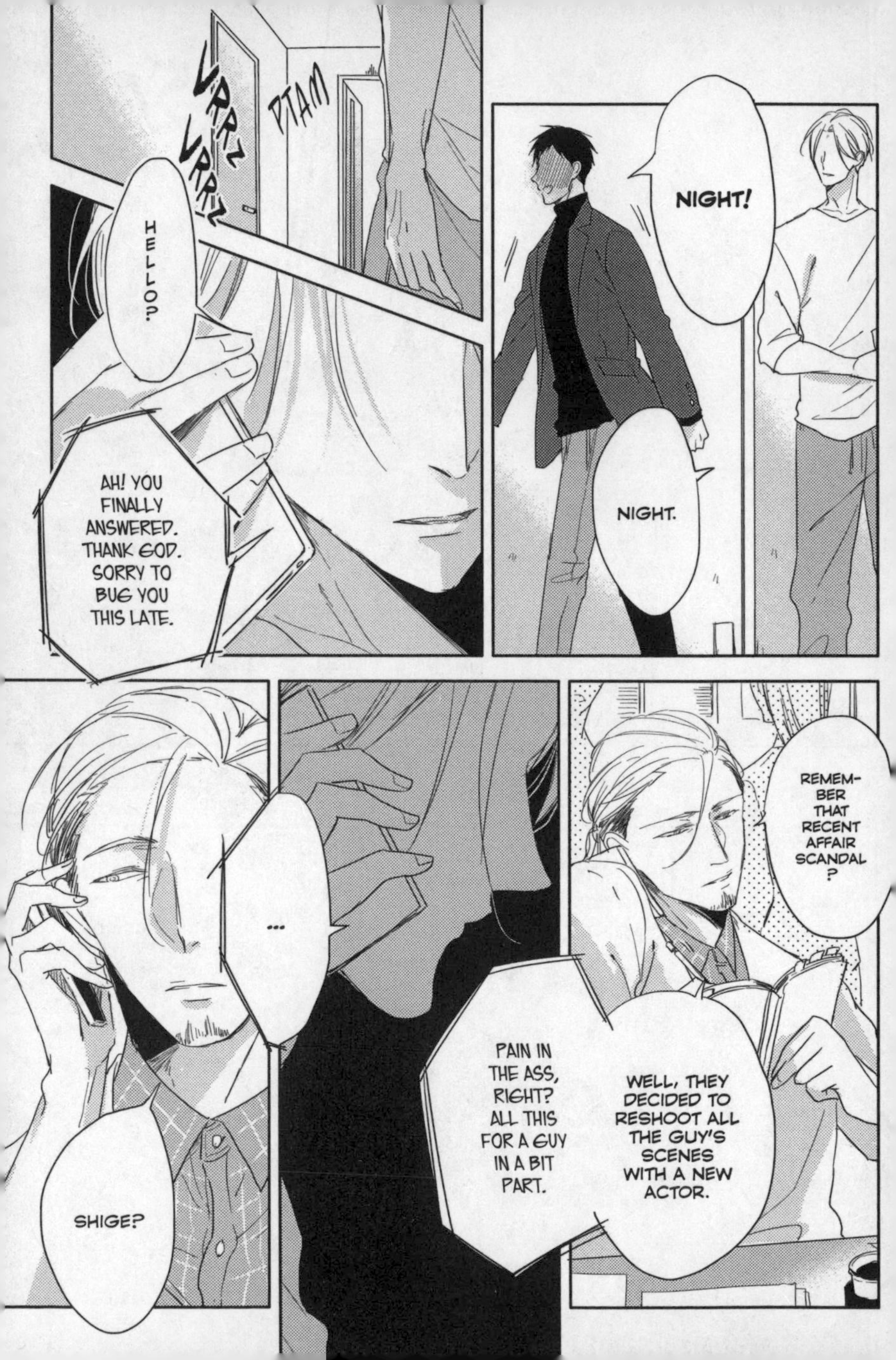
NIGHT!
NIGHT.
VRRZ VRRZ
PTAM
HELLO?
AH! YOU FINALLY ANSWERED. THANK GOD. SORRY TO BUG YOU THIS LATE.
REMEMBER THAT RECENT AFFAIR SCANDAL?
WELL, THEY DECIDED TO RESHOOT ALL THE GUY'S SCENES WITH A NEW ACTOR.
PAIN IN THE ASS, RIGHT? ALL THIS FOR A GUY IN A BIT PART.
...
SHIGE?

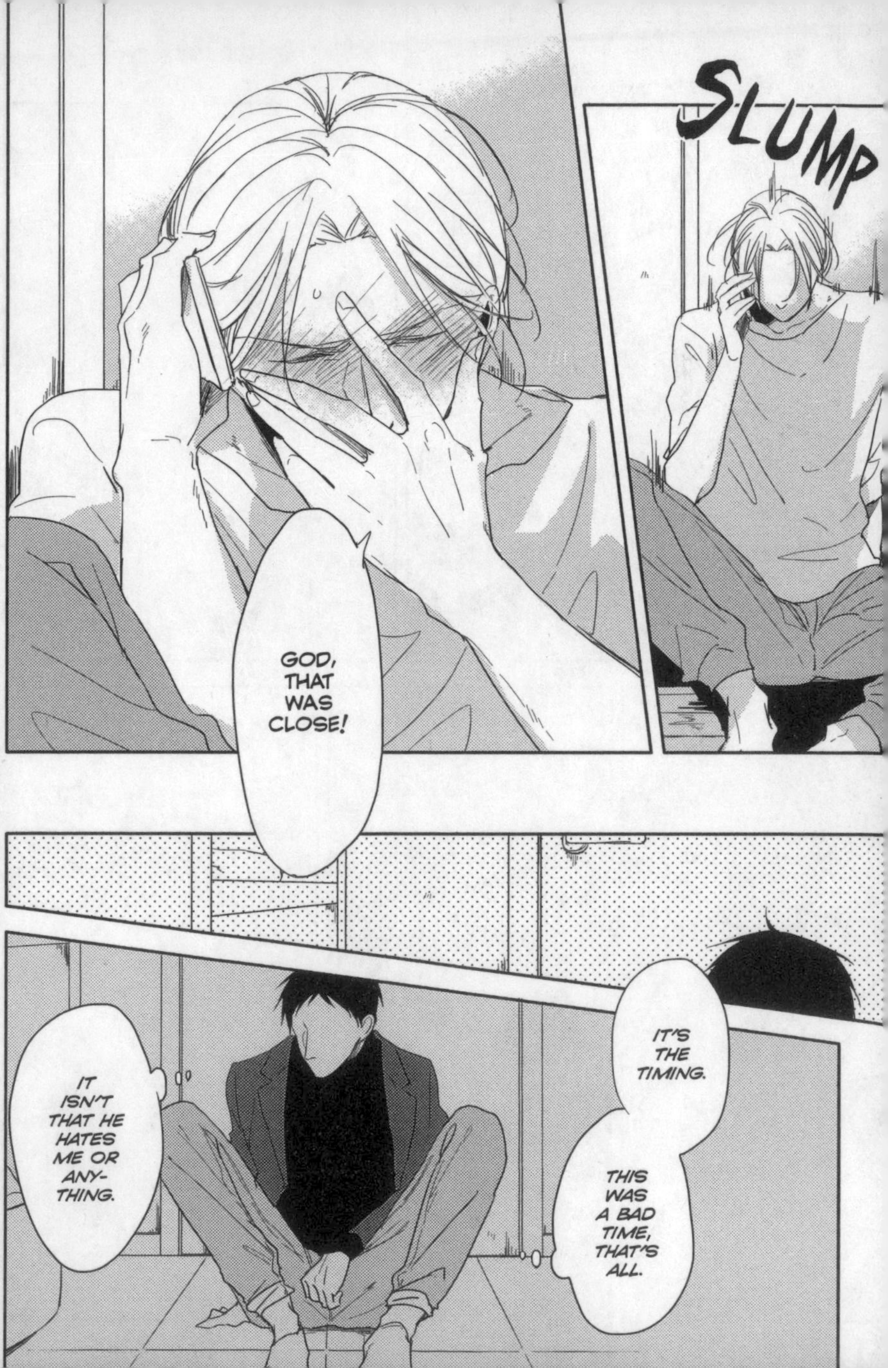
SLUMP
GOD, THAT WAS CLOSE!
IT'S THE TIMING.
THIS WAS A BAD TIME, THAT'S ALL.
IT ISN'T THAT HE HATES ME OR ANY-THING.

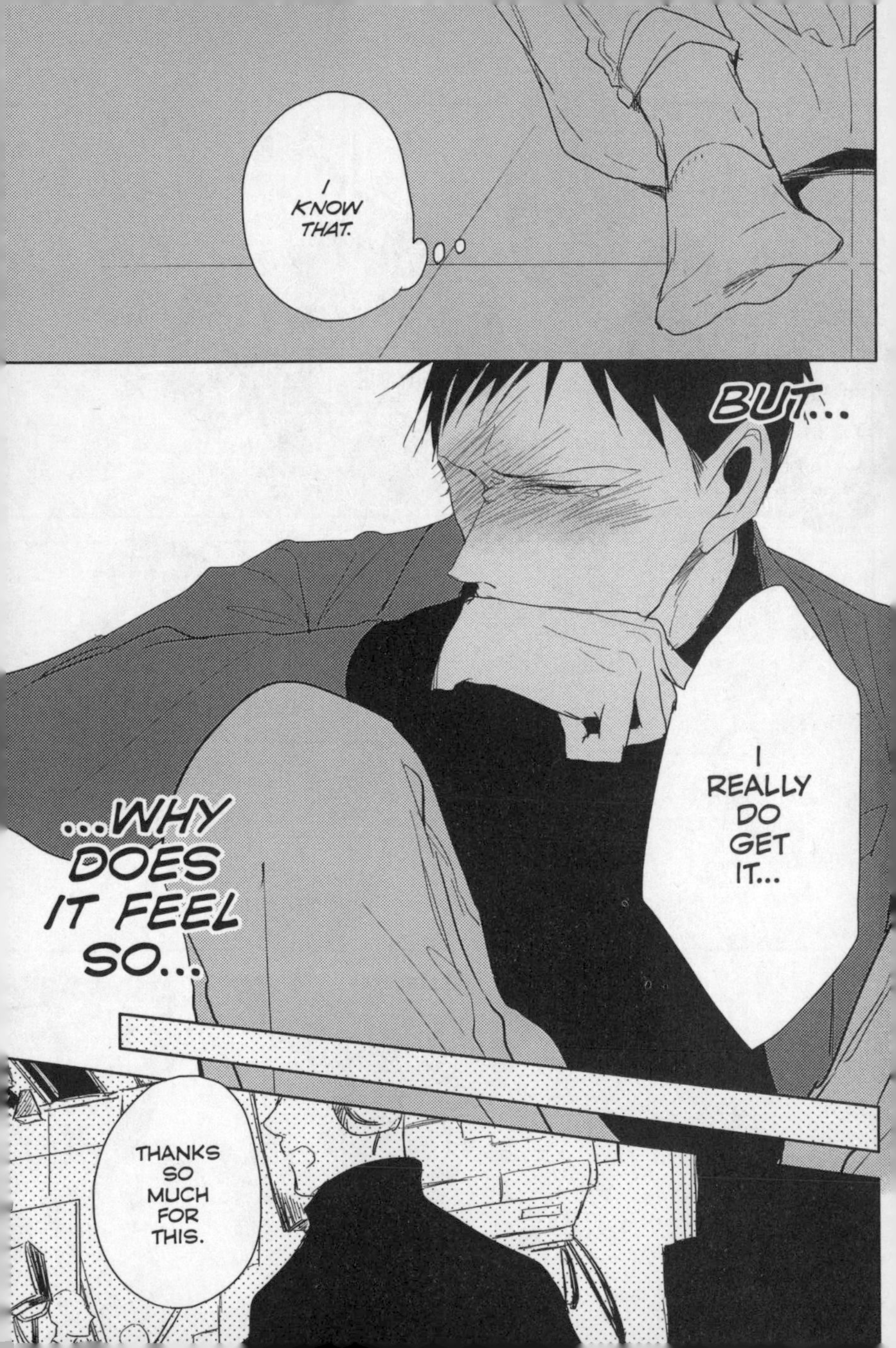
I KNOW THAT.
BUT...
I REALLY DO GET IT...
...WHY DOES IT FEEL SO...
THANKS SO MUCH FOR THIS.

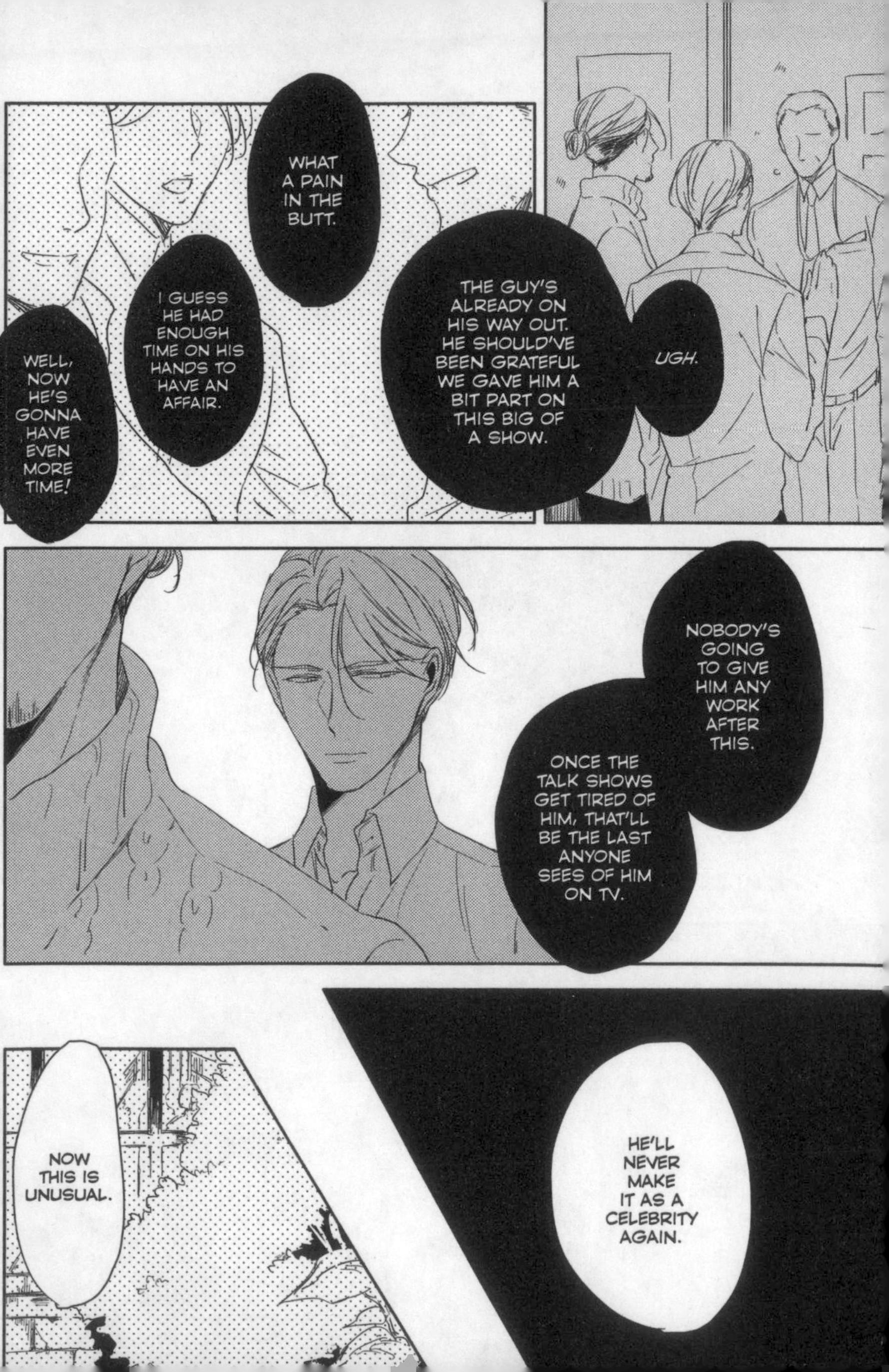
UGH.
THE GUY'S ALREADY ON HIS WAY OUT. HE SHOULD'VE BEEN GRATEFUL WE GAVE HIM A BIT PART ON THIS BIG OF A SHOW.
WHAT A PAIN IN THE BUTT.
I GUESS HE HAD ENOUGH TIME ON HIS HANDS TO HAVE AN AFFAIR.
WELL, NOW HE'S GONNA HAVE EVEN MORE TIME!
NOBODY'S GOING TO GIVE HIM ANY WORK AFTER THIS.
ONCE THE TALK SHOWS GET TIRED OF HIM, THAT'LL BE THE LAST ANYONE SEES OF HIM ON TV.
HE'LL NEVER MAKE IT AS A CELEBRITY AGAIN.
NOW THIS IS UNUSUAL.

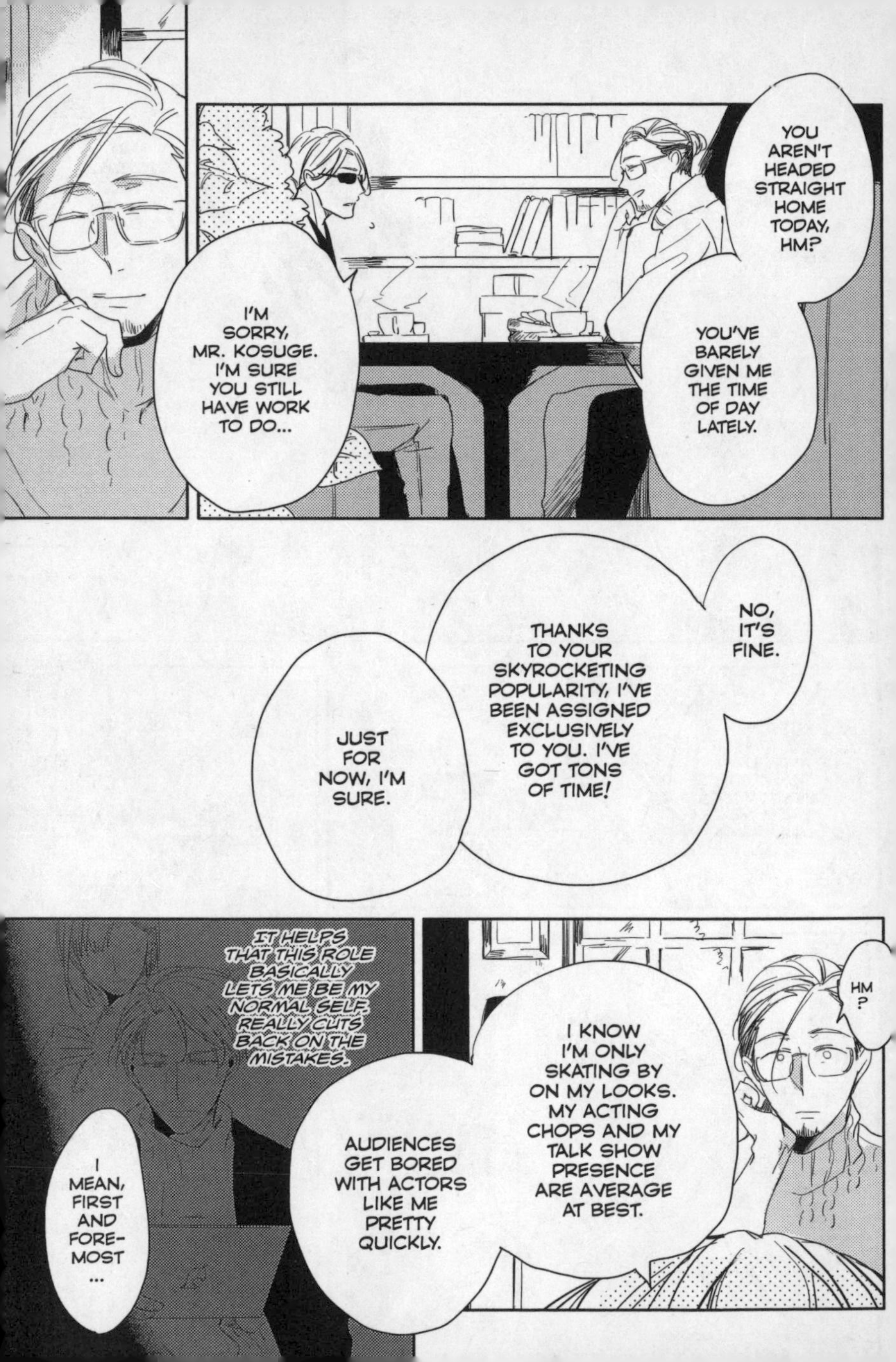
YOU AREN'T HEADED STRAIGHT HOME TODAY, HM?
YOU'VE BARELY GIVEN ME THE TIME OF DAY LATELY.
I'M SORRY, MR. KOSUGE. I'M SURE YOU STILL HAVE WORK TO DO...
NO, IT'S FINE.
THANKS TO YOUR SKYROCKETING POPULARITY, I'VE BEEN ASSIGNED EXCLUSIVELY TO YOU. I'VE GOT TONS OF TIME!
JUST FOR NOW, I'M SURE.
HM?
I KNOW I'M ONLY SKATING BY ON MY LOOKS. MY ACTING CHOPS AND MY TALK SHOW PRESENCE ARE AVERAGE AT BEST.
AUDIENCES GET BORED WITH ACTORS LIKE ME PRETTY QUICKLY.
IT HELPS THAT THIS ROLE BASICALLY LETS ME BE MY NORMAL SELF. REALLY CUTS BACK ON THE MISTAKES.
I MEAN, FIRST AND FORE-MOST...

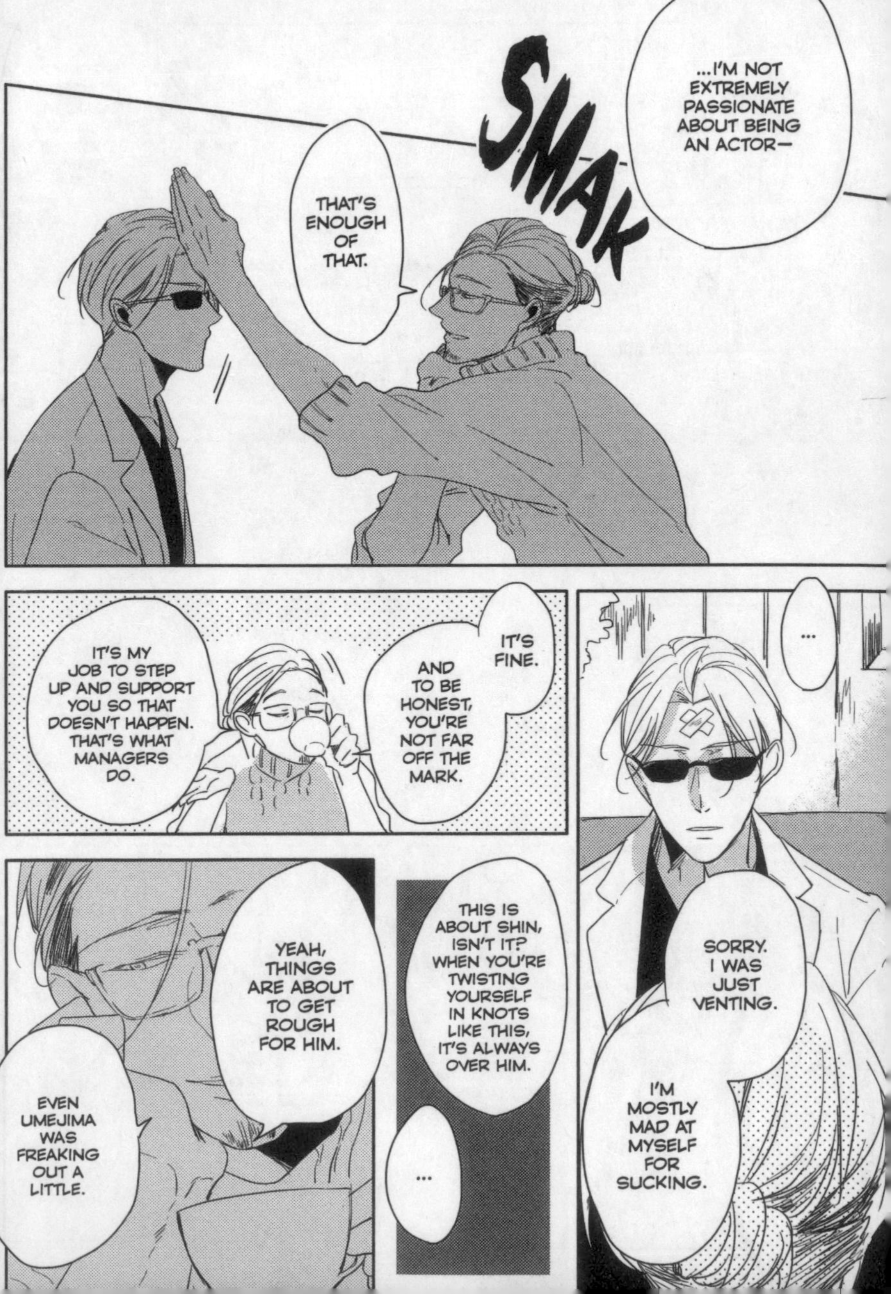
...I'M NOT EXTREMELY PASSIONATE ABOUT BEING AN ACTOR—
SMAK
THAT'S ENOUGH OF THAT.
...
SORRY. I WAS JUST VENTING.
I'M MOSTLY MAD AT MYSELF FOR SUCKING.
IT'S FINE.
AND TO BE HONEST, YOU'RE NOT FAR OFF THE MARK.
IT'S MY JOB TO STEP UP AND SUPPORT YOU SO THAT DOESN'T HAPPEN. THAT'S WHAT MANAGERS DO.
THIS IS ABOUT SHIN, ISN'T IT? WHEN YOU'RE TWISTING YOURSELF IN KNOTS LIKE THIS, IT'S ALWAYS OVER HIM.
...
YEAH, THINGS ARE ABOUT TO GET ROUGH FOR HIM.
EVEN UMEJIMA WAS FREAKING OUT A LITTLE.

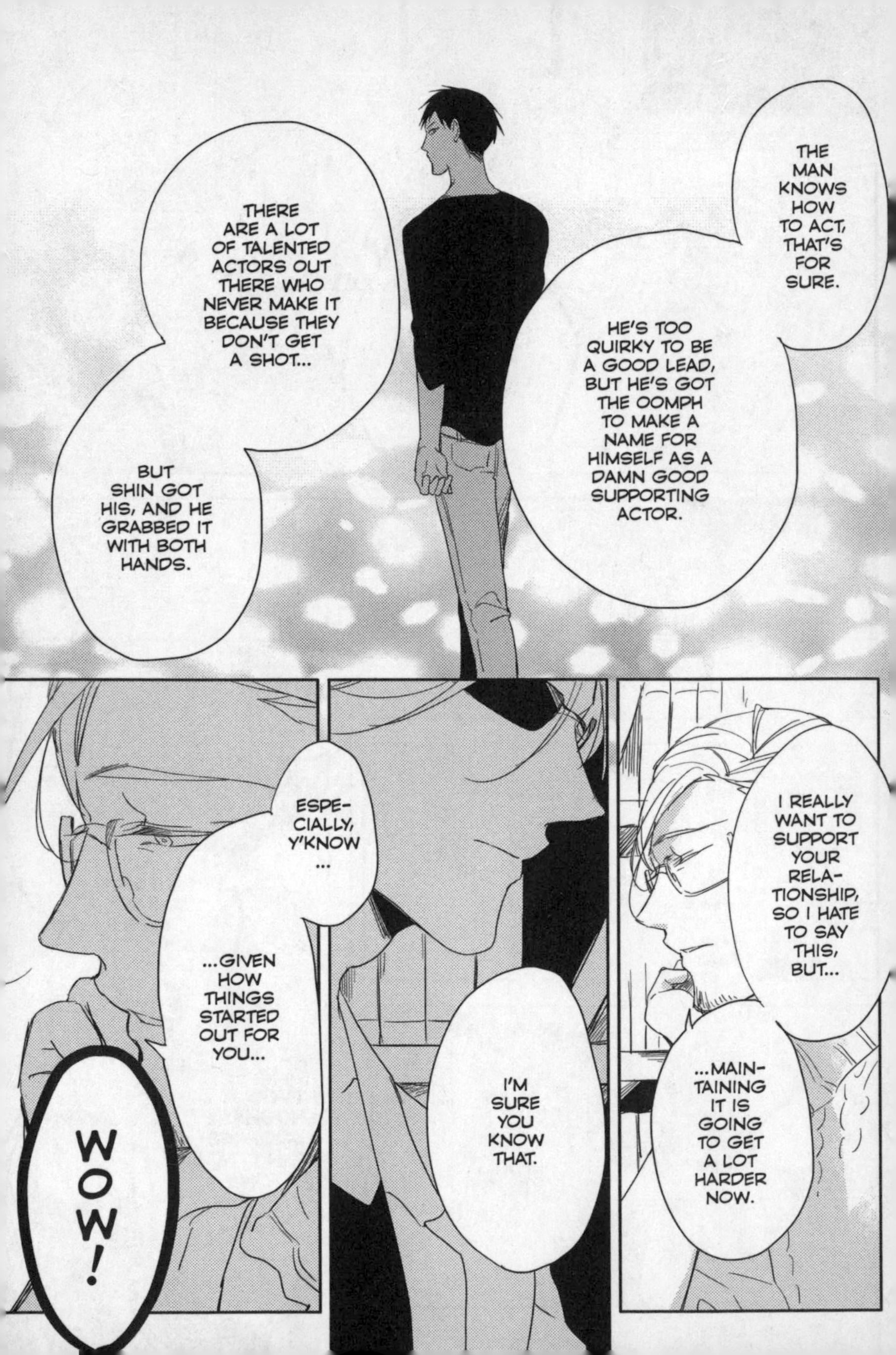
THE MAN KNOWS HOW TO ACT, THAT'S FOR SURE.
HE'S TOO QUIRKY TO BE A GOOD LEAD, BUT HE'S GOT THE OOMPH TO MAKE A NAME FOR HIMSELF AS A DAMN GOOD SUPPORTING ACTOR.
THERE ARE A LOT OF TALENTED ACTORS OUT THERE WHO NEVER MAKE IT BECAUSE THEY DON'T GET A SHOT...
BUT SHIN GOT HIS, AND HE GRABBED IT WITH BOTH HANDS.
I REALLY WANT TO SUPPORT YOUR RELA-TIONSHIP, SO I HATE TO SAY THIS, BUT...
...MAIN-TAINING IT IS GOING TO GET A LOT HARDER NOW.
I'M SURE YOU KNOW THAT.
ESPE-CIALLY, Y'KNOW ...
...GIVEN HOW THINGS STARTED OUT FOR YOU...
WOW!

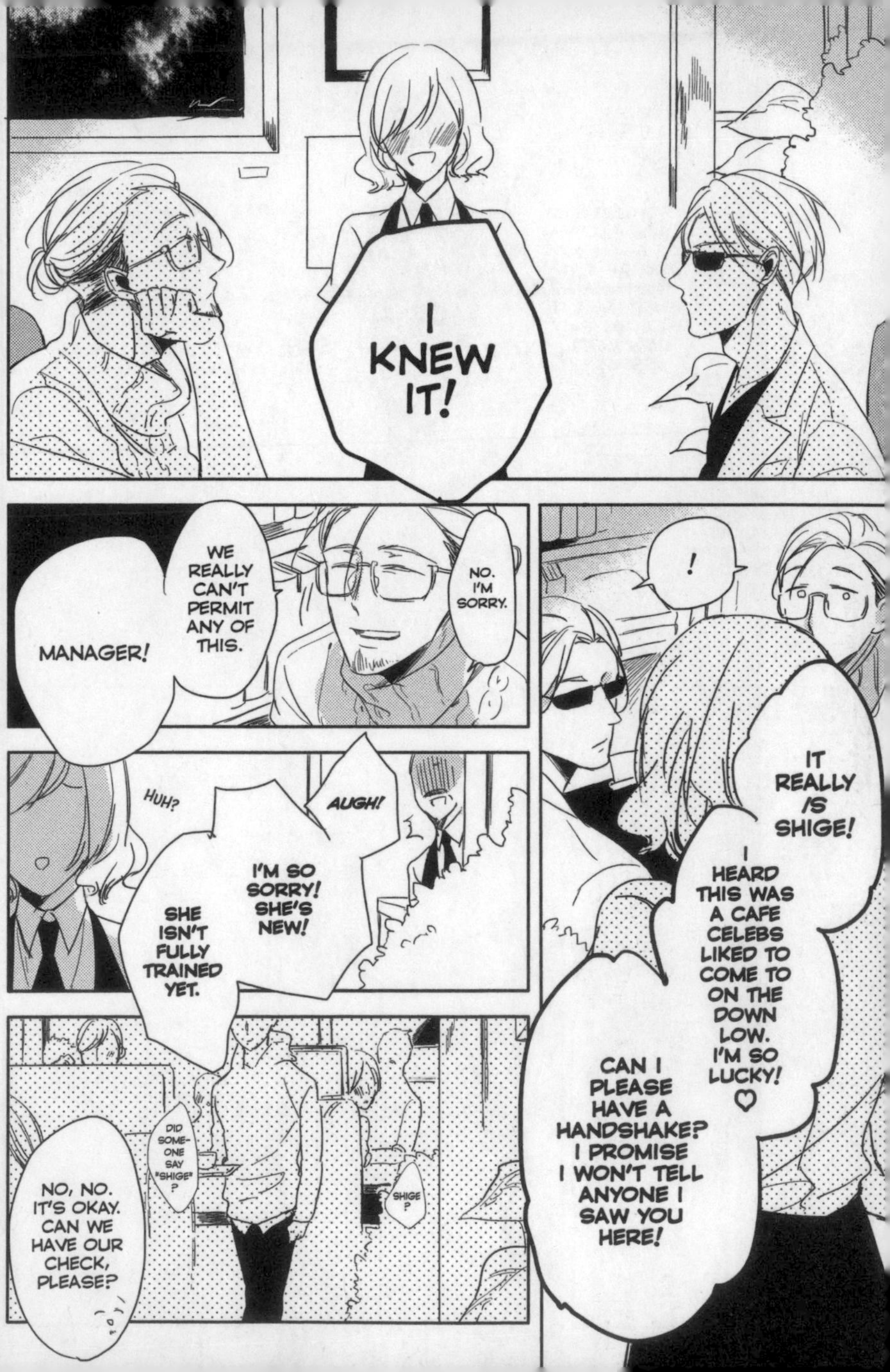
I KNEW IT!
!
IT REALLY IS SHIGE!
I HEARD THIS WAS A CAFE CELEBS LIKED TO COME TO ON THE DOWN LOW. I'M SO LUCKY! ♡
CAN I PLEASE HAVE A HANDSHAKE? I PROMISE I WON'T TELL ANYONE I SAW YOU HERE!
NO. I'M SORRY.
WE REALLY CAN'T PERMIT ANY OF THIS.
MANAGER!
AUGH!
I'M SO SORRY! SHE'S NEW!
SHE ISN'T FULLY TRAINED YET.
HUH?
SHIGE?
DID SOMEONE SAY "SHIGE"?
NO, NO. IT'S OKAY. CAN WE HAVE OUR CHECK, PLEASE?

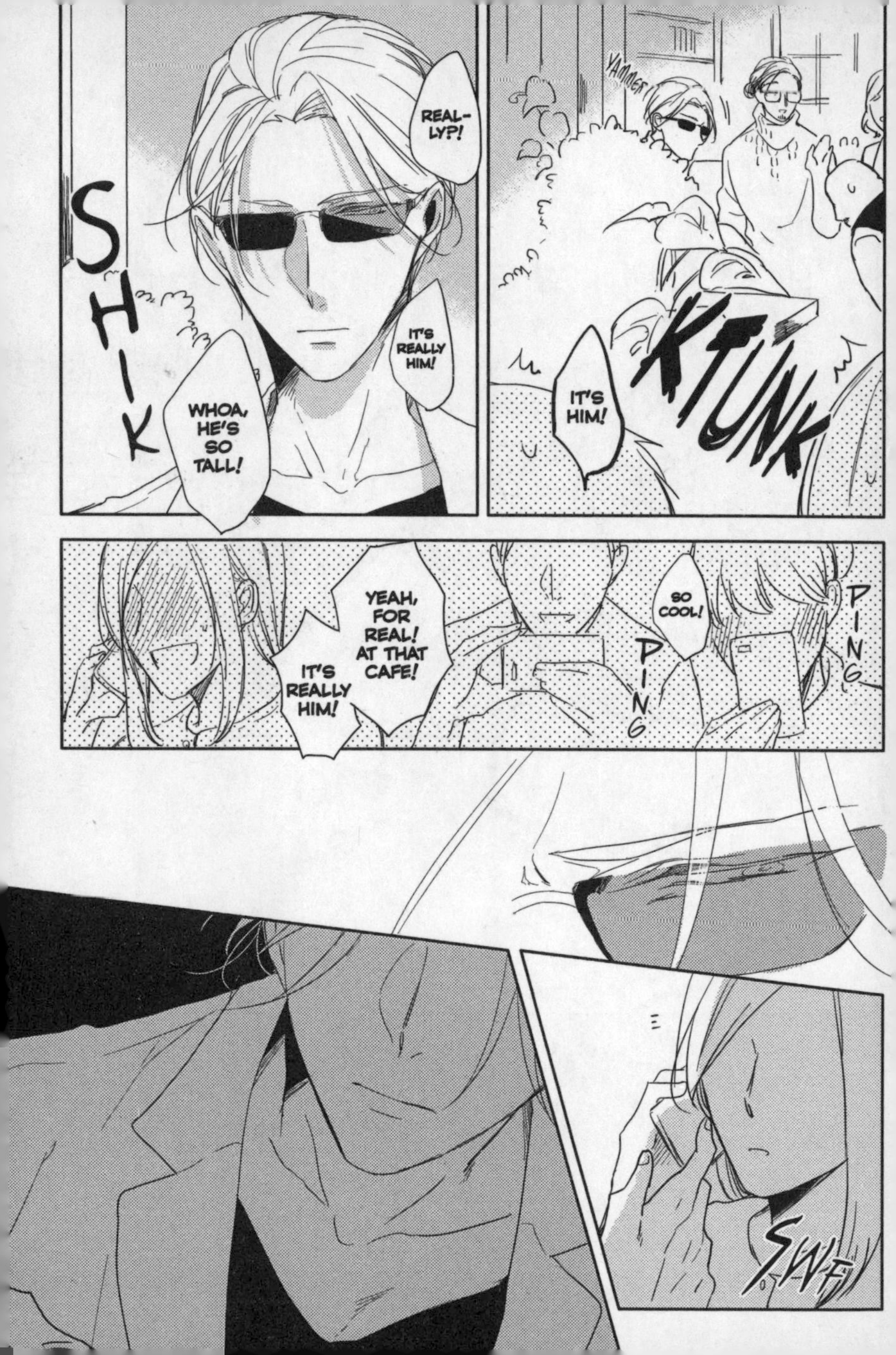
YAMMER
IT'S HIM!
KTUNK
REAL-LY?!
IT'S REALLY HIM!
WHOA, HE'S SO TALL!
SHIK
PING
SO COOL!
PING
YEAH, FOR REAL! AT THAT CAFE!
IT'S REALLY HIM!
SWF

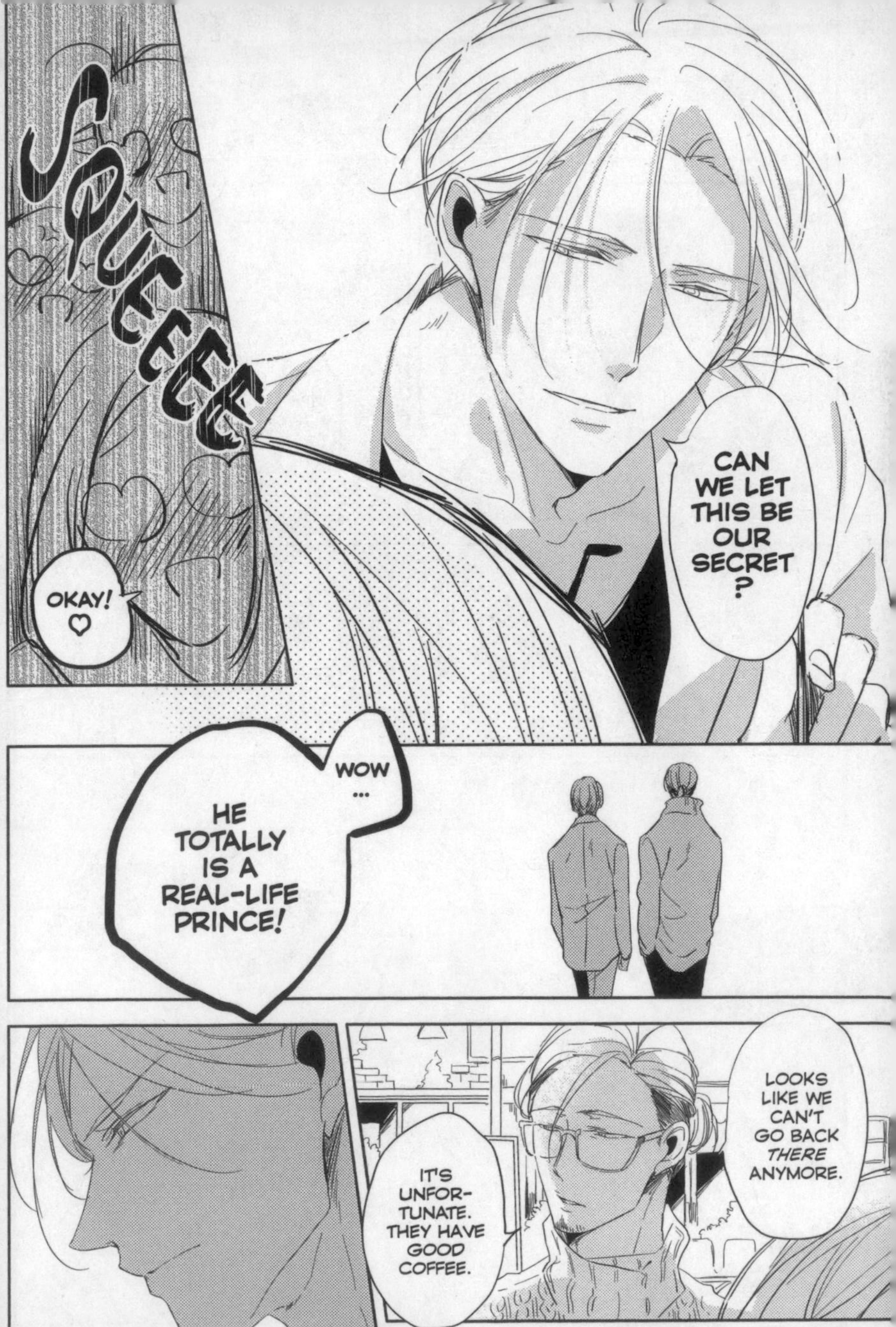
CAN WE LET THIS BE OUR SECRET?
SQUEEEE
OKAY! ♡
WOW ...
HE TOTALLY IS A REAL-LIFE PRINCE!
LOOKS LIKE WE CAN'T GO BACK *THERE* ANYMORE.
IT'S UNFORTUNATE. THEY HAVE GOOD COFFEE.

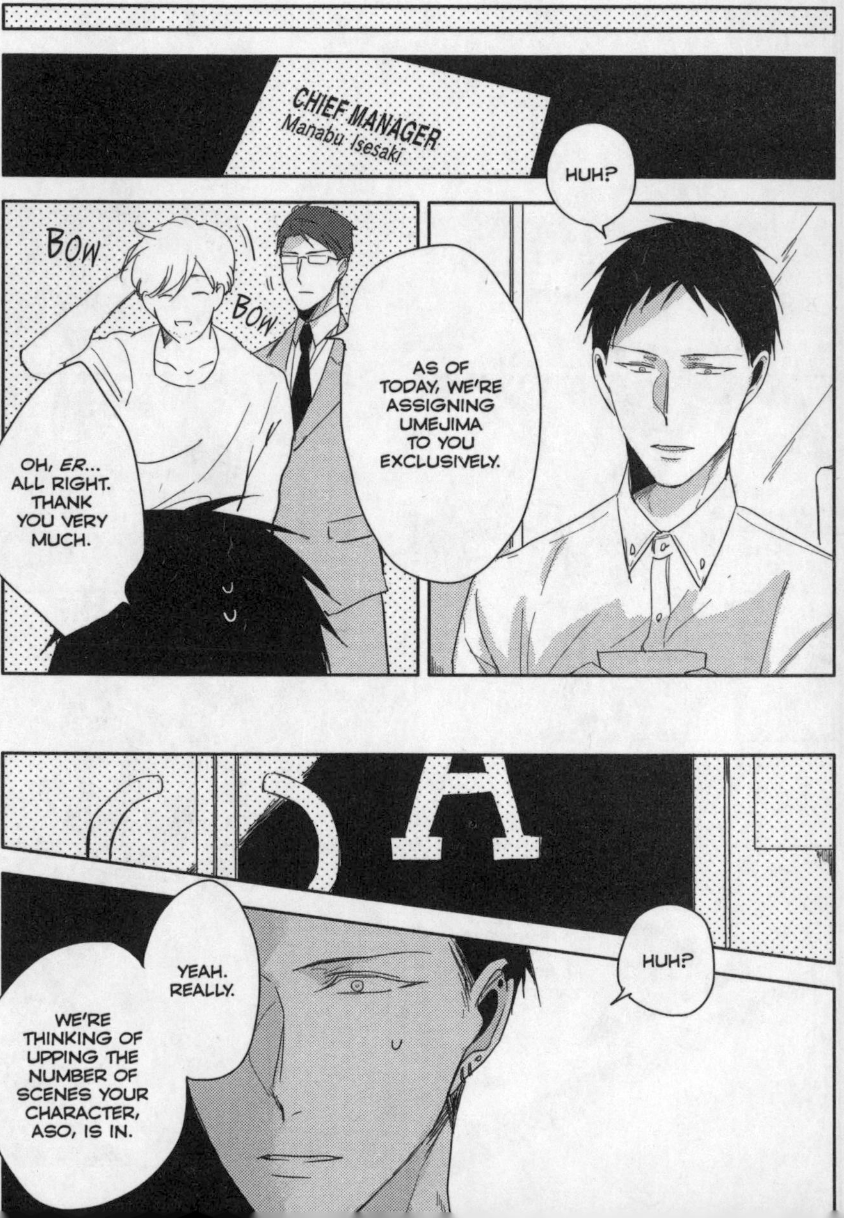
CHIEF MANAGER
Manabu Isesaki
HUH?
AS OF TODAY, WE'RE ASSIGNING UMEJIMA TO YOU EXCLUSIVELY.
BOW
BOW
OH, *ER*... ALL RIGHT. THANK YOU VERY MUCH.
A
HUH?
YEAH. REALLY.
WE'RE THINKING OF UPPING THE NUMBER OF SCENES YOUR CHARACTER, ASO, IS IN.

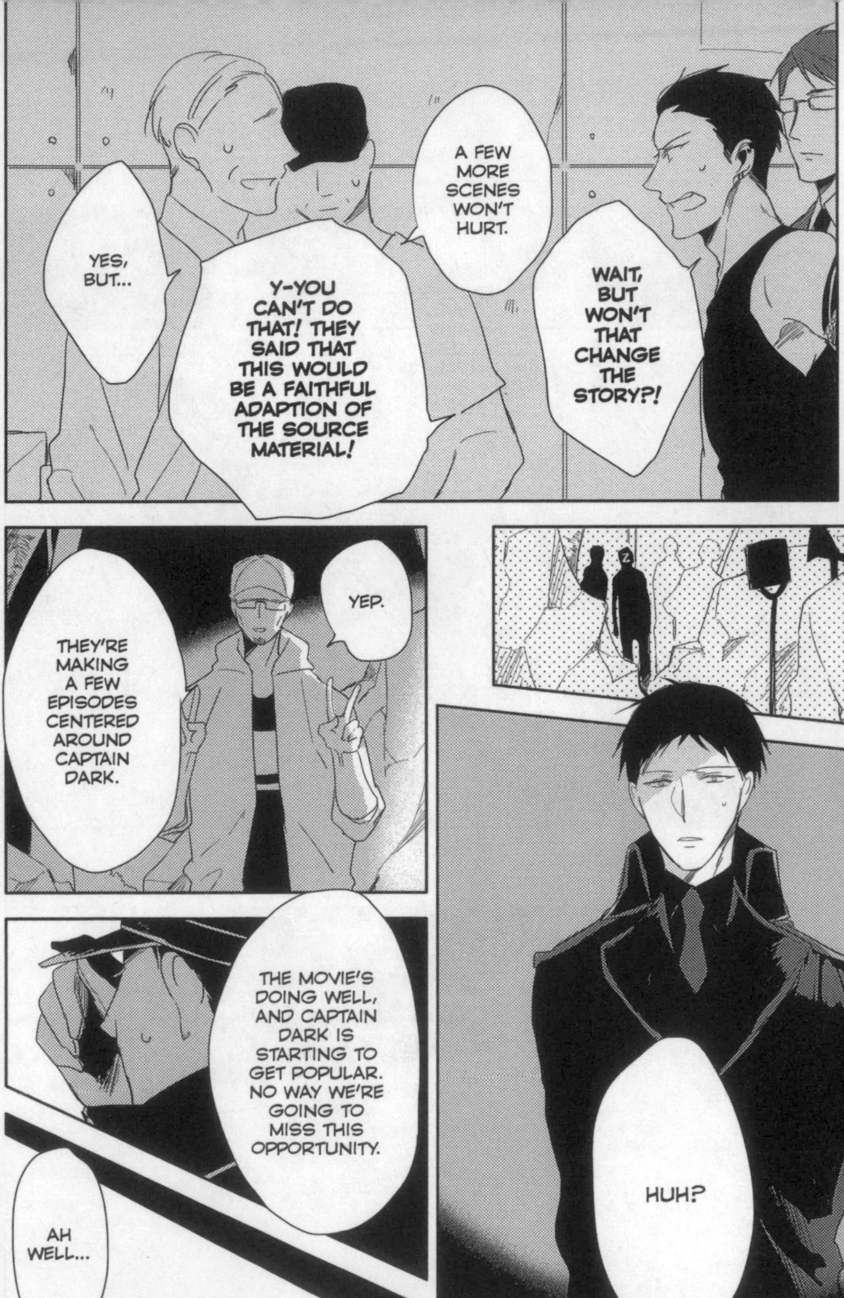
WAIT, BUT WON'T THAT CHANGE THE STORY?!
A FEW MORE SCENES WON'T HURT.
Y-YOU CAN'T DO THAT! THEY SAID THAT THIS WOULD BE A FAITHFUL ADAPTION OF THE SOURCE MATERIAL!
YES, BUT...
HUH?
YEP.
THEY'RE MAKING A FEW EPISODES CENTERED AROUND CAPTAIN DARK.
THE MOVIE'S DOING WELL, AND CAPTAIN DARK IS STARTING TO GET POPULAR. NO WAY WE'RE GOING TO MISS THIS OPPORTUNITY.
AH WELL...

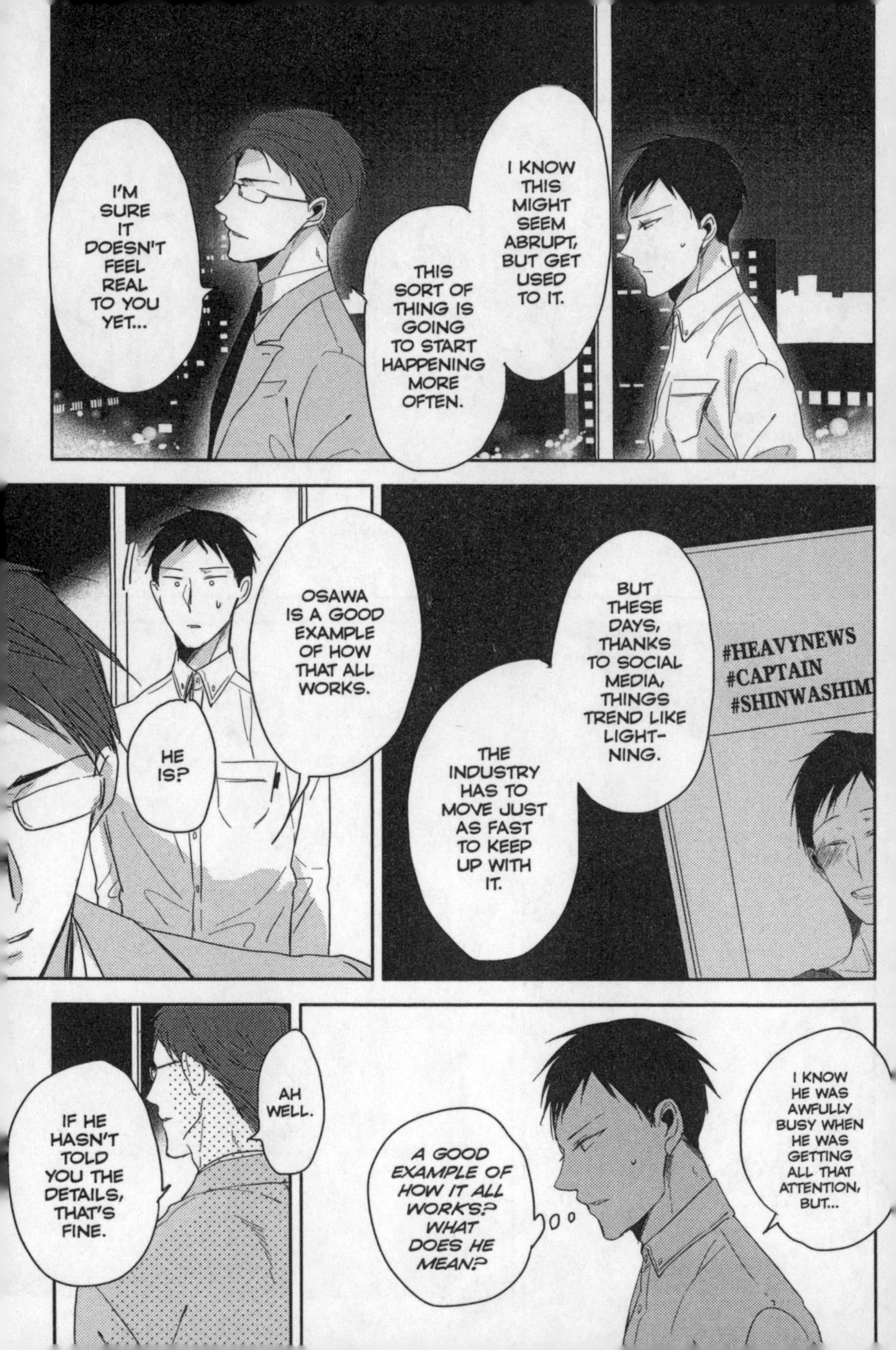
I KNOW THIS MIGHT SEEM ABRUPT, BUT GET USED TO IT.
THIS SORT OF THING IS GOING TO START HAPPENING MORE OFTEN.
I'M SURE IT DOESN'T FEEL REAL TO YOU YET...
#HEAVYNEWS
#CAPTAIN
#SHINWASHIM
BUT THESE DAYS, THANKS TO SOCIAL MEDIA, THINGS TREND LIKE LIGHTNING.
THE INDUSTRY HAS TO MOVE JUST AS FAST TO KEEP UP WITH IT.
OSAWA IS A GOOD EXAMPLE OF HOW THAT ALL WORKS.
HE IS?
I KNOW HE WAS AWFULLY BUSY WHEN HE WAS GETTING ALL THAT ATTENTION, BUT...
A GOOD EXAMPLE OF HOW IT ALL WORKS? WHAT DOES HE MEAN?
AH WELL.
IF HE HASN'T TOLD YOU THE DETAILS, THAT'S FINE.

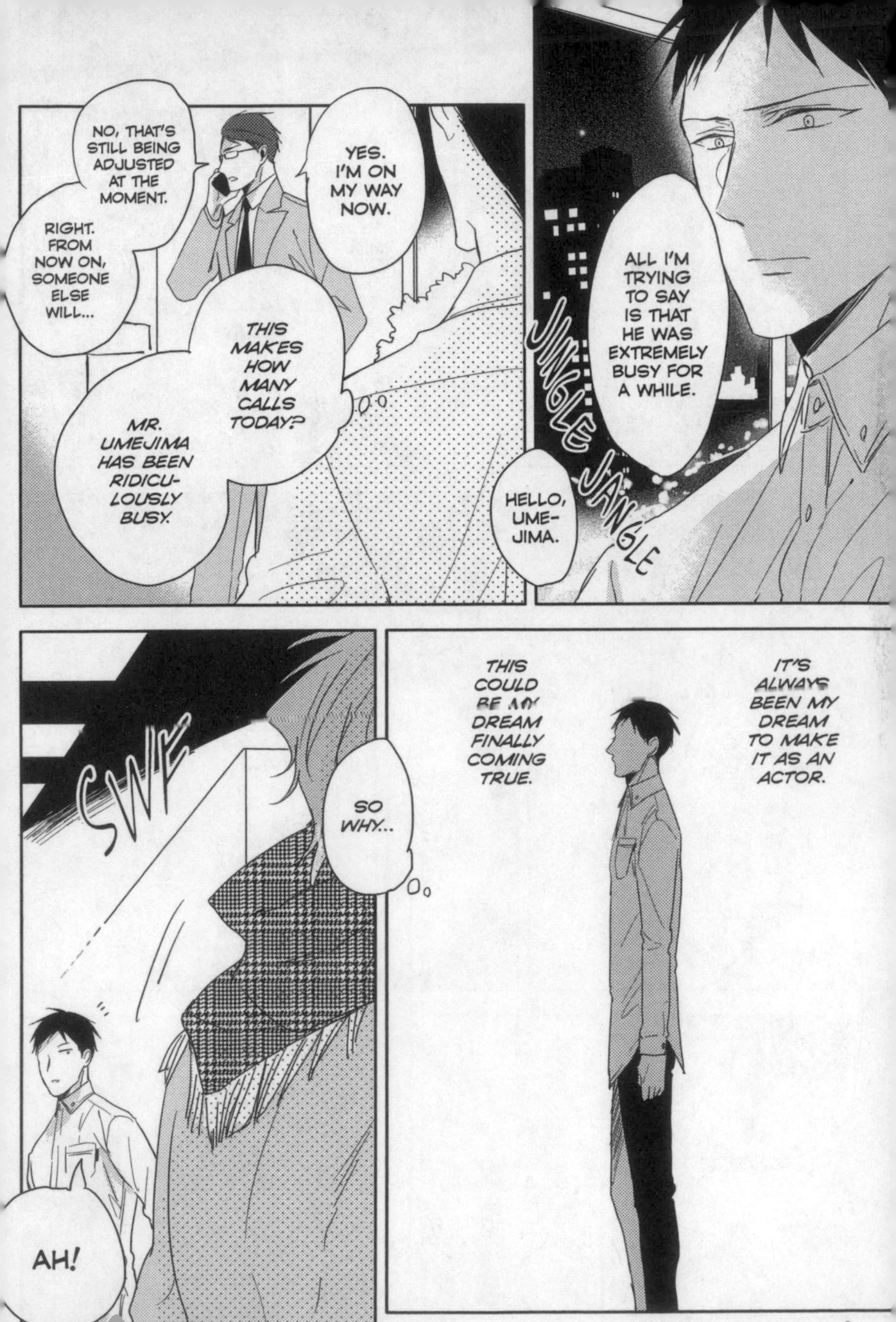
ALL I'M TRYING TO SAY IS THAT HE WAS EXTREMELY BUSY FOR A WHILE.
JINGLE JANGLE
HELLO, UME-JIMA.
YES. I'M ON MY WAY NOW.
NO, THAT'S STILL BEING ADJUSTED AT THE MOMENT.
RIGHT. FROM NOW ON, SOMEONE ELSE WILL...
THIS MAKES HOW MANY CALLS TODAY?
MR. UMEJIMA HAS BEEN RIDICU-LOUSLY BUSY.
IT'S ALWAYS BEEN MY DREAM TO MAKE IT AS AN ACTOR.
THIS COULD BE MY DREAM FINALLY COMING TRUE.
SO WHY...
SWE
AH!

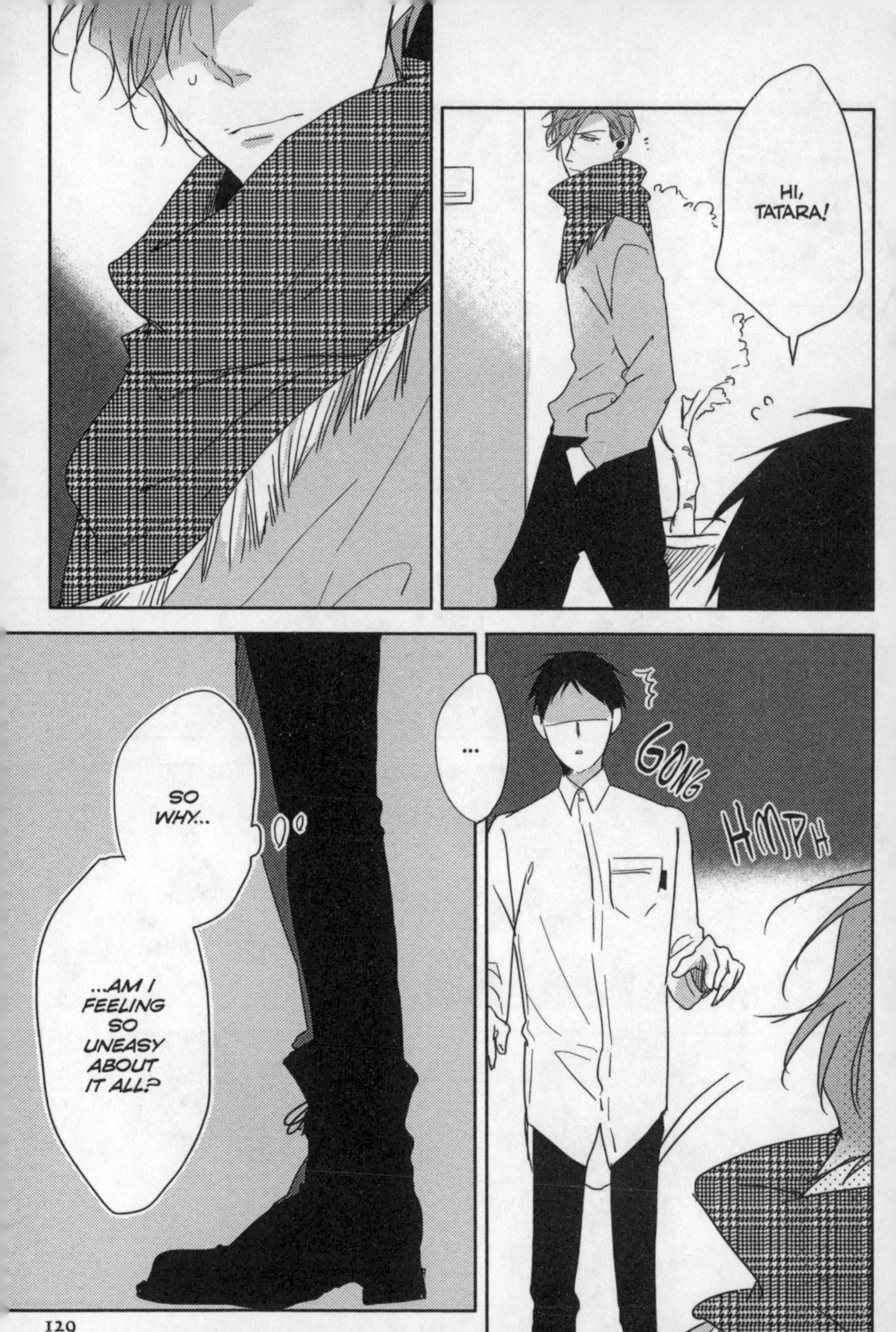
HI, TATARA!
GONG
HMPH
...
SO WHY...
...AM I FEELING SO UNEASY ABOUT IT ALL?

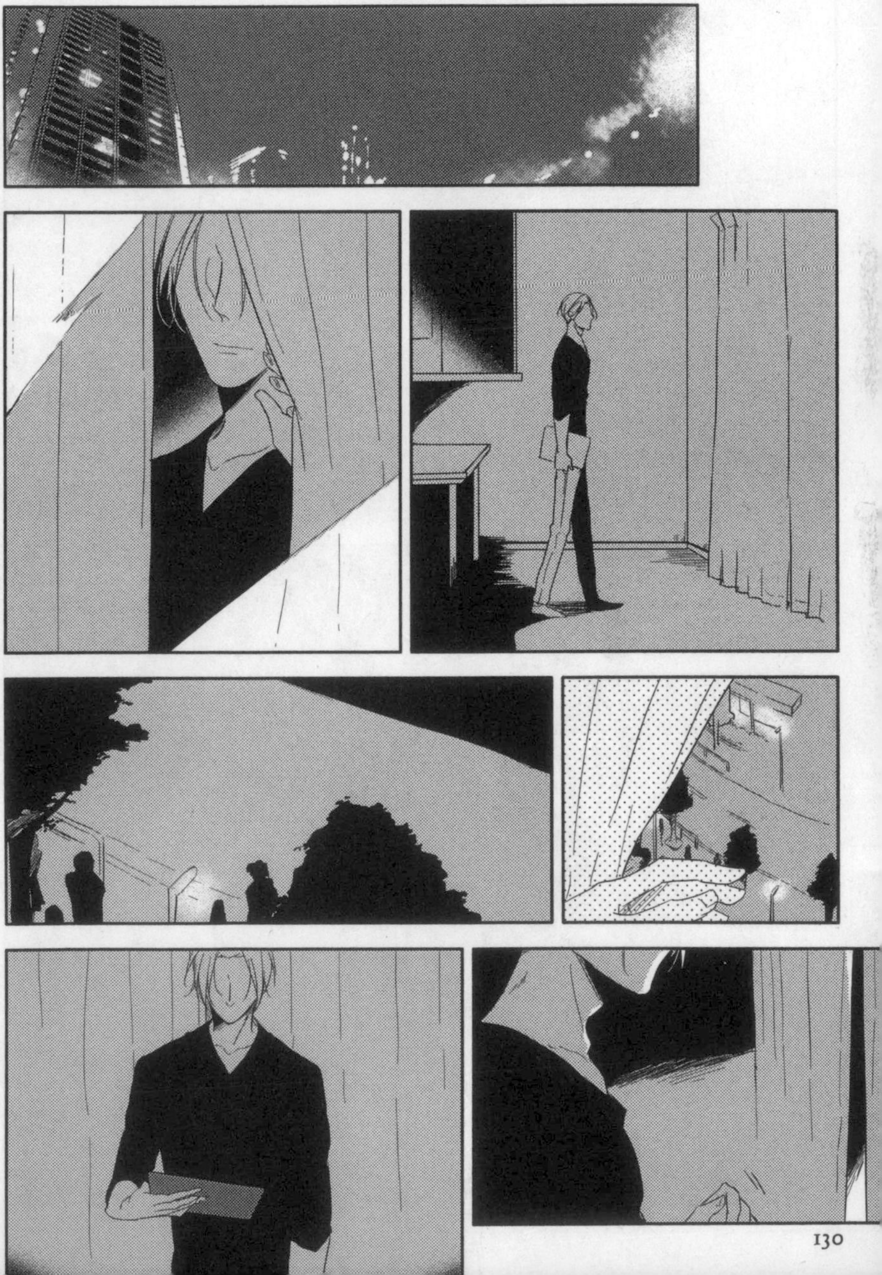

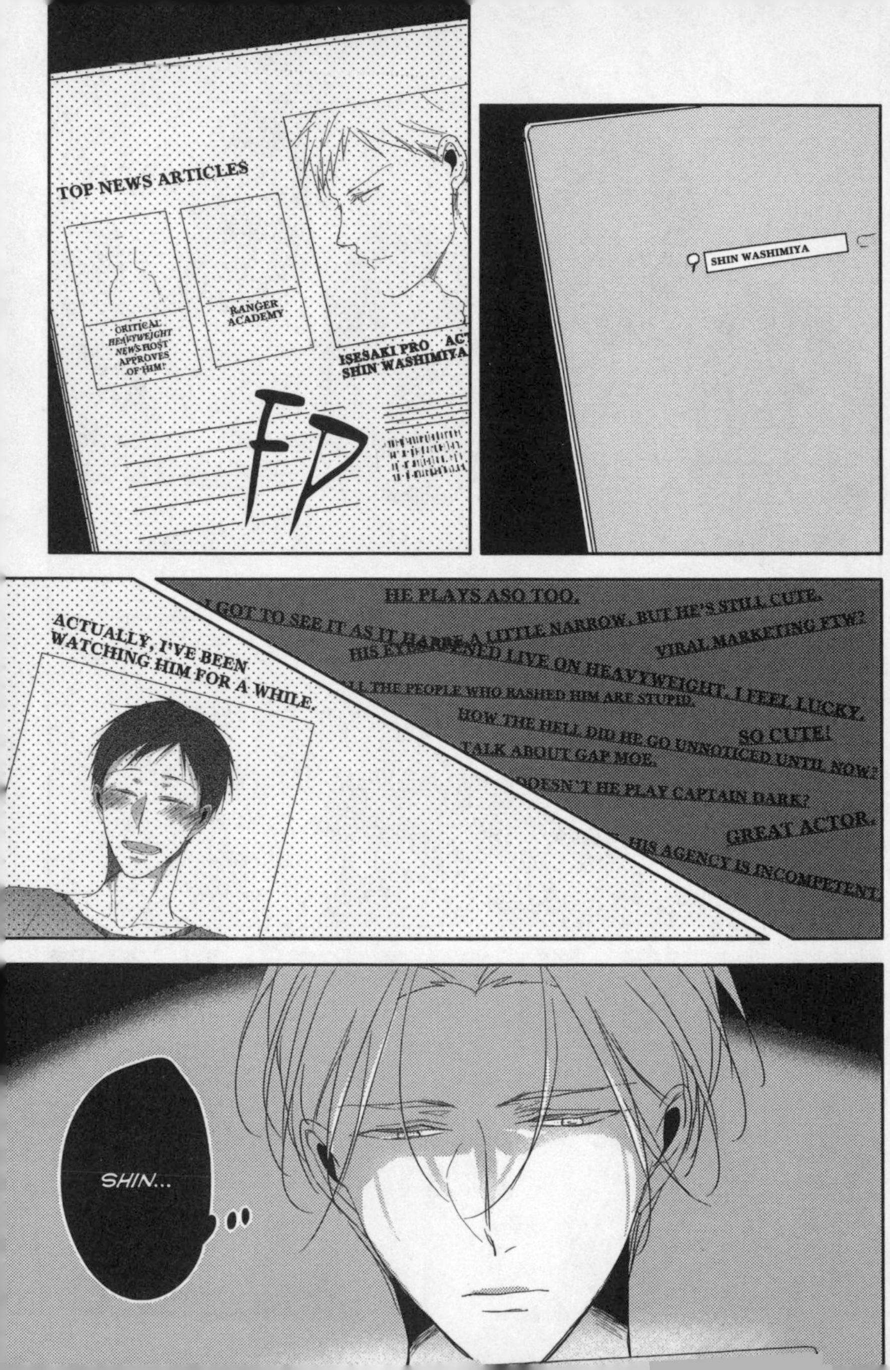

SHIN WASHIMIYA
TOP NEWS ARTICLES
CRITICAL HEAVYWEIGHT NEWS HOST APPROVES OF HIM!
RANGER ACADEMY
ISESAKI PRO ACT SHIN WASHIMIYA
FP
HE PLAYS ASO TOO.
A LITTLE NARROW, BUT HE'S STILL CUTE.
VIRAL MARKETING FTW?
LIVE ON HEAVYWEIGHT. I FEEL LUCKY.
THE PEOPLE WHO BASHED HIM ARE STUPID.
HOW THE HELL DID HE GO UNNOTICED UNTIL NOW?
SO CUTE!
TALK ABOUT GAP MOE.
DOESN'T HE PLAY CAPTAIN DARK?
GREAT ACTOR.
HIS AGENCY IS INCOMPETENT.
ACTUALLY, I'VE BEEN WATCHING HIM FOR A WHILE.
SHIN...

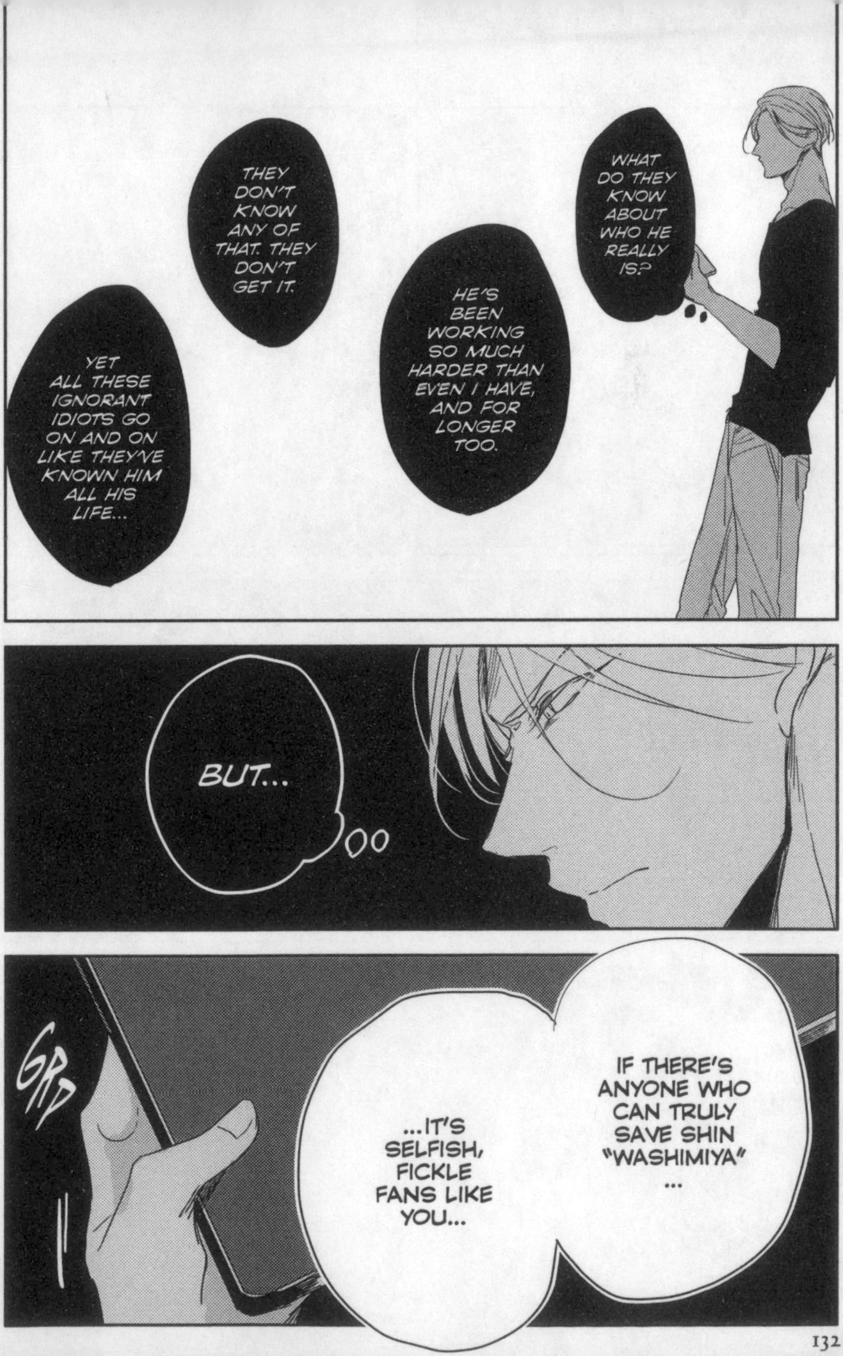
WHAT DO THEY KNOW ABOUT WHO HE REALLY IS?
HE'S BEEN WORKING SO MUCH HARDER THAN EVEN I HAVE, AND FOR LONGER TOO.
THEY DON'T KNOW ANY OF THAT. THEY DON'T GET IT.
YET ALL THESE IGNORANT IDIOTS GO ON AND ON LIKE THEY'VE KNOWN HIM ALL HIS LIFE...
BUT...
IF THERE'S ANYONE WHO CAN TRULY SAVE SHIN "WASHIMIYA" ...
...IT'S SELFISH, FICKLE FANS LIKE YOU...
GRP

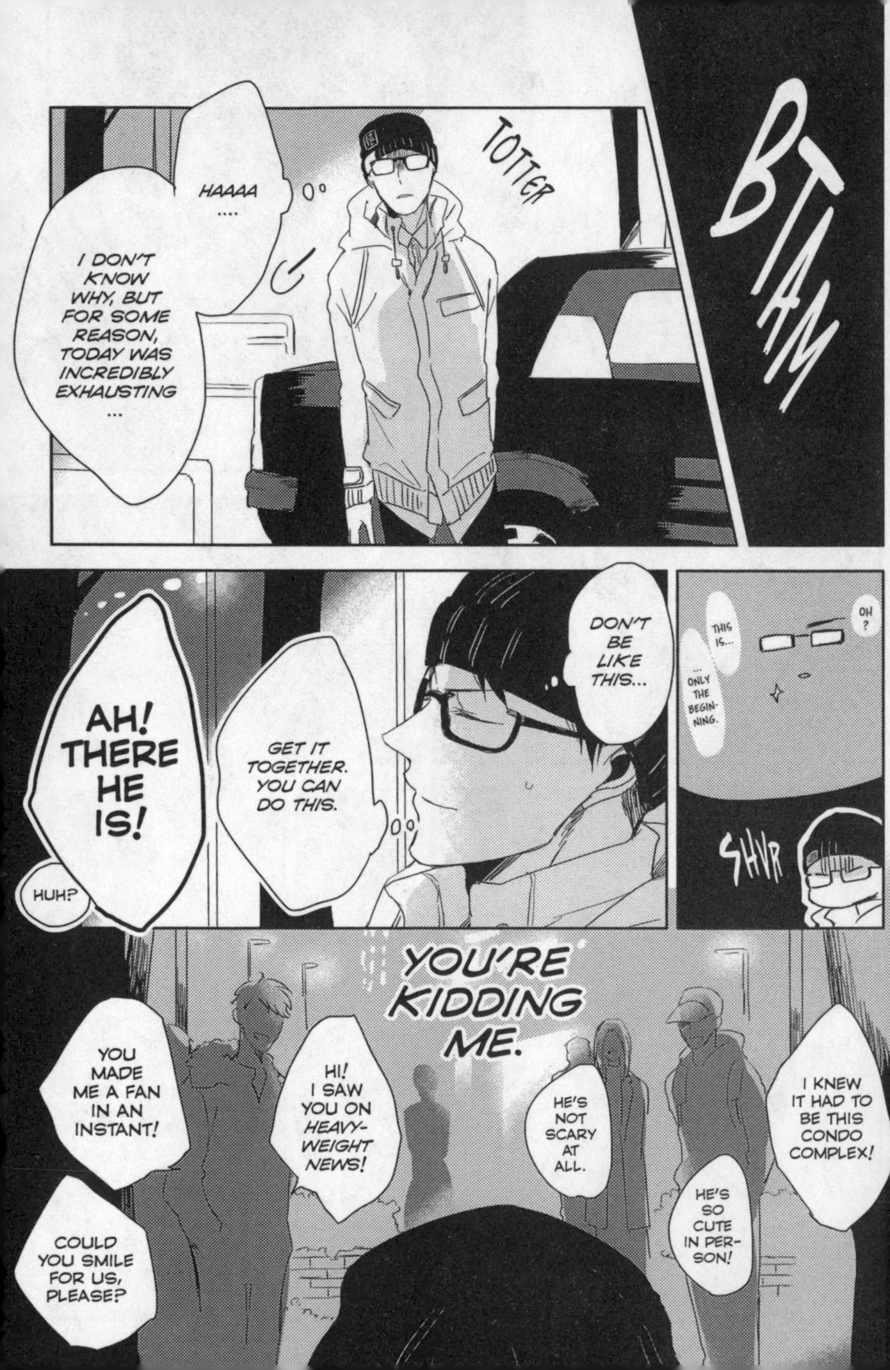
BTAM
TOTTER
HAAAA ....
I DON'T KNOW WHY, BUT FOR SOME REASON, TODAY WAS INCREDIBLY EXHAUSTING ...
OH ?
THIS IS...
... ONLY THE BEGIN-NING.
SHVR
DON'T BE LIKE THIS...
GET IT TOGETHER. YOU CAN DO THIS.
AH! THERE HE IS!
HUH?
YOU'RE KIDDING ME.
I KNEW IT HAD TO BE THIS CONDO COMPLEX!
HE'S NOT SCARY AT ALL.
HE'S SO CUTE IN PER-SON!
HI! I SAW YOU ON HEAVY-WEIGHT NEWS!
YOU MADE ME A FAN IN AN INSTANT!
COULD YOU SMILE FOR US, PLEASE?

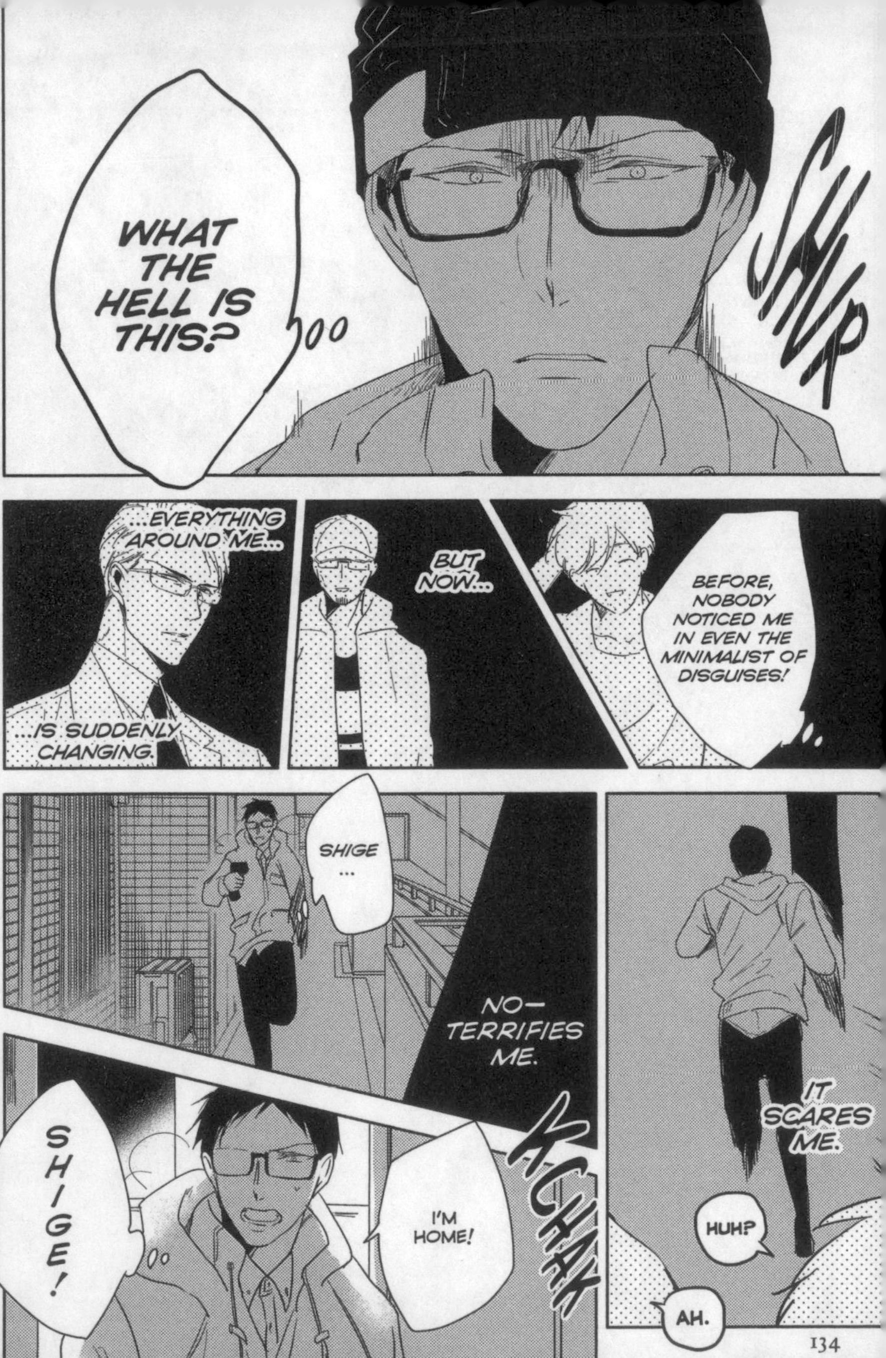
SHUR
WHAT THE HELL IS THIS?
BEFORE, NOBODY NOTICED ME IN EVEN THE MINIMALIST OF DISGUISES!
...
BUT NOW...
...EVERYTHING AROUND ME...
...IS SUDDENLY CHANGING.
IT SCARES ME.
HUH?
AH.
SHIGE ...
NO— TERRIFIES ME.
KCHAK
I'M HOME!
SHIGE!

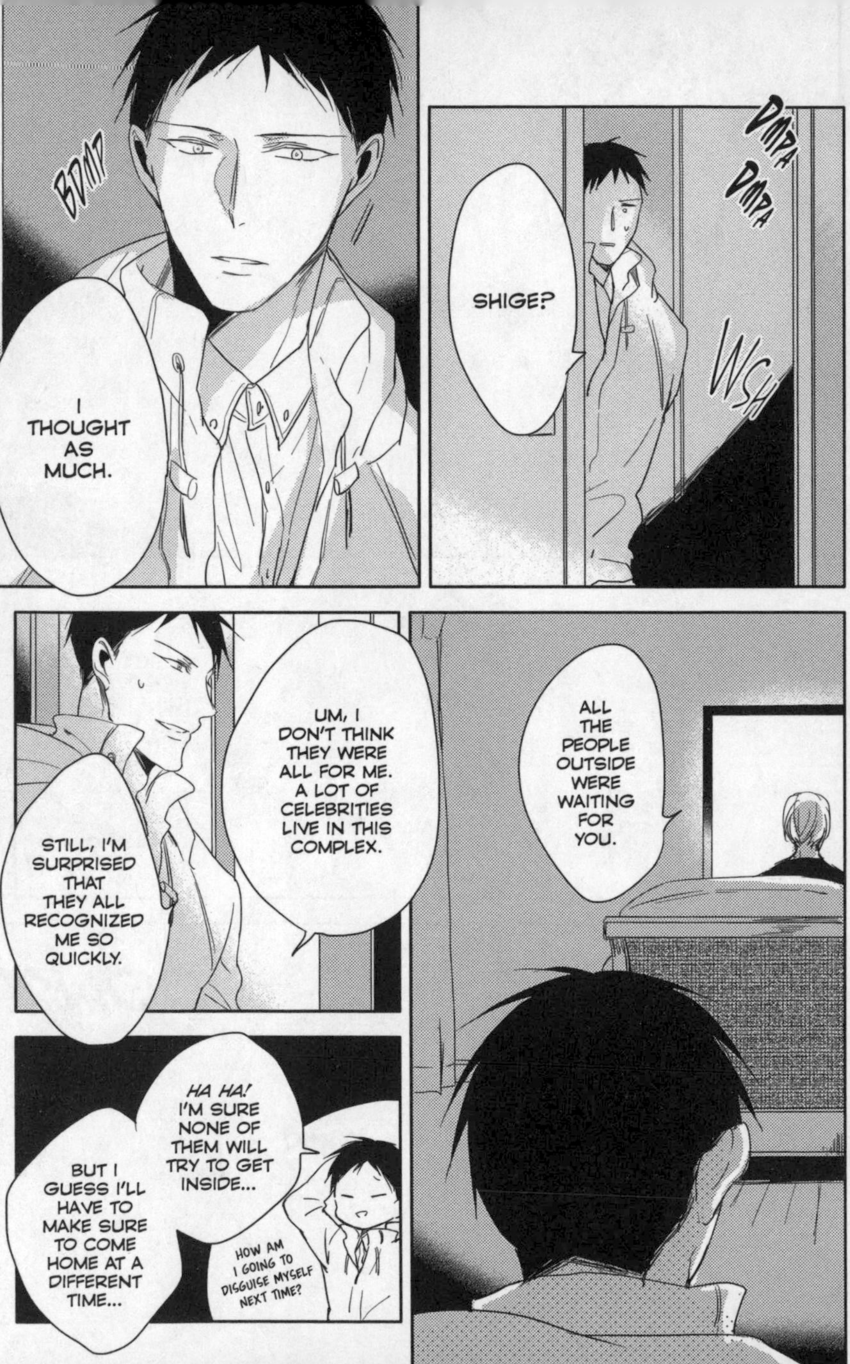
DMPA DMPA
SHIGE?
WSH
BDMP
I THOUGHT AS MUCH.
ALL THE PEOPLE OUTSIDE WERE WAITING FOR YOU.
UM, I DON'T THINK THEY WERE ALL FOR ME. A LOT OF CELEBRITIES LIVE IN THIS COMPLEX.
STILL, I'M SURPRISED THAT THEY ALL RECOGNIZED ME SO QUICKLY.
HA HA! I'M SURE NONE OF THEM WILL TRY TO GET INSIDE...
BUT I GUESS I'LL HAVE TO MAKE SURE TO COME HOME AT A DIFFERENT TIME...
HOW AM I GOING TO DISGUISE MYSELF NEXT TIME?

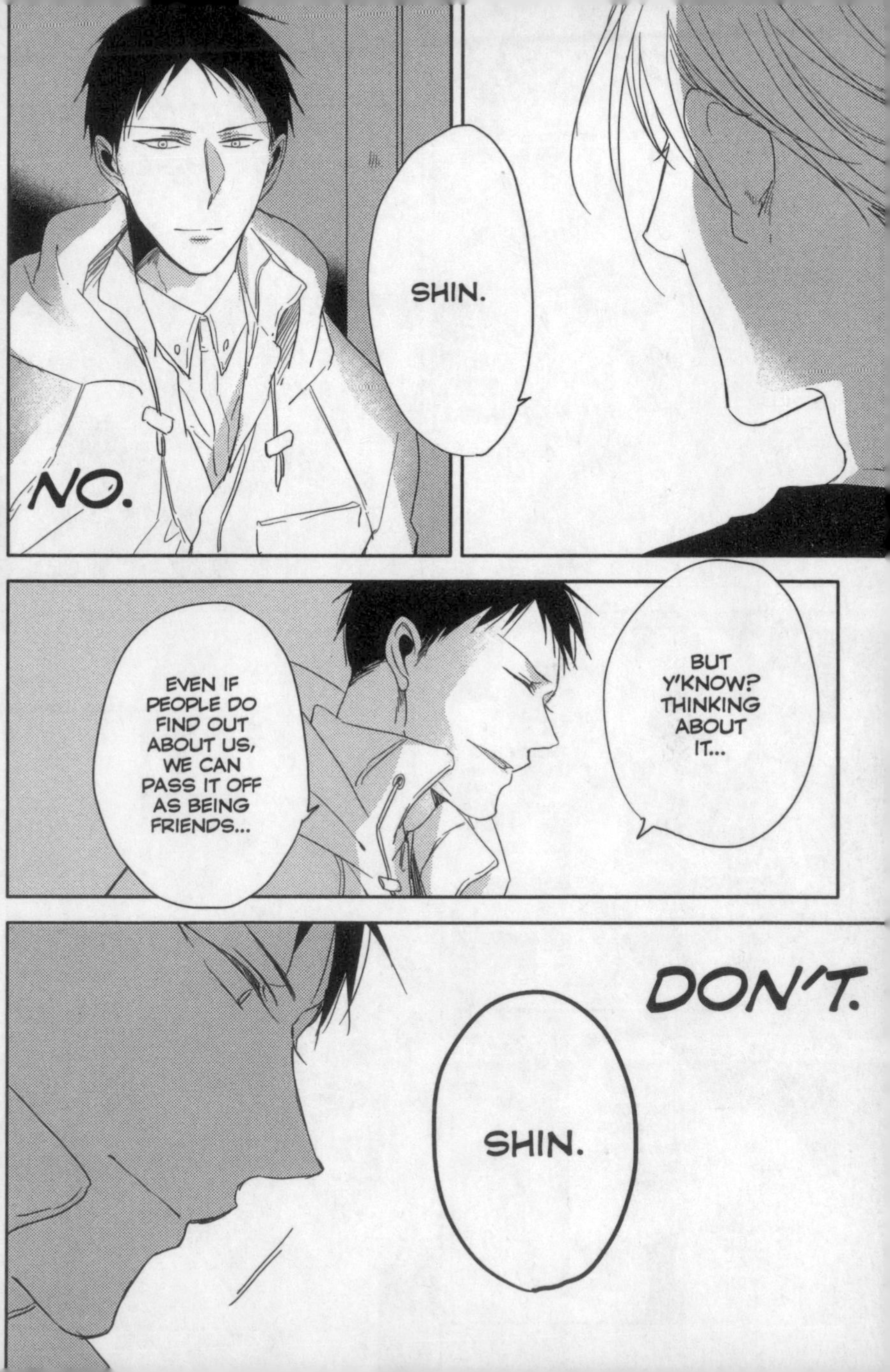
SHIN.
NO.
BUT Y'KNOW? THINKING ABOUT IT...
EVEN IF PEOPLE DO FIND OUT ABOUT US, WE CAN PASS IT OFF AS BEING FRIENDS...
DON'T.
SHIN.

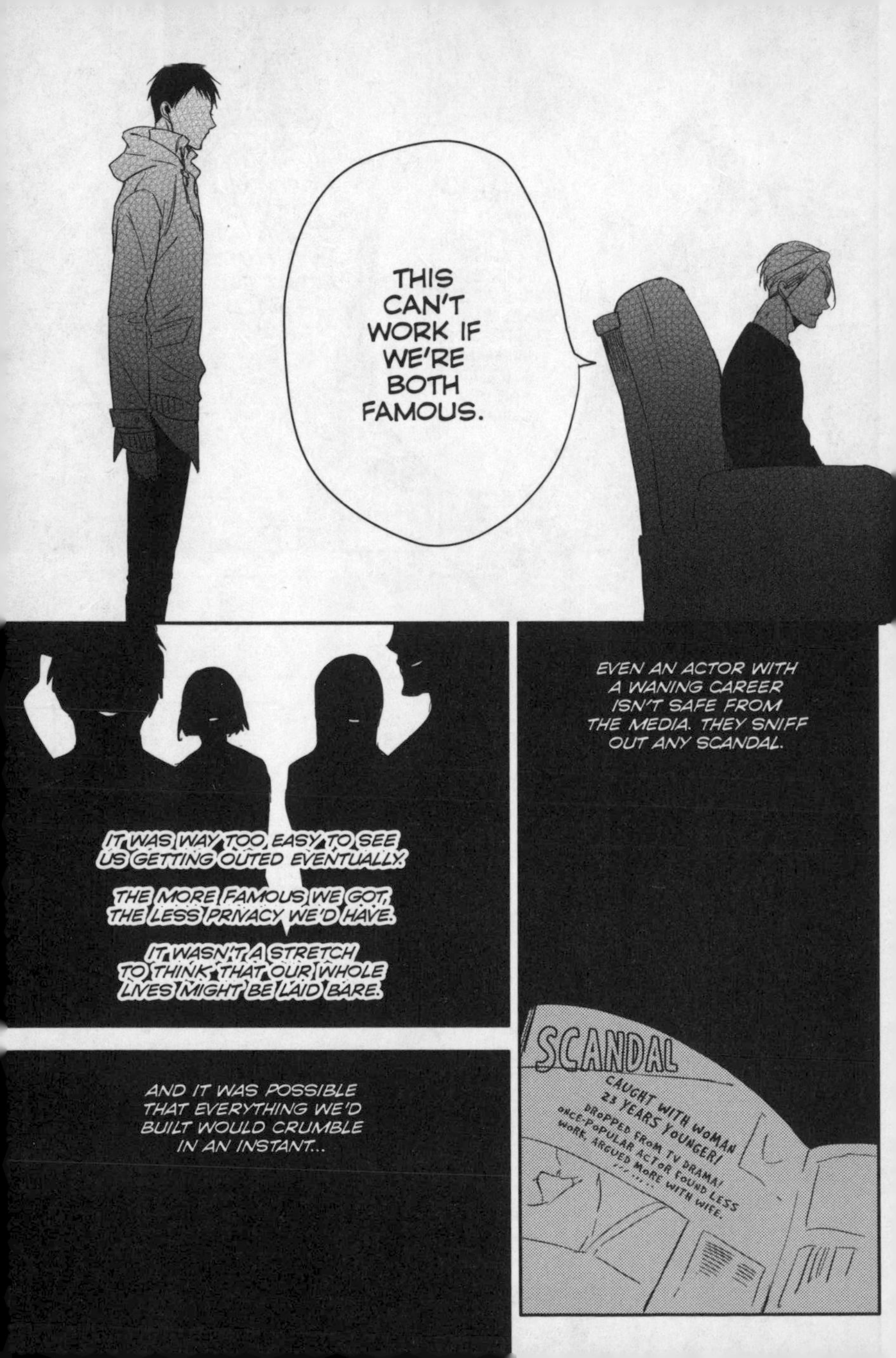
THIS CAN'T WORK IF WE'RE BOTH FAMOUS.
EVEN AN ACTOR WITH A WANING CAREER ISN'T SAFE FROM THE MEDIA. THEY SNIFF OUT ANY SCANDAL.
SCANDAL
CAUGHT WITH WOMAN 23 YEARS YOUNGER!
DROPPED FROM TV DRAMA!
ONCE-POPULAR ACTOR FOUND LESS WORK, ARGUED MORE WITH WIFE.
IT WAS WAY TOO EASY TO SEE US GETTING OUTED EVENTUALLY.
THE MORE FAMOUS WE GOT, THE LESS PRIVACY WE'D HAVE.
IT WASN'T A STRETCH TO THINK THAT OUR WHOLE LIVES MIGHT BE LAID BARE.
AND IT WAS POSSIBLE THAT EVERYTHING WE'D BUILT WOULD CRUMBLE IN AN INSTANT...

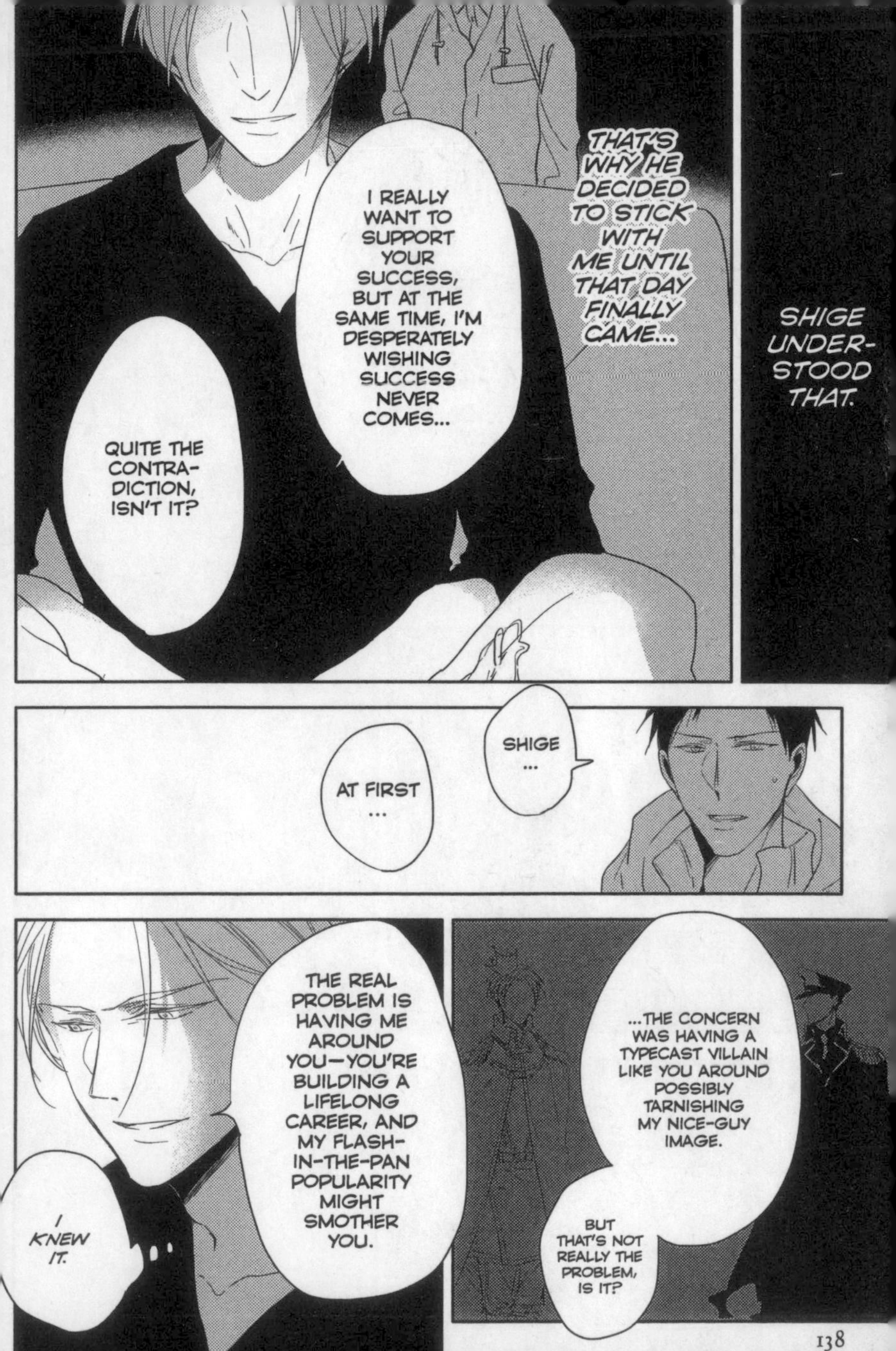
SHIGE UNDERSTOOD THAT.
THAT'S WHY HE DECIDED TO STICK WITH ME UNTIL THAT DAY FINALLY CAME...
I REALLY WANT TO SUPPORT YOUR SUCCESS, BUT AT THE SAME TIME, I'M DESPERATELY WISHING SUCCESS NEVER COMES...
QUITE THE CONTRADICTION, ISN'T IT?
SHIGE...
AT FIRST...
...THE CONCERN WAS HAVING A TYPECAST VILLAIN LIKE YOU AROUND POSSIBLY TARNISHING MY NICE-GUY IMAGE.
BUT THAT'S NOT REALLY THE PROBLEM, IS IT?
THE REAL PROBLEM IS HAVING ME AROUND YOU—YOU'RE BUILDING A LIFELONG CAREER, AND MY FLASH-IN-THE-PAN POPULARITY MIGHT SMOTHER YOU.
I KNEW IT.

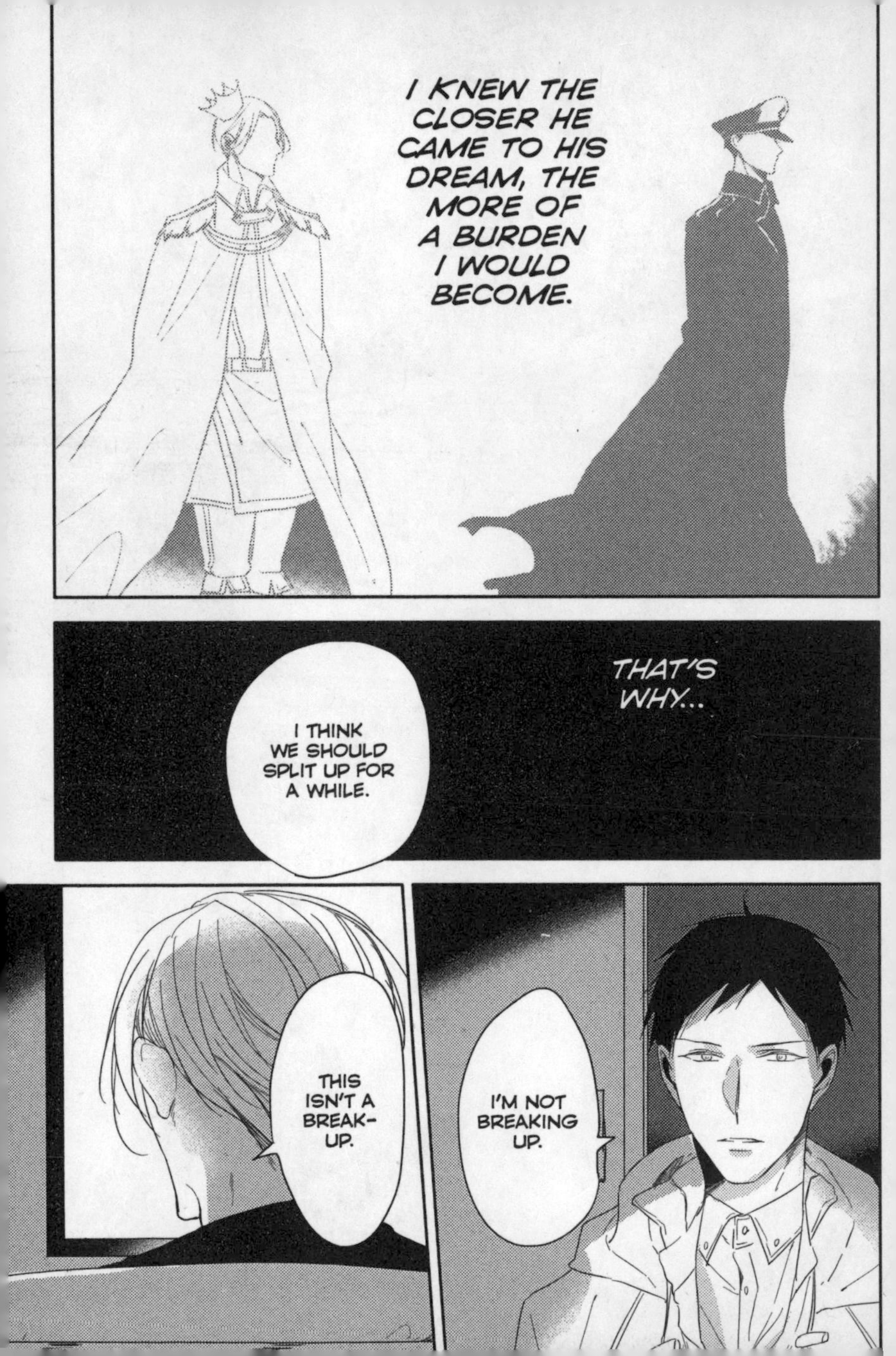
I KNEW THE CLOSER HE CAME TO HIS DREAM, THE MORE OF A BURDEN I WOULD BECOME.
THAT'S WHY...
I THINK WE SHOULD SPLIT UP FOR A WHILE.
I'M NOT BREAKING UP.
THIS ISN'T A BREAK-UP.

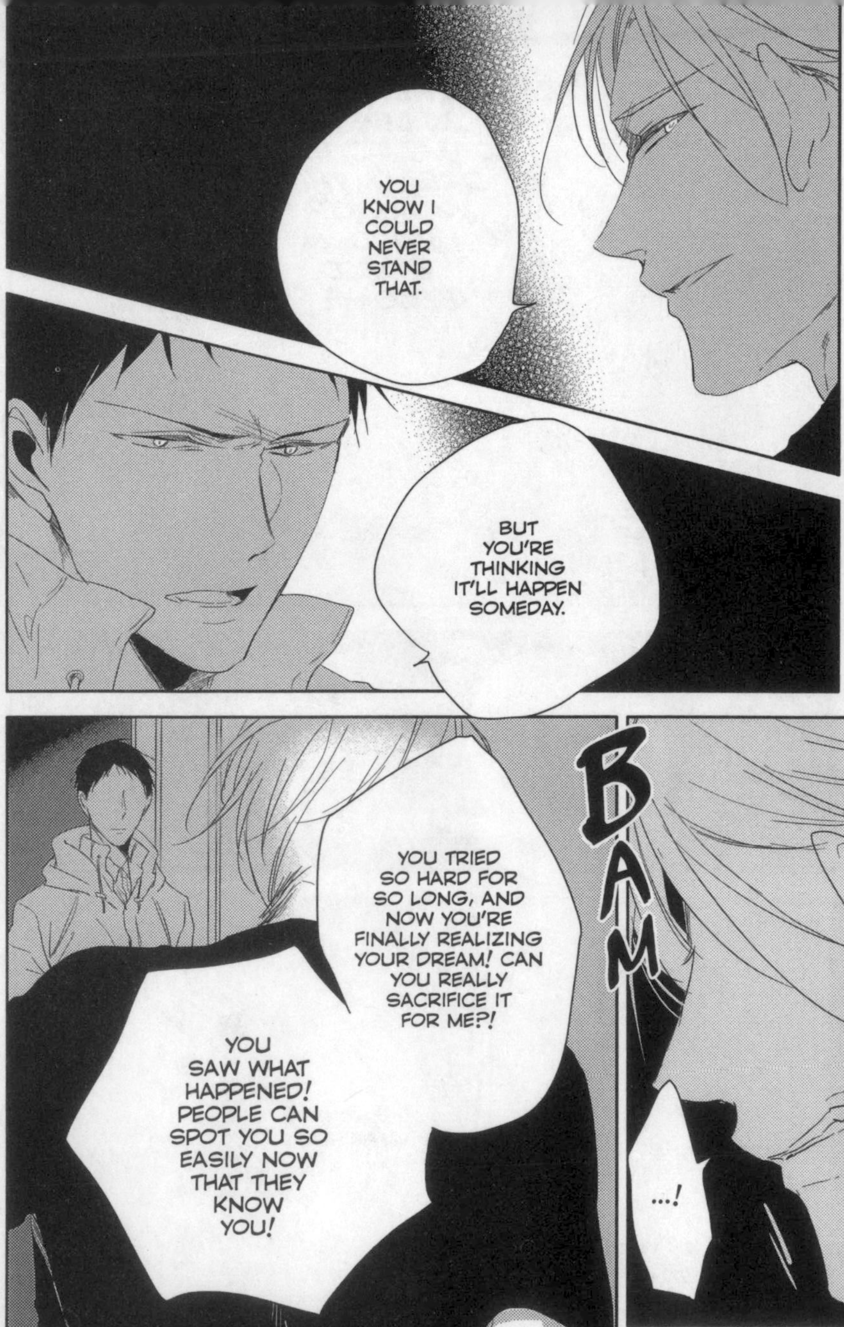
YOU KNOW I COULD NEVER STAND THAT.
BUT YOU'RE THINKING IT'LL HAPPEN SOMEDAY.
BAM
...!
YOU TRIED SO HARD FOR SO LONG, AND NOW YOU'RE FINALLY REALIZING YOUR DREAM! CAN YOU REALLY SACRIFICE IT FOR ME?!
YOU SAW WHAT HAPPENED! PEOPLE CAN SPOT YOU SO EASILY NOW THAT THEY KNOW YOU!

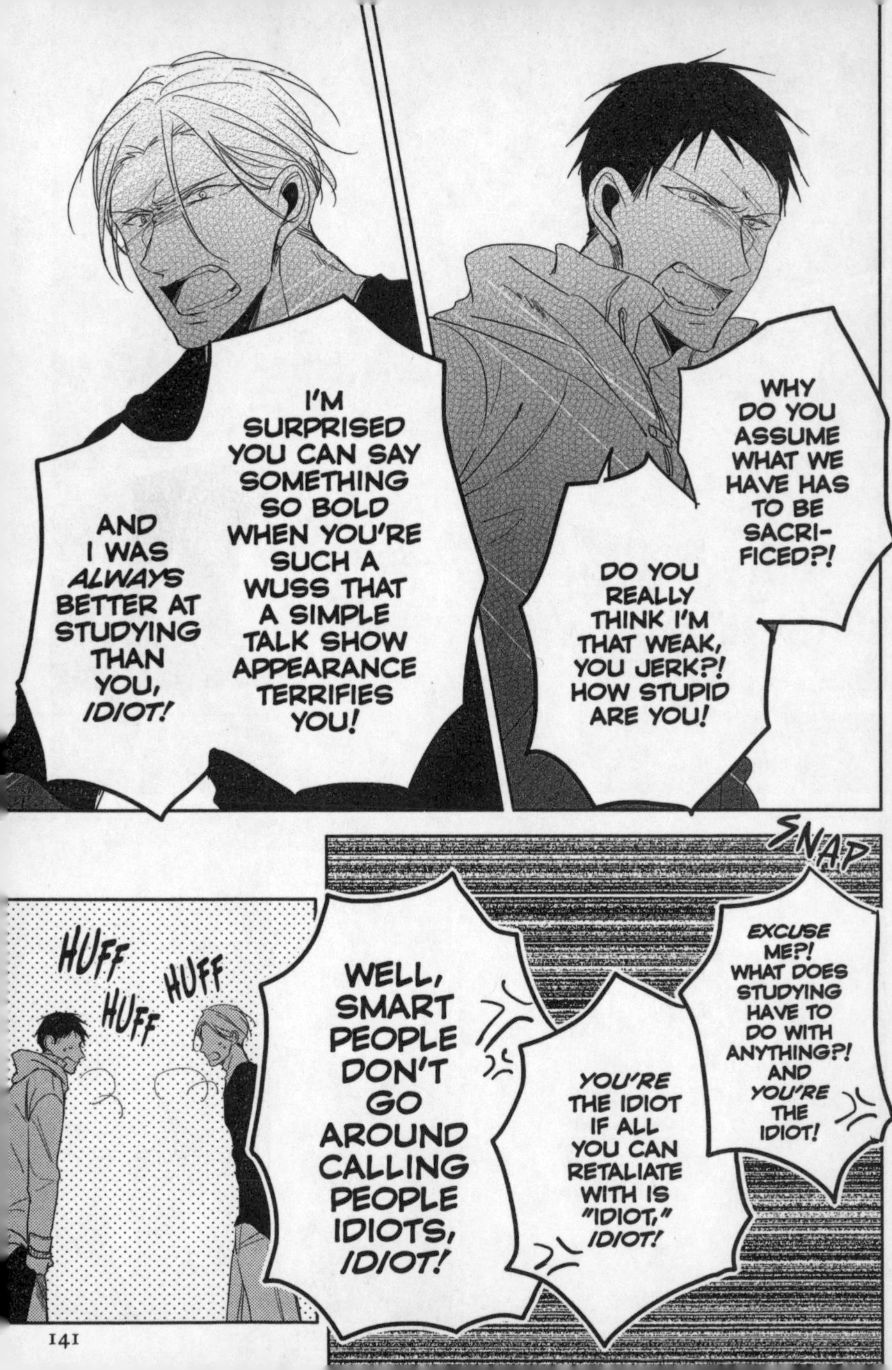
WHY DO YOU ASSUME WHAT WE HAVE HAS TO BE SACRI-FICED?!
DO YOU REALLY THINK I'M THAT WEAK, YOU JERK?! HOW STUPID ARE YOU!
I'M SURPRISED YOU CAN SAY SOMETHING SO BOLD WHEN YOU'RE SUCH A WUSS THAT A SIMPLE TALK SHOW APPEARANCE TERRIFIES YOU!
AND I WAS *ALWAYS* BETTER AT STUDYING THAN YOU, *IDIOT!*
SNAP
EXCUSE ME?! WHAT DOES STUDYING HAVE TO DO WITH ANYTHING?! AND *YOU'RE* THE IDIOT!
YOU'RE THE IDIOT IF ALL YOU CAN RETALIATE WITH IS "IDIOT," *IDIOT!*
WELL, SMART PEOPLE DON'T GO AROUND CALLING PEOPLE IDIOTS, *IDIOT!*
HUFF
HUFF
HUFF

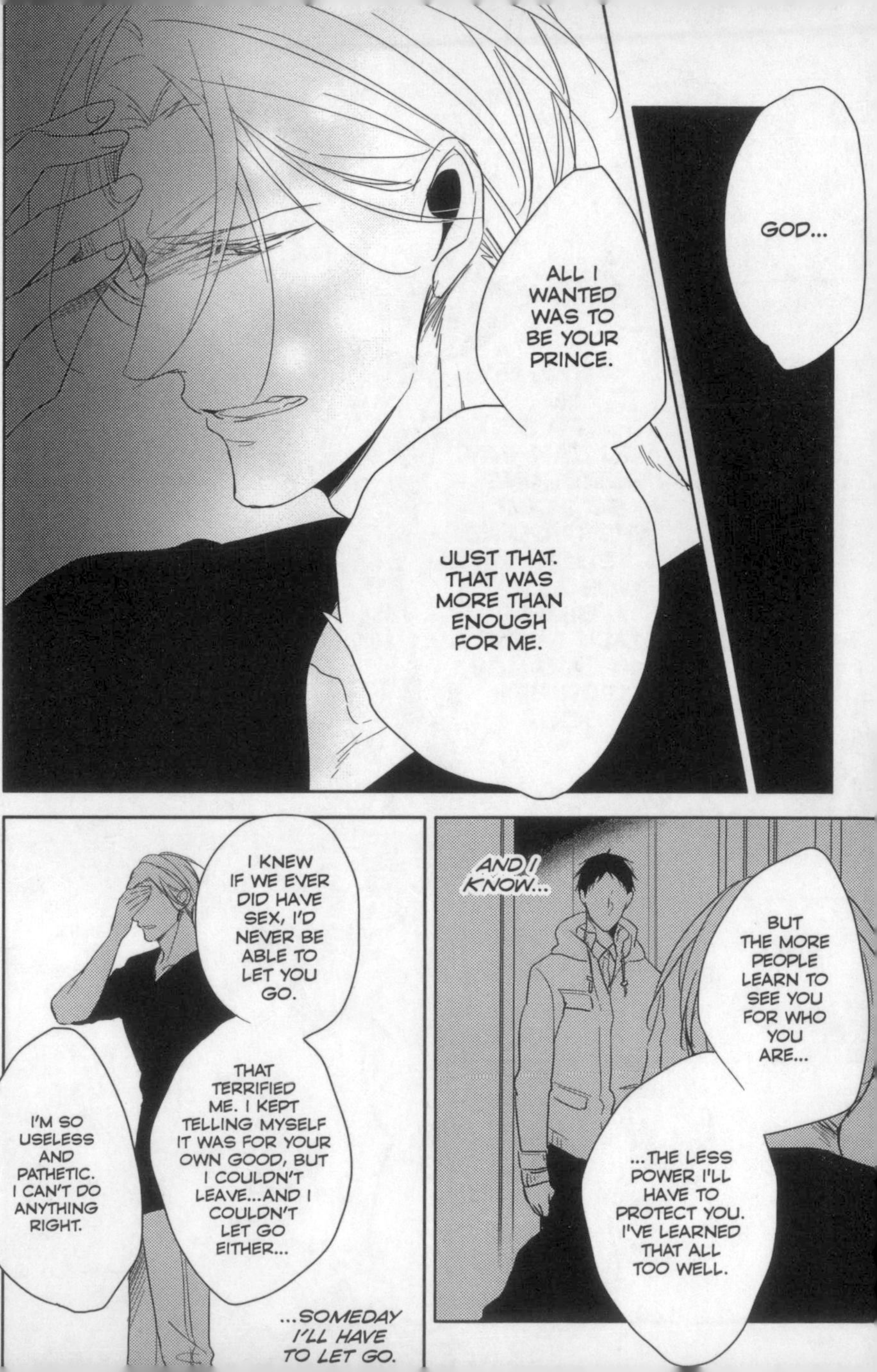
GOD...
ALL I WANTED WAS TO BE YOUR PRINCE.
JUST THAT. THAT WAS MORE THAN ENOUGH FOR ME.
BUT THE MORE PEOPLE LEARN TO SEE YOU FOR WHO YOU ARE...
...THE LESS POWER I'LL HAVE TO PROTECT YOU. I'VE LEARNED THAT ALL TOO WELL.
AND I KNOW...
I KNEW IF WE EVER DID HAVE SEX, I'D NEVER BE ABLE TO LET YOU GO.
THAT TERRIFIED ME. I KEPT TELLING MYSELF IT WAS FOR YOUR OWN GOOD, BUT I COULDN'T LEAVE...AND I COULDN'T LET GO EITHER...
I'M SO USELESS AND PATHETIC. I CAN'T DO ANYTHING RIGHT.
...SOMEDAY I'LL HAVE TO LET GO.

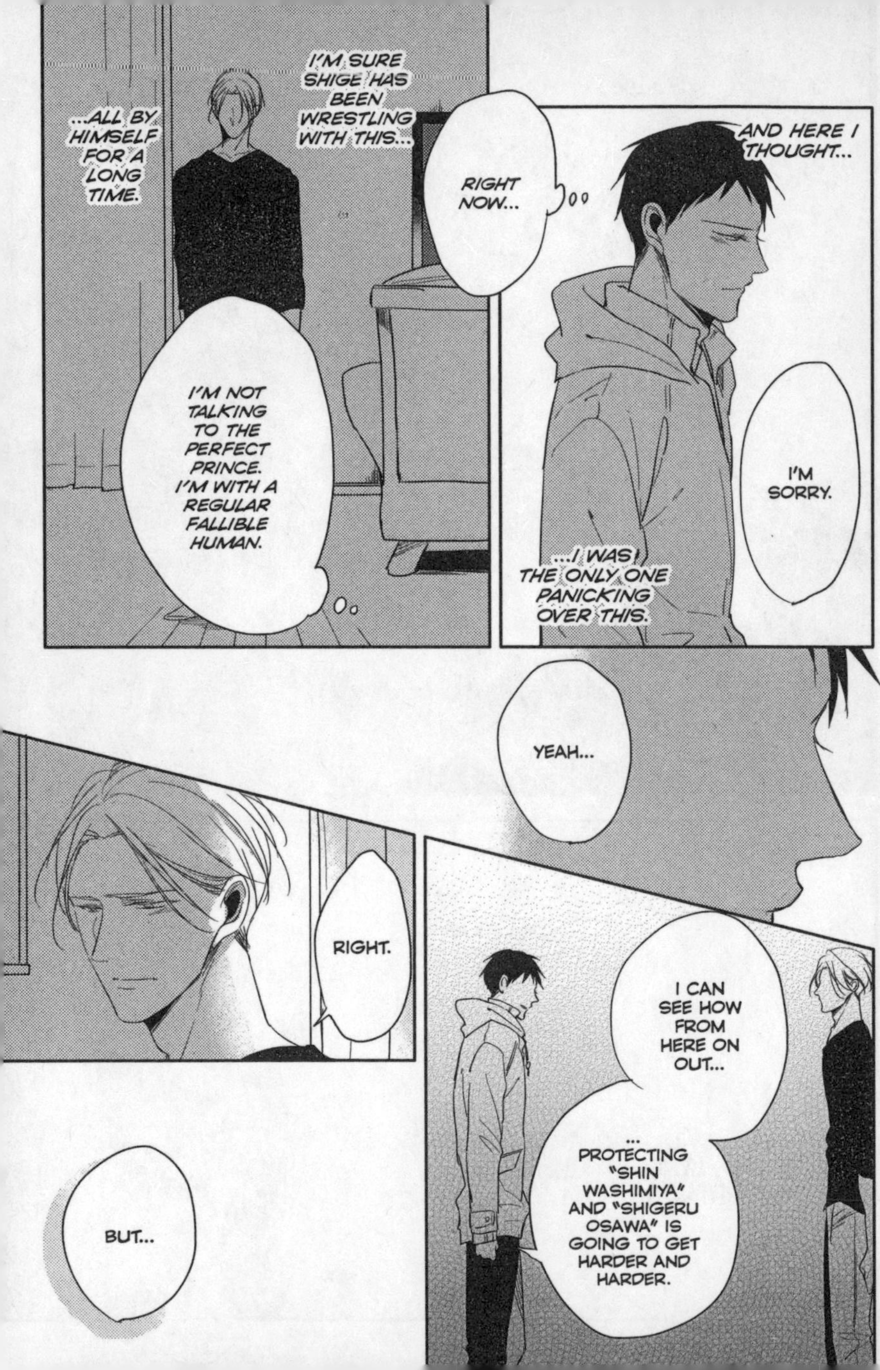
AND HERE I THOUGHT...
...I WAS THE ONLY ONE PANICKING OVER THIS.
I'M SORRY.
I'M SURE SHIGE HAS BEEN WRESTLING WITH THIS...
...ALL BY HIMSELF FOR A LONG TIME.
RIGHT NOW...
I'M NOT TALKING TO THE PERFECT PRINCE. I'M WITH A REGULAR FALLIBLE HUMAN.
YEAH...
RIGHT.
I CAN SEE HOW FROM HERE ON OUT...
...PROTECTING "SHIN WASHIMIYA" AND "SHIGERU OSAWA" IS GOING TO GET HARDER AND HARDER.
BUT...

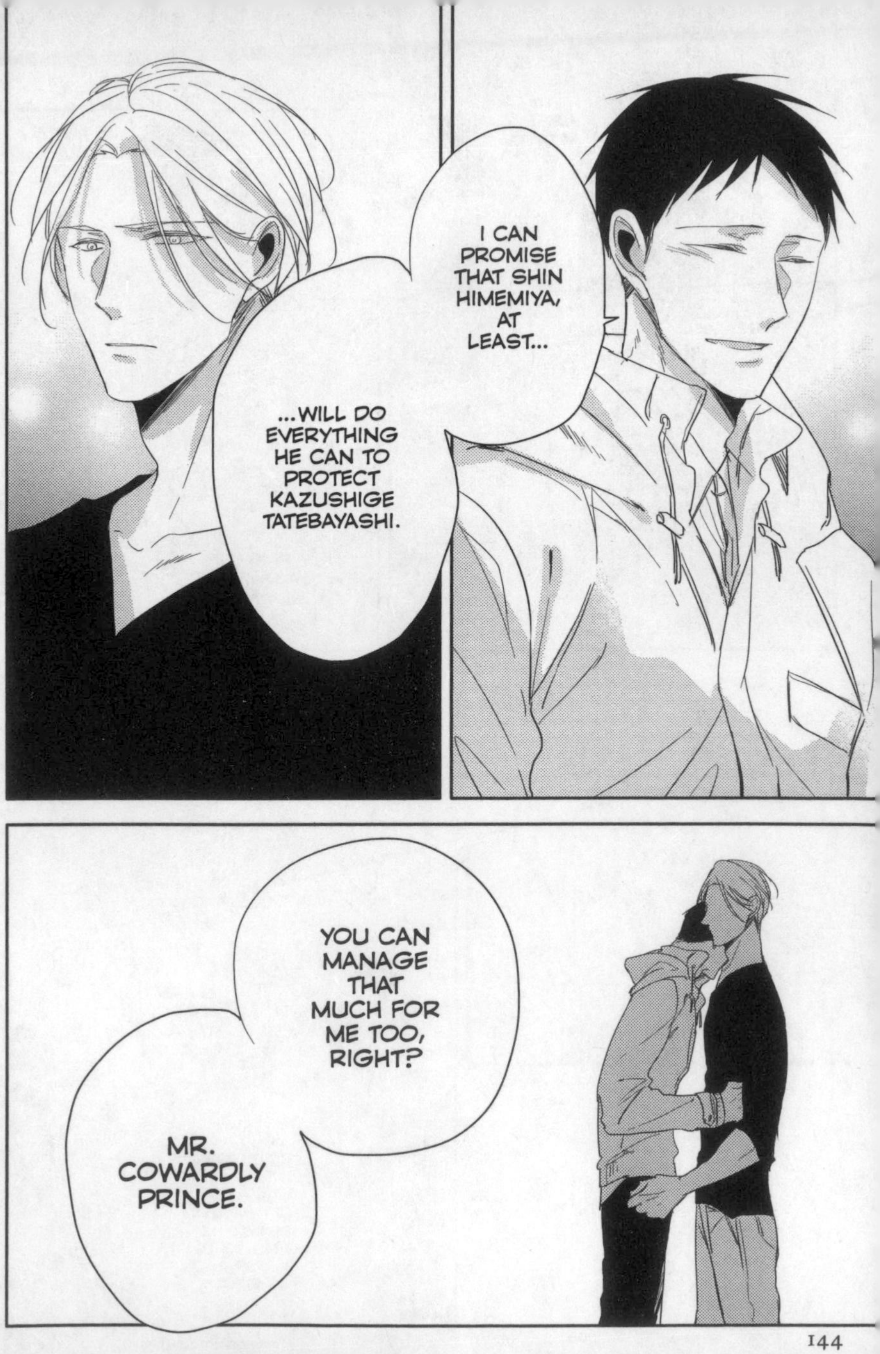
I CAN PROMISE THAT SHIN HIMEMIYA, AT LEAST...
...WILL DO EVERYTHING HE CAN TO PROTECT KAZUSHIGE TATEBAYASHI.
YOU CAN MANAGE THAT MUCH FOR ME TOO, RIGHT?
MR. COWARDLY PRINCE.

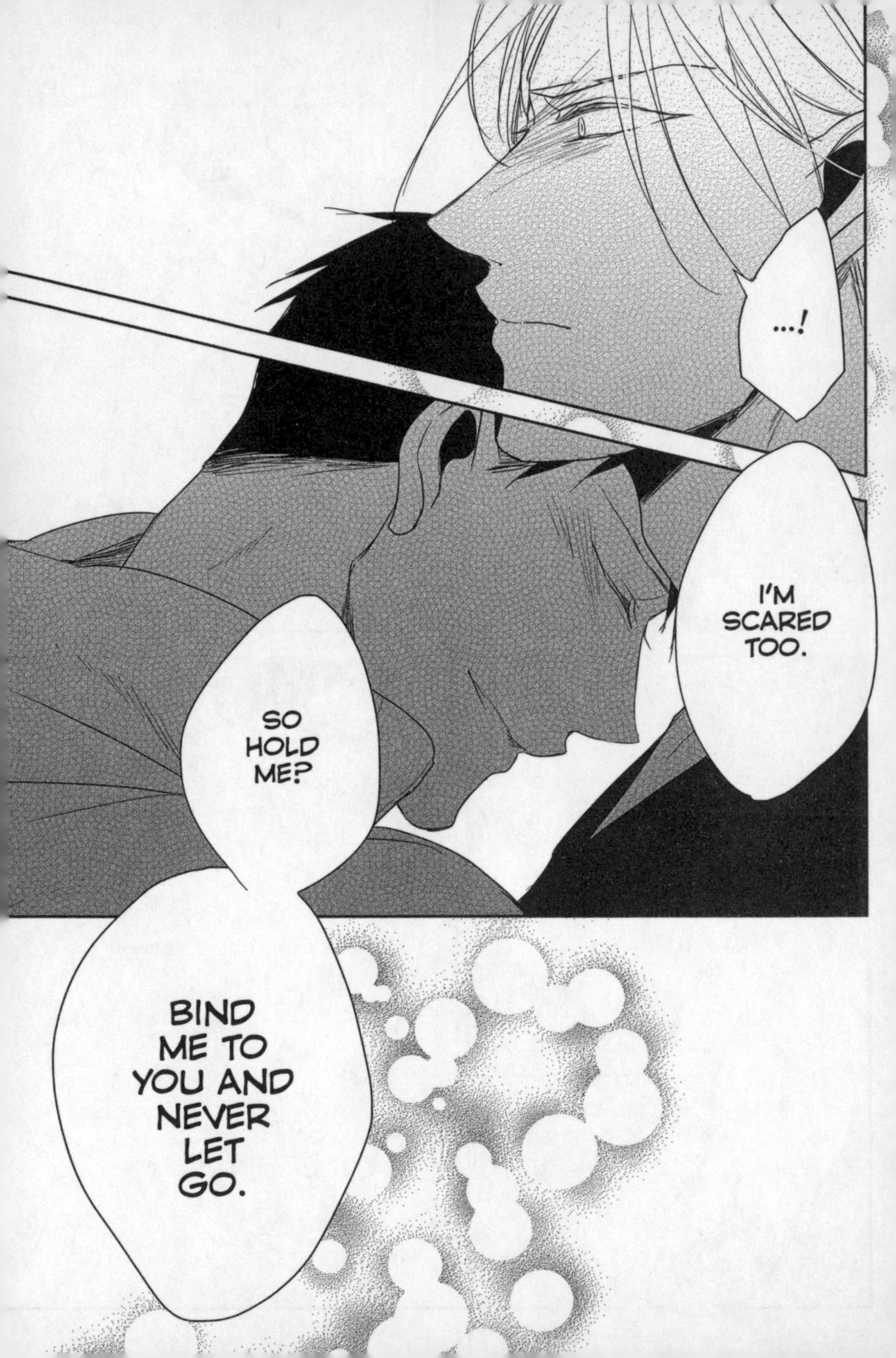
...!
I'M SCARED TOO.
SO HOLD ME?
BIND ME TO YOU AND NEVER LET GO.

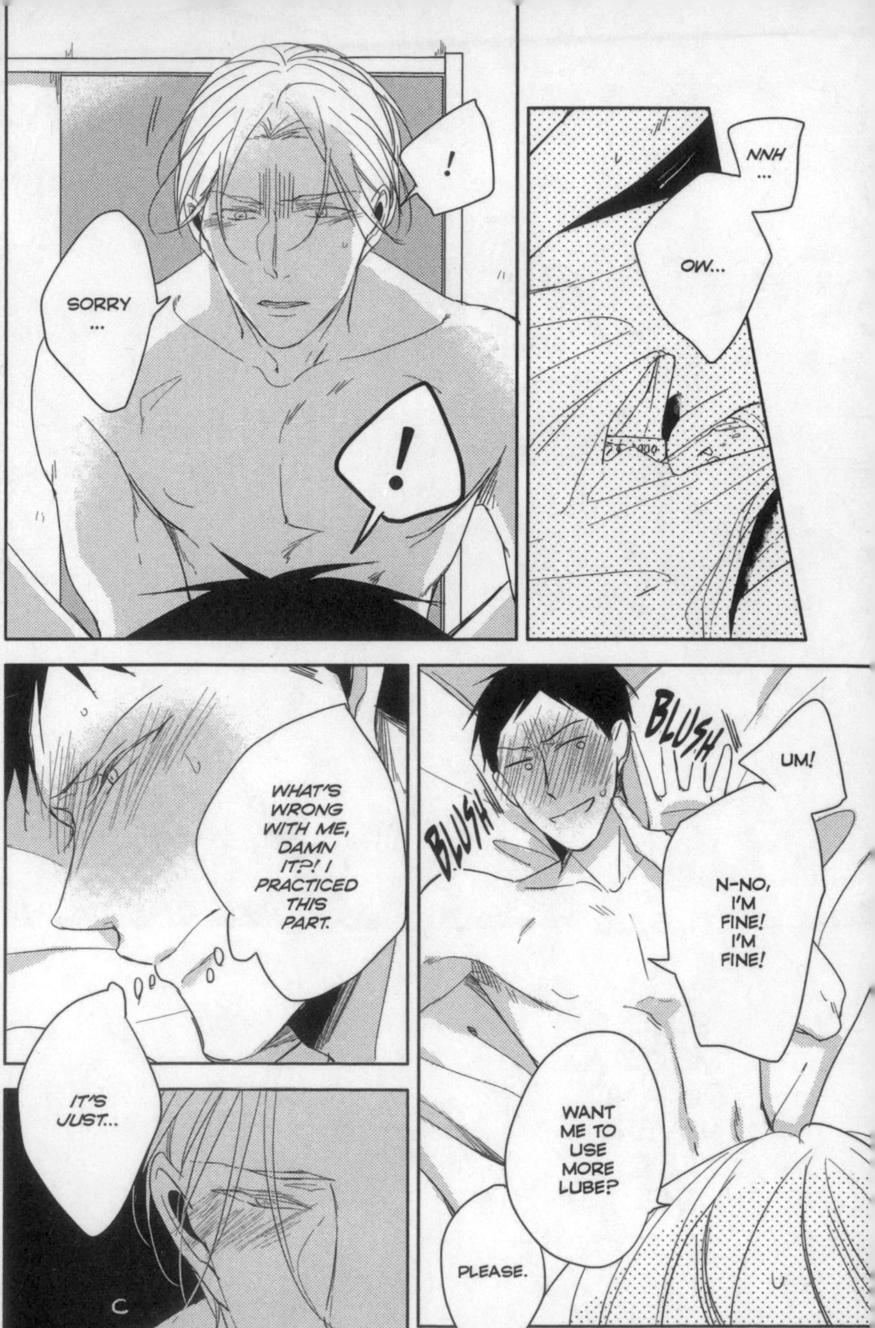
NNH ...
OW...
!
SORRY ...
!
BLUSH
UM!
BLUSH
N-NO, I'M FINE! I'M FINE!
WANT ME TO USE MORE LUBE?
PLEASE.
WHAT'S WRONG WITH ME, DAMN IT?! I PRACTICED THIS PART.
IT'S JUST...

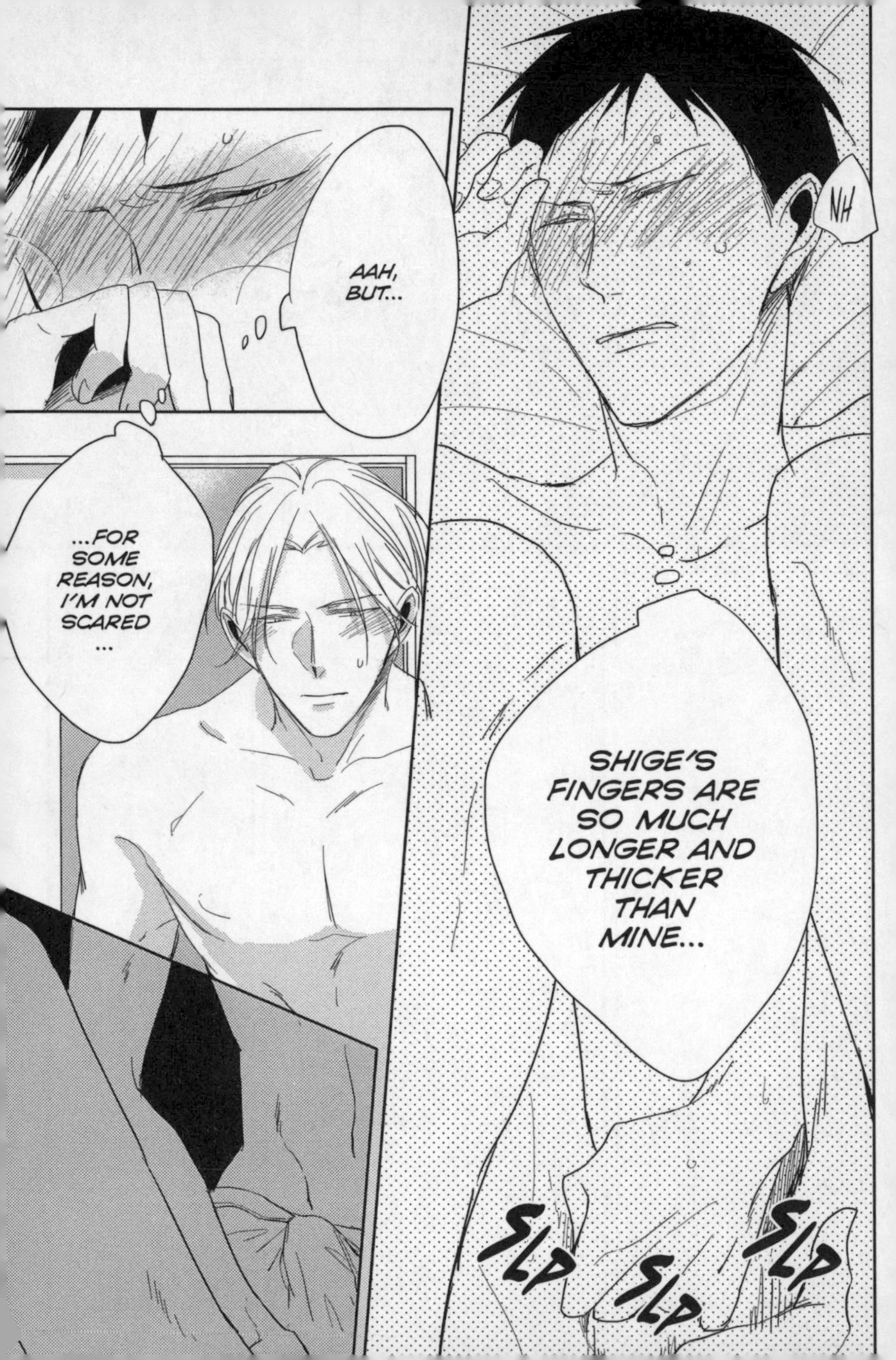
NH
SHIGE'S FINGERS ARE SO MUCH LONGER AND THICKER THAN MINE...
SLP SLP SLP SLP
AAH, BUT...
...FOR SOME REASON, I'M NOT SCARED ...

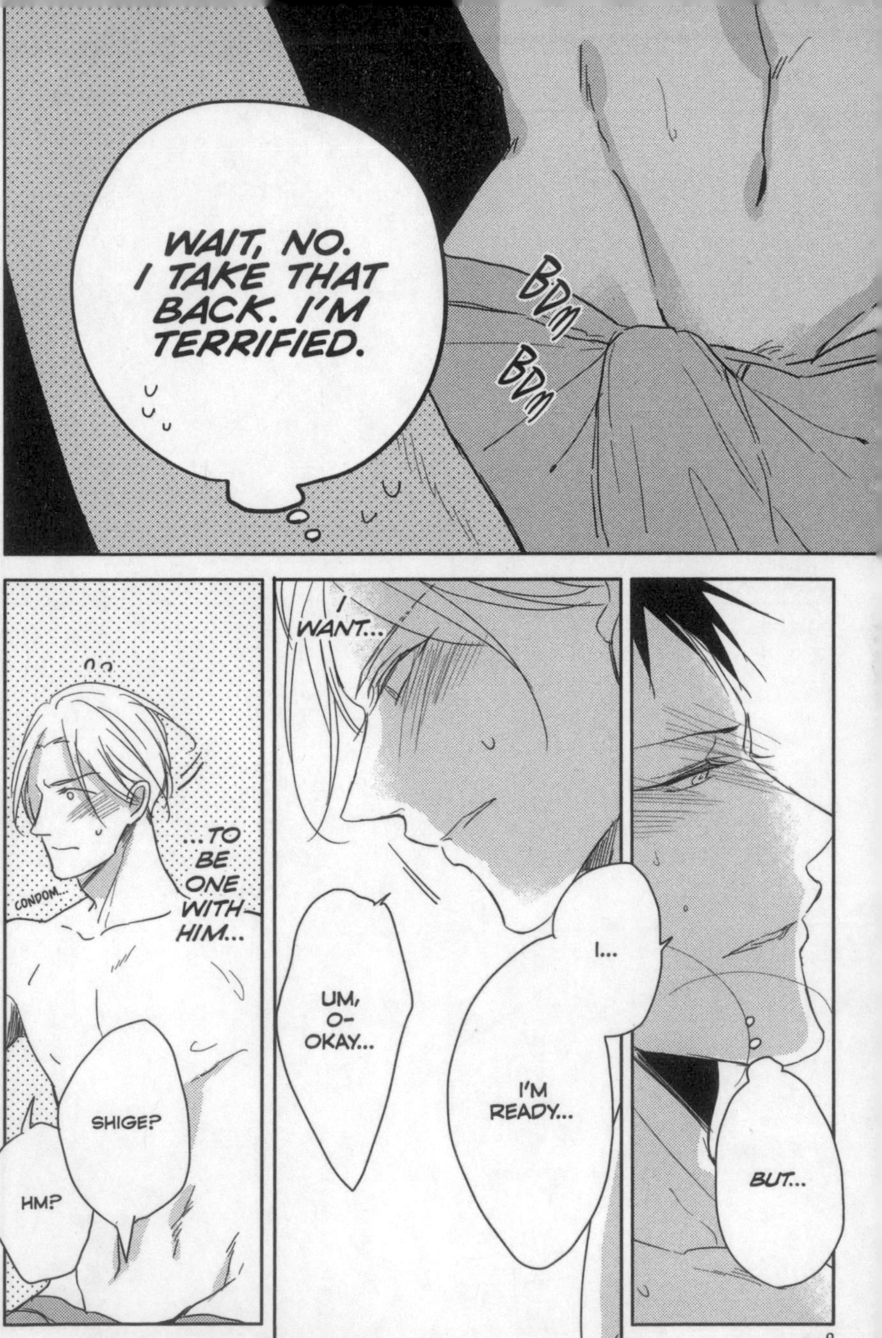
WAIT, NO. I TAKE THAT BACK. I'M TERRIFIED.
BDM BDM
I...
I'M READY...
BUT...
I WANT...
UM, O-OKAY...
...TO BE ONE WITH HIM...
CONDOM...
SHIGE?
HM?

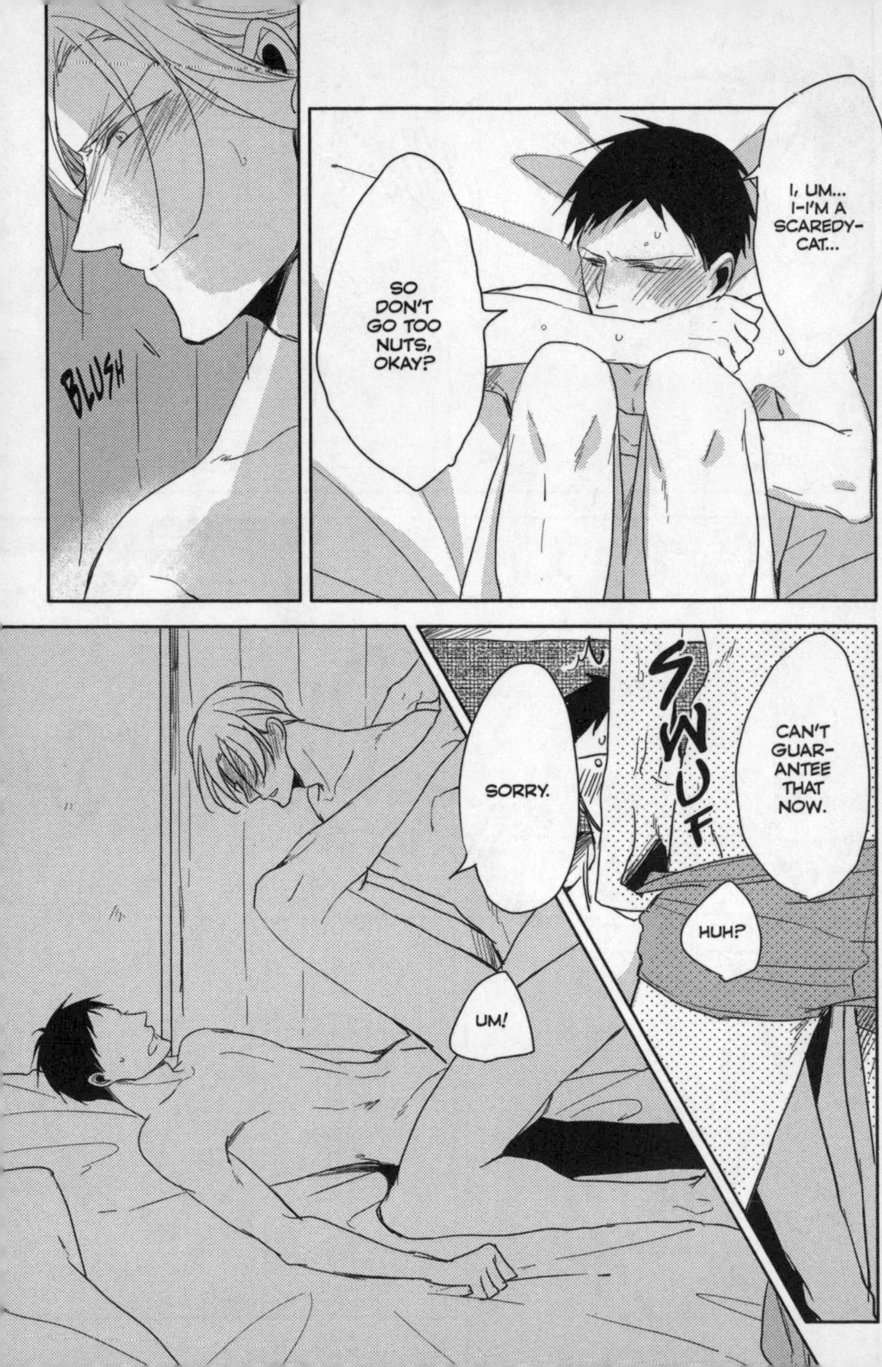
I, UM... I-I'M A SCAREDY-CAT...
SO DON'T GO TOO NUTS, OKAY?
BLUSH
CAN'T GUAR-ANTEE THAT NOW.
SWUF
HUH?
SORRY.
UM!

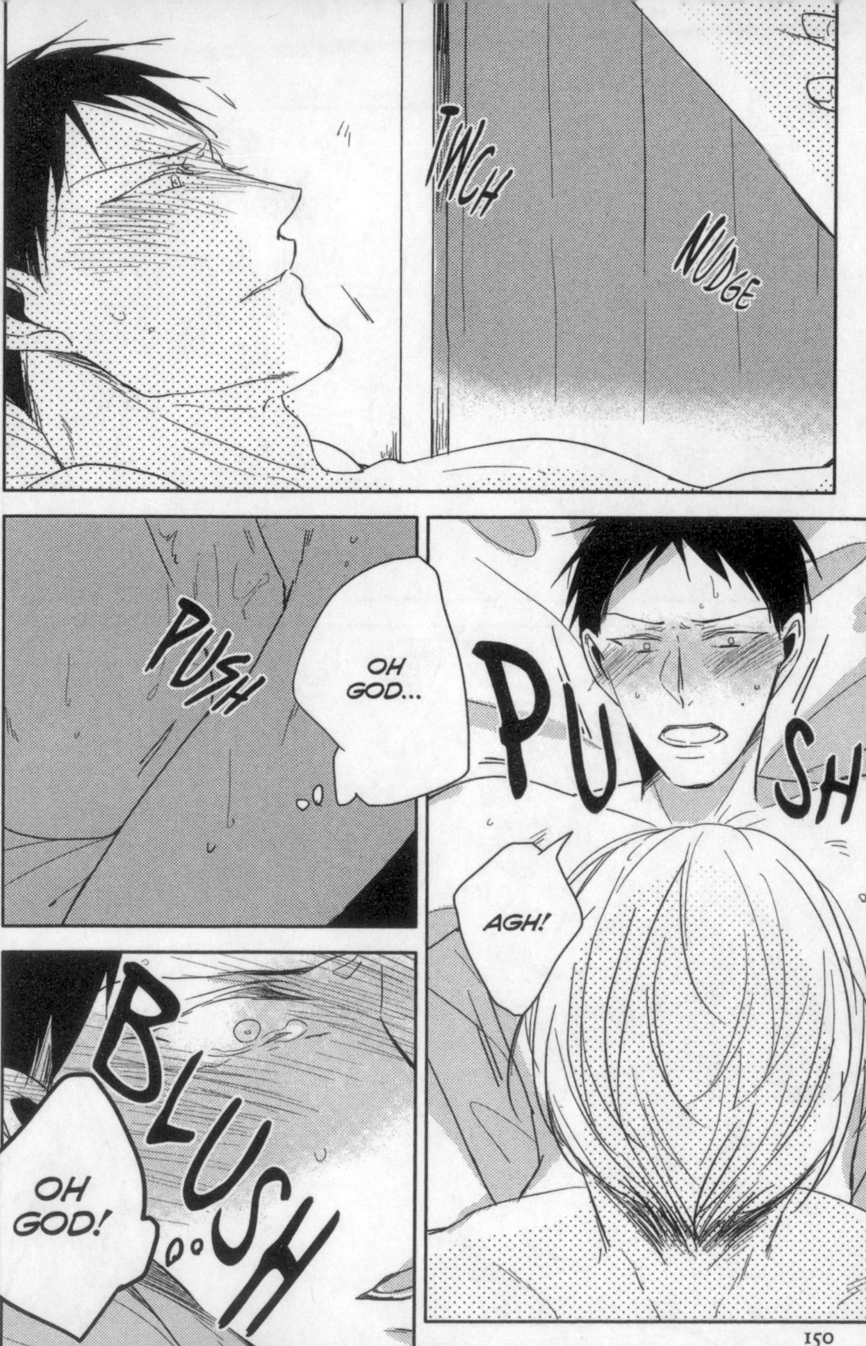
TWCH
NUDGE
PUSH
AGH!
PUSH
OH GOD...
BLUSH
OH GOD!

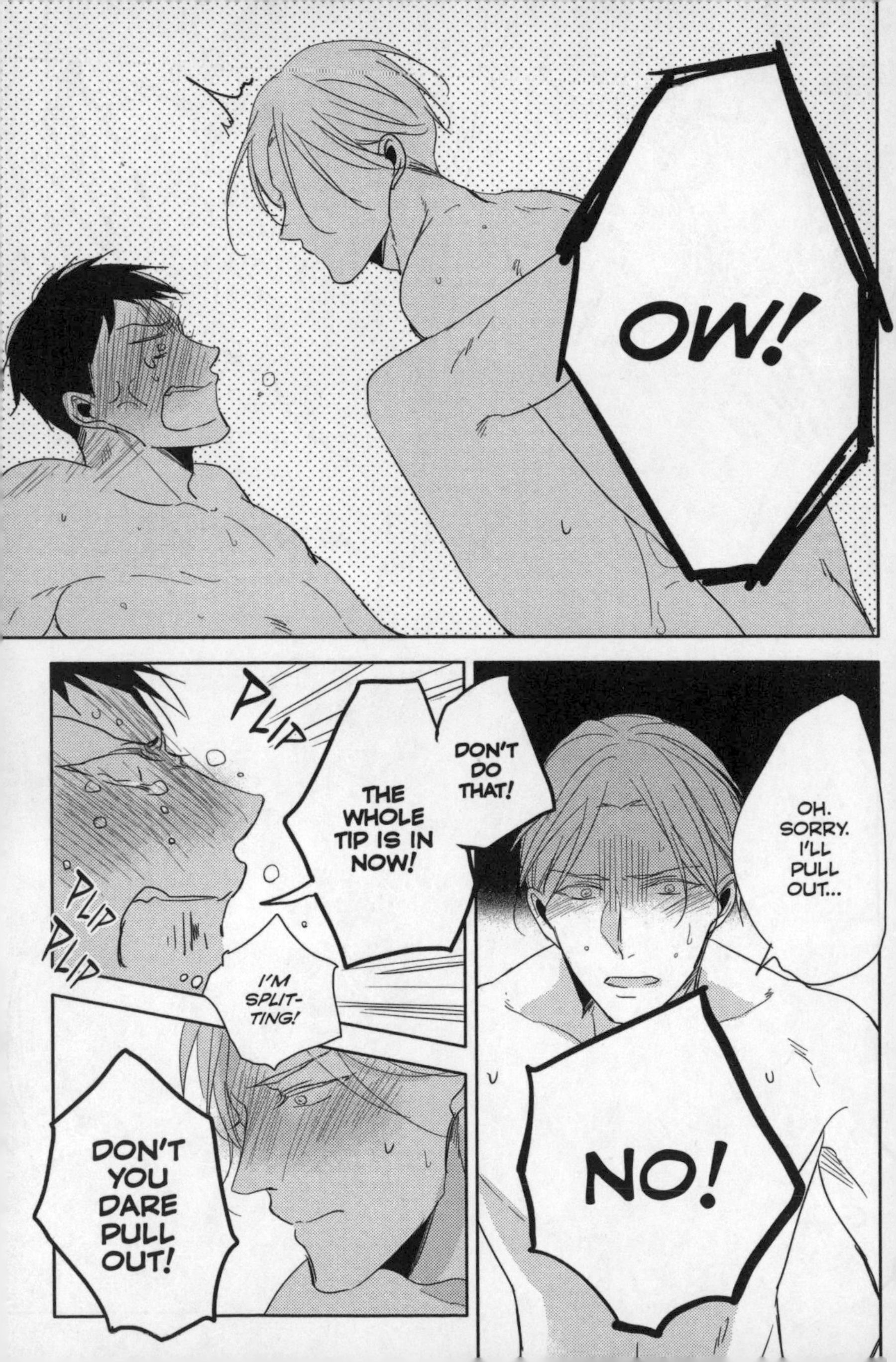
OW!
OH. SORRY. I'LL PULL OUT...
NO!
DON'T DO THAT!
THE WHOLE TIP IS IN NOW!
PLIP
PLIP PLIP
I'M SPLIT-TING!
DON'T YOU DARE PULL OUT!

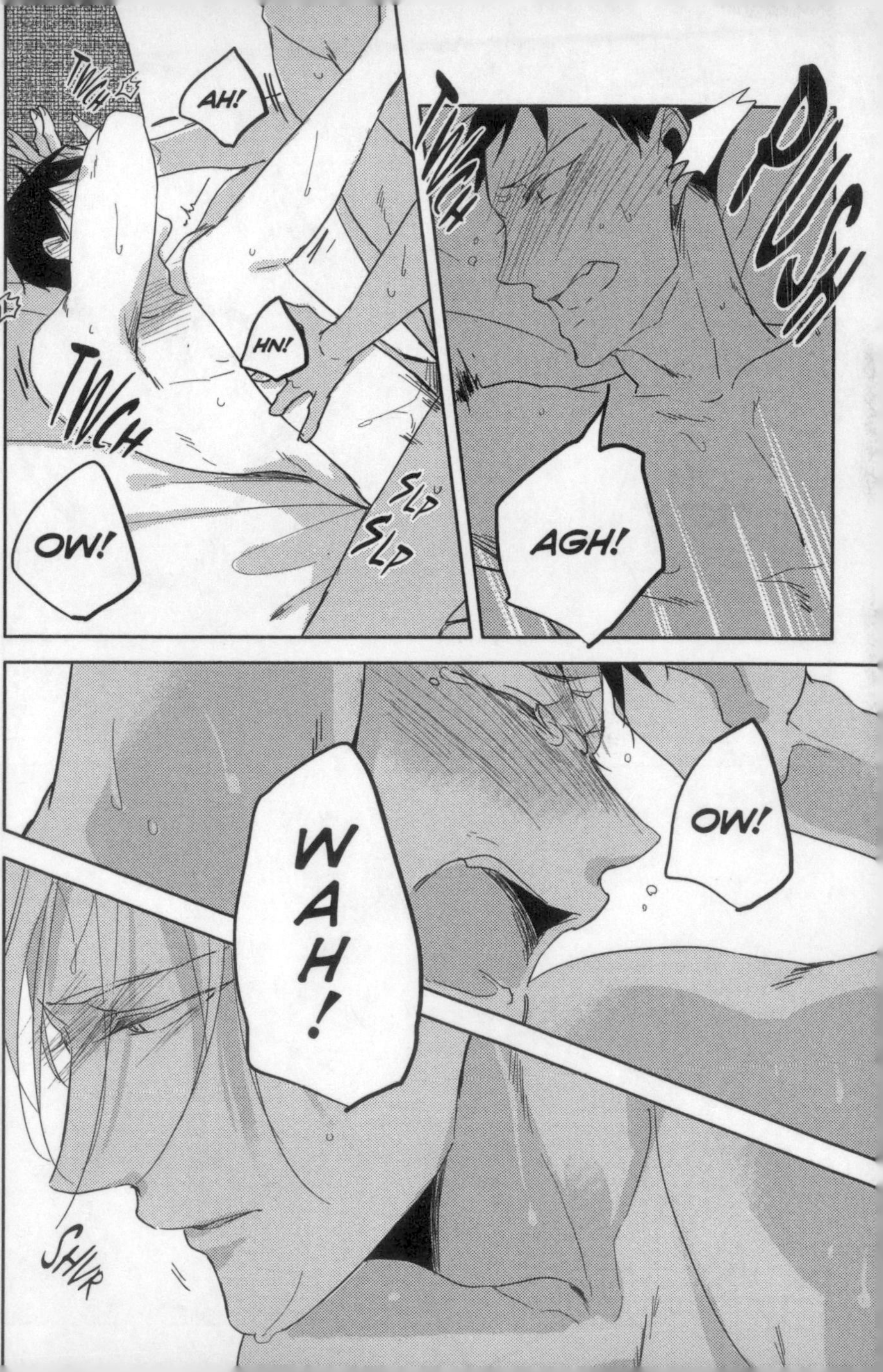
PUSH
TWCH
AGH!
AH!
TWCH
HN!
TWCH
SLP SLP
OW!
OW!
WAH!
SHVR

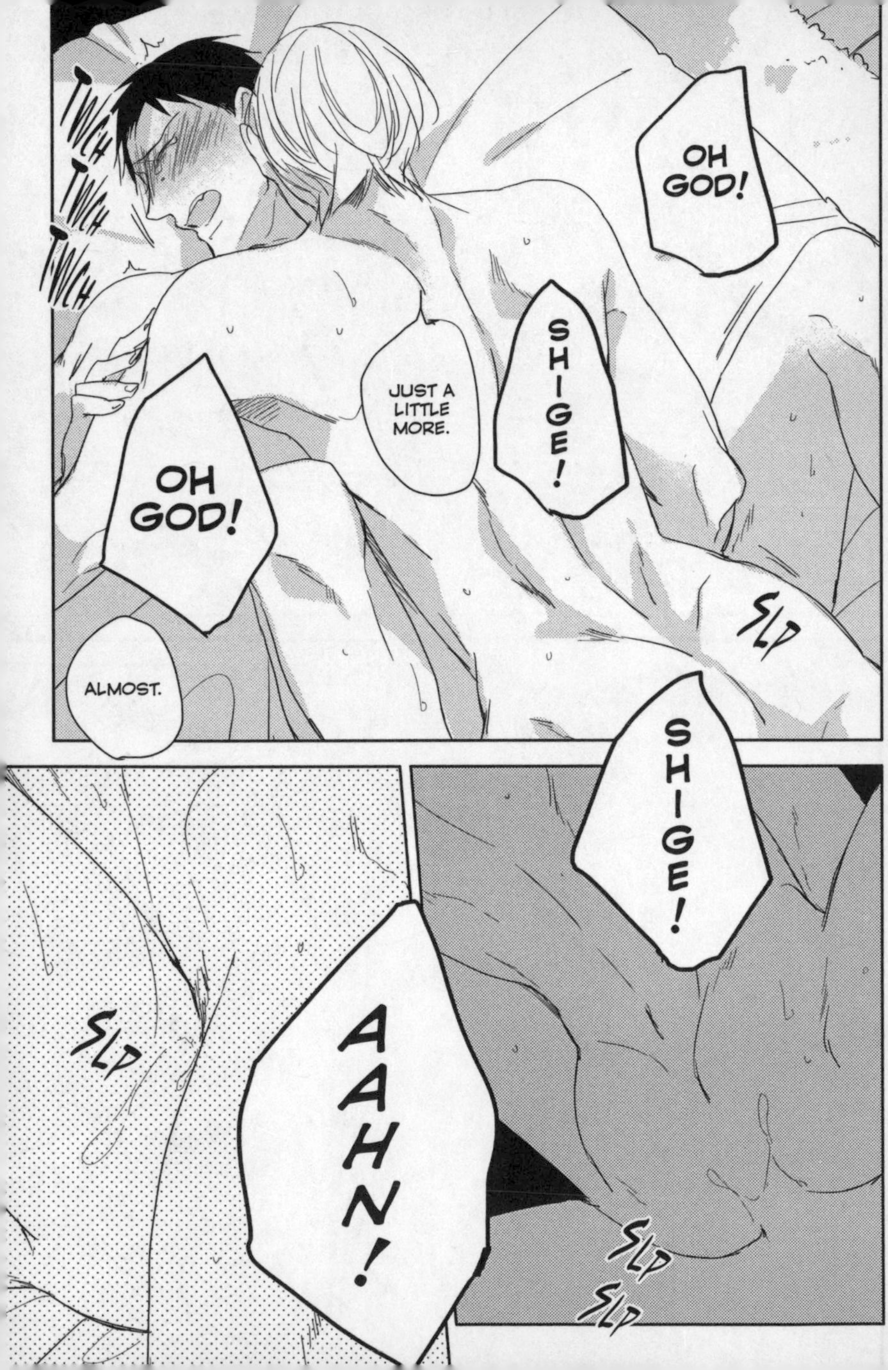
OH GOD!
SHIGE!
JUST A LITTLE MORE.
TWCH
TWCH
T-WCH
OH GOD!
SLP
ALMOST.
SHIGE!
AAHN!
SLP
SLP
SLP

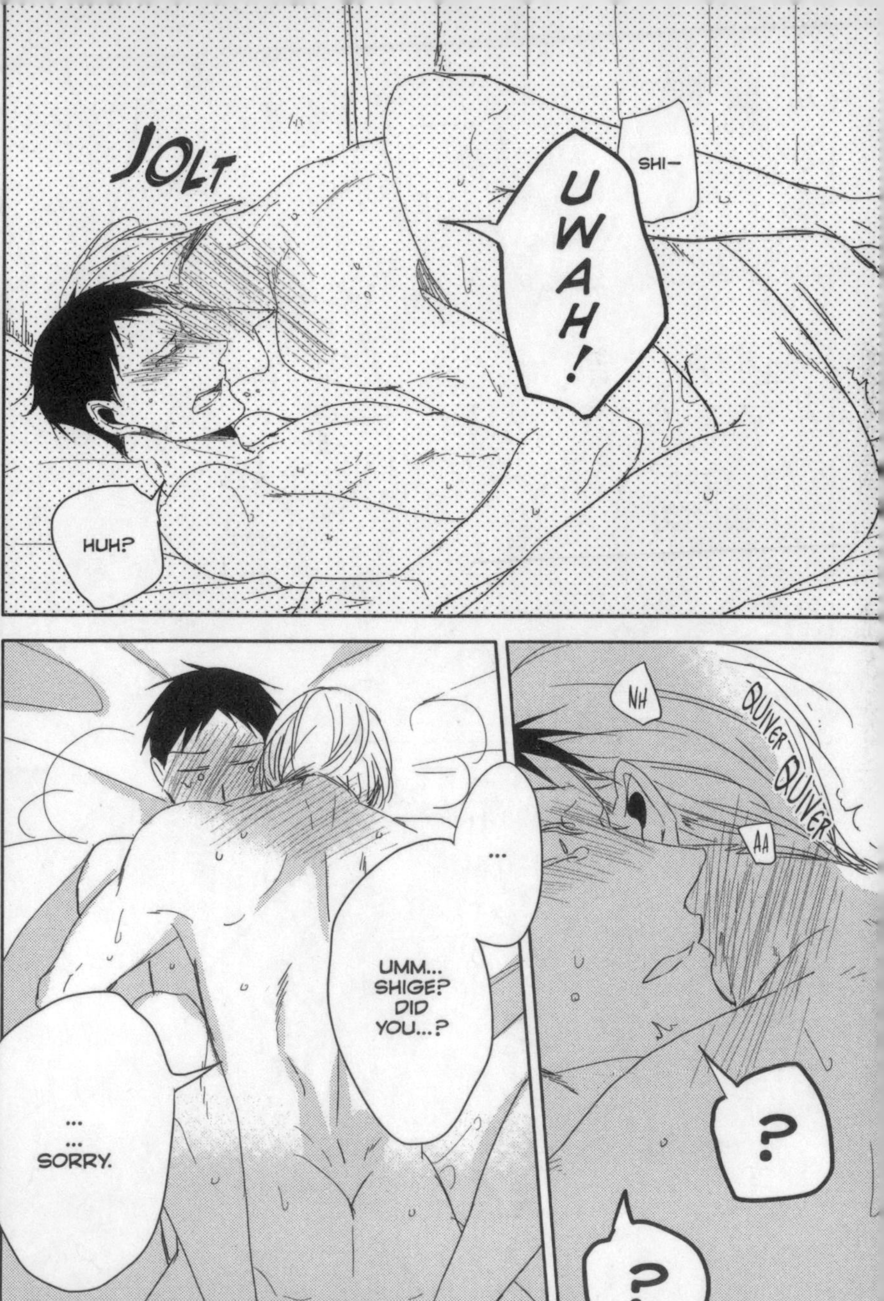
SHI—
UWAH!
JOLT
HUH?
NH
QUIVER QUIVER
AA
?
?
...
UMM... SHIGE? DID YOU...?
... ... SORRY.

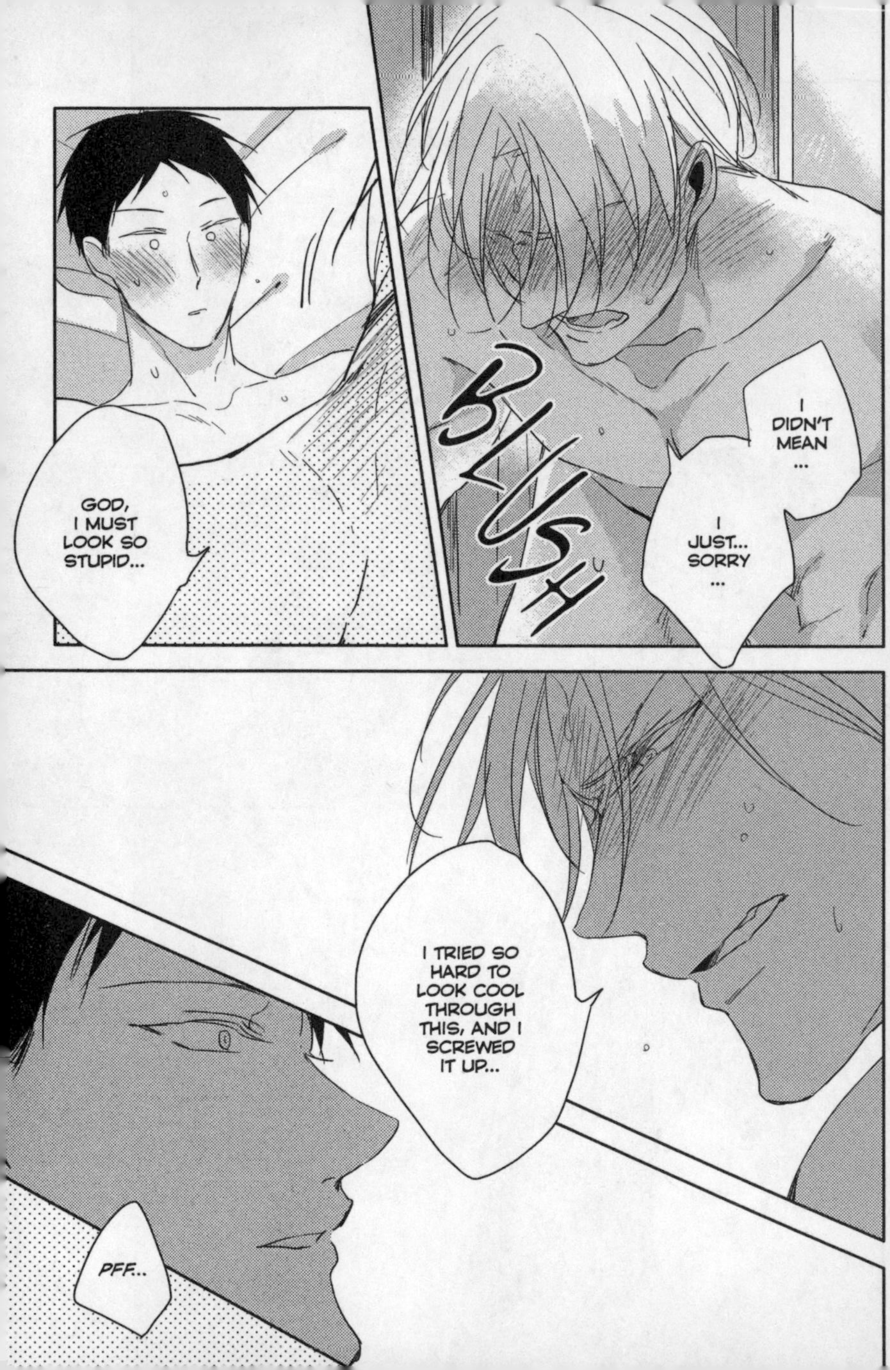
BLUSH
I DIDN'T MEAN ...
I JUST... SORRY ...
GOD, I MUST LOOK SO STUPID...
I TRIED SO HARD TO LOOK COOL THROUGH THIS, AND I SCREWED IT UP...
PFF...

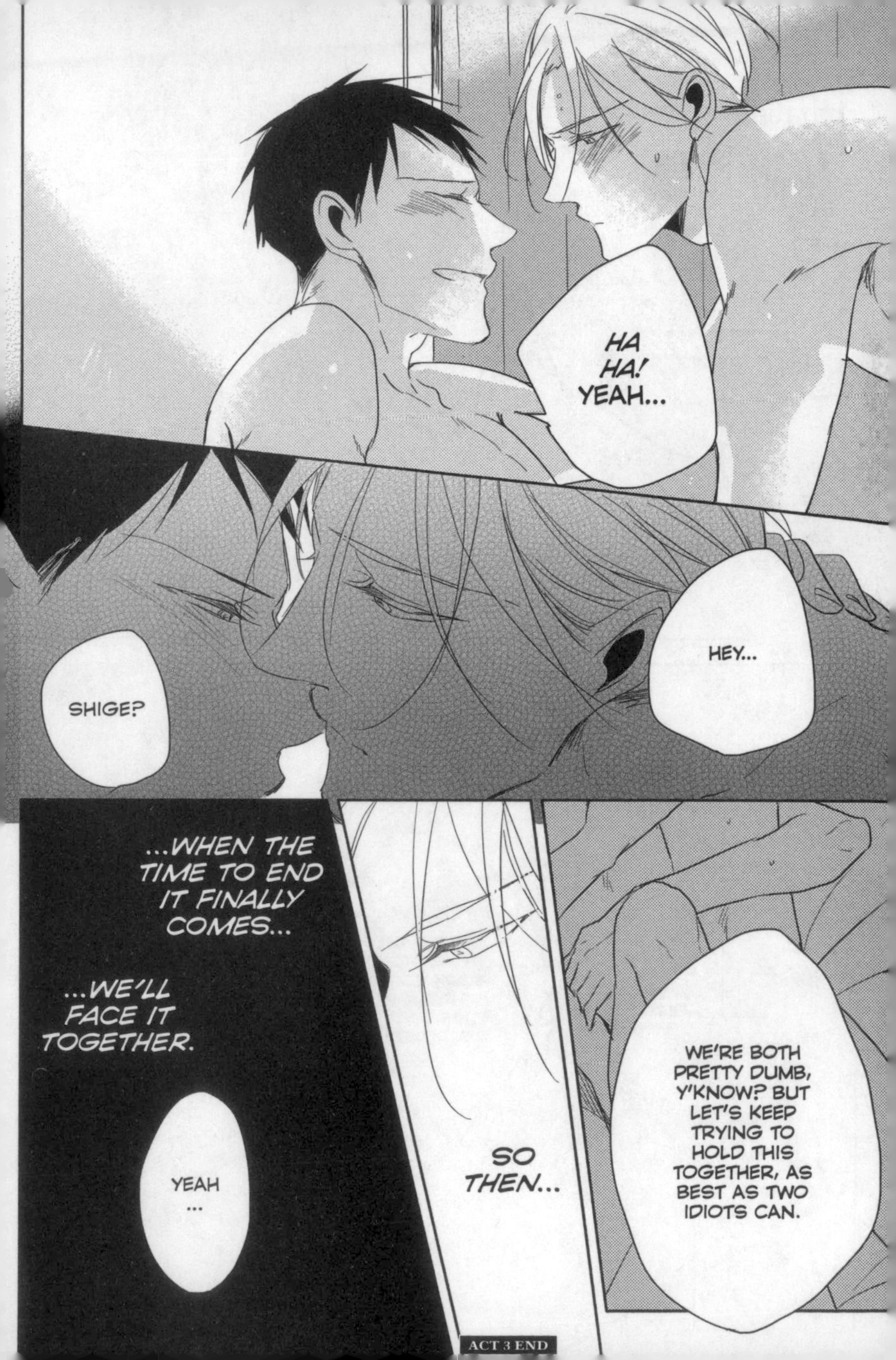
HA HA! YEAH...
HEY...
SHIGE?
WE'RE BOTH PRETTY DUMB, Y'KNOW? BUT LET'S KEEP TRYING TO HOLD THIS TOGETHER, AS BEST AS TWO IDIOTS CAN.
SO THEN...
...WHEN THE TIME TO END IT FINALLY COMES...
...WE'LL FACE IT TOGETHER.
YEAH ...
ACT 3 END

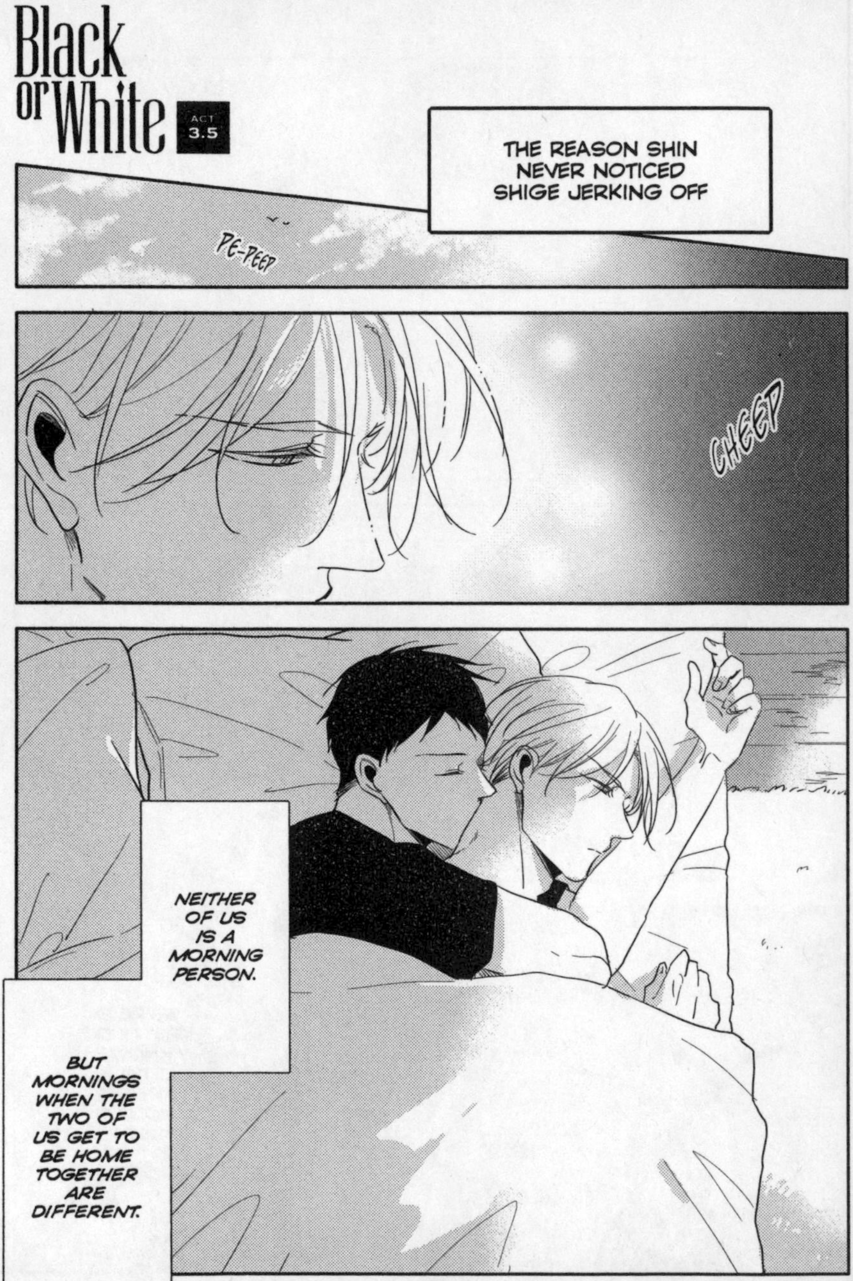
Black or White
ACT 3.5
THE REASON SHIN NEVER NOTICED SHIGE JERKING OFF
PE-PEEP
CHEEP
NEITHER OF US IS A MORNING PERSON.
BUT MORNINGS WHEN THE TWO OF US GET TO BE HOME TOGETHER ARE DIFFERENT.

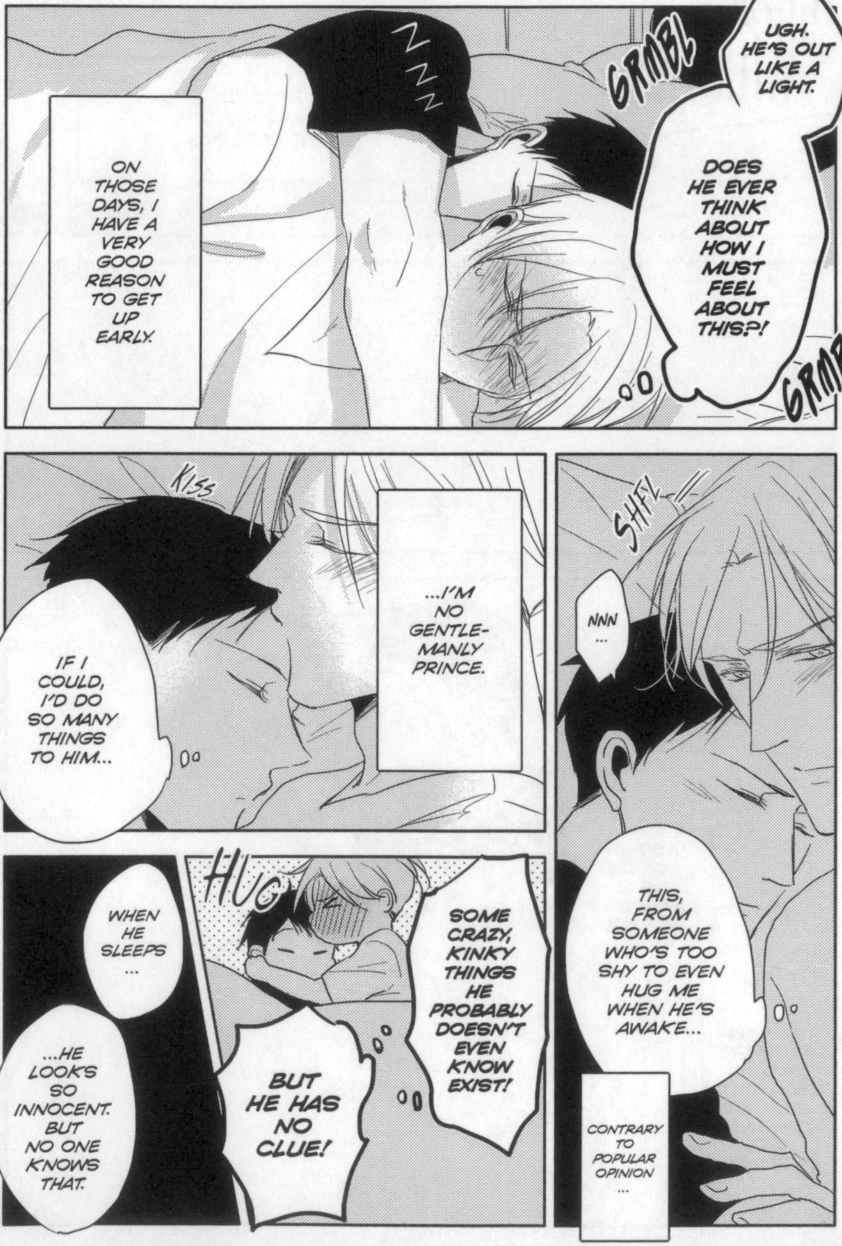
UGH. HE'S OUT LIKE A LIGHT.
GRMBL
DOES HE EVER THINK ABOUT HOW I MUST FEEL ABOUT THIS?!
GRMBL
ON THOSE DAYS, I HAVE A VERY GOOD REASON TO GET UP EARLY.
SHFL
NNN...
THIS, FROM SOMEONE WHO'S TOO SHY TO EVEN HUG ME WHEN HE'S AWAKE...
CONTRARY TO POPULAR OPINION...
KISS
...I'M NO GENTLE-MANLY PRINCE.
IF I COULD, I'D DO SO MANY THINGS TO HIM...
HUG
SOME CRAZY, KINKY THINGS HE PROBABLY DOESN'T EVEN KNOW EXIST!
BUT HE HAS NO CLUE!
WHEN HE SLEEPS...
...HE LOOKS SO INNOCENT. BUT NO ONE KNOWS THAT.

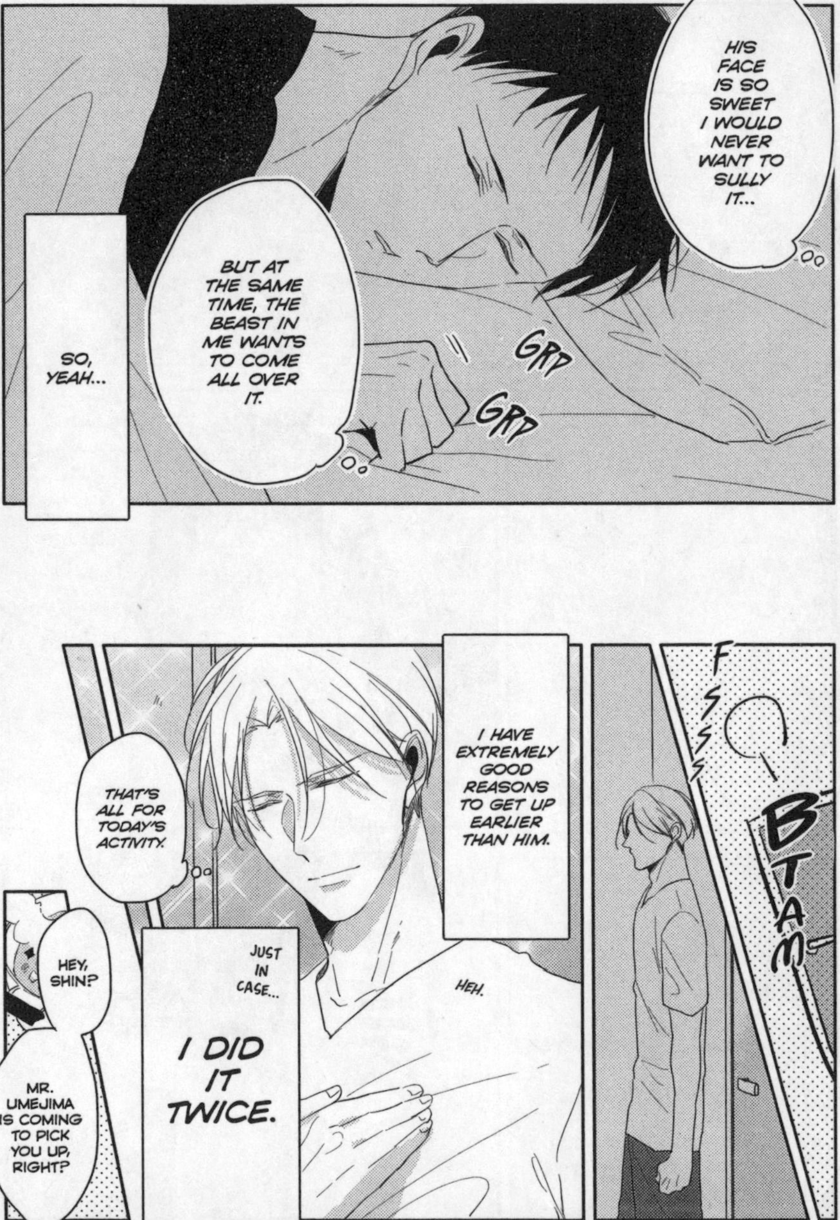
HIS FACE IS SO SWEET I WOULD NEVER WANT TO SULLY IT...
BUT AT THE SAME TIME, THE BEAST IN ME WANTS TO COME ALL OVER IT.
GRP
GRP
SO, YEAH...
FSSS
BTAM
I HAVE EXTREMELY GOOD REASONS TO GET UP EARLIER THAN HIM.
THAT'S ALL FOR TODAY'S ACTIVITY.
HEH.
JUST IN CASE...
I DID IT TWICE.
HEY, SHIN?
MR. UMEJIMA IS COMING TO PICK YOU UP, RIGHT?

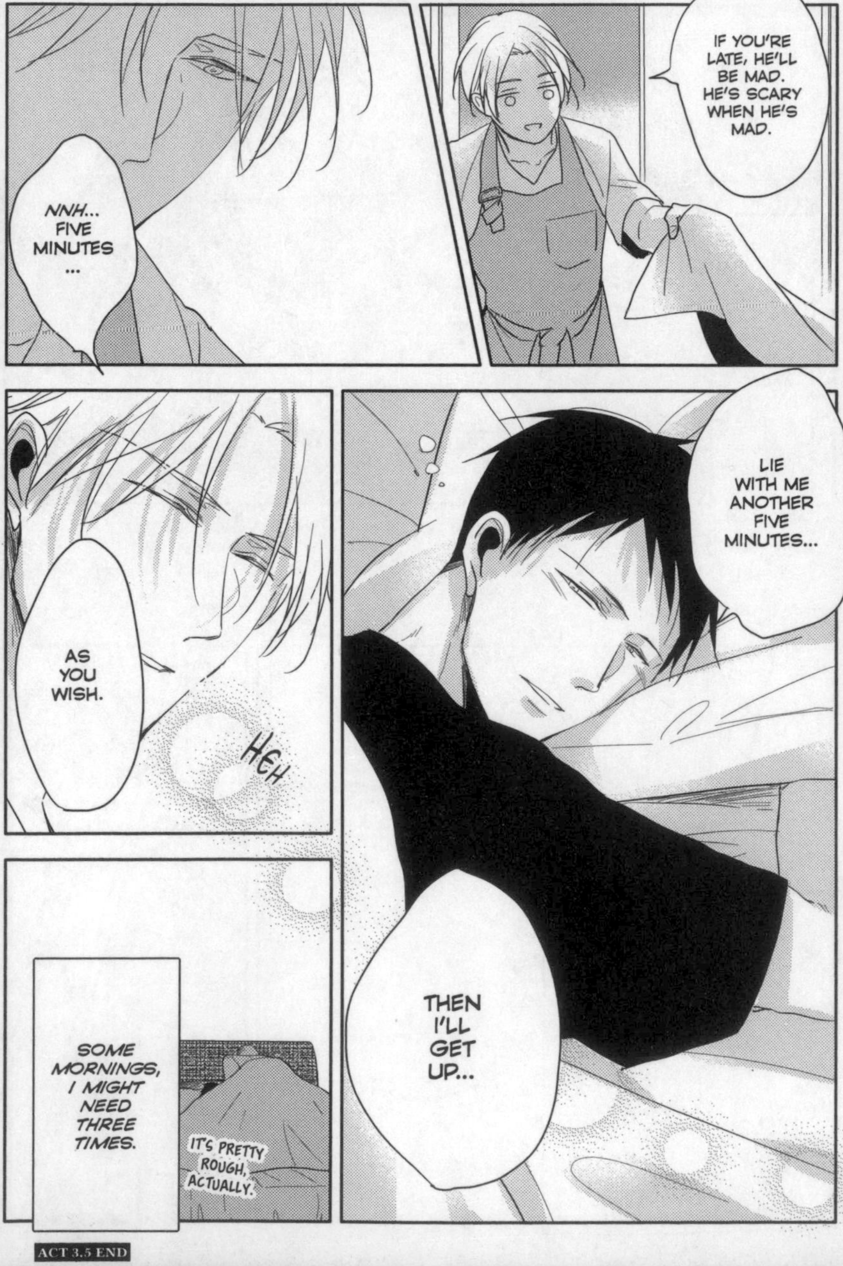
IF YOU'RE LATE, HE'LL BE MAD. HE'S SCARY WHEN HE'S MAD.
NNH... FIVE MINUTES ...
LIE WITH ME ANOTHER FIVE MINUTES...
THEN I'LL GET UP...
AS YOU WISH.
HEH
SOME MORNINGS, I MIGHT NEED THREE TIMES.
IT'S PRETTY ROUGH, ACTUALLY.

ACT 3.5 END

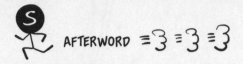

AFTERWORD

THIS IS THE FIRST SERIES I'VE PUBLISHED WITH KADOKAWA! YAY! AND HI. I'M SACHIMO.

THERE ARE ALL SORTS OF JOBS ONE CAN HAVE IN THIS WORLD.

ALTHOUGH I'M FORTUNATE ENOUGH TO BE A MANGA CREATOR, I'VE LONG HAD INTEREST IN THE WORLD OF CELEBRITIES. FOR PEOPLE WHO HAVE A LOT OF SECRETS, THEY'RE LEFT WITH LITTLE PRIVACY. I DON'T THINK THERE'S A CAREER OUT THERE AS BLATANTLY UNFAIR AS THEIRS.

I PLANNED FROM THE START FOR THIS TO BE VOLUME 1 OF A LONGER SERIES, A FIRST FOR ME. IT'S ALSO THE FIRST SERIES WHERE MY TWO LEADS START OUT AS A COUPLE. I'M FEELING A LOT OF THINGS OUT FOR THE FIRST TIME, BUT IT LOOKS LIKE THIS IS GOING TO BE A LOT OF FUN!

I'D BE HONORED IF YOU WOULD STICK AROUND FOR THIS SOMEWHAT LONGER RIDE!

さちも.
SACHIMO

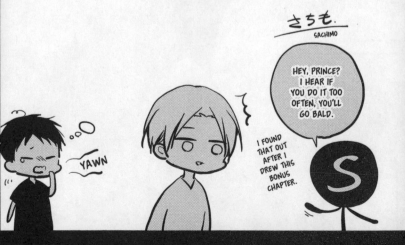

HEY, PRINCE? I HEAR IF YOU DO IT TOO OFTEN, YOU'LL GO BALD.

YAWN

I FOUND THAT OUT AFTER I DREW THIS BONUS CHAPTER.

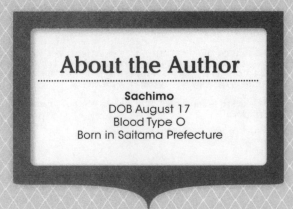

About the Author

Sachimo
DOB August 17
Blood Type O
Born in Saitama Prefecture

Black or White
Volume 1
SuBLime Manga Edition

Story and Art by **Sachimo**

Translation—**Adrienne Beck**
Touch-Up Art and Lettering—**Deborah Fisher**
Cover and Graphic Design—**Shawn Carrico**
Editor—**Jennifer LeBlanc**

First published in Japan in 2018 by KADOKAWA CORPORATION, Tokyo.
English translation rights arranged with KADOKAWA CORPORATION, Tokyo.

ASUKA COMICS CL DX

Printed in the U.S.A.

Published by SuBLime Manga
P.O. Box 77010
San Francisco, CA 94107

10 9 8 7 6 5 4 3 2 1
First printing, September 2021

M MATURE
PARENTAL ADVISORY
BLACK OR WHITE is rated M for Mature and is recommended for mature readers. This volume contains graphic imagery and mature themes.

SUBLIME
www.SuBLimeManga.com

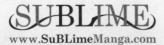

For more information

on all our products, along with the most up-to-date news on releases, series announcements, and contests, please visit us at:

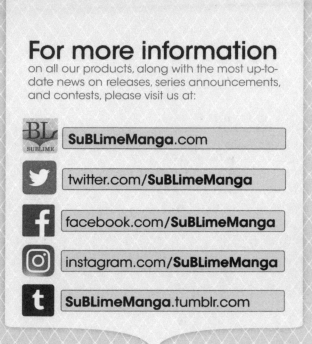

BL SUBLIME — **SuBLimeManga**.com

🐦 twitter.com/**SuBLimeManga**

f facebook.com/**SuBLimeManga**

📷 instagram.com/**SuBLimeManga**

t **SuBLimeManga**.tumblr.com

SUBLIME
MANGA

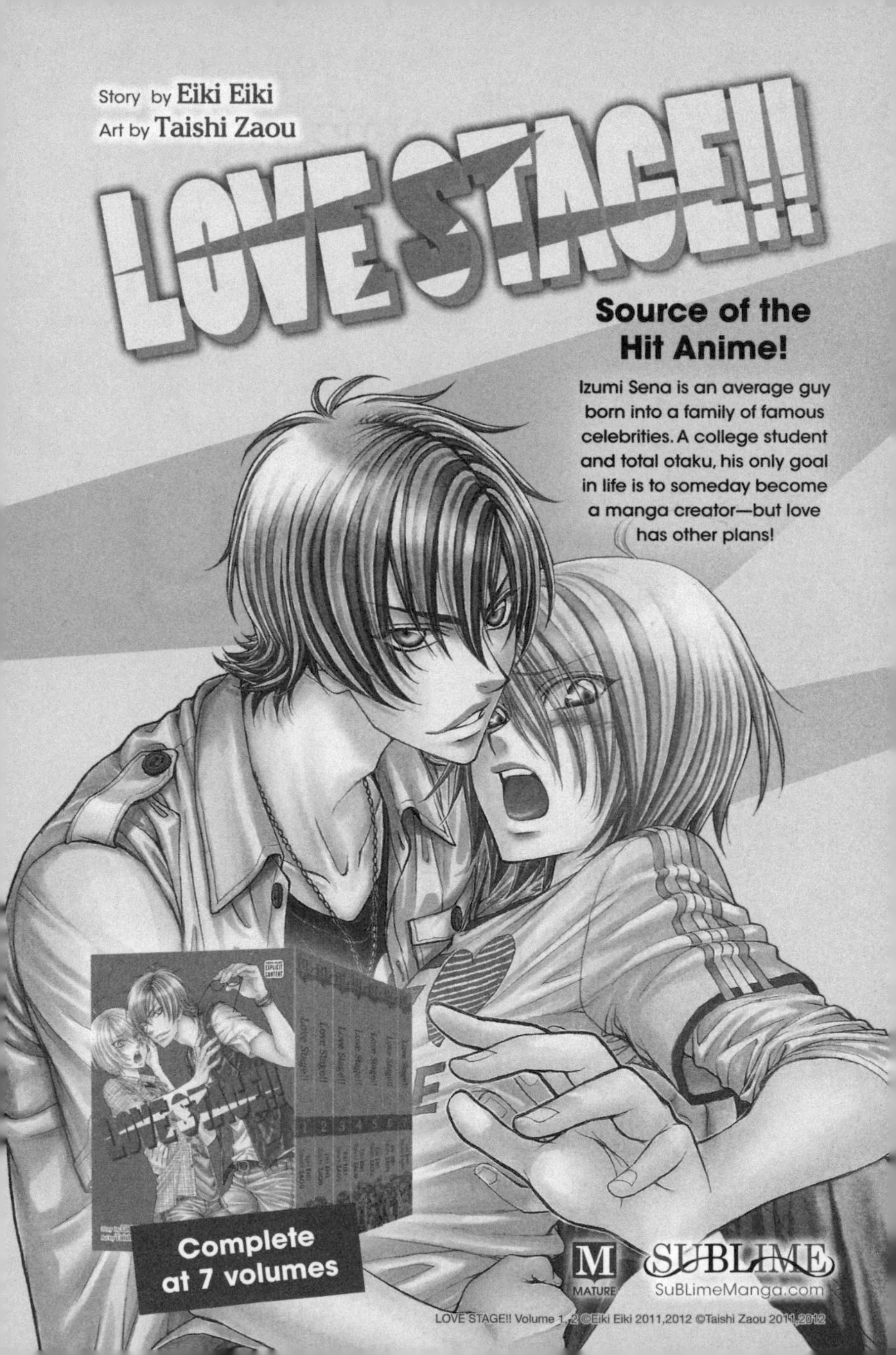

Story by **Eiki Eiki**
Art by **Taishi Zaou**

LOVE STAGE!!

Source of the Hit Anime!

Izumi Sena is an average guy born into a family of famous celebrities. A college student and total otaku, his only goal in life is to someday become a manga creator—but love has other plans!

Complete at 7 volumes

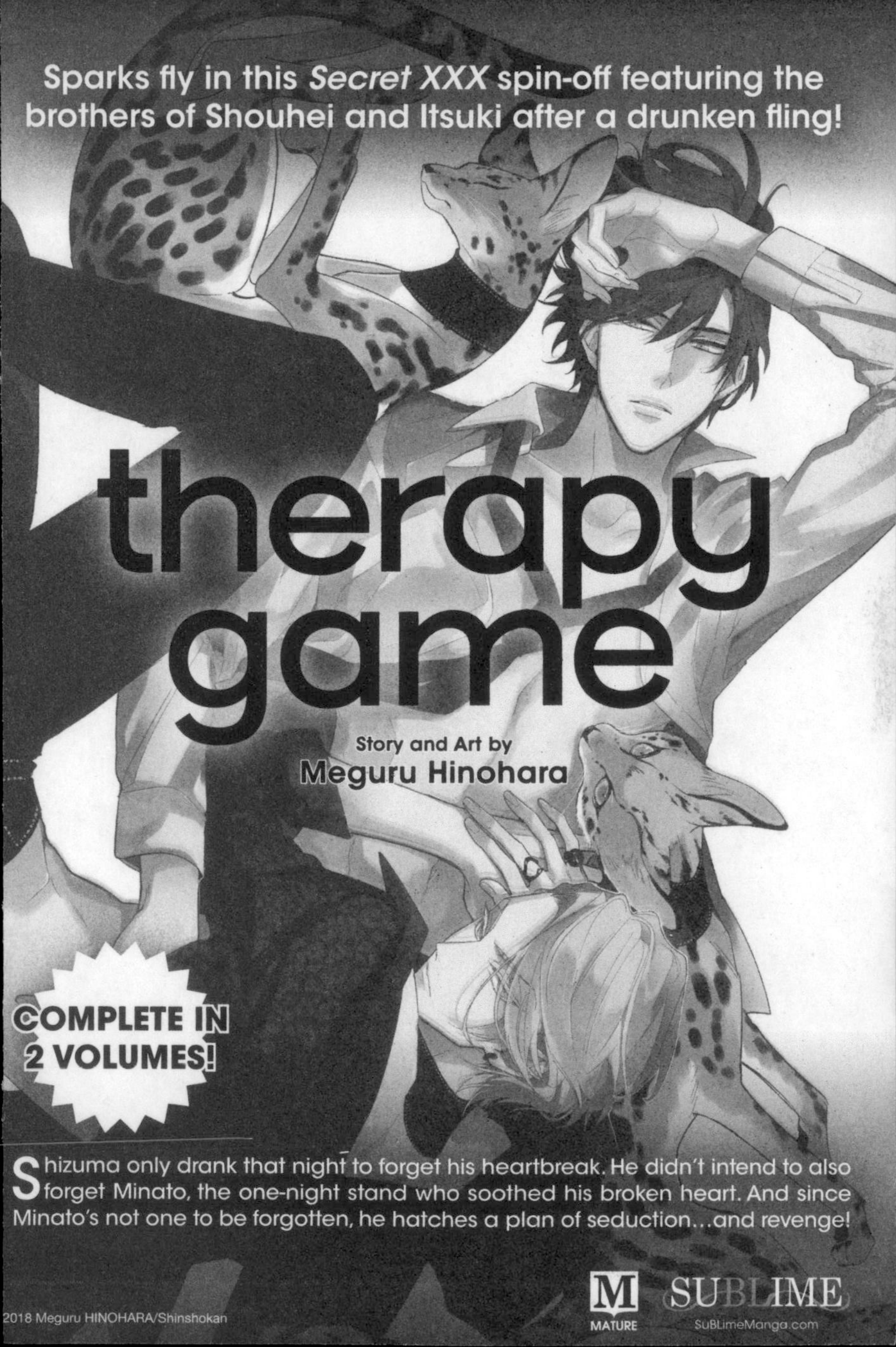

Sparks fly in this *Secret XXX* spin-off featuring the
brothers of Shouhei and Itsuki after a drunken fling!

therapy
game

Story and Art by
Meguru Hinohara

COMPLETE IN
2 VOLUMES!

Shizuma only drank that night to forget his heartbreak. He didn't intend to also
forget Minato, the one-night stand who soothed his broken heart. And since
Minato's not one to be forgotten, he hatches a plan of seduction...and revenge!

MATURE

SUBLIME

SuBLimeManga.com

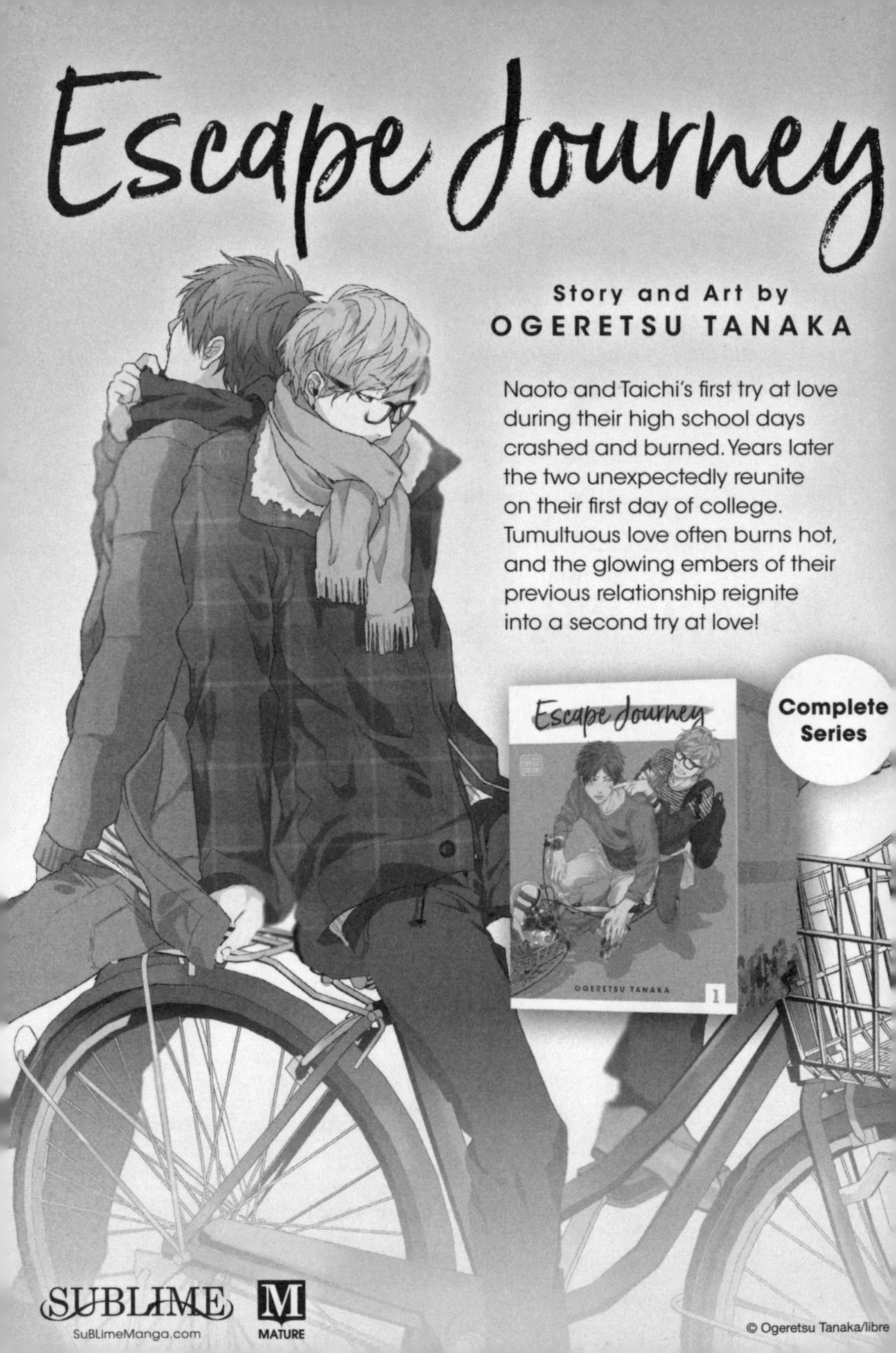
Escape Journey
Story and Art by
OGERETSU TANAKA
Naoto and Taichi's first try at love during their high school days crashed and burned. Years later the two unexpectedly reunite on their first day of college. Tumultuous love often burns hot, and the glowing embers of their previous relationship reignite into a second try at love!
Escape Journey
OGERETSU TANAKA
1
Complete Series
SUBLIME
SuBLimeManga.com
M
MATURE
© Ogeretsu Tanaka/libre

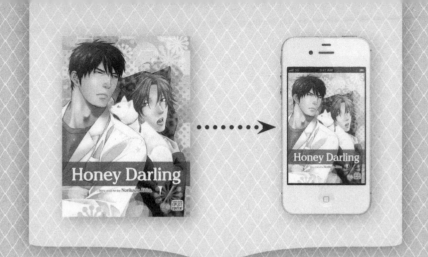

Downloading is as easy as:

1

2

3

SUBLIME

Your Toys Love Boys' Love

Own your SuBLime book as a convenient PDF document that is downloadable to the following devices:

- ♥ Computer
- ♥ Kindle™
- ♥ NOOK™
- ♥ iPad™, iPhone™, and iPod Touch™
- ♥ Any device capable of reading a PDF document

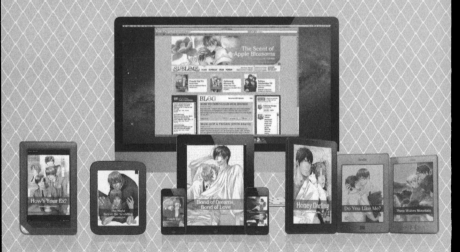

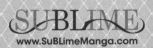

www.SuBLimeManga.com

More of the best digital BL manga from

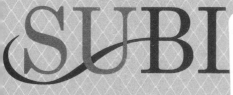

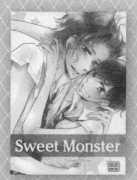

Sweet Monster
by Tsubaki Mikage

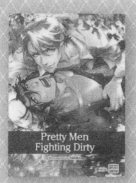

**Pretty Men
Fighting Dirty**
by Sakira

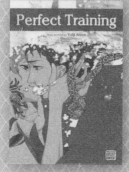

Perfect Training
by Yuiji Aniya

Available **Worldwide** in
Download-To-Own Format

Get them now for only **$6.99** each at **SuBLimeManga.com!**